D0079321

Japan's political system has been transformed gradually by a pluralizing trend since the postwar era. That is not to say, however, that many diverse, fluctuating groups now compete equally in Japan's political marketplace. Instead, small sets of well-organized, narrowly focused interest groups typically join specific bureaucratic agencies, groups of politicians, and individual experts to dominate policymaking in relatively self-contained issue areas. *Advice and Consent* offers a rare, penetrating examination of the critical role of interest-group politics in Japan.

One useful window onto interest-group politics is Japan's system of consultative councils. More than 200 of these councils, or *shingikai*, are attached to the ministries. Composed of businesspeople, bureaucrats, scholars, journalists, union members, and others, they deliberate on virtually every aspect of public policy. Frank Schwartz reviews the functions and operations of Japan's council system, and presents three case studies of specific governmental decisions involving the use of *shingikai* in the late 1980s. He explores how political conflicts of interest among economic groups are resolved in Japan with the help of consultative councils, makes broader observations about the political economies of Japan, and by extension, other advanced industrial economies.

Advice and consent

Advice and consent

The politics of consultation in Japan

FRANK J. SCHWARTZ
Harvard University

CAMBRIDGE
UNIVERSITY PRESS

PUBLISHED BY THE PRESS SYNDICATE OF THE UNIVERSITY OF CAMBRIDGE
The Pitt Building, Trumpington Street, Cambridge CB2 1RP, United Kingdom

CAMBRIDGE UNIVERSITY PRESS
The Edinburgh Building, Cambridge CB2 2RU, United Kingdom
40 West 20th Street, New York, NY 10011-4211, USA
10 Stamford Road, Oakleigh, Melbourne 3166, Australia

© Frank J. Schwartz 1998

This book is in copyright. Subject to statutory exception
and to the provisions of relevant collective licensing agreements,
no reproduction of any part may take place without
the written permission of Cambridge University Press.

First published 1998

Printed in the United States of America

Typeset in Ehrhardt

Library of Congress Cataloging-in-Publication Data
Schwartz, Frank J. (Frank Jacob), 1958–
Advice and consent: the politics of consultation in Japan / Frank
J. Schwartz.
p.   cm.
Includes bibliographical references (p.).
ISBN 0-521-58048-X
1. Pressure groups – Japan.   2. Political planning – Japan.
3. Business and politics – Japan.   4. Industrial policy – Japan.
I. Title.
JQ1669.P7S39   1998
322'.3'0952 – dc21   97–14943
                                             CIP

A catalog record for this book is available from the British Library.

ISBN 0-521-58048-X hardback

To my teachers

Contents

Tables and figures

Tables

Figures

Preface

In order to draw broader conclusions about Japan's political economy, this study explores how political conflicts of interest among economic groups are resolved with the help of consultative councils. Why interest groups? Why Japan? Why consultative councils?

I chose to focus on interest groups not because they are necessarily *the* crucial institution for explaining politics, but because in recent years the association has reasserted its place alongside the community, corporate hierarchy, market, and state as one of the key institutional bases of social order and social science.[1] That development reflects the expansion of functionally differentiated interests, the interpenetration of public and private decisionmaking, and thus the growing importance of associational as well as partisan representation.

The Japanese case is especially instructive for the study of interest-group politics. Japan is, above all, an *organized* society: A seven-nation survey of political participation found that more people belonged to some organization in Japan than in any other nation examined, including the United States (72 percent versus 61 percent).[2] As extended economic growth has differentiated and enriched society, established interest groups have won greater autonomy from, and influence over, state actors, and increasing numbers of new groups have developed the identity and capacity to organize and articulate demands. However, because most Western research has focused on bureaucrats or politicians, there is a curious gap in the literature on how interest-group politics relates to economic policymaking in Japan.[3]

The two most popular models of interest-group politics in Japan are currently the pluralist and the statist, but neither is adequate in itself. Although patterns naturally vary across issues and over time, what we most often see can be characterized as a bureaucratically led form of neopluralism. If the postwar era has witnessed a pluralizing trend in Japan, that is not to say that many diverse, fluctuating groups compete equally in the political marketplace. Rather, small and fairly stable sets of well-organized, narrowly focused interest groups typi-

[1] Streeck and Schmitter (1985); Hollingsworth and Streeck (1994).
[2] Quoted in Calder (1988), pp. 183–84.
[3] Calder (1993), pp. 10–11.

ix

cally join specific bureaucratic agencies, groups of politicians, and individual experts to dominate decisionmaking in relatively self-contained policy domains. This compartmentalization of politics generally follows the lines of ministerial jurisdiction, and agency officials are frequently able to adjust the policy conflicts that arise within their purviews in a deliberate and self-interested way. But in this context, bureaucratic leadership must be understood as coordinative, not imperative, and it must be emphasized that there are also domains where politicians (or even interest groups) exercise such leadership. The likelihood of bureaucratic leadership varies directly with the scope of administrative jurisdiction and inversely with the distributive nature of a policy. (The dependent variable here is thus the policymaking process itself rather than particular policy outcomes.)

Debates among students of Japan over whether bureaucrats or politicians dominate or whether bureaucrats enjoy much leverage vis-à-vis interest groups are long-standing. I believe that one reason they are long-standing is that they have not been framed in the most useful way. Whether or not other specialists find this particular synthesis convincing, a powerful consensus is emerging along these lines.[4]

Where politician-led neopluralism prevails (as in most policy domains in the United States), interest groups concentrate on lobbying the legislature; where bureaucratic agencies lead (as in most domains in Japan), access to administration is crucial, and one avenue of access is the consultative council. Composed of scholars, businesspeople, bureaucrats, journalists, unionists, and others, more than 200 consultative councils, or *shingikai*, are attached to Japanese ministries in order to examine virtually every aspect of public policy. Not all *shingikai* articulate and mediate conflicting interests, and *shingikai* are not the only institutions in Japan to perform those functions, but they do provide one means for state agencies to acknowledge those private actors whose preferences they regard as worthy of being taken into account, and to establish a formal means of incorporating those preferences into policymaking.

To borrow a forgotten author's metaphor, *shingikai* offer a handy "can opener": Often humble in themselves, they nevertheless help one get at something important, the nature of interest-group politics in Japan. That *shingikai* are auxiliary organs of bureaucratic agencies in no way implies their insulation from politics; quite the contrary. As Léon Dion observed, "The field of consultation extends far beyond pure administration, if only because the administrative apparatus, far from being autonomous, is closely bound to the whole political system. . . . Rather than using the expression 'consultative administration' we should speak of the politics of consultation."[5] With Japan's party politics now in flux, it is more necessary than ever to examine the bureaucratic–

---

[4] Cf. Samuels (1992), p. 38. For an alternative view, see Uriu (1996), p. 31.
[5] Dion (1973), p. 336.

interest group nexus and its politics of consultation. When associations were surveyed as to whether it was more effective to work through ministries or parties to attain their goals, the balance shifted from parity in 1980 (48 percent versus 46 percent) to a strong preference for ministries in 1994 (61 percent versus 31 percent).[6]

Chapter 1 briefly sketches the development of Western thinking about interest groups and the ways in which specific models have been applied to Japan to make an argument for the neopluralist approach. Chapter 2 introduces Japan's system of consultative councils, their history, functions, composition, and operation. How that system took on new functions in the 1980s is discussed in Chapter 3. Chapters 4, 5, and 6 present three case studies of concrete decisions made in the policy domains of labor, finance, and agriculture in which *shingikai* played a prominent part. The results of these case studies are compared in Chapter 7, which also returns to the broader issue that motivated this research: the relative applicability of Western models of interest-group politics to Japan.

Although this study's hypotheses were developed inductively in the course of analyzing the empirical material presented here, given the absence of a commonly accepted paradigm in comparative politics, it is best to announce one's assumptions at the outset. I believe that the most fundamental domestic determinants of economic policy are neither the rationality of monadic individuals, group dynamics, class struggles, nor national culture, but the institutions that mediate and structure the workings of those factors. The interests and ideas that drive policymaking are shaped, articulated, and advantaged – or disadvantaged – by the organization of a nation's state apparatus, electoral system, and principal producer groups, for example. Of course, institutions constrain rather than single-handedly and deterministically cause political strategies and outcomes, and the same institutions that structure relations of power are themselves created and changed in political struggles.[7]

As Arthur Bentley observed, "who likes may snip verbal definitions in his old age, when his world has gone crackly and dry."[8] If only for the sake of precision, though, it is necessary to define one's terms. For the purposes of this study, an "interest group" will be defined as a set of individuals or corporate institutions that consciously pursues common, limited aims by means of public policy, but does not attempt to realize those aims by governing itself. This definition does *not* necessarily accord with those used by authors to be discussed.

All research is in some sense a collective effort. My greatest debt is to my teachers. It was Edwin Reischauer who first piqued my interest in Japan and

---

[6] Tsujinaka (1996), pp. 49, 52.
[7] Hall (1983), pp. 23–24; Hall (1986), p. 232; Thelen and Steinmo (1992), pp. 10, 22, 28.
[8] Bentley (1908), p. 199.

Terry MacDougall who nurtured that interest. Judith Shklar steered me around some major theoretical pitfalls with one of her characteristically penetrating critiques. I am grateful to all of my language instructors at Harvard University and the Inter-University Center for Japanese Language Studies for their unstinting efforts to teach an old and especially obtuse dog a new trick. While I was in Japan, Sone Yasunori provided me with invaluable help, both intellectual and practical. Upon my return to America, Peter Hall tried to inject some rigor into my thinking and Ezra Vogel gave me more of his scarce time than I had a right to expect. Both friend and adviser, Susan Pharr has helped me in too many ways to enumerate. At Cambridge University Press, Elizabeth Neal not only made publishing this book as painless as possible, but even permitted me to stand by my mistakes when I got pigheaded about it.

Institutions as well as individuals have been kind to me. The United States government granted me two Foreign Language and Area Studies Scholarships and a Fulbright Scholarship. In Japan, Keiō University was generous to a fault with its bountiful resources, ministry bureaucrats freely supplied me with more information than I could digest, and a Sanwa Bank Foundation Fellowship provided me with the wherewithal to begin writing up my research. In addition to supporting me materially, Harvard University's Lowell House offered as congenial an environment for scholarship as I can imagine. Finally, Harvard's Program on U.S.–Japan Relations was good enough to award me a postdoctoral fellowship to begin preparing my dissertation for publication, and the Program and Harvard's Center for International Affairs underwrote the compiling of this volume's index.

Although far more people have helped me than I can name here, I would nonetheless like to thank Gary Allinson, Eva Bellin, Tom and Sucharita Berger, Pat Boling and Mark Tilton, Bob Bullock, Gerald Hane, Ehud Harari, Chalmers Johnson, Deborah Milly, Elizabeth Norville and Peter Schwartz, and Tomo Rieko for their aid, advice, and encouragement. I am especially indebted to all of the individuals (listed in the Bibliography) who so hospitably shared their time and knowledge with me over the course of my interviews, interviews that I approached with such trepidation and from which I learned so much.

Except for the most familiar names (e.g., Tokyo, Osaka), the Japanese forms of proper nouns are used here. Japanese individuals' names are thus written surname first, and where those individuals themselves had chosen an English translation for their title, that translation is used. For figures from before 1985, conversions from yen to dollars are made at the prevailing exchange rate. Because the exchange rate began to fluctuate considerably after the Plaza Accord of 1985, all conversions for the several years that followed are made at a constant ¥140 to the dollar. Newspaper citations always refer to morning editions unless otherwise noted.

Abbreviations

AMA	Administrative Management Agency
DSP	Democratic Socialist Party
EA	Environmental Agency
EPA	Economic Planning Agency
FTC	Fair Trade Commission
GATT	General Agreement on Tariffs and Trade
ILO	International Labor Organization
JCP	Japan Communist Party
JNR	Japan National Railways
JSP	Japan Socialist Party
LDP	Liberal Democratic Party
MAFF	Ministry of Agriculture, Forestry, and Fisheries
MCA	Management and Coordination Agency
MFA	Ministry of Foreign Affairs
MHA	Ministry of Home Affairs
MHW	Ministry of Health and Welfare
MITI	Ministry of International Trade and Industry
MOC	Ministry of Construction
MOE	Ministry of Education
MOF	Ministry of Finance
MOJ	Ministry of Justice
MOL	Ministry of Labor
MOT	Ministry of Transportation
MP	member of parliament
MPT	Ministry of Posts and Telecommunications
NHK	Japan Broadcasting Corporation
NIEs	newly industrializing economies (of East Asia)
NLA	National Land Agency
NPA	National Personnel Authority
NTT	Nippon Telephone and Telegraph
OB	"old boy," i.e., an alumnus (here, of a bureaucratic agency)
OECD	Organization for Economic Cooperation and Development

Abbreviations

PARC	Policy Affairs Research Council (of the LDP)
PMO	Prime Minister's Office
PR	proportional representation
STA	Science and Technology Agency
TSE	Tokyo Stock Exchange
USTR	Office of the United States Trade Representative

1

Interest-group politics in Japan: Competing interpretations

Which model of interest-group politics is most applicable to contemporary Japan? Not Marxism or a model of power elites: Some groups, like big business, have better access than others, but participation in policymaking is wide and widening. Not pluralism: A variety of competing groups have input, but interest-group participation remains structured. Not corporatism: Interest organizations influence the government's policymaking process from within, but broad peak associations do not dominate the articulation of private interests or engage in wide-ranging negotiations with one another. Not statism: Bureaucrats play a central role in the framing and implementation of policy, but ministries are increasingly constrained by markets, their clienteles, and elected politicians. Although patterns of interest-group politics vary across issues and over time, to generalize, neopluralist models offer the best lens through which to examine Japan today. What follows is a brief review of these models and an exploration of their relative applicability. Readers familiar with or uninterested in the more theoretical literature may choose to proceed directly to the more empirical discussion of the Japanese case, which begins with the section "Culturalist Models."

Theories of interest-group politics

Political theory has gradually moved from an almost exclusive concern with what is right to a greater concern with what is, and the study of interest groups has reflected that shift. Traditionally, the interest group was accepted "in the way that the typhoid bacillus is, as an organism that is a feature of civilized existence but that must be eradicated if society is to develop and prosper."[1] Modern empirical models differ on the internal organization of groups, on the relations of interest groups to one another and to the state, and, most clearly, on the relative weights and distribution of political resources. These competing approaches are most easily distinguished, that is to say, by their respective designations of what Eric Nordlinger called "effective demand groups," or those

---

[1] Truman (1971 [1951]), p. 46.

private actors whose policy choices tend to prevail. For Marxists, the effective demand groups are the classes that control the means of production; for pluralists, virtually all cohesive and determined groups; for neopluralists, only well-organized groups with narrow interests; and for corporatists, monopolistic, centralized, functional associations.[2] Statists look less to the demands of private actors than to the independent initiatives of public officials.

Traditional conceptions of the public interest

As a naturally independent person, Jean Jacques Rousseau asserted, each individual has a particular will concerned with merely private interests; as a citizen, on the other hand, he or she shares in the "general will," a higher, communitarian will concerned with the public interest. Rousseau recognized that every political society is composed of smaller societies, and every association of individuals creates its own general will for their common good, but if it is general for the members of the association, that will is particular vis-à-vis, and thus pernicious to, society at large. "It is therefore essential, if the general will is to be able to express itself, that there should be no partial society within the State. . . ."[3] This idea was not peculiar to Rousseau. On the contrary, it was the accepted wisdom. Although Rousseau's political philosophy was anathema to Edmund Burke, he similarly argued that "Parliament is not a *congress* of ambassadors from different and hostile interests, which interests each must maintain, as an agent and advocate, against other agents and advocates; but Parliament is a *deliberative* assembly of *one* nation, with *one* interest, that of the whole."[4]

Philosophically, such communitarianism still enjoys wide currency; empirically, it has long since been overtaken by events. In the wake of the industrial and democratic revolutions, the social universe of Rousseau and Burke, to say nothing of earlier Western and all non-Western theorists, changed beyond recognition, and with it the properties and perceptions of interest groups. It was with the division of labor, not market competition, that Adam Smith began *The Wealth of Nations*, and new associations emerged as an advancing division of labor engendered structural differentiation. The growing interdependence of specialized spheres of society prompted state coordination, and as the state adopted a more interventionist role, multiplying interest groups had more of an incentive to attempt to influence its actions. Democracy facilitated those efforts. Modern interest-group politics thus owes its existence to both the push of social differentiation and the pull of state activism and popular government.

[2] Nordlinger (1981), pp. 44–46.
[3] Rousseau (1946 [1762]), pp. 22–23.
[4] Edmund Burke. 1826 [1774]. "Speech to the Electors of Bristol." In *The Works of the Right Honorable Edmund Burke*. Boston: Wells and Lilly; v. II, p. 11.

Marxism

The first major philosopher of our era, Georg W. F. Hegel accepted modern society on its own terms, drawing a distinction between "civil society" and the state. Civil society is the world of the market, where each person is pitted against every other in a contest of unrestrained egoism. The state, on the other hand, is neither an aggregate of private interests nor the guarantor of those interests. The state transcends self-interest: It is a unity characterized by solidarity. Hegel thus opposed the universalism of the state to the particularism of civil society. If he, too, subordinated the person to the citizen, the worldliness of economic activity to the ideal of political participation, Hegel nonetheless broke with Rousseau in allowing a place for egoistic interests in civil society.

Karl Marx accused Hegel of mystifying the dialectic of history, of leaving it "standing on its head." The state is not prior to civil society; rather, civil society is prior to the state. Marx formulated a materialist conception of history that regards relations of production as the real foundation of society, the "structure" that conditions, and in the last instance determines, the "superstructure" of political life. Whereas Smith saw in functional interdependence a new way to integrate society, Marx argued that each historical phase in the development of the division of labor tends to produce two hostile classes whose interests are mutually exclusive: a minority who owns the means of production and a majority whose labor the minority exploits. "Every class struggle is a political struggle," and, conversely, "all struggles within the State . . . are merely the illusory forms in which the real struggles of the different classes are fought out among one another."[5] Marx thus saw modern interest-group politics in terms of capitalists' attempts to maintain their class rule through the oppression of workers, and workers' efforts to resist that oppression and overthrow the property relations that make it possible.

While agreeing that groups dominate social life, a heterogeneous school of pluralists has defined class in terms of source of income or functional position in the division of labor, criteria that cut across Marx's fundamentally dichotomous scheme to yield a plethora of different classes. More to the point, they have contended that classes rarely act as wholes because of the kaleidoscopic and cross-cutting diversity of private interests, and that politically meaningful differentiation extends far beyond merely economic groupings.

Pluralism

Although Rousseau had argued that the public interest would tend to prevail in small, direct democracies, James Madison countered that, paradoxically, the

---

[5] Marx and Engels (1978 [1848, 1846]), pp. 481, 160–61.

dangers inherent in interest groups are to be overcome by their multiplication within an extended republic: "Extend the sphere and you take in a greater variety of interests; you make it less probable that a majority of the whole will have a common motive to invade the rights of other citizens; or if such a common motive exists, it will be more difficult for all who feel it to discover their own strength and to act in unison with each other."[6]

While conceding the inevitability of interest-group activity, Madison was eager to limit its influence. Alexis de Tocqueville, on the other hand, celebrated it: "In democratic countries the science of association is the mother of science; the progress of all the rest depends upon the progress it has made."[7] For Tocqueville, the distinguishing feature of modern society is not a polarizing class structure but a growing equality of conditions, and interest groups help check the grave threats to liberty posed by the leveling of feudal hierarchy. By teaching individuals to cooperate, interest-group activity guarantees against both the "tyranny of the majority" and "individualism," or the willingness of members of the community to isolate themselves from society at large.

Arthur F. Bentley and (later) David B. Truman constructed a systematic theory of group politics. In opposition to the formal-legalism that dominated American political science, which examined laws rather than what people in government actually did, Bentley regarded the various groups operating *behind* formal institutions as "the raw material of government." Truman asserted that they fill social needs, stabilizing social relations disturbed by differentiation. Although the two are often accused of simplistically arguing that public policy is the calculable "resultant" of conflicting vectors of group pressure, the charge does not do them justice. First, with every individual belonging to a variety of cross-cutting groups, they contended that associations must moderate their demands in order to avoid antagonizing subsets of their members. Second, Bentley and Truman argued that accepted "rules of the game" further constrain group activity. Finally, given that they can be *expected* to act if their interests are sufficiently threatened, the two men maintained that even inactive, "potential" interest groups influence policymaking. They shared a confidence that the results of interest-group politics will generally be just and desirable because groups tend to reconcile their differences and more general interests tend to defeat narrower ones.

Pluralism reached an apogee of optimism in the early work of Robert A. Dahl, who concluded that industrialization has gradually replaced a cohesive, uniformly advantaged oligarchy with multiple sets of leaders, each of which commands a different combination of political resources. Whereas one group might enjoy numbers, votes, and organization, another might boast money, control

---

[6] Madison et al. (1961 [1788]), p. 83.
[7] Tocqueville (1945 [1835]), v. I, pp. 200–2; Tocqueville (1945 [1840]), v. II, p. 118.

over economic resources, and social status, and a third might possess expertise, access to the mass media, and a positive public image. If inequalities persist, they now tend to be noncumulative, or dispersed, and no group of any size is entirely lacking in political resources.

In the neoclassical model of competition, firms on the same side of the market restrain one another: Sellers restrain other sellers. John Kenneth Galbraith theorized that the very process of industrial concentration that impaired or destroyed competition in numerous markets has replaced it with another regulatory mechanism, "countervailing power," which appears not on the same side of the market but on the *opposite* side: Industrial concentration begets strong suppliers and buyers as well as strong sellers. Although Galbraith acknowledged that weaker groups like workers and farmers often require state assistance, he attributed the property of "self-generation" to countervailing power, making interest-group politics self-regulating.

As the pluralist study of interest groups spread throughout the world, Gabriel A. Almond posited that all political systems carry out the same basic functions. Among those functions, interest articulation is of crucial importance, linking society and polity. Although many different kinds of institutions can articulate interests, because associational groups are specialized to perform that function, they play a regulatory role in "processing" raw claims, and the greater the frequency of interest articulation by associational groups, the better the "boundary maintenance" between society and polity and among the sub-systems of the polity. If Almond reintroduced a notion of pathology to the study of interest groups with his idea of boundary maintenance, it was no longer the *presence* of vocal interest groups that was unhealthy, but their *absence*. Interest groups were more than functional: They had come to be viewed as indispensable.

For pluralists, then, almost all politically active groups (and some merely potential groups) represent effective demand groups. Because society is highly fractionated by cross-cutting cleavages and because the ready availability of a wide variety of political resources keeps the barriers to entry low, a plethora of diverse, fluctuating groups compete freely in the political marketplace. Conflicting interests tend toward a dynamic equilibrium: If many groups control a disproportionate share of some particular resource, inequalities are dispersed, and no one group can prevail for long without its opponents or the state mobilizing countervailing power. No sooner had this model carried the day than scholars began to challenge it. Americanist critics never coalesced around a single rival paradigm, and they continued to prize the voluntarism and fluid competition of pluralism as ideals, so they have been referred to as "neopluralists."[8] Many Europeanists, on the other

---

[8] Nordlinger (1981), pp. 44, 45.

hand, mounted a sustained attack on the most basic assumptions of pluralism, gathering in support of an entirely different, "corporatist" research program.

Neopluralism

In asserting that conflicts tend to interfere with and temper one another, pluralists' unspoken assumption was that there is a kind of equality of conflicts. Politics deals with the competition of conflicts, however, and there exist any number of potential cleavages in a society that will not materialize because its institutions do not and cannot treat conflicts impartially. "All forms of political organization have a bias in favor of the exploitation of some kinds of conflict and the suppression of others because *organization is the mobilization of bias*," E. E. Schattschneider aphorized (italics in the original).[9] Peter Bachrach and Morton Baratz enlarged on this argument. They acknowledged that "of course power is exercised when A participates in the making of decisions that affect B. But power is also exercised when A devotes his energies to creating or reinforcing social and political values and institutional practices that limit the scope of the political process to public consideration of only those issues which are comparatively innocuous to A."[10] In concentrating on the decisionmaking process, pluralists fail to heed the "nondecision-making process," the prevention of policy debates that might threaten the status quo.

Schattschneider also criticized pluralists for having failed to realize that the outcome of any conflict is determined by its scope, by the number of people involved: "*The most powerful private interests want private settlements* because they are able to dictate the outcome as long as the conflict remains private" (italics in the original).[11] Empirical research increasingly revealed how interest groups succeed in carving out niches for themselves within ostensibly public decisionmaking bodies, how the U.S. government acquiesces in the privatization of conflict by hiving off programs for the benefit of small, particularistic constituencies.

Emphasizing the decentralization of America's national government, J. Leiper Freeman led the way by taking the study of policymaking below the general level of executive, legislature, and political party to examine the autonomous "subsystems" that they cloak. "Since the parties do not have clear control over the Administration and Congress, and since neither of the latter two consistently maintains an internal cohesion, interest group spokesmen frequently find it more profitable and more promptly effective to cultivate those subordinate units of Congress and the Administration dealing directly with a

---

[9] Schattschneider (1960), p. 71.   [10] Bachrach and Baratz (1962), p. 948.
[11] Schattschneider (1960), p. 40.

special field of interest."[12] Narrow issues tend to be resolved by coalitions (subsequently labeled "iron triangles" or "subgovernments") of corresponding executive bureaus, legislative committees, and favored interest groups that interact with one another independently of the larger political world. Grant McConnell went even further, asserting that "what emerges as the most important political reality is an array of relatively separated political spheres" beholden to particular interests, isolated from countervailing influences, and liable to reach settlements favoring existing elites at the expense of the public.[13]

In a similar vein, Theodore Lowi complained that "broad-gauged" models like pluralism were not related to observable cases and proposed a new, policy-oriented framework for analysis. When defined in terms of their impact on society, all domestic policies can be categorized as distributive, regulative, or redistributive, he contended. As exemplified by clientele services and "pork-barrel" public works, "distributive policies are characterized by the ease with which they can be disaggregated and dispensed unit by small unit, each unit more or less in isolation from other units and from any general rule."[14] Because regulatory policies must be made by application of a general rule, they are incapable of the same level of disaggregation, and redistributive policies approach whole social classes in the breadth of their impact. With the type of policy at stake determining the pattern of political interaction, "the political process" has to be approached as an aggregation of political process*es*. And with a vulgar pluralism equating democracy with access and pretending that intergroup bargaining and the diffusion of public authority obviate the need for coercion, a dysfunctional ideology of "interest-group liberalism" has elevated conflict of interest into a veritable principle of government in the United States.[15]

Although such an abdication of government responsibility has been justified by the pluralist assumption that organized groups represent most citizens' interests adequately and keep one another in check, many interests never get represented at all. By focusing on how group size affects member calculations, Mancur Olson demonstrated why individuals often fail to cooperate. Because individual action is sufficient to provide ordinary goods, organizational activity is characteristically geared toward "collective" or "public" goods, which cannot practically be withheld even from someone who has not helped pay for them (e.g., national defense). Because every group member will benefit from the provision of a collective good whether or not he or she contributes, everyone has an incentive to shirk paying his or her share of the cost. A collective good *can* result from the voluntary, self-interested action of

---

[12] Freeman (1965), p. 58.   [13] McConnell (1966), p. 244.   [14] Lowi (1964), p. 690.
[15] Lowi (1969).

individuals if a group is small enough for each member to enjoy a substantial portion of the total gain, but the more numerous the members, the less any individual member can expect to receive and the more attractive the free-rider option becomes. Accordingly, "the organized and active interests of small groups tend to triumph over the unorganized and unprotected interests of larger groups."[16]

A widely influential example of this approach is George Stigler's theory that regulation is generally designed and operated for the benefit of the industry concerned rather than for that of the public at large.[17] Robert Salisbury, on the other hand, pointed out that hierarchical institutions like corporations differ in crucial respects from the voluntary associations focused on by Olson and his predecessors alike. Given their size and complexity, institutions tend to have a broader range of policy concerns, and with more discretionary resources and more autonomous leaderships, they have greater latitude to enter politics and less need to justify such efforts by reference to their "memberships," such as they are. As a result of these differences, Salisbury concluded that "institutions have come to dominate the processes of interest representation in American national politics."[18]

If Olson underscored how "organizability" poses important barriers to entry in the political process, Hugh Heclo pointed to "a dissolving of organized politics and a politicizing of organizational life throughout the nation."[19] Washington has delegated the responsibility for more and more policies to intermediary organizations, be they state and local governments or private interest groups. At the same time, however, policymaking has increasingly become an "intramural activity" among experts, and there now exist subcultures of policy specialists who share a detailed understanding of particular issues and move easily between the public and private sectors. For Heclo, "issue networks" of these individuals tie together the otherwise contradictory tendencies of widening organizational participation and narrowing technocratic specialization.

America has not been the only object of neopluralist analysis. Joseph LaPalombara's examination of Italy led him to conclude decades ago that "the process whereby groups exert influence over organs of the state is structured rather than fluid. . . . The notion of structured influence is an overriding generalization."[20] He distinguished between two broad patterns of institutionalized ties between the national bureaucracy and interest groups: *clientela*, in which an interest group becomes the favored representative of a social sector dealt with by an agency, and *parantela*, in which a hegemonic political party intervenes in the administrative process on behalf of its constituencies. (Unfortunately, LaPalombara's nice distinction is not observed, and interests enjoying either

---

[16] Olson (1965), p. 144.   [17] Stigler (1971), p. 3.   [18] Salisbury (1984), p. 64.
[19] Heclo (1978), p. 89.   [20] LaPalombara (1964), pp. 258–59.

clientela or *parantela* are now undiscriminatingly referred to as "clientele groups.")

The expanding scope and complexity of governmental responsibility tend to fragment and specialize policymaking in all advanced industrial societies, neopluralists argue. The bulk of public decisionmaking is said to be dominated by relatively autonomous "policy communities" or "policy networks"[21] composed of bureaucrats, interest groups, politicians, experts, and, on occasion, other actors who share a specific policy focus, if not a special constitutional status. Across sectors, let alone countries, policy subsystems vary in size, composition, inclusivity, and integration.[22] For John C. Campbell, policy communities lie somewhere between subgovernments and issue networks. Where interest groups are powerful and politicians active or when it is resisting outside pressures for change, a policy community looks more like a subgovernment. Where there is a more intellectual approach to policymaking or when an interest in change is generated internally, it looks more like an issue network.[23] Carrying such conceptual differentiation even further, Michael Atkinson and William Coleman have categorized individual policy networks as pluralist, corporatist, or statist (among other things) on the basis of state agencies' and organized interests' structural properties.[24]

Rather than the attributes and activities of individual organizations, recent network analyses have focused on how relationships *among* organizations construct structures of power and affect policy outcomes. Specifically, researchers have attempted to identify – and quantify – such factors as the relative importance of information versus political support networks, the distributions of organizational reputations and participation in issues, and the locations of organizations occupying the most central network positions.[25] The results of such research have varied, however. Heinz, Laumann, Salisbury, and Nelson found that in the United States, "networks of representatives are arranged in spheres with hollow cores" characterized by "the absence of a centrally positioned group of elites that is capable of coordinating or integrating disparate interest group demands."[26] With a much more diverse set of interest groups now participating in a broader range of relatively open, competitive political arenas, pluralism does not represent America's past, but its future. The "organizational state" perspective of Edward Laumann and David Knoke, on the other hand, approaches the ideal type of neopluralism:

---

[21] Some authors use only one term; others use both terms but distinguish between them. With definitions varying from author to author, no convention on usage exists.

[22] Wilks and Wright (1987), pp. 306–7.

[23] Campbell et al. (1989). See also Atkinson and Coleman (1992), p. 160.

[24] Atkinson and Coleman (1989).

[25] Laumann and Knoke (1989), p. 58.

[26] Heinz et al. (1993), pp. 377, 22.

> The scope of policy-making is narrow. Most policy events occur within
> specialized spheres, or domains, having restricted access. These policy
> domains develop fairly stable power structures dominated by a core of peak
> associations and governmental actors. . . . The tendency of policy-making
> [is] to be an exclusionary process – locking out both actors and alternatives
> – rather than an inclusionary one.[27]

It is important to note that neopluralists do *not* contend that subgovernments
or policy communities are all there is to policymaking. Although they frequently
succeed in monopolizing decisionmaking in their own particular domain, they
must compete with alternative policymaking processes, and the most salient
decisions will often be handled by the chief executive, the floor of the legislature,
and other heavyweight actors in the general political arena.[28] Nevertheless, with
the partial exception of Heclo and some network analysts, whose work represents a return to pluralism,[29] all those scholars labeled here as neopluralist agree
that pluralism fails to recognize that the effective demand groups are limited to
what Lowi called "the most interested and best organized," and that these
private actors not only enjoy preferential access to the state, but are often
delegated powers of implementation. Neopluralists thus reject pluralists' optimism concerning fluid competition, dispersed inequalities, and countervailing
power.

Corporatists echo these criticisms. They agree that public and private power
are frequently merged in the formulation and implementation of public policies,
but whereas neopluralists (looking primarily at the American case) focus on
relatively narrow interests, corporatists (looking primarily at European cases)
focus on nationally organized, densely populated peak associations representing
whole sectors of the economy. And if neopluralists portray state–society relations as highly compartmentalized, corporatists examine instances in which
associational leaders deal directly with one another, as well as with state actors,
on a regular basis.

Corporatism

Just as neopluralists had ceased to regard interest groups as outsiders that
participate only intermittently in American policymaking, analysts like Andrew
Shonfield, Stein Rokkan, and Samuel Beer demonstrated how some European
countries had institutionalized schemes of functional representation that
brought government and producer groups into intimate and continuous contact.[30] Rokkan, for example, described a two-tiered system in Norway that
comprised both a formal "electoral-legislative" and an informal "organizational-
corporate" channel of decisionmaking.

[27] Knoke et al. (1996), pp. 8, 27.   [28] Campbell (1989), pp. 5–7, 18, 86.
[29] Jordan (1981), p. 101.   [30] Shonfield (1965); Rokkan (1966); Beer (1969).

> The crucial decisions on economic policy are rarely taken in the parties or in Parliament: the central area is the bargaining table where the government authorities meet directly with the trade union leaders, the representatives of the farmers, the smallholders, and the fishermen, and the delegates of the Employers' Association. These yearly rounds of negotiations have in fact come to mean more in the lives of rank-and-file citizens than the formal elections.[31]

These studies laid the groundwork for a paradigmatic revolution, and 1974 saw the near-simultaneous, independent publication of essays on corporatism by the German Gerhard Lehmbruch, the Britons Ray Pahl and Jack Winkler, and the American Philippe Schmitter. Because corporatism quickly acquired as many definitions as authors who addressed the subject, this discussion concentrates on the ideas of Schmitter, its single most influential theorist.

In opposition to the ideal type of pluralism, which portrays a multiplicity of overlapping, voluntary, competitive, weakly disciplined, ever-shifting interest groups that lobby state actors from the outside while maintaining their autonomy, Schmitter defined corporatism as

> a system of interest representation in which the constituent units are organized into a limited number of singular, compulsory, noncompetitive, hierarchically ordered and functionally differentiated categories, recognized or licensed (if not created) by the state and granted a deliberate representational monopoly within their respective categories in exchange for observing certain controls on their selection of leaders and articulation of demands and supports.[32]

This complex definition must be unpacked. Extensive government intervention in the economy has enabled privileged interest groups to overcome Olson's rational-choice dilemma, and in some countries, private associations coordinate the activities of whole economic sectors and social classes. Because permanent administrative staffs tend to become entrenched oligarchies, bureaucratized associations do not limit themselves to the passive transmission of preexisting interests, but often generate interests from within, independent of member preferences. Although the two can vary independently of one another, the trend toward hierarchy includes both concentration, the organizational integration of everyone occupying the same position in the division of labor, and centralization, the accumulation of decisionmaking power at the highest level of organization – the "peak" association, or association of associations.

Schmitter distinguished between two subtypes of corporatism with radically contrasting origins and relations of power. When delayed and dependent capi-

---

[31] Rokkan (1966), p. 107.
[32] Schmitter (1979 [1974]), p. 13.

talist development engenders a weak bourgeoisie, an authoritarian state will attempt to enforce social peace by deliberately destroying incipient pluralism, repressing the autonomous articulation of subordinate class demands through the imposition of interest organizations from above. The result is "state corporatism" (e.g., *Franquista* Spain). Although characterized by stable bourgeois dominance, the welfare state, on the other hand, requires collaborative class relations and the incorporation of subordinate classes into the political process, and corporatism spontaneously emerges from below to displace pluralism and penetrate the liberal democratic state. The result is "societal corporatism" (e.g., the "Social Partnership" of postwar Austria). In the eyes of many theorists, societal corporatism represents first and foremost an attempt to coopt organized labor.[33]

In the 1970s, the European Michel Crozier, the American Samuel Huntington, and the Japanese Watanuki Jōji perceived a full-blown "crisis of democracy" due in part to "an overload of demands on government, exceeding its capacity to respond."[34] Low barriers to political participation had increased the strength and assertiveness of particularistic groups, had *dis*aggregated interests, to an excessive degree. Corporatists responded by reversing Almond's advocacy of boundary maintenance to argue that corporatized interest groups can lighten the load of parties, parliaments, and public servants and contribute to governability by aggregating demands as well as articulating them, formulating and implementing policies as well as lobbying for them.[35]

Schmitter initially related the corporatization of interest intermediation to "basic imperatives" of capitalism,[36] but as Peter Katzenstein observed, successful examples of societal corporatism have been limited to small European states. Openness to and dependence on world markets follow from their size, and these features establish a "compelling need for consensus" that transformed conflict among their main social forces into cross-sectoral, compensatory bargaining to minimize the political costs of economic adjustment.[37] Although forced to limit domestic conflicts over economic issues, these states are also uniquely qualified. As Rousseau declared and Olson rigorously demonstrated, smallness facilitates cohesion, and centralization and concentration in interest organizations vary inversely with country size. For similar reasons, there has been a shift in research from the national level to the level of the economic sector, where corporatist arrangements may actually be older, stabler, and more widespread.[38]

---

[33] E.g., Panitch (1980).   [34] Crozier et al. (1975), p. 8.   [35] Heisler (1979); Schmitter (1981).
[36] Schmitter (1979), p. 24. Cf. Schmitter (1989), p. 72.
[37] Katzenstein (1985), p. 34.
[38] Lehmbruch (1992), p. 63; Cawson (1985) and Cawson (1986). The concept of "micro-corporatism," or corporatist arrangements on the level of the locality, the corporation, or even the individual factory, strikes this author as incoherent, however.

Statism

Over the last century, "while almost everywhere the role of the state grew, one of the few places it withered away was in political science."[39] In reaction against Hegelianism and formal-legalism, which focused on the state, Marxism and pluralism concurred in reducing the political to the socioeconomic. In recent decades, however, a movement to "bring the state back in" has gained momentum.

Marx did allow for independent state action under exceptional circumstances. There might temporarily exist no hegemonic class capable of imposing its will on the state, or an intensification of class conflict might produce a hyper-trophy of the bureaucracy. Since the mid-1960s, Marxists like Perry Anderson, Fred Block, Ralph Miliband, Claus Offe, and Nicos Poulantzas have attempted to develop a more systematic theory of the state. Structuralists have asserted that the state *must*, in fact, have a measure of autonomy: Only by acting against the interests of particular bourgeois, or against the short-run interests of the entire bourgeoisie, can the state sometimes maintain capitalist society. This autonomy can be no more than "relative," however: The state may be free from the active control of capitalists, but not from meeting the needs of capitalism.

Pluralists have pictured the state as little more than an arena in which group struggles are played out, or perhaps as the mediator of such struggles. At most, state actors are themselves considered interest groups. Tellingly, when Graham Allison demonstrated how international relations could be explained in terms of different levels of analysis,[40] it was his bureaucratic-politics model, his pluralist dissection of the state apparatus itself, that attracted the most notice.

If pluralists have generally concentrated on how interest groups affect the state, Harry Eckstein called attention to the other side of the equation. Because it gives private groups more to gain or lose from public policy, state activism creates politically active associations, and interest groups tend to resemble the agencies they seek to influence, for example.[41] Nordlinger went beyond a notion of the democratic state as an unwitting environmental influence on politics to conceive of it as a potentially autonomous, goal-oriented actor in its own right. Nevertheless, even he continued to define the state in terms of atomistic officials who occupy positions of authority and its preferences in terms of the resultant of those officials' preferences.[42] In contrast, a variety of theorists began to conceive of the state as "an organization-for-itself," "a bureaucratic apparatus and institutionalized legal order in its totality" with purposes and powers quali-tatively different from those of any other institution.[43]

---

[39] Stepan (1978), p. 3.   [40] Allison (1971).   [41] Eckstein (1960).   [42] Nordlinger (1981).
[43] Skocpol (1979), p. 27; Krasner (1984), p. 224.

J. P. Nettl observed that "the relative 'statelessness' of American social science coincides with the relative statelessness of the United States,"[44] but as American social science widened its scope, it confronted nations where the state's role is not so easily downplayed. In extending the earlier insights of Thorstein Veblen, Alexander Gerschenkron attacked the unilinear evolutionism of other modernization theorists to discern patterns of alternative "institutional instruments." Subsequent authors have elaborated whole syndromes of political as well as economic characteristics associated with early and late development, syndromes that stress the need for state initiative in the industrialization of late-developing nations.[45]

The study of revolutions in particular has lent support to these conclusions. Theda Skocpol noted that the new states that have emerged from revolutions from below have been stronger and more autonomous than those they replaced, and that "increasingly over 'world time,' opportunities and models have become available for using state power to promote national economic development."[46] Ellen Kay Trimberger and Alfred Stepan examined another source of state ascendancy in late-developing countries: revolutions from above. Trimberger noted how high officials who are personally dependent on the power of the state can become "dynamically autonomous" in a crisis situation, taking radical initiatives to save the state at the expense of vested economic interests, and Stepan examined how the army had emerged in certain Latin American countries as a new "strategic state elite" that used a strengthened state apparatus to impose its own programs.[47]

Other scholars have called attention to more limited examples of self-determined state activism in the advanced industrial democracies, often couching their models in terms of a distinction between "strong" and "weak" states. State strength has two dimensions: autonomy, or the ability of state actors to formulate goals that do not simply reflect societal demands, and capacity, the ability of state actors actually to implement their goals, especially in the face of societal resistance or unfavorable socioeconomic circumstances.[48] Katzenstein has conceptualized state capacity in terms of "policy instruments," institutional levers that state officials can bring to bear in pursuit of their aims, and policy networks that link public and private sectors. Theorizing that the number and range of policy instruments and the role of the state in policy networks vary directly with neo-mercantilism (versus liberalism), the tightness of policy networks, the centralization of state and society, and a lack of differentiation between the two, Katzenstein concluded that the role of the state is strongest in Japan and weakest in the United States.[49]

Although he recognized "modal differences" in state power across countries, Stephen Krasner qualified the strong state–weak state approach by observing

[44] Nettl (1968), pp. 561–62.   [45] E.g., Dore (1973).   [46] Skocpol (1979), pp. 285–86.
[47] Trimberger (1978); Stepan (1978).   [48] Skocpol (1985), p. 9.   [49] Katzenstein (1978).

how any state "may be strong in some issue areas and weak in others. There is no reason to assume a priori that the pattern of strength and weakness will be the same for all policies."[50] A state normally faces fewest challenges to its autonomy in foreign affairs. Charles Tilly has argued that it was precisely security pressures that provided the original impetus for the growth of the state and created a basis for potential autonomy vis-à-vis domestic groups.[51] In foreign economic policy, Krasner himself demonstrated how U.S. policies on overseas raw materials investment not only diverged from the demands of private actors but, structural Marxism to the contrary, actually undermined the coherence of America's capitalist society as a whole.

In examining the development of social policies in Britain and Sweden, Heclo provided evidence of state autonomy in domestic matters, too. Whereas political parties and interest groups have taken only an intermittent interest in the subject, civil servants are engaged in relatively constant analysis and review of societal problems and policy alternatives.[52] Skocpol and Kenneth Finegold's research on the New Deal echoed Heclo's findings about activist civil servants. In contrast to the administrative incapacity of much of the American state, the Department of Agriculture had already nurtured both an "administrative will to intervene" and a process of "political learning" about the possibilities of government intervention.[53]

Despite a resurgence in the 1980s of neoclassical economic models and minimalist theories of the state, the 1990s brought a reexamination of the state as an agent of industrial development. Recent analyses, however, attribute state effectiveness to the linking of public and private actors as a necessary complement to the insulation of coherent elites. Only a state that is capable of acting autonomously can provide essential collective goods like competitive markets, but only a state that is immersed in society can devise policies that respond to the perceived problems of private actors and rely on those actors for implementation. As Peter Evans noted, "transformative capacity requires a combination of internal coherence and external connectedness that can be called embedded autonomy."[54]

Although all of these arguments fall under the heading of "the new institutionalism," that label can equally apply to two methodologically distinct schools of thought. For historical institutionalists, like the authors cited earlier, institutions shape the ways political actors define their interests as well as mediate their relations. Rational choice institutionalists, on the other hand, regard institutions as the strategic context in which actors maximize interests

[50] Krasner (1978), p. 58. See also Atkinson and Coleman (1989), pp. 49–50, and Hollingsworth, Schmitter, and Streeck (1994).
[51] Tilly (1975), p. 42.
[52] Heclo (1974).   [53] Skocpol and Finegold (1982), pp. 274–75.
[54] Evans (1992), p. 176.

that are treated as exogenous variables. Although the first school thus assigns institutions a larger role, the second is even more radically statist in taking it for granted that elected and appointed officeholders pursue their own interests as much as, if not more than, those of citizens.[55]

It is important to note that statist theorists have not simply replaced society-centered explanations with state-centered explanations, turning their predecessors' ideas on their heads as Marx and the pluralists did to Hegel and the formal-legalists. Rather, they offer state-centered models as supplements and correctives to one-sided society-centered models, as contributions to the development of a balanced, nonreductionist, relational approach.

A fundamental problem for the whole approach, however, is the specification of state structures. When statist theorists speak of "the state," they are talking primarily, if not exclusively, about central government bureaucracies. With party government, wars, and increased state intervention in the economy all helping to shift the balance of power from the legislature to the executive, Aberbach, Putnam, and Rockman have traced successive images of the evolving relationship between politicians and bureaucrats. The classic Weberian distinction held that "politicians make policy; civil servants administer."[56] Although this remains the official norm in every state, the most "technical" problems can assume political significance, and because politicians often lack the expertise, information, and time to decide all policy questions, the drafting of most legislation has fallen to career civil servants.

Political scientists therefore began to acknowledge that both politicians and civil servants participate in policymaking, but in different ways: "Civil servants bring facts and knowledge; politicians, interests and values." Although this second image assigns the task of articulating and balancing diverse claims to politicians, empirical research has revealed how bureaucratic agencies themselves mobilize and mediate sectoral interests. Consequently, it was accepted that bureaucrats as well as politicians engage in policymaking and are concerned with politics, but "whereas politicians articulate broad, diffuse interests of unorganized individuals, bureaucrats mediate narrow, focused interests of organized clienteles. . . . Politicians are energizing to the policy system, whereas bureaucrats provide equilibrium."[57] Because this progression of images suggests a convergence of roles, a politicization of bureaucrats and a bureaucratization of politicians, Aberbach et al. asked whether the future might not hold the development of a "pure hybrid."

"While physicists stand on each other's shoulders, political scientists stand on each other's faces."[58] Nevertheless, despite their contrasts and the acrimony of

---

[55] Thelen and Steinmo (1992), pp. 7–9; Atkinson and Coleman (1992), p. 154.
[56] Aberbach et al. (1981), p. 4.
[57] Ibid., pp. 6, 9.
[58] Valerie Bunce, quoted in Lucian W. Pye, "Political Science and the Crisis of Authoritarianism," *American Political Science Review*; v. 84, n. 1 (March 1990), p. 17.

debates among their adherents, the various models outlined earlier can be regarded as heuristic devices; it is unnecessary to regard them as mutually exclusive. No abstract model is ever fully realized in an actual society. In fact, a country may look very different when examined at the macro level of national policymaking, the meso level of the region or industrial sector, or the micro level of the locality or single corporation. On any given level, different policy domains may be organized in different ways, and patterns of interest intermediation can change over time. Although a country may tend in one direction, and although certain policy domains do appear to have a greater propensity for one set of arrangements than for others, every political economy is in this sense "mixed."[59] The question, then, is not so much which model is "right" as how much each of them, treated as a formal ideal type, throws light on a specific historical case. How do Marxism, pluralism, neopluralism, corporatism, and statism illuminate or obfuscate the case of contemporary Japan?

Before answering this question, it is necessary to justify the whole enterprise of applying models designed in and for the West to Japan. Kumon Shunpei, for one, warned that it would be "ridiculous to expect a Western model to fit the Japanese 'muddle.'"[60]

Culturalist models

Theories of Japanese exceptionalism typically credit that nation with a unique, culturally derived ability to cooperate because individuals (and small groups) are willing to sacrifice their interests for the sake of the (larger) group. Eugene Kaplan popularized a vision of a "Japan, Inc." that works in part because of "a propensity, which all Japanese share, for a consensual approach to harmonizing differences," for example.[61] What this approach ignores is that the relative anti-individualism of Japanese values does not preclude conflicts so much as shape the forms that they tend to assume, and, as will be detailed, intense conflicts unquestionably *do* exist within the private sector, among government agencies, and between the two.

In a more sophisticated culturalist analysis, Nakane Chie has asserted that the primary basis of group organization in Japan is not some common "attribute" acquired by birth or achievement, but position in a locational or institutional "frame." An individual is identified, that is to say, less by family and occupation than by hometown, alma mater, and, most especially, employer, and within these groups, embracing individuals with different attributes as they do, members are tied vertically to one another in a hierarchical order. As a result, Japanese society is riven by competition among groups in the same field of

---

[59] Schmitter (1979), p. 28; Schmitter (1977), p. 14; Hollingsworth, Schmitter, and Streeck (1994), p. 8.
[60] Kumon (1992), p. 110.
[61] Kaplan (1972), p. 10.

activity and by factionalism within groups. Because people who share common attributes are located in different frames, they are more likely to view one another as competitors than as comrades, impeding the mobilization of socio-economic strata. Because the verticality of social relations hampers the development of balanced, horizontal links among subgroups, groups always run the risk of fission.[62]

Paradoxically, Scott Flanagan started out from the same groupism observed by consensus theorists only to arrive at what comes close to a conflict theory of Japanese politics. For Flanagan, intergroup competition is "an essential ingredient" in reinforcing group solidarity and mobilizing group energies, and "the greater the affective distance between the groups which are engaged in any conflict situation, the greater the likelihood that the conflict will move into the anomic domain where conflict may be unrestrained. It is therefore likely that conflict will be greatest among large interest groups and organizations operating at the national level."[63] Japanese collectivism is thus characterized by a multiplicity of competitive groups, and one reason consensus is so highly valued in Japan is precisely that the social order is so threatened.

Cultural differences cannot be gainsaid, and the relevance of analyses like Nakane's and Flanagan's to many aspects of Japan is too obvious to belabor. But even when it is not (mis-)used as an undifferentiated, residual category to "explain" whatever is different about Japan, appeals to culture suffer from serious limitations. Most obviously, culturalist theories are too broad to capture differences across time and policy domains: Sometimes Japanese cooperate, and sometimes they don't. How can slow-changing, widely held norms explain why there was more harmony among Japanese during the 1960s than during the 1950s or more in industrial policy during the 1960s than in educational policy? Explaining at one and the same time too much and too little, culturalist models tend to be applied in an arbitrary, ad hoc manner.

Behavior is often due less to diffuse considerations of culture than to the ways in which specific institutional settings condition individuals' perceptions and expectations.[64] The same people with the same values will behave differently when confronted with different circumstances, and Ruth Benedict long ago emphasized the highly "situational" nature of Japanese ethics.[65] Even when cultural differences clearly do exist, they must still be explained. Values are neither heritable nor immutable: They must be maintained and transmitted, and their reproduction allows for their re-creation by power holders. Although the preference for harmony observed today was, in fact, a part of previous generations' social consciousness, so too were other, antithetical attitudes that have been deliberately discouraged.

[62] Nakane (1972).   [63] Richardson and Flanagan (1984), pp. 151, 154.
[64] Hall (1986), p. 9; Reed (1993), p. 25.   [65] Benedict (1946).

In sum, the relationship between culture and political economy is dialectical rather than one-sidedly causal, and culturalist theories of Japanese exceptionalism are no more (or less) valid and enlightening than theories of American or Swedish exceptionalism. In the West, bureaucratized, democratic polities must resolve the conflicts of interest generated by capitalist (post)industrial economies; the same holds true in Japan. Norms of consensus and group solidarity may well play an important part in Japanese policymaking, but more for their influence on policy style than for their direct, determinative power.[66]

The statist model

There never was a need to "bring the state back in" to Japanese studies: Japan is commonly thought to have the archetypal strong state.[67] In his seminal work *MITI and the Japanese Miracle*, Chalmers Johnson elaborated a model of bureaucratic dominance that framed Western debate on Japan for years. A late industrializer, Japan is characterized by a "developmental," "plan-rational" orientation, with the state going beyond mere regulation actively to set substantive goals for society, Johnson argues. To operate effectively, the developmental state requires an implicit political division of labor whereby "the politicians reign and the bureaucrats rule." Thus, Japan's elite bureaucracy "makes most major decisions, drafts virtually all legislation, controls the national budget, and is the source of all major policy innovations in the system." Politicians, on the other hand, "provide the space for bureaucrats to rule by holding off special interest claimants who might deflect the state from its main developmental priorities, and . . . legitimate and ratify the decisions taken by bureaucrats."[68]

Proponents of the statist model underestimate the degree to which bureaucratic authority has ebbed in the postwar era. Officials have had to share more and more of their authority with elected politicians, and Japanese society has become increasingly autonomous as the processes of expansion, the easing of regulation, and internationalization have reduced the state's role in the economy. Moreover, political parties and private organizations have gradually routinized their recruitment and promotion of personnel, creating professional hierarchies distinct from the national bureaucracy.[69] The weight of current research suggests that Japanese bureaucrats exercise power most frequently and effectively via, in cooperation with politicians and private actors, rather than vis-à-vis, in control of them.

---

[66] For more on policy style, see Richardson and Gustafsson (1980) and Richardson, Gustafsson, and Jordan (1982).

[67] E.g., Katzenstein (1978).

[68] Johnson (1982), pp. 19, 154, 20–21.   [69] Allinson (1993a) and Allinson (1993b).

Bureaucrats and politicians

The phrase "party up, government [i.e., officials] down" (*tōkō seitei*) was widely heard in the 1980s. A variety of factors contributed to the increasing influence of (conservative) politicians over policymaking.

"The plan-rational system depends upon the existence of a widely agreed upon set of overarching goals for the society, such as high-speed growth," Johnson asserted.[70] The Pacific War discredited militaristic but not economic nationalism, and the latter combined with the harsh conditions of the 1940s to create just such a consensus on the priority of rapid economic growth. By the 1970s, however, Japan had succeeded in its century-long quest to overtake the West, and rapid growth no longer seemed so desirable when accompanied by industrial pollution, urban overcrowding, and stressful personal lives. Amaya Naohiro, an architect of Japan's postwar industrial policy, offered a vivid metaphor for this change of heart: "Just after the war, the Japanese people were like a greyhound pursuing the hare. When people are hungry, they have only one voice, one wish. But when their stomachs are filled, the confusion begins. People have lost their goals. Now, where is the hare we should pursue?"[71]

Civil servants have difficulty articulating broad, new national goals because the Japanese bureaucracy is riven by sectionalism. The flip side of a functional loyalty and sense of belonging *within* ministries is a dysfunctional us-versus-them attitude *among* ministries that creates tensions and hinders cooperation. Although ministries frequently rotate higher civil servants among bureaus and strongly encourage officials to identify with the ministry organization as a whole, competition is intra- as well as interministerial. With their compartmentalized structure (*tatewari gyōsei*, or "vertical administration"), every bureau, division, and section jealously protects its jurisdiction over some particular policy domain. "What actually exists is not *bureaucracy*, but *bureaucracies*," Muramatsu Michio declared. "The interests of every ministry and agency are different, and they participate on the stage of political competition."[72]

If anything, bureaucratic conflicts have become more frequent and open. In the prewar and early postwar years, the need to defend against external threats and the subordination of other objectives to economic growth helped repress centrifugal tendencies. Those days are gone. Since the late 1960s, new technologies, structural economic shifts, and Japan's growing role on the world stage have created a slew of broad, complex problems that straddle or fall outside traditional administrative boundaries, sparking heated turf battles. In the mid-1980s, for example, the Ministry of International Trade and Industry (MITI) alone clashed with the Ministry of Finance (MOF) over capital market liberali-

---

[70] Johnson (1982), p. 22.   [71] *The Wall Street Journal* (7 December 1992).
[72] Muramatsu (1981b), p. 96.

zation, with the Ministry of Posts and Telecommunications over value-added networks, with the Ministry of Education over copyrights for software, with the Ministry of Agriculture, Forestry, and Fisheries over the liberalization of agricultural imports, and with the Fair Trade Commission over the legality of administrative guidance.[73] As Johnson himself has pointed out, these turf wars present politicians with "numerous opportunities to support one ministry against another, or to profit from the deadlocks by offering real supra-bureaucratic leadership, or in other ways to expand their powers at the expense of the bickering bureaucrats."[74]

In truth, politicians' growing weight in policymaking owed less to bureaucratic weakness than to the gradual institutionalization of (one-)party government, but Japanese parties have always been better at articulating interests than at aggregating them and mobilizing support for integrated programs. Throughout the postwar period, the involvement of individual politicians in policymaking has tended to concentrate in specialized areas because Japan's electoral system made them highly sensitive to constituency pressure and rewarded distributive politics. There are now a total of 500 members in the more powerful lower house, 300 elected from local, single-member districts, with voters casting ballots for individual candidates, and 200 elected from 11 regional, proportional-representation (PR) districts, with voters casting ballots for political parties. Until 1994, however, 511 lower house members were elected by means of a single, nontransferable ballot from 129 multimember districts with two to six seats. By forcing candidates from any party that sought a significant number of seats to vie with one another for the same votes, this system made very small shifts in support crucial to politicians' election and required them to build their own personal support organizations (kōenkai) and attach themselves to intraparty factions. Japanese electoral politics has thus revolved around personalistic appeals and intraparty competition over the servicing of specific constituencies – especially well-organized interest groups in domestically oriented sectors like agriculture, small business, and construction – rather than interparty conflict over principles. Once elected, Diet members have served primarily as intermediaries or "pipes" (paipu) between these particularistic constituencies and the national government.

Factionalism and clientelism may have inhibited politicians from playing comprehensive programmatic or even coordinating roles in policymaking, but as Aberbach et al. noted, civil servants labor under an inescapable constraint:

> The norms of representative democracy . . . endow elected politicians with a monopoly on one essential ingredient in policymaking – legitimacy as the final decision-making authority. However expert and imaginative a civil servant in substantive terms, however skilled in winning consent from

---

[73] Eads and Yamamura (1987), p. 451.   [74] Johnson (1986b), p. 25.

organized interests, however adept in coordinating his initiatives with others, however successful in implementation, he needs endorsement from
political leaders for his actions.[75]

Japan's postwar constitution states unequivocally that "the Diet shall be the
highest organ of state power, and shall be the sole law-making organ of the
state." Bureaucrats thus have no choice but to depend on politicians to propose
and pass bills on their behalf, and as changing circumstances have repeatedly
forced agencies to draft new legislation requiring Diet approval, party politics
has intruded into Japanese policymaking more than was previously the case. If
not the United States, Japan exceeds many other democracies in the extent to
which rank-and-file politicians participate in policymaking.[76]

Of equal importance to the 1947 constitution was the 1955 unification of
conservative Diet representatives into the Liberal Democratic Party (LDP).
The LDP provided every prime minister from its birth until its schism in 1993,
a record unsurpassed among the advanced industrial democracies with the sole
exception of the Social Democrats' rule of Sweden from 1932 to 1977. If voters
repeatedly punished the party for improprieties or for tardiness in adapting
public policies to new demands, they were unwilling to accept the risk of
empowering an untested and fractious opposition.[77] Stable one-party dominance
forced government agencies to collaborate closely with the LDP.

On the surface, the Japanese bureaucracy is notable for its insulation
from outside intervention. Whereas the American president doles out about
3,000 administrative jobs, the Japanese prime minister allots fewer than 30,
appointing only cabinet ministers and political vice-ministers. The primary
consideration behind these appointments has been the need to balance
intraparty factions, not the qualifications of individual politicians, and because
there have always been more LDP Diet members with the requisite seniority
than there are posts, there has been fairly rapid turnover in order to give
everyone who qualifies the chance to serve: The average term of a cabinet
minister has been less than a year.

Under the circumstances, the norm has been for ministers to entrust the
details of administration to their nominal subordinates, the permanent bureaucratic staff. The ministries do not exist in a political vacuum, however. As
Gerald Curtis has observed, officials' behavior has always been marked by a
process of "anticipated reaction." Because they understood that a party in
control of the Diet has the ultimate power to bend them to its will, "the
bureaucracy was responsive to LDP needs without necessarily having to be
ordered to be."[78] If alternations of the party in power typically bring policy shifts

[75] Aberbach et al. (1981), p. 248.
[76] Calder (1993), pp. 66, 211; Campbell (1989), p. 11.
[77] Allinson (1993b), p. 39.   [78] Curtis (1988), p. 108.

and pressure for the politicization of administration, the seeming permanence of LDP rule dissipated that pressure.

Bureaucrats have thus maintained a measure of autonomy and been free to take policy initiatives – as long as they cooperated with the LDP and remained within the bounds of accepted conservative politics. Although few other students of Japanese politics have followed them, Mark Ramseyer and Frances McCall Rosenbluth draw on the principal-agent analysis of rational choice theory to take this line of argument to a polemical extreme: Precisely because of the ease with which ruling-party politicians can intervene in administration, they seldom need to, thus giving the *impression* of bureaucratic autonomy. "Real Japanese bureaucrats . . . administer in the shadow of the LDP."[79]

The legislative process exemplifies the limits of bureaucratic autonomy. The ministries do initiate and draft most laws, but because Japan's is a parliamentary rather than a presidential system, the Diet should not be expected to compete with the executive branch, and the lack of meaningful *Diet* involvement in policymaking has in no way entailed a lack of *ruling-party* participation. Ministry officials have had to consult with the LDP at every stage of policymaking, and it has been party leaders, not their bureaucratic authors, who have decided which bills were to be introduced in the Diet, what priorities they were to be assigned, and how they were to be amended. As Katō Junko has emphasized, bureaucrats must therefore exert their influence through an active involvement in politics, not insulation from it.[80]

Whether by taking advantage of the relative ignorance of politicians or, conversely, by strategically sharing their knowledge with politicians, bureaucrats are generally assumed to gain leverage from their superior policy information and technocratic expertise, and it cannot be denied that individual Diet representatives lack alternative resources available to their American counterparts. Members of the U.S. House of Representatives hire as many as 22 people to staff offices in Washington and their home districts, and other aides assist them in committees; in 1994, the number of government-paid staffers working for Japanese Diet representatives rose from two to three.[81]

Nevertheless, the LDP's Policy Affairs Research Council (PARC) has an elaborate structure of divisions (*bukai*), each of which corresponds to a ministry and a Diet standing committee, and a large number of less formal commissions and special committees. In the early years of the LDP, Johnson noted, division "meetings were occasions for bureau or section chiefs from the appropriate ministry to lecture on the bills that they intended to introduce in the Diet during a current session. LDP members were thus instructed on policy, but they did not in turn instruct."[82] And yet, due precisely to this educative function and the

[79] Ramseyer and Rosenbluth (1993), p. 120.   [80] Katō (1994).
[81] *The Los Angeles Times* (26 December 1994).
[82] Johnson (1986a), p. 36.

longevity of LDP rule, veteran Diet representatives gradually acquired expertise and connections in specific policy domains that came to equal, and sometimes surpass, those of their erstwhile bureaucratic masters, who individually
remain at any specific post for only two or three years.

Labeled *seisaku zoku*, or "policy tribes," groups of these MPs came to wield
great influence. "Simultaneously policy specialists, representatives of interest-
group and ministry interests, and mediators among those interests," *zoku* have
accumulated enough know-how to resist bureaucrats and regulate rapid social
change that the ministries no longer can.[83] The end of rapid economic growth in
the 1970s hastened the rise of *zoku*: As fiscal constraints turned budgetary
politics into more of a zero-sum competition for resources, the level of
politicization rose sharply in Japan, with LDP Diet members increasingly intervening on behalf of their constituencies.[84] The 1970s brought increasing intervention by conservative politicians on broader policy questions, too. Reduced
government revenues forced the party leadership to take a more active role in
setting priorities, a decline in electoral support forced the LDP to address issues
it had previously ignored, and the growing diversification and internationalization of the economy greatly expanded and complicated the concerns of constituents, forcing all representatives to interest themselves in a wider range of
policies.

Johnson has questioned whether the LDP can be said to control bureaucrats
when bureaucrats fill its ranks: "The bureaucracy staffs the LDP with its own
cadres to insure that the party does what the bureaucracy thinks is good for the
country as a whole."[85] A variety of statistics appear to support the proposition
that officials have moved the LDP from within. Of all conservatives elected to
the lower house of the Diet between 1955 and 1983, 21 percent came from the
higher civil service; only former local politicians were more numerous. The
ministries provided an even higher fraction of the LDP's leadership, with
retired bureaucrats occupying the prime ministry for 20 of the first 25 years after
1955.[86]

The dominance of ex-bureaucrats within the LDP was transitory, however.
Given their expertise and experience, retired officials did advance more rapidly
than other Diet members in the early years of the LDP, but the gradual
routinization of promotion on the basis of seniority eroded that advantage. If
only for reasons of age, the trend since the early 1970s has thus been for the
politically ambitious to leave the civil service when they are still junior or
middle-ranking bureaucrats. Between 1958 and 1969, 62.9 percent of the former
officials elected for the first time had achieved the rank of bureau chief or above;
this was true of only 28.2 percent of the former officials elected between 1972

---

[83] Sone (1986), p. 311.   [84] Okimoto (1988), p. 325; Ramseyer and Rosenbluth (1993), p. 49.
[85] Johnson (1982), p. 50.   [86] Fukui (1984), p. 393; Okimoto (1989), p. 219.

and 1983.[87] These younger bureaucrats have naturally lacked the leadership assets that lent so much weight to the senior officials who entered the LDP in its early years, when the party organization was still rudimentary.

Rather than demonstrating bureaucratic dominance, the very fact that civil servants seek elected office is a tribute to politicians' power. "The bureaucrats can't just use Diet members the way their predecessors did," observed a former lobbyist. "So increasingly they are thinking that it's better to be politicians themselves."[88] An official's ambitions has ensured that he or she will play ball with the LDP while still a bureaucrat, and once elected, ex-officials have provided the LDP with the prestige, connections, and firsthand knowledge of policymaking and administration that were formerly sources of bureaucratic leverage vis-à-vis the party.

Although Aberbach et al.'s "pure hybrid" has yet to emerge, with veteran politicians gaining the expertise of administrators and ex-bureaucrats becoming socialized as politicians, the distinction between the two has become less significant over time. To debate the relative dominance of politicians or bureaucrats can be misleading: It does not have to be an either-or, zero-sum game. Each acknowledges and depends on the other, and cooperative alliances that cut across the two groups in specific policy domains are more common than general conflicts between politicians qua politicians and bureaucrats qua bureaucrats. Thus, Nathaniel Thayer referred to LDP politicians and bureaucrats as "two peas in the conservative pod" and Satō Seizaburō to an "integrated LDP-bureaucratic structure."[89]

The debate continues, however. Although the LDP was once called the "party that will rule half an eternity," its 38-year grip on power was finally broken when two ostensibly reformist groups of rebels broke away in 1993. A key tenet of the eight-party government that replaced the LDP was the need to rein in bureaucrats – its watchwords were the easing of regulation (*kisei kanwa*) and decentralization (*chihō bunken*) – but preoccupied with coalition politics and the fight for political reform, the new Hosokawa Administration was soon regarded as helplessly dependent on the ministries. The slogan of the day shifted from the easing of regulation to "bureaucrats up, politicians down" (*kankō seitei*). In response to a 1994 poll, 63 percent of the high-level administrators surveyed reported that it was they, not elected politicians, who were taking the initiative in policymaking. "In present-day Japan, there is the problem of ministries but no government," complained the retired official Amaya.[90]

What of the future? In the short run, political turmoil has doubtless reinforced bureaucratic authority. Japan saw a succession of five prime ministers

[87] Curtis (1988), pp. 92–93; Satō and Matsuzawa (1984), p. 94.
[88] *Newsweek* (7 July 1986).
[89] Thayer (1969), p. 226; Satō S. (1984), p. 74.
[90] *The New York Times* (10 April 1994); *Asahi Evening News* (4 April 1994).

(Miyazawa, Hosokawa, Hata, Murayama, and Hashimoto) from four parties in three years. But in the past, if the party always had its own agenda, it was the LDP's continuous reign that provided ministries with the political support and stability necessary to formulate and implement policies and made it possible for certain agencies to retain a measure of autonomy.[91] The temporary banishment of the LDP to the opposition caused confusion in officialdom. Thus, intensified electoral competition and the alternation of parties in power might over the long run encourage bureaucratic neutrality and greater political intervention in administration. The continued relevance of multiple parties could also bring greater political interference due to the need to satisfy the varying goals of shifting coalition partners.

To date, the evidence is ambiguous. The minister of MITI forced the resignation of the chief of the Industrial Policy Bureau in 1993, and the minister of Health and Welfare in 1996 ordered the release of hidden documents proving that it had banned the importation of sterilized blood even as it ignored warnings that domestic blood supplies were contaminated with human immunodeficiency virus (HIV). It was unclear, though, whether to attribute greater significance to these assertions of political control or to the shock and outcries that accompanied them. Besides, the first incident was linked to factional struggles within MITI and among politicians, and the maverick politician who overcame the recalcitrance of Health and Welfare officials lamented that "being a minister is like being a tiny, lone coconut pushed into the vast, hostile ocean."[92]

Bureaucrats and the private sector

It is often overlooked that Japan's is a small state, the smallest (in relative terms) of the advanced industrial democracies. Repeated campaigns for "administrative reform" have checked bureaucratic expansion by freezing the number of posts within the national ministries and delegating many functions to local governments, semipublic corporations, and the private sector. In 1994, there were only 40 government workers for every 1,000 people in Japan compared to 68 in Germany and 86 in the United States.[93] Small government is cheap government: Japan perennially ranks near the very bottom of all developed nations in its ratios of tax revenues and state expenditures to gross domestic product. Industrial ownership has been almost exclusively in private hands since the turn of the century, and the government has been denationalizing many of the enterprises it once owned. It is the supposedly weak state of America, not Japan, that heavily regulates a long list of fields like occupational safety and industrial concentration and enforces that regulation with strong legal sanctions.[94]

[91] Katō (1994), pp. 14, 233; Okimoto (1988), p. 325.   [92] Itagaki (1996), p. 26.
[93] Journal of Japanese Trade & Industry (January/February 1997), p. 25.
[94] Okimoto (1989), pp. 2–3; Haley (1986), pp. 111–12; The New York Times (17 November 1996).

If the Japanese state is clearly interventionist in orientation and bureaucrats have drawn on an unusually wide range of policy tools, the last several decades have witnessed a significant erosion in bureaucrats' leverage over the private sector. Although credited in the past with enormous power, MITI's statutory authority is limited. It has had to employ indirect, market-conforming methods of intervention in the economy since it lost the absolute powers bestowed by Occupation authorities with the expiration of the Temporary Materials Supply and Demand Control Act in 1952.[95] MITI could still exert effective control as long as Japan remained a closed economy; the Foreign Exchange and Foreign Trade Control Act gave MITI the power to grant or deny firms access to raw materials, foreign technology, and foreign markets at its own discretion. Trade and capital liberalization began under foreign (and domestic) pressure in the 1960s, however, and were carried out in earnest from the late 1970s. The Foreign Exchange and Foreign Trade Control Act was drastically revised in 1979 and the Foreign Capital Act was abolished in 1980. The trend is not linear – MITI *gained* leverage over industries facing severe adjustment problems as a result of the oil shocks, the auto industry as a result of voluntary export re-straints, and a variety of mature "sunset" industries, for example – but a gradual (if admittedly halting) tendency toward the easing of regulation does exist.

Shorn of its express legal powers, MITI continued to carry out much the same policies as before by means of "administrative guidance" (*gyōsei shidō*), that is, by the persuasion of private actors to cooperate on matters over which an agency has broad jurisdictional competence even if no specific statutory author-ity. Although administrative guidance is by definition legally unenforceable, its recipients typically do comply. Its power derives from long-standing business–government relationships, respect for bureaucrats – and sanctions. A coopera-tive firm is more likely to receive government assistance; an insubordinate firm or its allies face retaliation.

Administrative guidance has its limits, too, however. It is rarely imposed on a recalcitrant private sector: Administrative guidance normally reflects the de-mands of "guidees" as well as those of the government, and it is often issued at the request of private industry itself.[96] Even so, with Japan ceasing to be a follower economy from the mid-1970s, successful companies have come to feel that they no longer need – indeed, have come to resent – MITI supervision, and a series of challenges has curtailed the use of administrative guidance. The practice came under severe attack in 1991 following a stock-loss compensation scandal that was blamed in part on cozy ties between MOF and the securities industry, and the Administrative Procedures Act of 1994 was designed to make regulation more transparent by pushing ministries either to eliminate or codify

---

[95] Johnson (1982), p. 240.
[96] Okimoto (1989), p. 941; Haley (1986), p. 108. See also Tilton (1996) and Uriu (1996).

non-statutory rules. Independent initiatives by MITI and MOF to reestablish a measure of statutory authority suggest that the utility of administrative guidance has diminished.[97] (It should be noted, though, that these ministries have failed in most of their attempts to strengthen their statutory authority in the past.)

By influencing the supply and cost of capital, MOF has wielded enormous leverage over the private sector, and it played a pivotal role in helping allocate investment funds during the years of recovery and high-speed growth, but its power, too, has declined. During the 1950s and early 1960s, when investment funds were scarce and capital markets undeveloped (the government positively discouraged equity and bond financing), large enterprises obtained the bulk of their funds through loans from a dozen or so "city," or commercial, banks. Because these banks, in turn, were overextended and had to borrow heavily from the Bank of Japan, MOF could ration and guide the flow of credit to some extent by means of "[discount] window guidance." The ministry also used money from the postal savings and insurance systems to provide additional low-cost funds to selected industries. Finally, by keeping domestic capital markets strictly segmented and insulated from international markets, MOF was able to administer interest rates. All of these preconditions of bureaucratic direction of industrial credit slowly unraveled from the early 1970s.

Given the explosive growth of Japan's economy, the supply of savings eventually came to exceed investment demand, dependence on the central bank shrank rapidly, and the state's share of industrial financing fell. In the wake of the first oil shock, rising international competitiveness and expansionary monetary and fiscal policies enhanced corporate profitability and multiplied internal funds just as a slump in economic growth, an increase in foreign protectionism, and a structural shift in the Japanese economy away from capital-intensive sectors all reduced companies' demand for credit and thus their dependence on banks. Bank lending as a fraction of corporate financing fell from an average of 84 percent in 1970–1974 to 44 percent in 1984.[98]

Even as corporate liquidity rose and bureaucratic leverage fell, the state's own finances weakened considerably, forcing the government to *compete with* industry and *depend on* banks for capital. In fiscal year 1975, when tax revenues dropped sharply because of the recession that followed the first oil shock, the government's bond dependency ratio shot up from 9.4 to 25.3 percent,[99] and as welfare expenditures began to take off and the government pursued stimulative policies in the years that followed, national budget deficits spiraled. The government's need for revenue weakened MOF's bargaining power vis-à-vis the financial institutions that bought national bonds, and the ministry gradually loosened regulations. Borrowing from the Bank of Japan became less attractive

---

[97] Mabuchi (1993).   [98] Calder (1993), p. 214.   [99] Mabuchi (1993), p. 140.

to commercial banks, Japanese firms gained access to cheap funds overseas (by 1984, the Euromarket[100] provided 36.2 percent of all Japanese corporate financing[101]), and as domestic capital markets became more responsive to market forces and open to international influences, the ability of the government to administer interest rates waned. In acknowledgment of these changes, the Bank of Japan formally abolished window guidance and the Diet passed landmark legislation to end the segmentation of the financial industry in the early 1990s.

Even when ministries pursue organizational goals rather than national ones, they rely on the cooperation of industries under their jurisdiction and seek to avoid controversy, so ministries have no choice but to be receptive to the preferences of interest groups and their political allies.[102] Furthermore, the Japanese state is not monolithic, so it is necessary to make distinctions among (and, to some extent, even within) the various ministries, and MITI and MOF actually stand out among bureaucracies for their relative cohesion and ability to parry outside pressures. With their more fragmented organizations and their extensive regulatory controls over particular sectors, ministries like Construction, Health and Welfare, Posts and Telecommunications, and Transportation all attract far more political intervention and have been significantly clientelized by the groups they regulate.

Although it has its defenders, the accumulation of evidence undercutting the bureaucracy-dominant perspective has emboldened critics to propose increasingly assertive alternatives. Richard Samuels has argued that business is not, in fact, induced to accept government goals; rather, "market objectives are more commonly achieved through the state than state objectives are achieved through the market."[103] Samuels perceives a process of "reciprocal consent" in which firms acknowledge state jurisdiction over markets in return for their continuing control over those markets and institutionalized access to public goods. Rosenbluth maintains that final decisionmaking authority lies in the political arena and that the very possibility of politicization ensures that policy outcomes are consonant with the respective political resources of the private interests involved. "The bureaucracy does not control any group in society; rather, it orchestrates according to a score it did not compose."[104]

Contending that Japanese officials are, on the whole, cautious, reactive, and stability oriented, Kent Calder has reconceptualized the Japanese political economy in terms of "corporate-led strategic capitalism": It is a "hybrid public-private system, driven preeminently by market-oriented private-sector calcula-

---

[100] Originally developed in Europe, Euromarkets consist of funds that are denominated in a currency other than that of the host country and are free of all regulatory control.
[101] Rosenbluth (1993), p. 112.
[102] Uriu (1996), pp. 24–25, 256.
[103] Samuels (1987), p. 261.   [104] Rosenbluth (1989), p. 216; Rosenbluth (1993).

tions, but with active public-sector involvement to encourage public spirited-ness and long-range vision."[105] Turning the bureaucratic-dominance approach on its head, Robert Uriu contends that it is private actors who have been the driving force behind industrial policymaking. Thus, "It is absolutely necessary to analyze the interests of industry actors – or perhaps even to make these interests our central focus."[106]

But to what extent are these "private" actors truly private? The direction of elite circulation in Japan is virtually always from the government to the private sector, and the very word for the employment of retired bureaucrats by companies – *amakudari*, literally "descent from heaven" – is redolent of statist attitudes. Johnson has maintained that the bureaucracy consciously distributes its officials to help coordinate state-led economic growth: "preferential access to the government for the strategic industries in Japan is . . . an objective of the developmental state. This is the true significance of *amakudari*."[107]

Actually, as Johnson himself concedes, *amakudari* is largely due to the inter-nal dynamics of the Japanese bureaucracy. Because civil service promotions are governed by rigid seniority rules and a sharp narrowing of opportunities at the upper reaches of the hierarchy, officials must retire young, by their early or mid-fifties. More to the point, major corporations now rely far more on insiders who have risen through the ranks, so rather than shoring up state ties to a select number of industry leaders, a disproportionate number of retired officials enter second-tier companies. "*Amakudari* thus operates to *broaden* the access of the less-connected portion of the corporate world to government information, and frequently to *co-opt* and to *undermine* bureaucratic efforts at strategic dirigisme" (emphasis in the original).[108] Patterns of elite mobility thus point to the same conclusion as do trends in the use of policy tools: Relationships between agen-cies and interest groups in their jurisdictions now tend more toward negotiation than notification.

The loss of state influence over the private sector should not be exaggerated. It is in the interests of officials to play down their role: Ministries cannot be held accountable for what they do not (admit to) control, and bureaucratic self-effacement deflects foreign criticism by suggesting that the Japanese economy does, in fact, operate by means of "free" markets. Ironically, the very countries that once complained about Japanese bureaucrats' grip on industry now turn to those same bureaucrats to resolve trade and investment tensions. Further, as noted earlier, the trend is by no means unilinear: The government once again began playing a more interventionist role as a result of the bursting of the "bubble economy" in the early 1990s, and Steven Vogel has detailed how often recent campaigns for liberalization (i.e., the introduction of more competition)

---

[105] Calder (1993), pp. 101–2, 16.   [106] Uriu (1996), p. 252.   [107] Johnson (1982), p. 70.
[108] Calder (1993), p. 69; Calder (1989). See also Radin (1997).

have entailed not deregulation, but *re*regulation.[109] Over the long run, though, the growth in private-sector autonomy seems irreversible.

The ruling triad model

To reverse the question, how much power does the private sector wield over the state? The unpopularity of explicitly Marxist models notwithstanding, one of the most influential earlier images of postwar Japanese politics postulated that the bureaucracy has shared power with the LDP and big business to form an interdependent triumvirate (*sei-kan-zai no yuchaku*), a power elite that effectively controls most policymaking. At its simplest, the model resembles the game of paper, scissors, stone: Conservative politicians depend on the campaign contributions of business, businesspeople depend on the administrative rulings of the bureaucracy, and bureaucrats depend on the legislative authority of the ruling party. The model dismisses interest groups other than big business (and, to a lesser extent, farmers) as inconsequential. Although it defines the scope of participation in policymaking more broadly than the statist model, the ruling triad model is no less inadequate. It assumes that the triumvirs are internally united and cooperative in their relations with one another. Neither of these assumptions is borne out. Sectionalism and factionalism are endemic in Japanese bureaucracies and parties. What of the business sector and its relationships to state actors?

Some observers have attributed extraordinary political power to big business. Yanaga Chitoshi, for example, characterized its role in the most sweeping terms. "Business feels that government is much too important to be left entirely to professional politicians and administrators and has seen to it that its representatives are directly involved at all levels. . . . The power of life and death over the government has been exercised by organized business."[110] If there was ever any truth to these assertions, they are patently false today. Businesspeople are not directly involved in governing Japan, "organized business" has become significantly less organized, and the business community's influence is limited even among the conservative politicians who represent it.

In marked contrast to the United States, the routinization of political and administrative recruitment has limited the lateral entry of businesspeople into elective and appointive office in Japan. In the postwar era, not a single prime minister or major LDP faction leader has come from big business, and although prime ministers are constitutionally obliged to appoint no more than a bare majority of cabinet ministers from among members of parliament, they almost

[109] S. Vogel (1996).
[110] Yanaga (1968), pp. 71, 141. For more recent assertions along these lines, see, e.g., Boyd (1987), pp. 72–73.

never go outside the Diet in their choices. Professional politicians and former bureaucrats have always been more numerous than businesspeople in the LDP's Diet delegation. Former staffers now outnumber them, too, and representatives with a "business" background naturally include small merchants as well as owners or executives of large enterprises.

There is no denying that the business sector has been highly organized and politically mobilized in Japan. Top politicians meet business leaders on a regular basis, and major corporations are in close contact with the ministries under whose jurisdictions they fall. On a higher level, industry associations attempt to build intraindustry consensus on relevant matters of government policy. At the peak of business interest aggregation stand four broad-based, nationwide economic organizations, the *zaikai* associations. (Literally "financial world," *zaikai* refers to an elite of major business leaders who speak not for their specific companies or industries, but for *all* companies and industries and, in their eyes at least, for all of Japanese society.)

Chief among them is the Federation of Economic Organizations, or Keidanren. With about 110 industry associations and over 800 of Japan's largest corporations as members, Keidanren encompasses virtually all of big business and finance. The Japan Federation of Employers' Associations, or Nikkeiren, organizes some 30,000 employers into prefectural associations and over 50 industry associations. Although Nikkeiren has taken up a variety of issues, the organization is preeminent and its task clearly defined only in the field of labor relations, and it represents employers in the annual, national-level *shuntō* ("spring struggle") wage negotiations with organized labor. The Japan Chamber of Commerce and Industry, or Nisshō, has a local, grassroots base and defends the interests of small business. Finally, the Japan Council for Economic Development, or Keizai Dōyūkai, has focused on the development of a new capitalist ideology suited to the postwar era.

Despite this impressive panoply, the power of these business associations is easily exaggerated. The very success of Japanese business has contributed to the decline of its peak associations: As corporations have gained strength, their dependence on government agencies and the associations that petition them has declined. Although the peak associations have banded together when businesspeople perceived Japan's economic or political stability to be at stake, such as during the Security Treaty crisis of 1960, the very existence of four national organizations underscores the repeated failure to create a comprehensive association that could represent the entire business community.

Conversely, precisely because they do bring together businesspeople from many sectors of the economy, Japan's *zaikai* associations are able to unite their memberships on only the most limited issues. The peak associations have therefore been losing influence to smaller groups like trade associations. This devolution of power has brought a diminution of power: Business-group influence now tends to be sector-specific, these groups cannot monopolize policymaking even within their own sectors, and there is political as well as economic competition among these groups. Trade associations themselves are not immune to pluralizing tendencies and sometimes cannot prevent individual firms from breaking ranks and pursuing independent strategies. Gregory Noble has called attention to the proliferation of "maverick" firms that are willing to undermine majority coalitions, and "the appearance of stubborn firms . . . [is] not accidental but a natural result of the growing sophistication and diversity of the Japanese economy."[111]

The fragmentation of business interests is clearly visible in the field of campaign financing. Even more than in the United States, politics revolves around money in Japan. Traditionally, politicians are expected to give cash gifts at constituents' graduation parties, weddings, and funerals; Diet members themselves must pay for district offices, official cars, travel, newsletters, mail, and any staff in addition to three government-paid employees; and forced for many years by multimember electoral districts to compete with one another for the same conservative votes, LDP candidates have had more of an incentive to outspend their rivals than to try to distinguish themselves on the basis of policy positions. Until the 1994 revamping of the electoral system, the average member of the lower house had roughly half as many constituents as the average House representative in the United States, and until 1996, Japanese candidates were restricted in their ability to broadcast political commercials, the largest expense for many Americans. Nevertheless, it was estimated in 1992 that the typical lower house member spent about $2 million during a two-year election cycle – approximately *four times* as much as the average House representative (and almost *ten* times the legal maximum).[112]

The LDP has always depended on business for financial support. In the party's early years, it was big business that provided most of the LDP's political funding, funneling donations through the party apparatus and faction leaders. In restricting the size of corporate contributions, however, a 1976 reform lowered the maximum amount corporations could contribute, decentralizing political funding by impelling individual politicians to raise more money themselves just at the time when a new stratum of provincial businesses was replacing the Keidanren establishment as the most important source of contributions. Campaign "reform" thus removed the buffer that had separated LDP backbenchers from the sources of their funding, and businesspeople pursuing specific, concrete payoffs have come to play a larger role in the political process.[113] In other words, it is often businesspeople, not "business," who wield real influence over conservative politicians. With the split of the LDP in 1993, Keidanren

---

[111] Noble (1988), p. 35.   [112] *The Washington Post* (6 September 1992).
[113] Curtis (1988), pp. 184–87.

abandoned altogether its tradition of mediating the political contributions of businesses.

The changes introduced in 1994 are unlikely to suppress Japan's "money politics." Among other things, the reforms: forbade companies, unions, and other organizations from contributing to individual politicians during campaigns; drastically lowered the threshold for reporting contributions; made candidates responsible for campaign violations committed on their behalf; and mandated public financing in accordance with the votes and seats won by each party in the last election. Nevertheless, even if the reforms sought to direct contributions to parties rather than to individuals, those contributions may be informally steered to a specific politician or group of politicians, and candidates can simply change their personal support organizations (kōenkai) into local branches of their parties. Furthermore, Japan's new system permits candidates to run on PR lists as well as in single-member districts in such a way that some politicians will still compete with, and have an incentive to outspend, colleagues within their own party.[114]

The real flaw in the proposition that business interests are unrivaled is that in a democracy like Japan, the LDP has had to be a party of many interests if it was to win sufficient votes to remain in power. Although each of the major opposition parties failed to broaden its base of support much beyond a single narrow interest group, the longevity of LDP rule has testified to its success in appealing to a wide variety of groups. Daniel Okimoto has referred to the LDP as "truly a grand coalition," one so encompassing that the party has not only been free of domination by any one interest group, but has frequently been compelled to choose among the competing claims of its different constituencies.[115]

Those choices have not always favored big business. Although the LDP is first and foremost committed to establishing a favorable business climate, Calder has demonstrated how distributive benefits from the government have been skewed to the small, often at the expense of the large.[116] Because rural areas and small businesses offer more votes, have more political options, and have a greater need for political assistance than big business, they have extracted major compensation for their support when the LDP has felt threatened at the polls, for example. Until the party split in 1993, big business, on the other hand, had no alternative to supporting the LDP: Any threat to abandon it would have lacked credibility in the absence of another conservative party.

Reputational surveys concur on the limited nature of business influence. Muramatsu found that party politicians and civil servants tend to regard one another as equals and to belittle the influence of all other actors, including big

---

[114] Christensen (1994a) and Christensen (1994b); *Asahi Evening News* (2 October 1996).
[115] Okimoto (1989), pp. 182, 179.   [116] Calder (1988a), pp. 156–57.

business. The evaluations of politicians and bureaucrats were seconded by business groups' own low appraisals of their influence.[117] When asked by Kabashima Ikuo and Jeffrey Broadbent who had more influence over Japanese life, a wide variety of elites rated the mass media first, followed by either politicians or bureaucrats. LDP leaders actually ranked business as inferior to labor, and business leaders ranked themselves lower than farm groups as well.[118] If anything, business associations' self-evaluations of their influence have declined significantly over time.[119] These responses call into question the statist model, with its emphasis on bureaucratic dominance, as well as the ruling triad model, with its assumption of business parity.

In summary, then, business leaders unquestionably enjoy preferential access to state actors, but big business is no more monolithic than the central bureaucracy or the LDP, and government policies do not necessarily favor large enterprises in their conflicts with other interests.

Corporatist models

Although its political economy bears little resemblance to those of the small European states Katzenstein described, a number of Western analysts (e.g., Shonfield) have labeled Japan corporatist and, indeed, it is not unusual for bureaucrats and interest groups to hammer out agreements that are later ratified by the Diet. MITI itself has described Japan in vaguely corporatist terms.[120] There is also some evidence of corporatism along the dimension of interest organization. Muramatsu found peak associations to be in closer contact with both the LDP and the ministries than other business and labor organizations and to evaluate their political efficacy more highly.[121]

There are two major variants of the corporatist model in Japanese studies, both focusing on the place of labor in society. Although T. J. Pempel's position has shifted with the times,[122] he and Tsunekawa Keiichi made an influential argument that perceived threats from abroad have historically led to pushes toward corporatism on the part of both the state and uncompetitive economic sectors. Weakened in the immediate postwar period, even big business was corporatized for a time, but it regained its autonomy as it regained its strength. Internationally vulnerable, agriculture and small business were corporatized early on and have remained so. The ruling coalition has always incorporated labor at the plant level but managed to exclude it at the national level. For Pempel and Tsunekawa, Japan thus presented an anomalous case of "corporatism without labor."[123]

---

[117] Muramatsu (1981b), pp. 27–28; Muramatsu (1981a), p. 79.
[118] Kabashima and Broadbent (1986), p. 339.   [119] Tsujinaka (1996), pp. 54–55.
[120] E.g., Kaplan (1972), p. 13.   [121] Muramatsu (1985), pp. 355–57.   [122] E.g., Pempel (1987).
[123] Pempel and Tsunekawa (1979).

The second model gives greater weight to the inclusionary aspects of Japanese labor relations. Japan boasts the favorable outcomes attributed to societal corporatism (e.g., peaceful industrial relations and effective, consensual management of the economy) despite its lack of the institutional underpinnings normally associated with it (e.g., a comprehensive, hierarchically organized union organization and labor participation in government). A number of authors have therefore suggested that the integration of labor within the enterprise and the coordination among unions seen during nationwide rounds of collective bargaining serve as functional equivalents of macro-corporatist arrangements.

As Schmitter himself observed, these attempts to apply corporatist models to Japan are ad hoc and unconvincing.[124] Blurring the distinction between industrial relations on the macro and micro levels robs the concept of corporatism of precision and disregards a defining characteristic of the Japanese labor market: its dualist structure.[125] For Japanese workers, the inclusion of a few is made possible only by the exclusion of many. And if Pempel and Tsunekawa were justified at the time in pointing to the weakness of organized labor, union participation in national policymaking has expanded since they proposed their model.

Japanese unionism has been handicapped by its low and uneven coverage, its decentralized structure, and internal divisions. In relative terms, organized labor has not grown at all since the end of the Occupation: Union membership hovered around 35 percent until 1975 and has been in steady decline since then, falling to 24.1 percent in 1994.[126] Unions are concentrated in large private enterprises and the public sector, leaving unorganized the workers in Japan's many smaller businesses.

More than 90 percent of Japan's private-sector unionists belong to enterprise unions that are organized vertically within individual factories or firms rather than to craft or industrial unions that cut horizontally across companies. By Western standards, the membership qualifications of these unions are both too broad and too narrow. On the one hand, enterprise unions serve as the sole representative of *all* employees, so blue- and white-collar workers are included in the same organizations, whatever the differences in their attitudes toward management. On the other hand, only permanent, full-time employees of a specific enterprise are eligible to join. "Temporary" workers, part-time workers, and the employees of subsidiaries and subcontractors do not qualify for membership even if they do the same work at the same place for the same number of hours. The unemployed are also excluded. And because union officers can be

---

[124] Schmitter (1989), pp. 59–60.
[125] For a comparison of corporatism and dualism, see Goldthorpe (1984).
[126] Japan Institute of Labour (1996), p. 48. In the United States, the unionization rate fell from 35 percent in the 1950s to 14.5 percent in 1996.

elected only from among the current employees of an enterprise, professional union leaders are relatively rare.

In addition to the contrasts between large and small firms and between core and marginalized employees within large firms, the postwar Japanese labor movement was long split between the public and private sectors. Enterprise unions are naturally sympathetic to the firms on which their members' livelihood depends, and big companies have deliberately structured their internal labor markets in ways that heighten the dependence and loyalty of those workers who enjoy union membership. But while private-sector unions evolved toward economic unionism and labor-management cooperation, public-sector unions moved in exactly the opposite direction as a result of the retraction of public employees' right to strike in 1948. Because their wage settlements require government approval, public-sector workers inevitably engage in political unionism; the deliberalization of labor laws succeeded only in radicalizing these unions and ensuring conflictual labor relations.

The politicization of the public sector contributed to the fragmentation of both the labor movement and the opposition political camp. Linkages between the local and national levels of the Japanese labor movement have been tenuous: Every enterprise union is an autonomous organization, and most of them have never been affiliated with any federation. To make matters worse, the labor movement was divided into two major and several minor "national centers" from the 1950s through the 1980s. Unions opposed to the radical policies of the General Council of Trade Unions of Japan, or Sōhyō, broke away in 1954 to form a rival national center that became the Japan Confederation of Labor, or Dōmei. Sōhyō was weighted toward public-sector unions, Dōmei toward the private sector. Although they both tried to achieve the greatest possible economic gains for their members through collective bargaining, Sōhyō sought to transform the existing political system through the Japan Socialist Party (JSP), whereas Dōmei accepted the status quo as a given and tried to participate in policymaking through the Democratic Socialist Party (DSP).

Until the Socialists participated in the coalition that replaced the LDP in 1993, Japan had not had a single government that received substantial support from organized labor since 1948. The Japanese labor movement and its political representatives nevertheless have had an impact on policymaking, an impact that has grown over time. First, although unions' contact with the LDP may be infrequent, their access to state agencies has provided them with the opportunity to make their views known. Surprisingly, a higher percentage of labor unions reported having frequent contact with the ministries than did either big or small businesses.[127] Second, changes within the labor movement have encour-

---

[127] Tsujinaka (1996), pp. 46–47; Muramatsu (1985), p. 346; Kabashima and Broadbent (1986), p. 341.

aged greater participation in policymaking. Finally, in its single-minded determination to remain in power, the LDP has often preempted opposition programs and, increasingly, coopted the labor movement itself.

Reflecting internal debates over Marxist orthodoxy and a growing consciousness of Dōmei competition, Sōhyō started to play a more active role from the mid-1960s. Declining rates of economic growth and the aging of the Japanese population raised such issues as structural unemployment and increasing medical needs, issues that could be addressed adequately only by the national government, and public criticism mounted of the labor movement's concentration on the narrow interests of the small minority of organized workers, so Sōhyō began to bestir itself on a wider range of issues on behalf of a broader constituency in the 1970s.[128]

Economic trends encouraged ever greater participation by Dōmei, too. With the "Nixon shock" of abolishing fixed exchange rates in 1971, the oil shock of 1973, and growing demands for the opening of Japanese markets, organized labor came to share a sense of crisis with management. As Japanese manufacturing became more dependent on exports, unions became more conscious of how wage increases and the emergence of newly industrializing economies threatened the international competitiveness of their firms. Private-sector unions were willing to restrain wage demands in return for government compensation like tax reductions and some of the world's strongest employment-maintenance policies.[129]

Union overtures to the government coincided with a greater receptiveness to labor input. Since the crisis that attended renewal of the Security Treaty with the United States in 1960, the LDP has been reluctant to ride roughshod over the strenuous objections of a united opposition, and as ideological polarization and conservative majorities declined in the late 1960s and especially in the 1970s, the LDP made compromises to facilitate the legislative process. The opposition's growing role in policymaking was reflected in a sharp increase in the number of bills adopted with their approval. During the years of near-parity in the Diet in the late 1970s, the JSP voted for more than 80 percent of all successful legislation and the DSP for more than 90 percent.[130]

Concretely, the LDP had to respond to rising exchange rates, inflation, and unemployment after the shocks of the early 1970s. These problems called for government cooperation with private-sector unions as well as business, and the creation of informal consultative forums such as the Industry–Labor Roundtable (Sanrōkon) encouraged the unions to cultivate ties to all three legs of the conservative establishment. The LDP naturally supported its own clienteles in conflicts of interest with organized labor but, mindful of the shrinking

---

[128] Harari (1986), p. 12.   [129] Garon and Mochizuki (1993), p. 163; Kume (1988).
[130] Curtis (1988), p. 39.

portion of the electorate accounted for by its traditional farm and small business allies and always on the lookout for new sources of electoral support, it was reasonably responsive to union demands and increasingly overt in its courting of the employees of big companies.[131]

The 1980s witnessed a striking failure by unions to adapt to structural transformation, declining radicalism, and political divisions. As noted earlier, the labor movement has always been more successful in organizing large firms than small ones – in 1970, 58 percent of workers in firms with more than 1,000 employees belonged to unions compared to less than 5 percent of workers in firms with fewer than 100, and these percentages did not budge over the next 20 years – but nearly all the new jobs created during this period were in small firms, so the national unionization rate steadily fell. Although it can be traced back to the 1950s and 1960s, labor moderation spread pari passu with growing affluence; workdays lost as a result of labor disputes plummeted from 8 million in 1975 to fewer than 220,000 in 1989.[132] On the political front, the LDP on the one hand tried to coopt private-sector unions by granting unprecedented access to top officials, and on the other launched an assault on the public-sector unions affiliated with the JSP by denationalizing and dividing public corporations. Mike Mochizuki has chronicled how defiance cost unions heavy losses, and cooperation won economic gains at the expense of unions' political goals.[133]

These trends amounted to a crisis for labor, and union leaders responded with a push for unity under the banner of pragmatism. In 1987, Dōmei and two other national centers disbanded and joined with Sōhyō's private-sector unions to form the National Confederation of Private-Sector Trade Unions (Rengō). When Rengō absorbed the rest of Sōhyō to unify public- and private-sector unions two years later, it embraced 78 industrial federations and 7.7 million members, who comprised 9 percent of Japan's voters, 17 percent of its entire labor force, and 65 percent of the nation's organized workers,[134] making it the third largest union federation in the world (after America's AFL-CIO and Britain's TUC) and the largest federation in Japanese history.

Rengō's ability to function as a peak organization is limited: Rather than concentrating power at the center, it has no formal authority over the 12,000 enterprise unions of its constituent industrial federations. But the confederation has expanded labor's ability to influence policymaking by creating direct channels of communication with central government ministries. In industrial relations, Rengō follows the moderate line championed by Dōmei, avoiding strikes and direct confrontations with management. It has concentrated on workers' job security and general living standards rather than on wage hikes, which should engage the federation in an increasingly active dialogue with the government.

---

[131] Carlile (1994), pp. 611–12; Knoke et al. (1996), p. 134.
[132] Allinson (1993b), pp. 23–24, 47–48.   [133] Mochizuki (1993).   [134] Tsujinaka (1993), p. 200.

The confederation permits its member unions to support whichever party they please and, significantly, the LDP actually encouraged its formation. Although it was split over the LDP–JSP coalition established in 1994, the birth of Rengō has set the stage for much more flexible cooperation between unions and any conservative ruling coalition.

How then best to conceive of labor's policymaking role? In response to a 1980 survey, at least 65 percent of the organizations in each of a variety of categories claimed to have had a favorable policy adopted recently. But if interest groups close to the LDP were more successful at having advantageous policies adopted, labor was among the most successful in exercising a veto.[135] Thus, as Samuels aphorized, "labor is incorporated [into the political system], albeit in a peculiar way: it has entered the conservative mansion through the tradesman's entrance."[136] Its participation does not take the form of corporatist bargaining among centralized, hierarchical peak associations.

(Neo)pluralist models

Western research has increasingly focused on the institutionalization of interest-group ties to the state and on the autonomy and capacity of the state apparatus itself. Just the reverse is true in Japan, and a growing number of scholars – particularly Japanese scholars – are advancing models that they forthrightly label pluralist.

Inoguchi Takashi has propounded a theory of "bureaucracy-led, mass-inclusionary pluralism," and Satō Seizaburō and Matsuzawa Tetsuhisa coined the catch phrase "compartmentalized pluralism channeled by an LDP-bureaucracy compound," but Muramatsu and Ellis Krauss have proposed what is perhaps the most elaborate model of Japanese pluralism. Although the LDP promoted economic growth in order to bolster its electoral fortunes, an unintended consequence was pluralization of the political system, they argue. Because growth increased surplus resources that the government could distribute, groups had more of an incentive to influence public policy, and because the new affluence strengthened interest groups, the government had more of an incentive to accommodate their demands. Muramatsu and Krauss describe the contemporary policymaking system in Japan as "patterned pluralism." It is pluralistic in that influence is dispersed among a wide variety of competing actors, there are many points of access to the policymaking process, and interest groups penetrate the government yet remain free of government control. At the same time, policymaking is patterned in that interest groups' political alliances have (in the past) been relatively fixed due to one-party dominance, the framework provided by the bureaucratic apparatus, and ideological cleavage.[137]

---

[135] Muramatsu and Krauss (1987), p. 534.   [136] Samuels (1987), p. 282.
[137] Muramatsu and Krauss (1987).

Whatever their differences, these qualified pluralisms all point to the coexistence of competition and cooperation in Japanese politics. Relationships among interest groups, bureaucracies, and political parties are too flexible and variable to call corporatist but more structured and stable than those pictured by the ideal type of pluralism. In a word, these models resemble those offered by American neopluralists, which do, in fact, illuminate such features of Japanese government as the overlap between public and private, the privatization of conflict, the reliance on informal decisionmaking, and especially the segmentation of policy domains.

The notion of Japan as a strong state par excellence to the contrary, many scholars have pointed out how Japan's government has become more disjointed. Gary Allinson contends that the distinguishing trend of postwar Japanese society has been "structural fragmentation" and an attendant dispersal of power. Pempel, who previously spoke of the "bureaucratization of policymaking" and then of "corporatism without labor," has written more recently of the "fragmentation, decentralization, and debureaucratization" of the conservative camp and of the "numerous entrenched pockets of power that have developed in the country over the years, each with its own vested interests." Sone Yasunori argues that Japan's contemporary political economy is best conceptualized in terms of distinct "policy clienteles" defined by ministerial jurisdictions. Calder speaks of "circles of compensation" that combine government and private actors with common interests in a specific public policy and that systematically discriminate against outsiders.[138] Japanese politicians themselves complain of their government's fragmentation. Ozawa Ichirō, for one, has observed that it is "scattered among many institutions and interests."[139]

What exists in Japan is not a single policymaking process pitting bureaucrats, politicians, private interests, and other concerned parties against one another, but an assortment of distinct, fairly self-contained policymaking processes that bring predictable sets of these actors together.

A broad consensus is emerging on this state of affairs, and analysts are beginning to treat it as a central organizing principle rather than as a peripheral observation. Okimoto has constructed a whole typology of "segmented political configurations" on the basis of the bureaucratic division of labor that orders interest aggregation and the routinized political transactions that have bound interest groups to the LDP. Big business and financial interest groups, for example, have provided the LDP with money in return for a stable, pro-business environment, but it is the bureaucracy-industry nexus with MITI and MOF that is the critical linkage for them. Farmers and small businesses,

---

[138] Allinson (1993b); Pempel (1974); Pempel (1979); Pempel (1987), pp. 287, 274; Sone (1993); Calder (1993), p. 246. See also Calder (1988a), p. 160, and Calder (1993), pp. 120–21.

[139] Quoted in Edward W. Desmond, "Ichiro Ozawa: Reformer at Bay," in *Foreign Affairs* (September–October 1995), p. 121.

on the other hand, have provided the LDP with votes in return for favorable legislation, subsidies, and generous tax treatment, but with the Ministry of Agriculture and the Small and Medium Enterprise Agency vulnerable to LDP interference and penetrated by the groups that they ostensibly regulate, it is the party-interest group nexus that has been critical.[140]

On the basis of Lowi's policy-determines-politics approach, Brian Woodall characterizes Japan as "a dual political economy in which segmented policy markets generate separate but interactive 'policy regimes' that operate under different equilibrium conditions."[141] On the one hand, policies for potential growth sectors, internationally competitive industries, and sectors deemed vital to the national interest emerge from a "strategic policy market" dominated by government bureaucrats and private-sector elites. On the other hand, elected politicians play a leading role in the subgovernments of the "structural policy market," which encompasses domestic sectors in which the public is often the client (e.g., agriculture, small business, public works). Because they offer ample opportunities for distributive policies and those policies reap electoral rewards, both the demands and the incentives for political intervention increase in the latter of the two.

Campbell has made explicit use of the language of neopluralism. In the late 1970s, he wrote that, "over time, quite stable and accepted clusters of actors have developed within each policy area. These may be thought of as policy 'subgovernments' made up essentially of one ministry, its corresponding division in the LDP Policy Affairs Research Council, and a number of interest groups."[142] Renewed electoral success in the 1980s provided the LDP with an opportunity to restore some coherence to Japanese policymaking, to suppress the many pockets of autonomy that had emerged over the years. As will be discussed later, the effort was made – and failed. Accordingly, Campbell has gone beyond subgovernments to adopt an even looser, policy-community perspective.

With its fragmented political system, Japan lacks the capacity for central leadership and coordination, Campbell contends: The Japanese prime minister is probably the weakest chief executive among the advanced industrial democracies, LDP involvement in policymaking has always been heaviest at the specialized level, bureaucratic power is concentrated in individual ministries, and there is little corporatist bargaining across policy areas. Although invented in the United States, the policy-community approach may be even more applicable to Japan. Japanese bureaucracies provide a stabler core than is available to American policy communities, and competitive policymaking processes like comprehensive proposals by a party or the chief executive, partisan or individual

---

[140] Okimoto (1989), pp. 194–202; Okimoto (1988), p. 335.
[141] Woodall (1996), p. 5.   [142] Campbell (1977), p. 40.

interactions in the legislature, grassroots social movements, and intellectual trends are less important in Japan than in the United States.[143]

Although the atomization of Japanese policymaking has yet to approach the level of Heclo's "issue networks," commentators have been applying the concept of networks to Japan. Rejecting any hard, "Manichaean" distinction between state and society, Okimoto stresses the interdependence of the two: "Instead of labeling Japan a 'strong' state, therefore, perhaps it would be more accurate to call it a 'societal,' 'relational,' or 'network' state, one whose strength is derived from the convergence of public and private interests and the extensive network of ties binding the two sectors together."[144] For Okimoto, public-private corporations, study groups, personal relationships developed in the course of government-industry contact, school ties, and the like gather government officials and leaders from the private sector to formulate public policy in an "intermediate zone."

Characterizing Japan more broadly as a "network society," Kumon, too, emphasizes the ubiquity of both formally institutionalized and informal networks. Although there is active sharing of information and consensus formation within Japanese networks, because that can take place effectively only on the basis of long-standing and stable relations of mutual trust, those networks tend to be closed and selfish, and thus protective of vested interests, he observes.[145] In explicitly attacking the bureaucracy-dominant and corporatist models, Tsujinaka Yutaka posits that state and society in Japan have become a system of "osmotic networks" whose links are "relatively weak and soft; they contrast with centralized, hierarchical patterns of authority that possess distinct boundaries and formal relationships."[146]

Japanese bureaucrats themselves have an implicitly neopluralist perspective on their work. When Muramatsu surveyed officials as to the advantages of interest-group contacts, they most frequently replied that such contacts help them: explain the meaning of policies and seek cooperation, obtain needed information, and adjust complex interests. Officials apparently feel the need for cooperation from interest groups, but cooperation on policies that interest groups do not necessarily have a hand in initiating themselves, casting doubt on both the statist and pluralist approaches. The chief disadvantages cited by bureaucrats – only powerful groups become the objects of consideration, there is a danger of administration's becoming fragmented, and officials might lose decisionmaking autonomy – are the classic pathologies associated with neopluralism.[147]

To include both Japan and the United States under the same rubric is counterintuitive, to say the least, and should not obscure the marked contrasts

---

[143] Campbell (1989), pp. 6–7, 18.   [144] Okimoto (1989), p. 145.   [145] Kumon (1992).
[146] Tsujinaka (1993), p. 202.   [147] Muramatsu (1981b), p. 220.

between them. A higher degree of what Nettl called "'stateness' in the intra-societal field" still distinguishes Japanese- from American-style neopluralism. As Susan Pharr and Frank Upham have observed, both countries may witness the frequent privatization of conflict, but if it is advantaged interest groups that typically seek this goal in the United States, in Japan it is the state itself. By relying on informal consultations and compromises rather than statutory authority and universalistic rulings subject to judicial review, bureaucrats avoid accountability, control access to the policymaking process, and discourage the formation of interest groups that might disrupt the process.[148]

More important, though, is the question of leadership. All the necessary qualifications aside, Japanese bureaucracies are typically more powerful than their American counterparts, and the American Congress is more powerful than the Japanese Diet, so the narrow arenas that handle the bulk of policymaking are more likely to be led by bureaucrats in Japan and by politicians in the United States.[149] (A third alternative, privately led policymaking, can be found where the state delegates the achievement of public objectives to private actors, such as cartels or professional associations,[150] or is thoroughly penetrated and clientelized by them.)

Other neopluralist analyses and the original research of this study suggest that two of the best predictors of whether bureaucrats or politicians are more likely to lead on a specific issue in Japan are the divisibility of benefits and the scope of bureaucratic jurisdiction. First, the more distributive the policy, the greater the demands and incentives for political intervention. Second, the more encompassing an agency's jurisdiction over a policy domain, the greater its motivation and ability to manage it.[151] A single bureau will lead on the narrowest of questions, a single ministry when the most important aspects of a problem fall within its jurisdiction, and politicians when an issue spills over bureaucratic boundaries to create a conflict among ministries.[152] Roughly speaking, this study's labor case falls in the first category, its business case in the second, and its farm case in the third. Given the distributive nature of the farm case (and only the farm case), politicians' leadership there was overdetermined.

It is crucial to note that officials' jobs have become increasingly difficult over time and that bureaucratic leadership does *not* imply bureaucratic dominance. In this context, leadership refers less to confrontational clout than to the ability to coordinate conflicting interests. "Coordination" is a slippery concept, especially in Japan. Although numerous words approximate it, some scholars have

---

[148] Pharr (1990); Upham (1987).
[149] Campbell (1989), p. 8; Heinz et al. (1993), p. 378; Knoke et al. (1996), p. 212.
[150] See Streeck and Schmitter (1985) on such "private-interest government" in general and Tilton (1996) on the Japanese case in particular.
[151] Rosenbluth (1993), p. 126.
[152] McKean (1993), p. 89.

gone so far as to argue that the concept does not really exist in Japanese, and the most commonly used term, *chōsei*, can be translated as "regulation," "adjustment," "reconciliation," or "control" as well as coordination.[153] This ambiguity is due precisely to its centrality, however. As Margaret McKean remarked, "coordination – collaboration, bargaining, negotiation, networking, reciprocity, and so on – in the relationships between government and interest groups in Japan . . . is the quintessential feature of state-society relationships that one must understand." John Haley has likewise referred to "governance by negotiation" and Allinson to "Japan's negotiated polity."[154]

Falling in the ambiguous middle ground between coercion and compliance, coordination can take many different forms, of course, three of which appear repeatedly in this study. Steven Reed has proposed a *"nemawashi* model" of business-government relations in Japan that aptly describes situations of relative bureaucratic weakness (or the initial stages of many negotiations). *Nemawashi*'s literal meaning is to bind a tree's roots in preparation for transplanting; its metaphorical meaning is carefully to lay the groundwork for an agreement. Why should Japanese officials strive to build a consensus in support of their policies? "One could argue that the bureaucracy seeks a consensus because it believes that consensus decision making produces better decisions than authoritative orders. A simpler explanation is that the bureaucracy seeks consensus because it lacks the power to enforce policy without it."[155] Officials are sometimes referees rather than players.

Situations of relative bureaucratic strength, on the other hand, often feature a pattern of policymaking that Vogel has labeled the "bureaucratic-led bargain." Although officialdom is not autonomous in the sense of being insulated from societal pressures, because private interests are divided on most issues and bureaucracies play a substantial role in the formulation as well as implementation of legislation, they can inject their own preferences into policy while they negotiate with, and sometimes manipulate, those interests.[156] Even Uriu, who describes MITI as "permeated" and "responsive," concedes that ministries enjoy greater autonomy when they mediate among conflicting private interests.[157]

As Beer pointed out, the problem is frequently not what programs to devise, but how to win understanding and acceptance of public policies that private actors did not originate or mandate themselves, how to "mobilize consent." The policymaking process itself can serve this end if it features "continuous, intimate interchange between authority and those subject to authority," particularly the producer and professional groups whose information and expertise the state

[153] Johnson (1980), pp. 98–99.
[154] McKean (1993), p. 91; Haley (1987); Allinson (1993b), p. 49.
[155] Reed (1993), p. 116.   [156] S. Vogel (1994), pp. 220–23.   [157] Uriu (1996), pp. 34, 224, 253.

needs to rule effectively. Government ministries will therefore consult and bargain with their organizations in extraparliamentary forums.[158]

Pace its many detractors, bureaucratic as opposed to political leadership commonly permits a more direct reflection of private interests in public policies. Politics constitutes a distinctive arena "close to but slightly separate from the state," with a dynamic all its own, noted Peter Hall. Any government must maintain both a coalition with electoral constituencies to remain in office and a coalition with producer groups to implement its economic policies, but the two may be built on different bases and require contradictory tasks.[159] Thus, if Almond argued that parties ought to stand between interest groups and the state, Eckstein countered that:

> Parties, in their very nature, tend to aggregate opinion on a very broad scale, rather infrequently, and for limited purposes, such as elections. . . . In attempting to win mass support, necessarily from a large variety of groups, they do not so much "aggregate" opinions (as Almond thinks) as reduce them to their lowest and vaguest denominators, sometimes distorting the perspectives and goals they seek to mobilize out of all recognition. One may doubt whether such systems could persist if groups did not have readily available outlets other than the parties through which to pursue their political goals.[160]

With parties often falling short in mediating between public and private interests, bureaucratic channels have broadened.

The existence of a single-party dominant regime does not change that fact. LaPalombara long ago observed that whereas *clientela* bestow "relatively permanent bridgeheads inside the system" whereby a client group renders itself indispensable and its pressure activities may not even be perceived as such, intervention based on *parentela* "creates neither a permanent connection with the bureaucracy nor a channel of access that both the bureaucrats and the group leaders view as normal and acceptable."[161] *Parentela* are therefore a second-best option for interest groups incapable of forming *clientela*, and Japanese politicians are more likely to react to bureaucratically initiated policies as advocates of disgruntled interests than to initiate policies themselves.

Virtually every government agency requires channels of communication to private actors to formulate and implement its policies; virtually every interest group seeks direct access to its government's policymaking process. These complementary movements are often institutionalized in consultative councils attached to central bureaucracies. More than 60 years ago, Harold Laski declared that "the first great need of the modern State is adequately to organise

[158] Beer (1966), pp. 46, 36–37.   [159] Hall (1986), pp. 271, 273.
[160] Eckstein (1960), p. 162.   [161] LaPalombara (1964), pp. 391–92.

institutions of consultation."[162] The continued differentiation of society and the growth of state responsibilities have only multiplied and intensified the relations between public and private actors since that time, enhancing the significance of these institutions. In the words of Léon Dion, consultative councils now act as "a bridge between the social system and the political system" that makes possible "the confrontation and reconciliation of the demands and supports of the social agents, as well as the expressions of the wishes and possibilities of the political agents."[163] Accordingly, such councils offer an ideal vantage point from which to analyze interest-group politics.

Whatever their differences, every school has acknowledged the role of *shingikai*, Japan's consultative councils. Johnson: "To the extent that laws are scrutinized and discussed at all in Japan by persons outside the bureaucracy, it is done in the councils." Pempel: advisory bodies "have become major organizational tools in overall policy formulation." Muramatsu and Krauss: "There are constant attempts to coordinate and structure the keen intra- and intersectoral competition. The use of *shingikai* to hammer out acceptable policy solutions among competing interests is one such coordinating device." Campbell: "Consensus within the policy community is virtually prerequisite for an idea to be taken seriously by others. Such a consensus is usually embodied in the formal report by the legally established advisory committee for that policy area." Kumon: *Shingikai* are "the most representative form" of network organizations connecting industrial, political, mass media, and academic spheres to one another.[164]

Although innumerable case studies in English have touched on the actions of particular councils, only a single non-Japanese scholar, Ehud Harari, has conducted systematic research on the subject. What are the origins of Japan's *shingikai*? What functions do they perform? Who serves on them? How do they operate?

---

[162] Harold J. Laski, *A Grammar of Politics*, 2nd ed. (New Haven: Yale University Press, 1931), p. 80.
[163] Dion (1973), p. 335.
[164] Johnson (1982), p. 47; Pempel (1974), p. 658; Muramatsu and Krauss (1987), pp. 538–39; Campbell (1989), p. 16; Kumon (1992), p. 126.

2

The shingikai *system*

Statist models would predict that *shingikai* ensure the authorization of officials' own initiatives. Marxist and ruling triad models would predict that the business community employs councils to secure policies advantageous to capital. Corporatist models would predict that commissions serve as a locus for extraparliamentary bargaining among peak associations. Pluralist models would predict that a wide variety of interest groups participate in advisory bodies on roughly equal terms to lobby pervious ministries. Bureaucratic leadership is much in evidence, in fact, but as a neopluralist perspective would lead one to expect, given the segmentation of Japanese policymaking, no single generalization captures the *shingikai* system in its entirety.

Historical background

The use of advisory bodies has a long history in Japan: The forerunner of today's Council on the Legal System was established in 1893. But contemporary commissions differ from their prewar cousins in nomenclature, legal basis, membership, and function. Agencies now distinguish *shingikai* from purely administrative committees that do not include participants from outside the government (*iinkai*); prewar officials made no such distinction. Throughout most of the postwar era, it has been necessary to establish advisory bodies by law; although prewar authorities did establish several councils by law, they generally bypassed the Diet by means of imperial edicts, cabinet orders, or ministerial ordinances. Today, people from all walks of life sit on commissions, and the inclusion of incumbent bureaucrats is discouraged; in the past, few extragovernmental individuals other than scholars and leading businesspeople were consulted, and the proportion of officials was relatively high.

Finally, whereas contemporary *shingikai* play a variety of roles, prewar councils performed very limited functions. Plagued then as now by sectionalism, the Japanese government sought ways to coordinate the planning and implementation of policies among ministries, and commissions sometimes filled this need.[1]

---

[1] Abe (1978), p. 9; Katō K. (1971), p. 45.

Important industry-related *shingikai* facilitated interest adjustment among private enterprises or between the government and *zaikai*: The Commerce and Industry Council created in 1927, for example, included all the leading businesspeople of the time and set the stage for modern industrial policy.[2] Under the prewar system of barely tempered bureaucratic absolutism, however, authorities generally restricted the recommendations of advisory bodies to a simple "yes" or "no" in response to officials' plans that at most might result in minor revisions of the original proposal.

Occupation authorities established the current system of consultative councils in order to limit bureaucratic power, open up and better integrate state administration, and pluralize participation in government policymaking, as well as to solicit outside advice.[3] Many Japanese citizens embraced the reform: "In aiming at the democratization of administration, the task of adopting such methods as committees and *shingikai* of every sort was considered more than anything an urgent necessity."[4] The bureaucrat Sakuma Tsutomu later reminisced about the same period from the other side of the fence:

> Whenever we proposed a bill and went to the Diet, we were questioned as to whose opinion we had asked. . . . When we said, "we have listened to the views of these sorts of people at this sort of *shingikai*," they would pass it for us easily. Then, because the public came to see that there would not be any official arbitrariness, that we would be operating the administration democratically if there was a *shingikai*, we sometimes created *shingikai* because we wanted to adopt such a pose.[5]

More than idealism and public relations were at work in firmly rooting the *shingikai* system. The continual struggles among and within ministries prompted officials to seek outside support. As one newspaper noted early in the postwar era, "Looking over the ministries, almost every bureau is attended by a *shingikai* in the form of that bureau's partisan. . . . If one bureau creates one, it seems other bureaus cannot be satisfied unless they cook up rival auxiliary organs, too."[6] Less cynically, Sakuma suggested that the establishment of commissions developed a momentum of its own: "Once you have one example, everyone comes to learn from it. With *shingikai* included in almost any law, there was then considerable reason to include one [in any new legislation] because it would not have looked right not to."[7]

In compliance with Occupation policy, *shingikai* were initially intended to be ad hoc. Even if the government has sometimes disbanded *shingikai* once they have completed a specific task (e.g., the Commission on the Constitution, 1957–64), most councils have been standing bodies that deal with a subject on a

---

[2] Johnson (1982), p. 102.   [3] Harari (1974), p. 539; Harari (1988), p. 149.
[4] Miyake (1971), p. 65.   [5] Sakuma et al. (1972), p. 39.   [6] *Asahi Shinbun* (1952).
[7] Sakuma et al. (1972), p. 39.

continuing basis. Some of these "permanent" bodies, too, have been abolished or reorganized when the problems they addressed lost their urgency, but that has been the exception rather than the rule, and the number of councils skyrocketed. As early as 1948, a (*shingikai*) report rapped the misuse of *shingikai* and called on agencies to avoid their reckless creation; a 1949 (*shingikai*) report called for the abolition of all but indispensable *shingikai*. Critics condemned the proliferation of commissions as a source of bureaucratic complexity and sought their consolidation.

These efforts were not entirely without effect. The first shakeup of the council system occurred in 1949, and with another reorganization in 1951, the more than 350 councils then in existence were pared down to 184.[8] An expansion of administrative duties inevitably accompanied economic growth, however, and the system began to expand once again. The *Asahi* newspaper observed in 1952 that "if left alone, it seems as if *shingikai* would soon multiply like bacteria. . . . We can say that '*shingikai* inflation' is one of the distinguishing features of postwar administration."[9] A high of 277 statutory *shingikai* was reached in 1965 before the government finally took action.

Because its four previous reports had not produced the desired results, the Council on Administration in 1960 recommended the establishment of "a nonpartisan, authoritative, ad hoc body on the model of America's Commission on the Organization of the Executive Branch of the Government (Hoover Commission) [1947–49] . . . to gather every kind of positive data, deliberate on the actual conditions of administration, and plan an epoch-making overhaul."[10] When the Administrative Management Agency (AMA), which was responsible for the inspection and improvement of government organizations, pressed for fundamental reform, it found willing support among business leaders, who had become impatient with what they took to be inefficiency and mismanagement on the part of government bureaucracies. Although public expenditures shot up from 17 to 24 percent of national income between 1952 and 1963, the ministries could not attribute the increase to their having taken on many additional functions.[11]

Established with the support of all parties except the Communists, an Ad Hoc Commission on Administrative Reform (<u>Rin</u>ji Gyōsei <u>Chō</u>sakai, or First Rinchō) was appointed by Prime Minister Ikeda Hayato in February 1962 to investigate administrative operations in their entirety. Its voluminous September 1964 report pointed to 16 areas in need of reform, the *shingikai* system among them. The First Rinchō (itself a PMO advisory body) was not unremittingly critical: It acknowledged that growth in the complexity and specialization of administration made an increase in the number of advisory bodies inevitable.

---

[8] Yamada (1972), p. 16; Satō C. (1962), p. 43; *Asahi Shinbun* (1952).
[9] *Asahi Shinbun* (1952).   [10] Shingikai Kenkyūkai (1963), p. 55.
[11] Pempel (1982), pp. 260–61.

Nevertheless, it blamed "a trend toward the reckless establishment of *shingikai* that do not adequately perform their function or whose raisons d'être resemble one another" for such abuses as a reduction in efficiency, an obscuring of responsibility, and the promotion of sectionalism.[12] To end these abuses, the First Rinchō recommended that the government make the most of public hearings, operate *shingikai* with broad jurisdiction flexibly through the use of subcommittees, attach clear deadlines to ad hoc bodies, and quickly abolish those *shingikai* whose necessity had been reduced by the completion of their duties or a change in social conditions.

The AMA negotiated with the ministries and the LDP's Policy Affairs Research Council, and 1966 saw the abolition of 10 councils and the consolidation of another 24. A year later, one scholar observed that this was "just a drop in the bucket. . . . Even if logical in theory, a drastic reorganization faces powerful resistance from bureaucratic sectionalism and political interests, and will be exceedingly difficult without a great deal of leadership."[13] Retrenchment did not, in fact, appeal to the bureaucratic establishment, which actively opposed it. The AMA, the press, the Cabinet Bureau of the Secretariat, and the Rinchō itself brought enormous pressure to bear on the cabinet, however.[14] The cabinet, in turn, repeatedly directed ministries to carry out the Rinchō's recommendations, and in accordance with the principle of "scrap and build," they managed to reduce the number of statutory advisory bodies from the peak of 277 in 1965 to 212 in 1978.

The situation has barely changed since then. In 1995, the cabinet promised a thorough reexamination of *shingikai* that had lost their utility. After a year, the ministries had resolved to investigate the abolition of two councils that had been inactive for more than a decade, and only one body had actually been eliminated. Because of the creation of another *shingikai*, the total number remained unchanged at 217.[15]

To a large extent, reform succeeded only in shifting the expansion of the *shingikai* system from statutory to unofficial or "private" councils (a trend that will be examined in Chapter 3). Agencies are still reluctant to do away with commissions even after they have completed their original tasks, sometimes keeping dormant bodies on the books without even appointing members to them. On other occasions, ministries create a consultative process of Byzantine complexity by multiplying *shingikai* beyond any obvious need. In the Ministry of Education in 1987, for example, "with advisory bodies A (Rinkyōshin), B (Daigaku Kaikaku Kenkyū Kyōgikai), C (Daigaku Shingikai), and D (Shiritsu Daigaku Shingikai), A creates B, and while B plans for C, it goes on to become C itself. While D changes in nature to become C's subordinate, C is promoted into a body that can infringe on the constitutional principle symbolized by

---

[12] Satō I. (1972), p. 7.   [13] Narita (1967), p. 50.   [14] Park (1972), p. 463.
[15] Sōmuchō (1996); *Nihon Keizai Shinbun* (8 August 1996).

D. . . ."[16] The now-entrenched policy of scrap and build has problems of its own, however. It is a perversion of administrative reform to make consolidation an end in itself. As one critic noted, "We often hear the view that because *shingikai* are too numerous, we must reorganize them, reduce their numbers. . . . But we should abolish unused *shingikai*, and maintain or newly establish effective or necessary ones, without regard to number."[17]

What is it, though, that makes councils "effective or necessary"? What functions do they perform?

Functions

The First Rinchō distinguished between "consultative bodies" (*shimon kikan*), which deliberate on policies, and "examining bodies" (*san'yo kikan*), which ensure the fair application of laws. Although this distinction is somewhat artificial, councils that most often perform one or another set of tasks do tend to differ in a variety of ways. The report of a *shimon* body is not legally binding; *san'yo* bodies participate directly in administrative decisionmaking, and their resolutions constrain bureaucracies. *San'yo* councils have greater authority than *shimon* councils, sometimes approaching in independence the strongest administrative committees. *Shimon* bodies tend to be active at a relatively early stage of the policymaking process, *san'yo* bodies at a late stage of administrative operations. And in terms of procedure, if *shimon* organs normally adopt a parliamentary style, many *san'yo* bodies behave in a more judicial manner.[18] The consultative type of commission is the more common of the two. By one estimate (allowing for double counting), 85 percent of all councils performed *shimon* and 30 percent *san'yo* functions in 1966; 20 years later, *san'yo* functions were attributed to about 18 percent of all *shingikai*.[19] This study focuses exclusively on *shimon* bodies and the functions performed by consultation.

As noted earlier, the original rationale of the postwar *shingikai* system was to introduce new ideas and to pluralize participation in governmental decisionmaking. Like all Occupation reforms, however, it inevitably underwent a process of naturalization, and today's councils not only carry out these duties in ways unforeseen by the reformers, but also function in ways downright inimical to their intentions.

Of the many functions attributed to advisory bodies, the most straightforward would seem to be the provision of outsiders' advice. The proposition that *shingikai* are capable of providing special insights has been questioned, however. "It is rather in administration that expert knowledge accumulates, so the value of using councilors diminishes and it seems to become a merely nominal matter of making use of their reputations. . . . Nonprofessional members cannot dis-

[16] Mori (1987), p. 66.   [17] Okabe (1969), p. 6.   [18] Kaneko (1985), pp. 124–25.
[19] *Toki no Hōrei* (1966), p. 72; Teshima (1986), p. 39; Harari (1974), pp. 539–40.

play sufficient ability and inevitably become officials' yes-men."[20] If a parent agency deliberately appoints insufficiently knowledgeable members to a commission, whether to make use of their prestige or to take advantage of their ignorance, that commission will be unable to make a substantive contribution to policymaking, of course. It would be a mistake, however, to downplay the expertise of qualified members, even vis-à-vis trained administrators.

Max Weber made a useful distinction between two *types* of specialist knowledge: technical knowledge (*Fachwissen*), and "knowledge growing out of experience in the service [*Dienstwissen*], for [bureaucrats] acquire through the conduct of office a special knowledge of facts and have available a store of documentary material peculiar to themselves."[21] Despite its lofty reputation, Japanese themselves sometimes deride their "amateur administration" and suggest that its authority rests more on officials' "knowledge of duties [*shitsumu chishiki*]" than on their "technical knowledge [*senmon chishiki*]."[22] Because elite bureaucrats are rotated through a variety of posts, they must often reach out for technical knowledge they lack, and consultation with private actors has become institutionalized through *shingikai*.

The council system is still a force for democracy in the eyes of some. In 1985, one Japanese observer wrote:

> Perhaps the most important of its basic raisons d'être is the democratization of administration. . . . Consideration of how the functions of contemporary administration are marked by quantitative increase and qualitative specialization reveals the limits of parliament's or administration's own faculty for dealing with the democratic control of administration. Direct, popular participation in administration is necessary as a compensatory measure, and *shingikai* are one form of that.[23]

The extent to which commissions democratize administration depends on one's definition of democracy, of course. Because public hearings are not widespread in Japan, the forums councils provide do help forestall arbitrariness or complacency on the part of bureaucrats. And unlike administrative investigations, the establishment, deliberations, and reports of advisory bodies usually attract press coverage, thus focusing citizens' attention on matters of concern and ensuring that bureaucrats' proposals are defensible.[24]

But if *shingikai* were to reflect, and not merely take into consideration, popular sentiment, citizens themselves would have to choose councilors. They do not. Although some advocates of grassroots democracy look forward to the day when commissions might institutionalize direct citizen participation,[25] the pluralizing influence of advisory bodies remains limited because parent agencies

---

[20] Satō C. (1978), pp. 5, 6–7.   [21] Weber (1947), p. 339.
[22] Ōmi (1958), p. 43; Imamura (1978), pp. 41–42.
[23] Kaneko (1985), p. 118.   [24] E. Vogel (1979), p. 89.   [25] Matsuoka (1985), pp. 38–39.

appoint their members. Looking on *shingikai* as vehicles of citizen participation can only lead people to mistrust government bureaucracies and undermines *shingikai*'s performance of their other duties.[26] The democratization of adminis-tration will continue to rest on its obligation to respect the will of the people as it is reflected through their elected representatives, and it is a dangerous mistake to exaggerate the significance of councils in this regard.

In part because of such misunderstandings, critics of the *shingikai* system are legion. Commissions in Japan are often portrayed as helpless or willing tools of their parent agencies, and they have been tarred as ministries' "robots," "cheer-leaders," "backers," "tunnel organizations" (i.e., secret means of influence), "sham bodyguards," and "ornaments."[27] The most common epithets are "kept body" (*goyō kikan*) and "invisibility-working fairy cloak" (*kakuremino*, i.e., a means of parrying criticism or obscuring bureaucratic responsibility). In this view, "the most prevalent way in which the council is put to use is as a support-ing device for the government," so "the [ostensible] reasons for establishing shingikai are no more than a pretense."[28] Advisory bodies themselves have long called attention to this practice: In 1959, the Council on Administration warned against the establishment of commissions that exist "to wangle agreement with government policies or to escape responsibility." Five years later, the First Rinchō echoed this admonition.[29] In the 1990s, the politician Ozawa Ichirō has advocated the outright abolition of *shingikai* as a means of checking bureaucratic power.

Advisory bodies can support their parent agencies in a variety of ways, some already touched upon. In the case of kept bodies dominated by members sym-pathetic to government aims, the referral of a problem to a commission may be no more than a stratagem to authorize a predetermined policy with the imprima-tur of seemingly disinterested citizens, in the process lending a semblance of democracy to the decision. In other words, advisory bodies can be good public relations. The inclusion of prestigious persons as members is especially useful in this regard, and agencies often choose councilors for their name value regardless of their expertise or ability to attend deliberations. Although their expertise may not be in doubt, Japanese scholars have many opportunities to express their opinions in the mass media, so bringing academics into the councils of govern-ment improves bureaucrats' chances of gaining an audience for their own views.[30] The appointment of journalists – and about half of all advisory bodies include representatives from the mass media[31] – can also be a ploy to ensure favorable publicity.

[26] Imamura (1978), p. 38.
[27] Satō C. (1962), p. 43; Ogita (1969), p. 37; Satō C. (1978), p. 5; Imamura (1978), p. 38; Harari (1986), p. 27.
[28] Park (1972), p. 455; Satō C. (1978), p. 4 .
[29] Yamada (1972), pp. 16–17.
[30] Fukunaga (1995), p. 18.   [31] Amano (1994), p. 296.

Within the government, commissions may defend one bureaucratic unit's claims against those of another in inter- or intraministerial confrontations. Struggling with one another to take the initiative in the information and communications industries, *shingikai* of both MITI and the Ministry of Posts and Telecommunications released identically named "vision" reports with similar contents in the same month of 1996.[32] Different advisory bodies often arrive at contradictory conclusions, however. During the budgeting process, although agencies' *shingikai* typically recommend increases in their appropriations, MOF's Council on the Financial System typically recommends cuts.[33] When interagency disputes overlay the division between operational ministries and MOF, the commissions of the concerned bureaucratic units may confront one another in "a maelstrom of three-cornered competition."[34] To put a more positive spin on it, the sectional multiplication of *shingikai* may prevent bureaucratic agencies from exceeding their authority.[35]

Ministers sometimes shift the blame for unpopular or mistaken decisions onto councils, of whose motives the public is less suspicious.[36] When some 2,000 hemophiliacs unnecessarily contracted HIV, officials implicated in the scandal testified in 1996 that they had entrusted such important decisions as whether to continue the use of unheated blood products to an acquired immunodeficiency syndrome (AIDS) study group. "Administrators are a group of amateurs. We respected the decisions made by medical experts." (The former head of the study group demurred, however: "I thought that the task of the study group was to make academic research," not to make administrative decisions.[37]) Of course, commissions can justify administrative *inaction* as well, either by prolonging deliberations or by endorsing the avoidance or postponement of change.[38] When the implementation of many provisions of a 1995 plan for deregulation was obscured by the stipulation that "investigation by *shingikai* is necessary," an advocate of deregulation angrily complained that officials were "trying to postpone implementation by using *shingikai* as a pretext."[39] It is no wonder that state actors should so resent the abolition or consolidation of their councils.

In 1972, Yung Ho Park published the first sustained examination of *shingikai* in English and one of the most influential studies in either English or Japanese. Japanese critics still approvingly quote Park's characterization of councils as "supporting devices for the government." Much of the rest of this chapter examines the overt and covert means by which parent agencies influence council

---

[32] *Nihon Keizai Shinbun* (8 August 1996).
[33] Park (1972), p. 455; Ebata (1965), p. 134.
[34] Shindō (1978), p. 19.
[35] *Nihon Keizai Shinbun* (9 August 1996).
[36] Fukunaga (1995), p. 18; Ogita (1972), p. 35.
[37] *The Japan Times* (24 July 1996).
[38] Harari (1974), p. 543.   [39] *Nihon Keizai Shinbun* (12 July 1995).

operations. Park's followers have served him poorly, however, in focusing almost exclusively on the shortcomings to which he called attention without paying heed to the way he was careful to qualify his accusations. Such epithets as *goyō kikan* or *kakuremino* are unquestionably justified – in certain cases. But the fact that some, perhaps many, commissions do little to pluralize administration or contribute expert advice does not preclude other commissions from doing so. In Park's own words, "their deliberations and reports often constitute an important preliminary in the totality of Japanese policy-making; and there are numerous instances of commissions having authored persuasive reports which culminated in administrative policies and legislation."[40] Furthermore, as Park himself pointed out, the *official* purposes of the council system do not exhaust its potentialities.

Decisionmakers have occasionally turned to *shingikai* as a last resort when they cannot solve their conflicts within the Diet or ministries. These commissions have the character of a "political committee" or "subcontracting organ" of the Diet.[41] Spawned by controversy, these bodies inevitably become controversial themselves. In 1966, for example, Prime Minister Satō Eisaku sought to revive the holiday National Foundation Day on February 11, a date Socialists opposed because it had come to be associated with a prewar rightist coup attempt. Although the Diet empowered the cabinet to select a date by decree, it also obliged the prime minister to respect the recommendations of a National Foundation Day Council in making his decision. (The Council eventually chose February 11, which Japanese now celebrate as a national holiday.) Critics harshly rebuked the Diet for abandoning its legislative function to an appointed advisory body.[42] Although the relevant committee of the Upper House considered the procedure "an exceptional expedient," the suspicion remained that it was downright unconstitutional, and even one of the *shingikai*'s members commented, "I can't help but wonder why they're entrusting this kind of important problem to a handful of learned people."[43]

Many commentators credit advisory bodies with enhancing the fairness and rationality of administrative decisionmaking. In the prewar era, officialdom ideally embodied a neutral public interest distinguished from private interests, which were ipso facto subordinate. In the postwar era, though, the assertion of those same private interests has gained greater legitimacy, and they are vigorously and publicly pressed, often in confrontation with bureaucracies whose own fairness is increasingly questioned. With the decline in officials' authority – by the end of 1996, fully 65 percent of the respondents to one poll said that they distrusted bureaucrats[44] – has come a need for the legitimation of administrative decisions by neutral outsiders.

[40] Park (1972), pp. 454–55, 457.   [41] Sugita (1967), p. 85.
[42] Park (1972), p. 461; *Mainichi Shinbun* editorial (4 June 1966); Hayashi (1966), p. 17.
[43] Arikura (1966), p. 54.   [44] *Asahi Evening News* (12 December 1996).

Paradoxically, councils are also expected to rationalize policymaking through the *inclusion* of once suspect private interests. Because direct pressure by competing groups on bureaucratic agencies can lead to sectionalism or to compromises worked out without regard to policy coherence, "what is important is to exclude disputes among interests from decisionmaking organs as much as possible by allowing the participation of interest representatives." Within the LDP, the Policy Affairs Research Council has helped soften and mediate interest-group confrontations before they reach more authoritative party bodies; within the ministries, commissions play that role. "We can thus say that *shingikai* are a means of making administrative unity possible through the coordination [*chōsei*] and settlement of all kinds of opposing interests."[45]

It is this coordination of interests within civil society and administration that is of greatest relevance to this study. As Japanese society has diversified and the sphere of state intervention has expanded, the postwar period has witnessed a marked increase in the need for administrative adjustment of public and private interests. This development is symptomatic of broad shifts in the political process. One scholar has argued:

> In a legislative state or a period of parliamentary supremacy, regulating [*chōsei*] the confrontations among various social interests and promoting political integration was the function of the legislature. With the administratization of the state, such a function of political integration is often played by the administration, too. In this case, one problem for administration is its lack of a mechanism to perform functions that have been achieved by means of the representational system of parliament, such as the gathering of information considered essential for integration or the adjustment [*chōsei*] of confrontations among interests. With the shift towards the administrative state, the *shingikai* system has been put to practical use because it is expected to perform such a function.[46]

Despite the postwar doctrine of parliamentary supremacy, it is a commonplace that the Diet is not the pivot of political integration, and however much information and expertise the ministries possess, they alone cannot bear the burden of interest adjustment either.

Advisory bodies contribute to the coordination of interests in a variety of ways. By allowing interested parties to express their opinions, councils serve agencies as a useful listening post. Rather than imposing policies from above, Japanese ministries typically sound out concerned parties (*sebumi o suru* – literally, "find out the depth of water by wading in it") and lay the groundwork (*nemawashi o suru*) for new initiatives, processes institutionalized by the *shingikai*

---

[45] Satō C. (1962), p. 42. See also Ebata (1965), p. 136.
[46] Abe (1978), p. 8.

Table 2-1. *The function most often played by* shingikai *(percentages)*

	Bureaucrats (n = 250)	LDP Diet reps. (n = 50)	JSP Diet reps. (n = 51)	Total (n = 351)
Enhance fairness of policies	30	34	22	29
Adjust societal interests	29	20	12	26
Obtain specialists' views	25	30	27	26
Authorize administrative decisions	15	12	25	16

Source: Muramatsu (1981b), p. 125.

system. Conversely, commissions offer private organizations a valuable means for learning the views and plans of agencies and of other interest groups with which they frequently interact.[47] Ministries rely on councils that include representatives of conflicting interests to recommend mutually acceptable policies. On the output side, *shingikai* facilitate policy implementation: As the price for formal, prior representation of their views, interest groups cannot entirely avoid cooptation, and they necessarily share some measure of responsibility for the success of policies they helped frame.

There are thus much more interesting and effective ways for commissions to support bureaucracies than by serving as kept bodies and fairy cloaks. They help embed state agencies in a concrete set of social ties that bind them to private actors and provide institutionalized channels for the continual negotiation and renegotiation of public policies.[48]

When surveyed on their perceptions of *shingikai* performance, Socialist representatives predictably emphasized the likelihood of government manipulation, but bureaucrats and ruling-party politicians both stressed the positive contributions that councils make to the policy process (see Table 2-1).

This study has distinguished among commissions' functions for analytical purposes; that is not to suggest that they each perform a single function, of course. There are commentators who feel that they should. "Aren't too many objectives vaguely expected of *shingikai*? With their composition and operation becoming vaguely multipurpose, isn't their essential specialization diluted?" one observer worried.[49] This attitude is unrealistic, however. A council may simultaneously play a variety of roles at any one point in time, and may sequentially perform different functions over the course of time as its environment and the needs of its parent agency change. It is to the actual performance of those functions that we now turn.

[47] Park (1972), p. 459.
[48] Cf. Evans (1992), p. 164.
[49] Okabe (1969), p. 13.

Legal basis

Article 8, Section 1 of the National Administrative Organization Act (implemented 1 June 1949) legally authorized the creation of advisory bodies:

> Within the scope of jurisdiction fixed by law, each Article 3 administrative organ [i.e., office (*fu*), ministry (*shō*), committee (*iinkai*), or agency (*chō*)] can establish consultative bodies by law for the purpose of having them take charge of such appropriate business as the investigation of or deliberation on important matters, the examination of complaints, and so on through consultation with persons of learning and experience and others.[50]

The National Administrative Organization Act referred only to "bodies of the council system" (*gōgisei no kikan*). Consultative councils have carried such diverse titles as *shinsakai* (12 percent of all official advisory bodies in 1986), *chōsakai* (3 percent), *iinkai* (3 percent), *kyōgikai* (2 percent), and *kaigi* (1 percent) as well as *shingikai* (79 percent), proportions that have changed little over the years.[51] *Kai* means "meeting"; the other Japanese roots mean "deliberation," "investigation," or "conference." There are no consistent rules for naming councils. (Just as it uses "council," "commission," and "advisory body" interchangeably, this study does not distinguish among the different Japanese names, subsuming them under the catchall *shingikai*.)

Consultative organs initially required a legal basis. This was long a point of contention. Japan's postwar constitution ushered in popular sovereignty, establishing the Diet as "the highest organ of state power" in complete opposition to the Meiji constitution's conception of imperial prerogative. But even if the creation and abolition of ministries were clearly matters requiring legislation, it remained open to question whether the details of their internal organization were necessarily the concern of parliament, too. Did the establishment of a *shingikai* require a Diet bill or just a government ordinance issued at the discretion of the parent agency? In the interest of flexibility, officials sought the latter; suspicious of any reassertion of executive prerogative, the Diet opted for the former, and the Diet prevailed.

The laws creating each ministry stipulated the raisons d'être of certain councils, individual laws of establishment founded some, and broader laws provided for many others.[52] This arrangement worked poorly. Requiring every creation, alteration, or discontinuation of a *shingikai* to be handled with legal nicety was meant to prevent their uncontrolled spread. Instead, it ossified the council system when it did not disorder it outright. To avoid the complexity and delay of legislation, agencies often created advisory bodies

---

[50] Satō I. (1965), p. 103.
[51] Sōmuchō (1986); Yamada (1972), p. 14; *Toki no Hōrei* (1966), p. 71.
[52] Yamada (1972), p. 14.

by cabinet decrees. Although the Diet, especially the opposition parties, strongly criticized such measures, officials defended themselves by claiming that the new commissions were only private gatherings, forums to hear individuals' opinions.[53]

The First Rinchō acknowledged the disadvantages of extreme legalism and recommended both that the cabinet have the right to alter internal bureaucratic organization and that most councils should be founded by government ordinance. The cabinet echoed this sentiment but the Diet stood pat, repeatedly rejecting government bills to revise the National Administrative Organization Act. In 1982, another Ad Hoc Administrative Reform Council, the Second Rinchō, called for an easing of regulations on administrative organization that would allow for the establishment of ministries' internal bureaus, sections, and commissions by government ordinance. When the government had originally proposed this in 1948, a young representative named Nakasone Yasuhiro had fulminated, "So is party politics useless in the eyes of the administration?"[54] On the basis of the Second Rinchō's report, however, Prime Minister Nakasone himself presented a similar bill to the Diet and cut a deal to win the support of the centrist opposition, prompting one disillusioned observer to lament that "with parliament legislating in a way that slights – that disowns – the existence of parliament, we can say that the suicide of parliamentary government is beginning."[55]

Despite such emotionally charged opposition, the government's revision of the National Administrative Organization Act passed, partially amended, in 1983. The bill clearly stated that, with only a few exceptions, "offices, ministries, committees, and agencies may establish *shingikai* by means of law or government ordinance." Although limited in its effect on existing councils, revision of the act did signify an important change in parliamentary-administrative relations: Whereas organizational reform of the latter was formerly a joint responsibility, bureaucracies now bear full responsibility for structural changes that fall within the scope of their new authority.[56] They have not hesitated to exercise that authority.

Although not unimportant, these matters are of interest primarily to the student of administrative law. Whether a consultative body is founded by law or government ordinance matters less to most observers than the question of exactly *who* is being consulted. As a former administrative vice minister at the Management and Coordination Agency succinctly put it: "Policy starts with the selection of people."[57]

---

[53] Okabe (1969), pp. 2–3.
[54] *Mainichi Shinbun* (17 January 1985).
[55] Ibid.; Mori (1987), p. 68.
[56] Masujima (1984), pp. 35–36.
[57] Fukunaga (1995), p. 18.

Membership composition

The regular members (*tsūjō iin*) of a *shingikai*, who are considered civil servants, have the right always to participate in that body's decisionmaking. Special members (*tokubetsu* or *rinji iin*), whose voting rights are limited to specific items, or expert members (*senmon iin*), who lack voting rights, can be appointed as the need arises.

The size of a commission is set by its law (or ordinance) of establishment, which indicates either a specific number of members or an upper limit. To pluralize decisionmaking, it is desirable to have numerous members in order to reflect the views of as many groups as possible. To promote efficiency, however, a smaller number is appropriate so that each member may take some part in, and some responsibility for, deliberations (as the Japanese say, *sendō ooku shite fune yama ni noboru* – a boat with too many sailors will end up on top of a mountain). In 1966 and 1967, the cabinet decided in principle to set an upper limit of 20 councilors per *shingikai* and encouraged ministries to use more expert and temporary members. To take an extreme example, the Council for the Encouragement of the Arts and Sciences had 420 members at the time.[58] But because it has been difficult to implement so arbitrary a limit, which does not take into account the diversity of councils' issue areas and functions, close to half of the commissions established between 1967 and 1985 violated that rule.[59]

It is a rare commission whose members have no fixed term, councilors most often serving for two years at a time. Because a *shingikai* might fall prey to inertia if it retains the same councilors for too long, the cabinet in 1963 came to an understanding that established the principle of limiting tenure in office to three terms of three years, or two terms of four or five years.[60]

A related issue is the concurrent membership of one individual in a number of different councils. With experts scarce and commissions numerous, multiple appointments are a natural outcome, especially when separate bodies deal with related problems. Awarding multiple posts to the same individual is convenient to bureaucrats because of that individual's familiarity with a councilor's duties. Less justifiably, though, it is also convenient for agencies repeatedly to appoint members whose positions harmonize with officials' desires, or whose prestige will lend authority to the conclusions of an advisory body whether they are actually in a position to contribute to deliberations or not.

Concurrent appointments led to clear abuses. Officials sometimes held ridiculously numerous posts: In 1964, MOF's administrative vice minister nominally served on 57 *shingikai*, and seven other vice ministers served on at least 30.[61] Such a situation naturally invited suspicion of undue bureaucratic influ-

---

[58] Okabe (1969), p. 7.   [59] Kaneko (1985), pp. 134–35.
[60] Satō H. (1978), p. 147.   [61] Ebata (1965), p. 132.

ence. The repeated appointment of *zaikai* was also common. In the eyes of the Marxist Satō Hidetake, for individuals to serve simultaneously on many advisory bodies constituted a "privatization" of the council system: "It's no exaggeration to say that various important policies of our country are formulated by this handful of people. The pretense that *shingikai* are established in order to contribute to the democratization of administration through the reflection of the views of all classes of the people is nothing more than a fiction," he charged.[62]

In addition to limiting the number of terms that a member could serve on one advisory body, the cabinet's 1963 understanding directly addressed the issue of representativeness:

> On the choice of candidates, fresh human talent must be appointed from as wide a collection of related fields as possible without being particular about school background or "name value."
>
> Officials must consider a member's frequency of attendance, ability to perform his duties adequately, and the effects of his health on attendance, and make strenuous efforts to avoid those people whose advanced age or many concurrent posts do not meet these conditions. Four will be regarded as the maximum number of concurrent posts.[63]

Critics were unimpressed. The First Rinchō pointed out that these guidelines were scarcely observed, an accusation that continued to be made into the 1980s.[64] Although the Rinchō was attacking a clear and present abuse, the complaint is now unfounded. Within 10 years of the cabinet understanding, ministries had dramatically reduced the number of councilors with five or more concurrent posts, and within 15 years, they had by and large ended the practice.[65]

It is very much open to question whether multiple appointments ever did enhance the influence of *shingikai* "regulars." Despite finding fault with concurrent appointments for concentrating power, Satō himself cast doubt on the ability of busy *zaikai* to play an active role in council deliberations and, precisely because it would tend to lower a member's attendance and thus dilute his or her contribution, one researcher has gone so far as to suggest that ministries single out *inconvenient* representatives for multiple posts.[66]

Even if councilors were limited to short terms on a single *shingikai*, there would still be nothing to prevent officials from creating kept bodies of agency apologists if they could exclude individuals critical of government positions. This is, in fact, a common indictment made against commissions: that bureaucrats set up advisory bodies that are more pliant than self-reliant, and under

---

[62] Satō H. (1978), pp. 133, 137.   [63] Ibid., p. 147.
[64] Park (1972), p. 463; Kaneko (1985), p. 135.
[65] Satō H. (1978), p. 141.   [66] Ibid., p. 133; Sone et al. (1985), p. 115.

Japanese law, an agency's choice of *shingikai* members is not subject to legal challenge.[67] No one doubts that antisystem radicals or champions of fringe positions receive few invitations to help frame public policy, but that is not the issue. Targets of exclusion need not be mavericks: Because the Ministries of Finance and Home Affairs clash over the distribution of revenue sources between national and local governments, they have sometimes blocked each other's nominations to the Council on the Tax System, for example.[68]

One political scientist managed to find several bureaucrats willing to confide that they did indeed prefer to exclude persons prone to get out of line; they added that they were not free to appoint only those people whom they considered suitable, however.[69] Although it is the head of the agency with jurisdiction, a cabinet minister or the prime minister, who formally appoints councilors, the actual selection of candidates is normally left to the particular bureaucratic unit concerned. A variety of limits constrain authorities. Some councilors serve ex officio; in other cases, nominations require the consent of both houses of the Diet, cabinet approval, or the recommendation of concerned parties.[70] The head of a parent agency is usually free to appoint members who meet specified criteria, but those qualifications can be quite detailed. Eight of the 20 members of the Central Social Medical Insurance Council must represent the providers of health, sailors', and national health insurance, the insured themselves, business proprietors, and ship owners; 8 must represent doctors, dentists, and pharmacists; and the remaining 4 must represent the public interest. Appointments to the first two categories are made from among those persons recommended by the groups concerned, and the four public-interest representatives' nominations must be approved by both houses of the Diet.[71]

Despite such precautions, it cannot be denied that agencies have excluded some groups even from advisory bodies in which they had a justifiable claim to representation. Long the bête noir of the Ministry of Education, the Japan Teachers' Union was barred from various commissions dealing with educational matters because of its militant antigovernment and left-wing stance, for example.[72] Nevertheless, the establishment of a *shingikai* is made public, and parent agencies must consider how their appointments will affect perceptions of that *shingikai*'s legitimacy and thus its authority. (Of course, canny bureaucrats might for that very reason include "a few awkward types on councils [merely] to give an impression of balance and conceal the degree to which they are actually in charge of things."[73])

Even a lack of formal restraints should not be confused with a free hand on the part of authorities because they never operate in a vacuum. Where the law stipulates that a commission include representatives of a specific interest, such

---

[67] Upham (1987), pp. 199, 219.   [68] Satō C. (1962), p. 43.   [69] Harari (1986), p. 32.
[70] Kaneko (1985), pp. 135–36.   [71] Sōmuchō (1986), p. 247; Park (1972), p. 438.
[72] Park (1972), pp. 438–41.   [73] Fukunaga (1995), pp. 19–20.

members will generally come from the largest organization of the interest concerned, regardless of whether or not it is sympathetic to the standpoints of the parent agency and the ruling coalition. Although representation is no guarantee of influence, of course, ministries are rarely able to "disenfranchise" such a group.[74] And even where the law fails to specify membership qualifications, *shingikai* tend to replace those councilors who are not reappointed with persons from the same organization. The consensual nature of Japanese politics is easily exaggerated, but the conservative establishment is clearly sensitive to the need at least to consult other views.

Moreover, the blame for an unrepresentative council is not invariably the government's alone. Although bureaucrats *are* wary of antiestablishment groups or individuals, it is not unknown for such groups or individuals to boycott advisory bodies to avoid being – or even appearing to be – coopted. For fear of lending a semblance of fairness and bipartisanship to what it considered a reactionary plot, the JSP refused to send representatives to the Commission on the Constitution in the late 1950s and early 1960s despite repeated invitations, more than halving the ranks of the *shingikai*'s antirevisionist minority. (In the end, if most members did support the LDP's attempt to amend the constitution, the minority of antirevisionist members whom the government had felt compelled to appoint still managed to minimize the partisan nature of the commission's report.[75])

Ehud Harari has argued that composition follows function. Ministries will indeed attempt to pack commissions with supportive members when authorities seek to legitimize their policies. But interest-group representatives will dominate when an agency is seeking to coopt them, and neutral members will when it genuinely needs policy guidance.[76] Because the ministries have developed a greater need for the cooperation of interest groups and for the contributions to policymaking that only relatively independent councils can make, the usefulness of kept bodies has declined.

Given that their respective roles have differed, a discussion of the membership composition of *shingikai* must distinguish among specific categories of councilors. The categories that have attracted the most critical attention have been members of parliament (MPs), bureaucrats, interest-group representatives, and the very Japanese class of "persons of learning and experience."

Members of parliament

The inclusion of MPs has engendered controversy for both constitutional and ethical reasons. First, because it involves the direct involvement of the legisla-

---

[74] Cf. Uriu (1996), p. 251n.   [75] Ward (1965), pp. 405–8, 417–18.
[76] Harari (1974), p. 547.

tive branch in administrative bodies, the appointment of Diet representatives to commissions strikes skeptics as a violation of the principle of separation of powers. Second, although some observers have supported their participation on the condition that they act as disinterested specialists or as representatives of the people,[77] the other argument against MPs is that they cannot help but participate as politicians, acting as mouthpieces for their parties or for special interests.

Many of the *shingikai* that include Diet representatives deal with public works and construction – pork-barrel projects. In the past, 10 of the 30 seats on the Railroad Construction Council went to parliamentarians. Operating in every electoral district, the nationally owned (now denationalized) railroads inevitably became the object of political pressure. It was said that the politicians left other members "virtually without the right to speak,"[78] and the council's proposal was always to build new lines. On purely practical grounds, it has been argued that the participation of Diet representatives may be a plus in implementation, increasing the chances of action on commission recommendations.[79] But prior consultation with the ruling party could achieve the same purpose, and the very inclusion of politicians can prevent *shingikai* from making any recommendations. As a result of conflicts among their politician members, seven successive Councils on Electoral Reform submitted multiple reports or no report at all. In 1989, on the other hand, when the council broke with tradition to include only neutral members, it produced a unified, compromise recommendation that was enacted largely intact.[80]

Thus, it is difficult to deny that direct parliamentary involvement in commissions is constitutionally suspect and politically pernicious. In 1959, the Council on Administration declared categorically that the government "must not" assign Diet representatives to administrative advisory bodies.[81] In the 1960s, under pressure from the AMA and the First Rinchō, the cabinet repeatedly resolved "in principle" not to appoint MPs to councils.[82] Although those resolutions were not always observed, the number of commissions containing Diet representatives did decline by half over ten years, falling from 20 in 1974 to only 10 (out of 214) in 1984.[83] Its drawbacks notwithstanding, the participation of MPs no longer constitutes a serious problem for the *shingikai* system.

---

[77] E.g., Okabe (1969), p. 5.
[78] Sone et al. (1985), pp. 32–35.
[79] Ebata (1965), p. 138; Sone et al. (1985), p. 38.
[80] Christensen (1994a), p. 60.
[81] Yamada (1972), p. 16.
[82] Satō H. (1978), p. 148; Satō I. (1972), p. 9; Yamada (1972), p. 16; Park (1972), p. 463; Narita (1967), p. 52.
[83] Harari (1986), pp. 8–9; Sone et al. (1985), p. 11.

Bureaucrats and "old boys"

Incumbent bureaucrats occupy far more council seats than Diet representatives, and their participation is equally controversial. The inclusion of officials is justified by their expert knowledge. One observer went so far as to assert that "because most subjects of deliberation are concerned with fields of administration, [*shingikai* deliberations] would be meaningless [if they] did not include persons with administrative experience."[84] The argument is specious. Because a council's parent agency provides it with data and is consulted on its views, there is no need for staff to participate as formal members. Besides, such a practice flies in the face of an advisory body's raison d'être, which is to seek advice from *outside* the government.[85]

Ideally, bureaucratic councilors would avail other councilors of their knowledge and experience in a disinterested manner. But they cannot avoid the suspicion of tendentiously promoting administrative interests, of guiding deliberations toward conclusions convenient to their agencies (*temori shingikai-ka* – literally, the "help yourself-ization of councils").[86] Although certainly warranted, this fear may be exaggerated precisely because the potential for abuse is so obvious. In 1959, the Council on Administration proposed the outright abolition, or at least reexamination, of commissions a majority of whose members were civil servants, and a cabinet decision the following year forbade bureaucratic councilors except under "special circumstances." The First Rinchō recommended that administrative staff should "in principle" confine their participation to *shingikai* secretariats, and cabinet resolutions have repeatedly echoed that proposal.[87]

Although some commissions established subsequent to these resolutions did include administrative staff,[88] progress has been made. Between 1973 and 1983, the proportion of councils containing bureaucrats fell from 43 to 21 percent, and the numerical weight of bureaucrats' membership was high in only a small minority of cases (see Tables 2-2 and 2-3). If anything, these numbers overestimate administrative influence because the single category "bureaucrat" suggests a monolith that simply does not exist. The category must be unpacked, the statistics disaggregated. As the severe sectionalism that characterizes Japanese bureaucracies would lead one to predict, in the overwhelming majority of *shingikai* that include officials as members, they belong to different ministries, and where more than one official comes from a single ministry, they tend to belong to different bureaus.[89] Their presence thus suggests the felt need for

---

[84] Ogita (1969), p. 43.   [85] Park (1972), p. 445.
[86] Satō H. (1978), p. 134.
[87] Yamada (1972), p. 16; Satō I. (1972), pp. 9, 11; Sone et al. (1985), p. 20.
[88] Satō H. (1978), pp. 139, 142.
[89] Harari (1986), p. 30.

Table 2-2. *Scope of membership, 1973 and 1983 (percentage of all active shingikai on which a group is represented)*

	1973	1983
University	85	89
Business and agriculture	78	79
Other *tokushu hōjin*[a]	60	54
Mass media (incl. NHK)	49	55
Government bureaucrats	43	21
Subnational governments	30	31
Labor	21	30
Public corporations and national enterprises	17	7
Lawyers	12	17
Women	10	11
Diet members	6	3

[a] Semigovernmental organizations other than public corporations and national enterprises.
Source: Harari (1986), pp. 8–9.

inter- and intraministerial coordination rather than a bid for bureaucratic domination.

The appointment of retired bureaucrats, or "OBs" (from the Japanese-English "old boys," or alumni), raises questions, too. Ministries sometimes use commissions as a dumping ground for superannuated officials (*kanryō no Ubasuteyama* – literally, "a mountain on which to abandon old bureaucrats to die"), and commission membership can serve as a form of retirement compensation.[90] In 1995, an advisory body survived despite having run out of subjects to investigate "because it's a study group for Ministry of Finance OBs," an official of that ministry explained.[91] Although this is surely true more often than OB councilors would like to believe, it does not tell the whole story. Like incumbent officials, OBs ostensibly participate as specialists in areas within their former ministry's jurisdiction. Like incumbent officials, however, OBs are widely suspected of acting on ministry instructions, or at least of being chosen by virtue of their sharing bureaucratic values and policy positions.

The government itself long ago recognized that the inclusion of OBs could damage a commission's legitimacy: The cabinet's 1963 understanding on the selection of councilors ruled that "in principle, current advisers or retired bureaucrats (particularly those who have just retired) should not be appointed as members of their agency's *shingikai*," and a year later, the First Rinchō recom-

[90] Satō C. (1962), p. 43; Craig (1975), p. 6.
[91] *Nihon Keizai Shinbun* (13 July 1995).

Table 2-3. *Relative numerical weight of participants, 1973 and 1983*[a]

	Mode		>50%		<1/3		<10%	
	1973	1983	1973	1983	1973	1983	1973	1983
University	85%	83%	6%	8%	88%	81%	28%	17%
Business and agriculture	100	100	22	13	54	60	15	14
Other *tokushu hōjin*	33	43	—	—	100	99	58	62
Government bureaucrats	75	71	5	9	72	66	26	18
Subnational governments	59	35	1	9	91	98	56	68
Labor	35	33	—	—	98	100	52	59
Public corporations and natl. enterprises	15	11	—	—	100	100	91	93
Lawyers	45	47	—	—	86	91	50	56
Women	15	29	—	—	100	100	87	91
Mass media (incl. NHK)	30	29	—	—	100	100	76	71

[a] In 1983, 83 percent was the greatest proportion of seats that university professors occupied in any *shingikai*; they constituted a majority in 8 percent of the *shingikai* on which they sat; made up one-third or less of the members in 81 percent of the *shingikai* on which they sat; and so on.
Source: Harari (1986), pp. 13–14.

mended that the appointment of OBs be kept to a minimum.[92] Even so, retired officials occupied close to 18 percent of all council seats in 1995, down only a few percentage points from a decade earlier.[93]

Although the role of OBs is ambiguous, Harari collected some suggestive survey data in 1973. Many of the retired officials were serving on commissions that were not attached to their former ministries, which would certainly mitigate any feelings of loyalty to their commissions' parent agencies. Furthermore, a large number of the OBs had assumed new positions outside the government at least ten years before, giving their new roles ample time to affect their perspectives.[94] When asked to whom they felt most responsible as councilors, although 32 percent of OBs indicated "the appointing authority" as opposed to only 19 percent of all respondents, 41 percent of the OBs felt responsible primarily to those who were affected by the policies under consideration, which differed

---

[92] Satō H. (1978), p. 147; Satō I. (1972), p. 9.
[93] Calculated from *Nihon Keizai Shinbun* (13 July 1995); Sone et al. (1985), p. 114.
[94] Forty percent of these ex-bureaucrats were associated with business or agricultural organizations, 25 percent with universities, and 12 percent with the mass media; none represented labor organizations. Harari (1982), p. 240.

little from the figure for all respondents. In addition, 55 percent of the OBs had retired from one of the three highest ranks in the civil service (bureau chief or above), so the officials allegedly controlling OBs were often former subordinates of theirs.[95] In such a situation, officials might well expect sympathy but not obedience. As one councilor put it, "bureaucratic OBs' right to speak is secure. Because they have a self-important feeling towards incumbent bureaucrats, they sometimes deprecate plans presented by those incumbents."[96]

It cannot be assumed that OBs will defend administrative views, and even when they do, the views they defend will be those of competing agencies, not of some undifferentiated bureaucratic establishment.

Interest-group representatives

It is ministries that deal with large, influential interest groups that have created the most *shingikai*.[97] In 1996, MITI had the largest number (33), followed by the Prime Minister's Office (25) and the Ministries of Health and Welfare (22) and Agriculture, Forestry, and Fisheries (22). The Ministry of Foreign Affairs had the fewest (2), followed by the Defense Agency (3) and the Ministry of Home Affairs (4).[98] (Because bodies whose jurisdictions do not fall neatly within the established province of any one ministry are assigned to the Prime Minister's Office, it is regarded as a "rubbish heap" for commissions.[99]) Over time, there has been a trend toward the appointment of more interest-group representatives to councils. When noneconomic groups are included, at least 90 percent of all *shingikai* contained such members in 1983, and 63 percent of all the national associations surveyed in 1994 had representation on some advisory body.[100] Commission membership lists generally identify the particular organizations to which councilors belong, sometimes gathering groups of them under functional subheadings like "the financial industry" or "workers."

However prevalent the practice, some Japanese question whether private actors should participate in public decisions on matters of interest to them. In the traditional Japanese view, just as in the traditional Western view, representatives of private interests naturally take a selfish standpoint and cannot judge the public interest fairly. Echoing prewar bureaucrats' refusal to accord legitimacy to any assertion of partial interests, the Council on Administration recommended in 1959 that the government "must not" establish commissions that gathered representatives of "special interest groups."[101] One critic pointed out, "There are legal restraints forbidding a member of parliament from participating in proceedings concerned with matters in which he or the business pursued by a relative have a direct interest relation. [Yet] there are no such regulations in

---

[95] Harari (1986), pp. 30–31.   [96] Sone et al. (1985), p. 16.   [97] Ibid., pp. 7, 10.
[98] *Nihon Keizai Shinbun* (8 August 1996).   [99] Inagawa (1985), p. 47.
[100] Harari (1986), p. 7; Tsujinaka (1996), p. 51.   [101] Yamada (1972), p. 16.

shingikai. . . . It is not unusual to act as a mouthpiece for a group's view from start to finish without trying to lend an ear to other members' views."[102] The Recruit scandal that rocked Japan in 1988 highlighted this conflict-of-interest issue: Prime Minister Nakasone was accused of using his position (in return for bribes?) to help install the chair of Recruit Cosmos on commissions considering matters with a direct bearing on that company's businesses.[103]

Although interest-group representatives are commonly blamed for drowning out the advice of disinterested specialists and for throwing *shingikai* deliberations into confusion, this is an unreasonable accusation: The orderliness of debate obviously depends in no small part on the subject debated, and strife cannot justly be attributed to the inclusion of interest-group councilors alone. The Rice Price Council failed to stifle divisiveness when it excluded producer and consumer representatives and attempted to conduct its deliberations on the basis of a purely "neutral" membership in 1968.[104] Growing diversity inevitably follows economic development, and commissions have come to reflect this situation. The scope of interest-group representation in the *shingikai* system is very wide, if sometimes of questionable fairness. Today's controversies usually have less to do with the legitimacy of their participation than with the relative access granted different groups.

Business and agriculture. Given the economic focus of postwar Japanese policy and its traditionally close ties to the LDP and the ministries, big business has naturally played a prominent role in commissions, a role that has attracted considerable critical attention. Park spoke for many when he posited *zaikai* "dominance" of *shingikai* in the following terms:

> Today advisory bodies provide big business with one of the major formal means of access to governmental decision-making. The major business groups . . . as well as major corporations or individuals associated with them are *invariably* given representation not only on economic advisory bodies but also on councils in areas not immediately relevant to economic matters. Furthermore, in many advisory councils and *every* economic advisory body, Zaikai representatives readily constitute a majority.[105] [emphasis added]

Appearing to substantiate these claims, Satō found in 1976 that *zaikai* occupied 56 percent of the seats on 11 important economic councils and government-tied representatives another 21 percent. In an extreme example like the Steel Subcommittee of MITI's Industrial Structure Council, a whopping 98 percent of the members were business representatives. Satō thus considered *zaikai*'s control of *shingikai* to be "watertight."[106] The Japan Communist Party (JCP)

---

[102] Miyoshi (1971), p. 35.   [103] *Asahi Shinbun* (17 March 1989), p. 2.
[104] Kaneko (1985), p. 138.   [105] Park (1972), p. 442.   [106] Satō H. (1978), pp. 130–32, 148.

conducted a similar survey of 20 major economic commissions in 1986. About half of the seats on these commissions went to *zaikai* and another 22 percent to individuals tied to the government or high-level bureaucratic OBs working in big business. These same groups also provided 19 of the 20 chairs. The JCP concluded that "it is natural that every kind of *shingikai* devised in this way will submit reports that on the whole serve *zaikai* exclusively."[107]

Even taken at face value, there is nothing particularly surprising about these figures if it is accepted that one of the main functions of these bodies is to adjust the competing interests of economic actors and administrative authorities. But this kind of research is tendentious in defining "*zaikai*" widely enough to embrace almost all businesspeople, and its choice of commissions is suspect. Although Satō's 11 and the JCP's 20 councils may well be important, they are not representative of all economic commissions, let alone the entire *shingikai* system. Looking at all 37 of the commissions attached to MITI in 1979, an American political scientist calculated that only 29 percent of their members represented "business groups" and 20 percent corporations,[108] and even these figures must be disaggregated.

Although business and agriculture were lumped together, Harari has collected the most detailed statistics. First, critics like Park and Satō were right to point to the ubiquity of business representatives: Business and agriculture together had the widest scope of membership of all categories of interest groups, sitting on fully 79 percent of all councils in 1983. (The percentage of councils on which they held a *majority* of seats did decline from 22 percent to 13 percent between 1973 and 1983, however; see Tables 2-2 and 2-3.) But Harari went on to distinguish among three levels of producer organizations: individual firms; *gyōkai*, or federations of firms in particular industries and the national federation of agricultural cooperatives; and the four *zaikai*, or peak, associations. In 1983, 34 percent of those *shingikai* including members from business or agriculture contained representatives of *zaikai*, *gyōkai*, and firms; 33 percent *gyōkai* and firms; 16 percent *gyōkai* alone; and 16 percent firms alone. Furthermore, *big* business sends a minority of those councilors representing individual firms: In 1974, only 20 percent of business councilors came from Japan's 100 largest corporations and 25 percent from other large corporations listed on the Tokyo Stock Exchange.[109]

Considering this multiplicity of organizations, it is safe to assume that business councilors spend more time trying to adjust their conflicting claims than imposing the dictates of monopoly capital on the government.

Labor. Park wrote that "it is not at all unusual that labor is excluded even from councils in whose activities labor is vitally interested. Furthermore, on councils

---

[107] Japan Communist Party (1986), p. 23.
[108] Richardson and Flanagan (1984), p. 316.   [109] Harari (1986), pp. 8, 15–19.

to which it is given access, labor is inequitably represented."[110] And yet, Harari described the scope of labor membership as "by no means negligible."[111] What accounts for this difference of opinion? Primarily the passage of time.

Labor representatives were never entirely excluded from the *shingikai* system. Established by a Socialist-led coalition in 1947, the Ministry of Labor's Central Council on Labor Standards and Central Council on Employment Security provided unions with representation equal to that of employers on important policymaking commissions for the first time. Particularly in the late 1950s, ministries created other tripartite forums that played crucial roles in devising important labor legislation.[112] For all its 4,200,000 members, Sōhyō was directly represented on only 29 of the nation's 241 advisory bodies in 1965.[113] This narrow participation was in part a result of self-exclusion, however – if Dōmei early on sought to join *shingikai*, where it took an accommodating line, Sōhyō long stressed open confrontation over behind-the-scenes conciliation – and from the mid-1960s Sōhyō, too, began to participate more actively in government policymaking.[114]

The Council on the Economy opened its doors to unions in 1966, and labor members began to sit on MITI's influential Industrial Structure Council in 1971. Between 1973 and 1983, the proportion of *shingikai* including union representatives rose from 21 to 30 percent. A majority of the commissions that *officially* include labor members are attached to the Ministries of Labor and Health and Welfare, the agencies that interact most intensively with unions and are most receptive to their views.[115] But labor participation is wider than membership lists suggest: Councils often form subcommittees (whose recommendations they tend to adopt), and subcommittees examining questions of concern to labor tend to include unionists whether their parent councils do or not. Even during the period when Sōhyō held a negative attitude toward participation in *shingikai*, its officials sometimes took part as specialist members or as the representatives of research organizations.

It must be admitted, however, that the widening scope of labor representation across commissions has not been matched by a commensurate increase in unions' relative weight within commissions. In no council do labor members constitute more than a third of the total, and unions hold no more than a tenth of the seats in a majority of the councils to which they send representatives (see Table 2-3). Moreover, even those unionists who do participate in *shingikai* do not feel quite so efficacious as other members. In response to a survey, business

[110] Park (1972), p. 441.
[111] Harari (1986), p. 9.
[112] Garon and Mochizuki (1993), pp. 157, 161.
[113] Park (1972), pp. 439–40.
[114] Harari (1986), p. 12.
[115] Sone et al. (1985), p. 12; Harari (1986), p. 44.

representatives and scholars rated the degree to which their commissions made a serious effort to improve public policymaking at 3.8 and 3.7, respectively, on a 5-point scale; the average labor response was 3.3. Both businesspeople and scholars rated the influence of their councils' reports on government decisionmaking at 3.5, unionists at 3.0.[116] Although unions may well make their presence felt in individual *shingikai*, there is no denying that labor influence within the *shingikai* system as a whole is still much weaker than that of businesses.

Japanese labor has been weak in part because it has been fragmented. As noted earlier, several national centers long dominated the postwar labor movement. On the level of a specific industrial or public-service sector, many unions joined *tansan* federations, with a single sector often supporting several *tansan* affiliated with different national centers (or with none at all). There were also *kyōgikai*, or groupings of several *tansan* in the private sector that cut across national-center affiliations. In 1983, 26 percent of the *shingikai* with labor members had representatives from the national centers alone; 31 percent from national centers, *tansan*, and/or *kyōgikai*; and 42 percent from *tansan* and/or *kyōgikai*. No representatives were merely enterprise union officials. If business executives get involved in public affairs independently of their *gyōkai* as well as through them, enterprise unions focus on bread-and-butter matters like wages, working conditions, and strikes and leave questions of public policy to higher-level union federations.[117]

The organizational structure of both labor and business representation varies with the scope of a commission's issue area: Commissions with the widest scope (e.g., the Council on the Economy) tend to include representatives of national centers as the only labor members and officials from *zaikai* business associations, whereas commissions that focus on a particular industry tend to include labor representatives from *tansan* and/or *kyōgikai* and officials of *gyōkai*. Labor membership has also mirrored union factionalism. In 1983, two-thirds of the councils with labor members included representatives associated with more than one national center, and councils with members from the national centers alone almost always included representatives from both Sōhyō and Dōmei.[118]

Political elites have accorded the labor movement less recognition in Japan than in most other advanced industrial democracies. As outlined in Chapter 1, however, recent trends have favored greater unity in the labor movement and a more inclusionary policymaking process. Whether or not Rengō becomes a major force in Japanese politics, its creation does set the stage for heightened labor participation in the *shingikai* system.

[116] Harari (1986), p. 43A.
[117] Ibid., pp. 21–22.
[118] Ibid., pp. 23–25, 47.

"Persons of learning and experience"

When laws set criteria for council membership, the most typical qualification is that a councilor be "a person of learning and experience" (*gakushiki keikensha*). In tripartite commissions, such members are also referred to as "neutral" (*chūritsu*) or "public-interest" (*kōeki*) representatives. Japanese themselves feel that the qualification of persons of learning and experience is distinctive of their *shingikai* system, and advisory bodies composed solely of such members are regarded as especially "council-like councils."[119] Although persons of learning and experience may be journalists, lawyers, staffers at research organizations, or bureaucratic OBs, they are most often scholars.

In principle, advisory bodies include these members for their special expertise and disinterested perspective, but these presumptions have come under attack. Unlike other formal qualifications, "person of learning and experience" is extremely vague, opening the door to arbitrariness or self-interested manipulation on the part of a parent agency in its selection of councilors. In the words of several faultfinders, "That persons chosen by authorities entirely lack either learning or experience is virtually impossible. . . . Provisions concerning persons of learning and experience are not a legal restraint on the right of administrative authorities to choose members, but rather a legalization of 'suit-yourself personnel.'" When invited to serve on commissions that deal with matters beyond their ken, persons of learning and experience are just lay persons. Even among bona fide experts, "each of the ministries and agencies carefully cultivates a stable of reliable tribe [i.e., *zoku*] academics" who act as their advocates. As a result, "depending on the method of choosing [persons of learning and experience], it is quite possible to predict the tendency of a report's contents, and the deliberation process is rather framed." Rather than vainly attempting to rationalize policymaking by excluding interest-group representatives and appointing ostensibly neutral members, the government would do well in some instances to exclude neutral members instead.[120]

To the extent that the inclusion of persons of learning and experience permits parent agencies to appoint councilors at their own discretion, it does contribute to the creation of kept bodies. As noted earlier, however, bureaucrats have so free a hand less often than critics suggest. This is particularly true when commissions include interest-group representatives. Because the participation of these groups is both voluntary and often necessary to ensure the legitimacy of proceedings, "bureaucrats consult with interest groups and even bargain with them – not only regarding the participation of officials of the groups involved or their rivals, but also regarding such supposedly neutral categories as academics

---

[119] Yasuhara (1978), p. 36; Sone et al. (1985), p. 10.
[120] Kaneko (1979), p. 161; Fukunaga (1995), pp. 18–19; Ōi (1965), p. 57; Sakuma et al. (1972), p. 45.

and members of the mass media." Although 46 percent of the nonbureaucratic respondents in one survey of councilors were interest-group officials, fully 65 percent reported that one of the reasons they became members was that some interest organization had asked them to do so.[121]

Of course, the consultation of interest groups does not in itself guarantee fairness: When officials consult only one set of groups and those groups have cultivated their own *zoku* scholars, then "we find ourselves in another classic triangle: power and favors circulate among bureaucrats, businessmen, and academics in a carbon copy of the better know 'Iron Triangle' of politicians, bureaucrats, and businessmen."[122] When multiple or less favored interest groups are represented, this becomes much more difficult, however. In 1965, for example, unions managed to delay the establishment of the Council on the Civil Servant System and to negotiate the inclusion of three labor scholars among the eight formally neutral members, two from a list presented by Sōhyō.[123] In typical Japanese fashion, political actors will thus maintain the pretense (*tatemae*) that persons of learning and experience do not represent particular interests while actually (*honne*) clashing fiercely over their selection.

Membership composition is probably the most crucial attribute of any advisory body, but the most representative commission would still serve as no more than a fairy cloak if it did not operate autonomously. "In the process of *shingikai* deliberations, it is possible for specialists' opinions to be twisted by high-level political interference," a commentator observed. "This suggests, in other words, that authorities exercise internal guidance in order to draw forth conclusions convenient to the government."[124] To what extent do parent agencies *consult* councils, and to what extent do they *manage* them?

Shingikai in operation

Shingikai fall outside the normal bureaucratic hierarchy. In their capacity as attached organs (*fuzoku kikan*), they submit to the supervision of higher-level administrative bodies without receiving orders from them, and thus should arrive at their decisions independently. Although Japanese law does not expressly provide for this independence, it follows logically from councils' raisons d'être. An advisory body cannot offer candid advice except on the basis of free deliberations, and in order for it to serve as a watchdog of bureaucratic fairness and rationality, it must operate unconstrained by that bureaucracy.

Some obvious guarantees of autonomy would be *shingikai*'s deciding their own rules of procedure, independent budgets, and security of membership status. Legal precedents ensure that advisory bodies do have the right to deter-

---

[121] Harari (1986), p. 33. [122] Fukunaga (1995), p. 19.
[123] Harari (1974), p. 567. [124] Okabe (1969), p. 18.

mine their own rules of procedure. If councils generally lack independent budgets, this is less crippling than might be imagined because their operating expenses are normally minimal. Although membership status is not legally guaranteed, parent agencies do not dismiss obstreperous representatives.

As part-time civil servants, councilors are paid, which raises the possibility of
coaxing cooperation in return for remuneration. That is unlikely, however. It
was estimated in 1995 that members were generally paid about ¥20,000–
¥40,000 ($220–$440) per meeting.[125] Rather than encouraging councilors to
curry favor with parent agencies, such honoraria may actually serve as a disin-
centive to participate at all. A famous writer was once reported to have resigned
from the Central Council on Education when he learned how small the consulting fee would be; he could make much more lucrative use of his time, he said, by
appearing on television or on panel discussions.[126]

There are more rewards to serving on a commission than direct financial
compensation, of course. Members enjoy what may be viewed as remuneration
in kind, like inspection missions abroad; forge personal connections that can
result in profitable opportunities inside or outside the government; enjoy access
to information that might otherwise be inaccessible, particularly data that have
already been refined by bureaucrats;[127] bask in prestige; or enjoy the satisfaction
of having their ideas reflected in public policy and making a contribution to
society. Few councilors profess suspicion of bureaucrats' motives – whereas
fully 74 percent of the respondents in one survey thought authorities appointed
them for their knowledge and experience and/or their fair judgment, only 7
percent felt that their sympathy with the appointing authority's position had
played a part[128] – and all indications are that councilors participate in order to act
as some group's advocate or out of public-spiritedness, not out of a concern for
officials' carrots and sticks.

Parent agencies do not have to bludgeon commissions through the imposition
of constricting rules of debate or outright bribery to influence their conclusions;
shingikai operations offer officials subtler means of intervention. Park neatly
summarized *shingikai* decisionmaking in the following way:

> The first sessions of a commission are usually devoted to such matters as
> the minister's report explaining the nature of the commission's new *assign-*
> *ment*, selection of a *chairman*, formation of subcommittees, creation of a
> *secretariat*, and other procedural matters. This is followed by the stage in
> which councilors examine *reference materials* furnished by the host ministry
> and various groups concerned with the outcome of the commission's delib-
> eration, conduct public hearings, and take field inspection trips. Then come

---

[125] *Asahi Shinbun* (18 June 1995); *Nihon Keizai Shinbun* (13 July 1995).
[126] Passin (1975), p. 268. See also Sakuma et al. (1972), p. 52.
[127] Kudo and Kakinuma (1994), p. 23; Fukunaga (1995), p. 19.
[128] Harari (1986), pp. 38–40.

extensive *deliberations and discussions* during which compromises and hard bargaining take place, and attempts made to identify acceptable courses of action. . . . The final stage of the commission's work is the making of a *draft report*.[129] [emphasis added]

Each of these facets of consultation will be examined in turn, but some deliberations of the Textbook Subcommittee of the Central Council on Education (CCE) can be cited as a worst-case scenario. The Ministry of Education (MOE)

> chose as chair a man known for his public statements in favor of the MOE position; the management of the CCE secretariat was placed under the Elementary and Secondary Education Bureau (the one closest to the *genba* [i.e., the issue at hand]) rather than the more far-sighted Planning Office; top MOE officials . . . attended virtually every meeting; while the council's "request for advice" was not too specific, the council used an LDP *zoku* report on textbook control (actually drafted by MOE officials) as a starting-point for its deliberations; when council members voiced opinions not totally in line with the MOE position, ministry officials were quickly sent around to "explain the problems with the member's points of view"; and the ministry secretariat, through its role in preparing the summaries of deliberations and the final report, brought the council's recommendations even more closely into line with the MOE position.[130]

Task assignment

Although some advisory bodies are empowered to study a problem and submit recommendations spontaneously, these and other commissions normally prepare a report only in response to a parent agency's formal inquiry. Several possible reasons for this passivity are that bureaucrats do not appreciate gratuitous advice, that the councils by themselves lack necessary information, or that councilors are simply too busy or unenthusiastic to take on extra duties voluntarily.[131]

Although it is often left to the discretion of bureaucratic agencies, many laws require them to "consult" or "ask the opinion" of *shingikai* before drafting bills in their issue area. The accepted interpretation of such laws has been that council deliberation is a prerequisite of valid administrative action only when the council in question is an examining (*san'yo*) body, or when it is a consultative (*shimon*) body acting to protect the rights and interests of concerned parties or to adjust conflicting interests. An administrative action would not be invalidated, in other words, just because an agency neglected its obligation to consult a commission on the abstract advisability of that action.[132] This line of argument

---

[129] Park (1972), pp. 447–48.
[130] Len Schoppa, *Education Reform in Japan* (New York: Routledge, 1990), p. 114.
[131] Tanaka M. (1972), p. 19.   [132] Kotaka (1986), p. 46; Satō C. (1962), p. 44.

is problematical on two counts. First, it is not always easy to distinguish between *san'yo* and *shimon* bodies, or between the protection of concerned parties' rights and interests on the one hand and a judgment of the abstract advisability of some action on the other. Second, as will be discussed, it is open to question whether it is admissible to slight *shingikai* because they are no more than advisory bodies.[133]

A parent agency can consult a commission in a variety of ways. It can have a *shingikai* examine a problem and submit its findings without making specific recommendations. A council may identify the pros and cons of a parent-agency proposal. Most often, though, an advisory body will deliberate and make recommendations on a problem along general guidelines laid down by the parent agency. Through the "frame" or "terms of reference" (i.e., instructions) it gives, a parent agency defines the task of a council and can influence the direction of its report. Exactly how it would go about exerting that influence is open to debate, however. Pempel argued that parent agencies determine the direction of recommendations by issuing specific instructions as to the direction an investigation should take.[134] Because it facilitates control of a commission's agenda and speeds deliberations, Harari agrees that a narrow frame of reference is expedient when a parent agency seeks to legitimize a policy initiative or, conversely, an open avoidance or postponement of change. But if an agency wished to divert pressure for action surreptitiously, it would equally be asserting control by *widening* the frame of reference and complicating the agenda, thus prolonging and perplexing *shingikai* deliberations.[135]

It is easy to exaggerate the leverage that frames of reference provide a parent agency. Narrow instructions may signify officials' genuine need for guidance on some specific issue, wide instructions a lack of consensus among them. The mandate of the extremely controversial Commission on the Constitution could not have been more vague – "to investigate and deliberate about the Constitution of Japan and related problems" – setting the stage for endless wrangling among commission members, yet the LDP was, in fact, seeking an endorsement of constitutional revision.[136] Harari himself takes pains to qualify his observations, noting that councilors are often consulted before the agenda is set, that they can raise the issue again from within a *shingikai*, and that whatever the formal frame of reference, councilors will necessarily interpret it.[137]

Chairs

Although commission chairs generally do not speak their minds as do ordinary members, they have the authority to set the agenda, preside over discussions,

---

[133] Kotaka (1986), p. 46.   [134] Pempel (1974), pp. 659–60.
[135] Harari (1974), pp. 543, 549.   [136] Ward (1965), p. 406.
[137] Harari (1986), p. 33; Harari (1974), p. 550.

Table 2-4. *Bureaucratic OB chairs, 1984 and 1995*

Ministry	Percent of chairs OBs	
	1984	1995
MFA	100.0[a]	—
MOJ	85.7[a]	—
MITI	48.5	45.2
MAFF	47.6	95.0
MOC	44.4	55.6
MOF	41.2	44.4
MHW	36.4	40.9
MOE	35.3	26.7
PMO	30.0	—
MOT	25.0	20.0
MPT	20.0	—
MHA	0.0[a]	—
MOL	—	21.4

[a] Because the Ministries of Foreign Affairs (MFA), Justice (MOJ), and Home Affairs (MHA) had among the fewest *shingikai* of all ministries, their figures are easily skewed and must be considered exceptional.
Source: Calculated from Sone et al. (1985), p. 13, and from *Nihon Keizai Shinbun* (13 July 1995).

and bring deliberations to a conclusion. Formally, members elect their chair; customarily, administrative *nemawashi* will settle on a mutually acceptable candidate in advance, with members simply ratifying that choice.

Beyond brokering the selection of chairs, administrative staff or even cabinet ministers occasionally fill these posts themselves, but the practice obviously flies in the face of advisory bodies' rationale and has been condemned repeatedly from within the government itself. Retired bureaucrats chaired 38.6 percent of all active *shingikai* in 1995, and in direct contravention of a cabinet resolution made that very year, almost 84 percent of those OBs chaired *shingikai* attached to the ministries in which they had previously worked.[138] More detailed statistics confirm this marked preference of agencies for retired officials in general and their own OBs in particular (see Table 2-4).

If OB chairs could be trusted to represent ministry positions, these figures would demonstrate the potential for considerable bureaucratic control. One cannot deduce ministry control from the mere presence of retired officials, however. As previously argued with respect to ordinary OB councilors, one

[138] *Nihon Keizai Shinbun* (13 July 1995); Sone et al. (1985), p. 13.

would expect an OB chair's susceptibility to manipulation to vary inversely with the final rank he or she attained and the years elapsed since retirement. An overwhelming 84 percent of OB chairs in 1975 had reached one of the top three grades of the civil service, and virtually all of the rest had risen at least to section chief. Where retirement dates could be ascertained, 93 percent of these OB chairs had retired no less than 10 years earlier, and 57 percent at least 20 years earlier.[139] These figures are significantly higher than those for ordinary OB councilors. Retired bureaucrats may be a safe choice from the perspective of incumbent officials in that "it's hard to imagine something like [their] throwing mud right at their former office or at government offices in general,"[140] but it would be a mistake to presume that OB chairs are willing tools of bureaucratic control.

Zaikai chairs have come under fire, too. "Appointing active *zaikai* as chairs of government *shingikai* or subcommittees deciding the course of future economic policies is like leaving traffic regulations to taxi drivers," in the words of one scholar.[141] *Zaikai* presided over 6 of the 11 "key" economic *shingikai* that Satō investigated and 10 of the 20 that the JCP surveyed.[142] But if the presence of businesspeople presumably testifies to the need for coordination among business and bureaucratic interests, MITI, the ministry most directly involved in industrial policy, appoints surprisingly few businesspeople to chair its councils: In 1984, *zaikai* or *gyōkai* officials constituted only 9.1 percent of the MITI council chairs who were not bureaucratic OBs. In addition, only a minority of these businessperson chairs represented one of the four *zaikai* peak organizations.[143]

Secretariat/information

Ideally, secretariats divorced from government influence would objectively gather information for councils. The First Rinchō called for the creation of such bodies, and it has been suggested more recently that secretariats be appointed by the Management and Coordination Agency, which would have no direct interest in the matters discussed.[144] With very few exceptions (e.g., the Commission on the Constitution), however, a council's parent agency acts as its secretariat. Even when an independent secretariat does exist, it is usually composed of parent agency staff, although outsiders are on rare occasions included. Secretariats handle such mundane matters as preparing a meeting place, drawing up minutes, and delivering documents. Secretariats' links to ministries could be overlooked if their functions ended there. They do not. In order for councils to engage in adequate deliberations and submit meaningful reports, they must

---

[139] Harari (1986), pp. 31–32.   [140] Sone et al. (1985), p. 114.   [141] Okabe (1969), p. 18.
[142] Satō H. (1978), p. 132; Japan Communist Party (1986).
[143] Sone et al. (1985), p. 14.   [144] Fukunaga (1995), p. 21.

obtain relevant data, and it is the secretariats that gather much of these data. The fairness with which they perform this function is disputed.

Critics have claimed that agencies are not above blatantly denying requests for information that might lead to conclusions inconvenient to them, and that they weave their own views into the data they do provide. To cite one particularly flagrant incident:

> At a time when the pros and cons of getting rid of streetcars was being noisily debated, the Ministry of Transportation dispatched a group of influential persons of learning and experience to foreign countries, guided them only to those cities where the discontinuation of streetcars had worked well and, after their return, succeeded in fostering a powerful group of supportive scholars. Although not a few places in the world had been successful in maintaining their streetcars, there was no evidence of members' having visited them, and they were subsequently criticized for acting as puppets of the Ministry of Transportation that had arranged the plans for the inspection trip.[145]

It has been alleged that bureaucrats do not treat all *shingikai* members equally, giving more study materials and special help to selected councilors in advance of meetings.[146] Conversely, consumer members of the Food Sanitation Council have publicly complained that officials distribute pertinent documents, including documents in foreign languages, only days before meetings in order to curb dissent.[147] A secretariat's influence is usually far more subtle, however. "Whenever we have a meeting," observed a member of the Council on the Tax System, "executives from MOF's Tax Bureau hand out thick sheaves of materials, and the meeting starts with them explaining what the materials mean. That usually sets the parameters for the discussion."[148]

Because advisory bodies are generally managed with extremely little money, most of which goes toward members' honoraria, the typical commission is unable to conduct extensive investigations by itself. Although the government at first spoke grandly of providing the First Rinchō, which included over 130 participants, with close to ¥3 billion ($8,000,000) over three years, it was ultimately budgeted only ¥37 million ($95,000) in 1962 and another ¥55 million ($150,000) in 1963. With the exception of four or five young assistant professors who worked part-time, the 70 research assistants who were responsible for the actual investigations of the First Rinchō were all incumbent bureaucrats. The commission thus had to entrust the research underpinning its proposals to representatives of the very targets of reform.[149]

---

[145] Ebashi (1985), p. 15.
[146] Fukunaga (1995), pp. 20–21.
[147] Patricia Maclachlan, personal communication.
[148] Kudo and Kakinuma (1994), p. 22.
[149] Shingikai Kenkyūkai (1963), pp. 56–57.

The knowledge and experience of any individual member may not suffice to arrive at an independent judgment. "Since a councilor's professional demands, his concurrent commission duties, and his personal needs prevent him from making efforts to obtain needed information, he is at the mercy of the secretariat," charged Park.[150] The problem is especially acute for lone persons of learning and experience, who lack the backing of an organization, and for unions, which lack the financial and analytical resources of businesses.[151] Councilors' dependence on parent agencies is not as extreme as some commentators suggest, however.

Bureaucracies' ability to screen information has declined over time. Nongovernmental organizations like trade associations, agricultural cooperatives, and research institutes have developed their own policy-related capabilities to the point where they can challenge agencies.[152] Not only are the representatives of organized interests, including labor, increasingly able to draw on such independent analytical resources, but individual councilors themselves can accumulate policy-related expertise. If an agency is advantaged vis-à-vis other actors thanks to its continuous and long-term involvement in a particular issue area, servicing a commission is generally one of many assignments performed by individual bureaucrats, and those bureaucrats' attachment to a commission tends to be of shorter duration than that of the councilors they assist. Although 41 percent of nongovernmental members pointed to the parent agency as their major source of information in one survey of consultative (*shimon*) councils, an almost identical 38 percent cited their own research and experience and another 9 percent in-house research by their councils. As councilors increase their independent contributions of information, their ability to elicit more information from bureaucrats also tends to increase pari passu.[153] Finally, it is unrealistic to presume that members are helpless in the face of administrative guidance. They are free to voice their opinions and draw their own conclusions even when their deliberations are based primarily on data presented by officials.[154]

Deliberations

Commissions vary tremendously in the frequency of their meetings, ranging from almost daily deliberations to total inactivity. *Asahi* was already complaining in 1952 that "an overabundance of purely nominal 'sleeping *shingikai*' stands out," and by the 1990s, there were bodies like the Central Council on Mediating Raw Milk Transactions that had been "sleeping" for 30 or 40 years.[155]

[150] Park (1972), pp. 449–50.   [151] Ōi (1965), p. 60.   [152] Harari (1988), pp. 154–55.
[153] Harari (1986), pp. 34–35; Harari (1982), p. 241; Harari (1988), p. 155.
[154] Hayashi (1966), pp. 15–16.
[155] *Asahi Shinbun* (1952); *Nihon Keizai Shinbun* (13 July 1995); Sōmuchō (1995), pp. 309, 440.

Needless to say, the casual appointment and then shelving of commissions has invited censure, and official proposals for reform have suggested attaching limits to commissions' lives.[156] In 1985, totally inactive councils accounted for 4.2 percent of all advisory bodies, those meeting fewer than 5 times a year 29.4 percent, those meeting from 5 to 19 times 41.1 percent, and those meeting 20 or more times 25.2 percent; only 11 councils met more than 100 times.[157]

With few exceptions, councilors do not serve full-time – cabinet resolutions have made this a matter of principle, in fact[158] – so whatever the frequency of meetings, members' professional duties sometimes prevent their attending. In the past, the abuse of concurrent appointment exacerbated this problem, of course. It has been argued that absenteeism among councilors greatly enhances bureaucratic influence. "Many absentees delegate their responsibility to proxies who tend to be ill-informed of the nature of the council's work . . . further dilut[ing] the potential strength of councilmen and contribut[ing] to the influential position of secretaries who serve as the sole major linkage between meetings," Park alleged.[159] Bureaucrats themselves can serve as members' proxies. What critics overlook is the bind in which this puts parent agencies, for which the presence of councilors provides formal legitimacy and substantive input.[160]

In one of the most informative accounts of the workings of councils, Ogita Tamotsu described their deliberations in the following way. Notable for its detached description of bureaucrats' involvement in the process, it deserves to be quoted at length.

> A *shingikai* will first hear the government's explanation of the draft it submitted for deliberation. There follow questions and answers, an airing of views with respect to a concrete plan if one is presented, or a discussion of how to take up the points at issue when there is an abstract proposal or none at all. Here, too, it is normal for the government to present a plan. In continuation of this, or parallel to it, the government will describe the existing state of affairs, and for this reason, a great deal of data is submitted. Members pose questions with regard to this, then start to decide for themselves what issues must be raised. As methods of inquiry, first-hand investigation may be conducted, or relevant groups, concerned interests, or specialists may be consulted. A *shingikai* with specialist members may delegate the investigation of a specific matter during this time, or divide and deliberate on the matter by means of sectional meetings or subcommittees. In either event, an examination of the facts, the airing of arguments and counterarguments, and discussion of certain points at issue is common

---

[156] Satō I. (1972), p. 7; Park (1972), p. 464; Narita (1967), p. 52; Satō H. (1978), p. 147.
[157] Sone et al. (1985), pp. 16–19.   [158] Narita (1967), p. 52; Satō H. (1978), p. 148.
[159] Park (1972), p. 450; Kaneko (1985), p. 142.
[160] Sakuma et al. (1972), p. 50.

in the process of deliberation. More than members' own opinions, it is often the case that comments of the Diet, the government, interested groups, or newspapers, or the views of knowledgeable people become the subjects of discussion at this stage. Members rather frequently question relevant government officials at this time, too. In our country, it may resemble the Diet on this point, with more give and take between the members and the government than among the members. Be that as it may, with a lot of such give and take between members and government, it turns out that the *shingikai* view will strongly reflect government inclinations. In *shingikai* that include concerned parties in an explicit way, on the other hand, there will ordinarily be heated arguments among those groups.[161]

According to a government survey conducted between the end of 1995 and the beginning of 1996, 95 percent or more of parent agencies publicly announced the creation or abolition of *shingikai*, the appointment or dismissal of members, and the submission of inquiries and reports. But if there are a few cases of laws or ordinances obliging advisory bodies to open their deliberations to the public and it is now common for parent agencies to release summaries of proceedings and even post them on databases or computer networks, councils normally meet behind closed doors: 51.3 percent opened neither their meetings nor their minutes to the public compared to 23.4 percent that closed their meetings but opened their minutes and only 24.7 percent that opened both.[162] That would seem to run counter to commissions' ostensible mission of democratizing government operations: "Established with the expectation of *opening* administration to the people and listening extensively to their views, it is ironic that *shingikai* have become a 'hotbed' of administrative secrecy," complained one observer.[163] It has even been suggested that some councilors personally profit from closed hearings by speculating on the basis of their inside information.[164]

The inclusion of journalists as councilors is especially problematic in this regard: Although the duty of reporters is to report, they run the risk of being coopted when they serve on bodies whose operations are confidential. In 1992, representatives of the mass media held seats in about 100 out of a total of 212 *shingikai*. The public television network NHK led the list, followed by the large national newspapers *Nihon Keizai*, *Asahi*, and *Yomiuri*. As councilors, reporters can obtain information from, and gauge the intentions of, government authorities, but they cannot report that information in any detail, and they are constrained in criticizing their bureaucratic sources. Ironically, journalists' participation may thus result in a *diminution* of disclosure. Media companies are thus ambivalent about letting their staff participate in councils – *Asahi* counsels

---

[161] Ogita (1969), p. 29.
[162] Sōmuchō (1996); *Nihon Keizai Shinbun* (8 August 1996).
[163] Satō H. (1978), p. 149.   [164] Ebashi (1985), p. 15.

its reporters to exercise restraint, for example – and one critic went so far as to demand that journalists withdraw from all *shingikai* because "it's self-evident that there's an intimate tie, a knitting together [*yuchaku*], with the bureaucrats who provide information and even briefings. . . . Individuals from the mass media camouflage the government's ulterior motives; they're accomplices, that is to say."[165]

Among the justifications cited for closed sessions are that corporations would stop providing confidential information without them or that council reports adequately document the contents of deliberations. There are more compelling reasons for excluding the public, however. First, an audience, especially one packed by interested parties, would constrain members' freedom of speech and prevent an honest exchange of views. When conflict is open, it is frequently the case in Japan that opponents become publicly committed to their positions and a loss of face on someone's part becomes inevitable.[166] Second, one of the unacknowledged raisons d'être of some consultative bodies is to offer a privileged point of access and communication, the effect of which is not just to facilitate the movement of ideas and representation of interests, but to integrate a small circle of government and private actors. Publicizing the process might invite the involvement of parties with conflicting interests.[167]

Critics charge that civil servants are inculcated with a culture of secrecy – "As much as possible, you simply don't give out information to the public; that's the first principle," confided one bureaucratic gadfly – and there is no question that the habit of secrecy is ingrained: Even the minutes of an advisory body that discussed how to enhance the transparency of government were not released. Commentators have proposed that the government at least publish commission minutes, and courts have set new precedents in this regard. In 1984, for instance, a local court ruled that the subsequent release of a council's records was, in fact, compatible with closing the council itself to the public.[168] Although the Hosokawa government fell before it could fulfill its promise to enact an American-style freedom of information law on the national level, grassroots groups began to push for such laws on the local level in the early 1980s, and dozens of local and prefectural governments now have them.

The battle is by no means over. When HIV-positive hemophiliacs sued the government over the distribution of tainted blood products, they demanded as evidence records of discussions held by the Health and Welfare Ministry's AIDS Study Group. As a result, bureaucrats at the ministry have reportedly taken to discarding internal documents to save themselves future trouble.[169]

---

[165] Fukunaga (1995), p. 20; Amano (1994), pp. 296, 302, 300, 298.
[166] Richardson and Flanagan (1984), p. 201.
[167] Boyd (1987), pp. 64–65.
[168] Kaneko (1985), p. 157; Ogita (1972), p. 33; Kotaka (1986), p. 51.
[169] Itagaki (1996), p. 28.

Disputes concerning the public's right to know regarding *shingikai* deliberations are sure to continue in the future.

Reports and their authority

Rather than trying to judge the quality of *shingikai* recommendations, this study examines only the process by which they are decided and the weight that they carry. Councils have been attacked on both counts, sometimes from different directions. In the span of one month in 1992, a telecommunications expert charged that "too many decisions are hashed out behind closed doors by special advisory panels in the Postal Ministry," and the very same ministry publicly declared that it adamantly opposed the report of one of those panels and had no plans to follow it.[170]

How a report is drafted is of critical importance; a Japanese saying has it that "the original draft is 70 percent of the battle" (*gen'an wa shichi-bu no tsuyomi*). There are a few commissions that permit specialized subcommittees to make decisions for the body as a whole (e.g., MITI's Industrial Structure Council). Otherwise, a *shingikai* may entrust the drafting of a report to a committee drawn from among its members (especially neutral or expert members), to its chair or some other select member, or to its (bureaucratic) secretary. When handed the job, the drafting committee or chair will themselves commonly work in cooperation with the secretariat or delegate the job entirely, only reviewing the draft produced.

Because government staff can participate in the drafting process in this way, there is no denying the possibility of their attempting to incorporate parent-agency positions into reports, but even if officials do generally draft reports – councilors have other duties to attend to, and writing reports is a burdensome, thankless task – the contents of those reports need not be identical to parent-agency designs. Reports reflect the opinions expressed by members over the course of deliberations, and where major disagreements exist, reports will reflect that, summarizing the contending positions (usually without naming names). Although councilors may be reluctant to go to the trouble of rewriting a secretariat's draft report, it cannot diverge sharply from the conclusions reached during a *shingikai*'s deliberations because every report must be approved by that *shingikai*.

Formally, most commissions make decisions by majority vote. Although this procedure is sometimes dictated by law, councils normally strive to achieve approval by consensus, and actual vote-taking usually signifies that attempts at mediation have failed. In one survey, 74 percent of the respondents replied that the most common way of adopting reports was by "consensus"; only 16

---

[170] *Business Week* (9 November 1992); *Japan Report* (October 1992).

percent replied "majority vote" and 5 percent "statement of [contending] positions." It is interesting to note that fully 78 percent of the labor members surveyed cited consensus, a higher percentage than for any other subset of councilors, suggesting that they felt that their views, too, win consideration. Seventy-seven percent of the respondents indicated a preference for consensual decisionmaking.[171]

Observers have advanced various explanations for this preference. Anthropologically, Japanese culture accords greater legitimacy to nonconfrontational modes of decisionmaking that forestall any participant's loss of face and to a principle of "fair share" that achieves balance rather than to one of "fair play" that produces winner-take-all outcomes. Legalistically, majoritarianism is out of place in advisory bodies because their members are not democratically elected and their respective numbers may not be representative. More practically, councils seek unanimity in order to bolster the impact of their recommendations.[172] Bureaucrats, in turn, dislike dissension because it suggests that government proposals are problematic and reflects badly on the officials in a *shingikai*'s secretariat. Conversely, though, a unified agreement can be misleading because

> the presentation of a report adopted by consensus does not necessarily signify the non-existence of conflict, [and] neither does it necessarily signify that conflict has been resolved. It can mean that conflict has been managed, in that the participants have to a certain extent changed their perceptions of the incompatibility of their goals or part of their goals, and/ or realized the futility of escalating their conflict behaviour and the possible benefits of de-escalating it.[173]

In any case, by the time a report is brought before a commission's plenary session, attempts will already have been made at the drafting stage to mediate conflicting viewpoints or to soften opposition by including ambiguous language. The chair will ask if there are any objections, and unless some especially contentious issue remains, councilors will adopt a draft unanimously. "Even if there are people dissatisfied with particular points, when that's not a serious problem, when they're not speaking out energetically, the original plan is carried."[174] Occasionally, the system breaks down. The Rice Price Council, which must navigate between the Scylla and Charybdis of producer and consumer (and governmental) interests, failed to produce its annual report five times between 1968 and 1982, for example. That is the exception and not the rule, however.

---

[171] Harari (1986), p. 36, and Harari (1982), p. 244.
[172] Harari (1974), p. 550; Ogita (1972), p. 33; Park (1972), p. 447.
[173] Harari (1989), p. 154.
[174] Ogita (1969), p. 31.

Because *shingikai* reports are considered internal administrative affairs that do not directly affect the rights or duties of private citizens, they are beyond legal challenge from outside the government.[175] Within the government, although parent agencies are generally held to have an obligation, and frequently a legal duty, to respect (*sonchō suru*) these reports, "respect" is not unambiguous. It could mean that the government is bound to carry out commission recommendations willy-nilly:

> Among the public, there is a tendency to look on officially announced *shingikai* reports as government policy in themselves. And it's not just the public: it seems common for *shingikai* themselves to think that government policy can be decided exactly in accordance with their reports. Even government authorities every so often vigorously warm up before a report comes out and execute it with reckless valor, without altering it one iota. Observing these phenomena, it would seem that *shingikai* determine important government policies and that government authorities do no more than carry out their decisions.[176]

Criticism of the government for not following *shingikai* recommendations implicitly rests on such assumptions. But to attribute decisionmaking authority to commissions is both constitutionally untenable and politically naive.

The government's Administrative Reform Committee publicly declared that "it is important that outsiders not overestimate the role of *shingikai*."[177] A handful of exceptions aside, advisory bodies exist to provide authorities with advice, so from a purely legal standpoint, *shingikai*'s rights and responsibilities are close to zero.[178] Nothing guarantees that they will accurately represent the will of the people, and final decisionmaking power could not be granted to commissions without their usurping legislative and administrative prerogatives. "It's no exaggeration to say that the government holds 'the power of life and death' over the conclusions of consultative bodies. Whether a report is adopted in toto, partially reflected in policy, or shelved is entirely up to the government."[179]

Officials have a vested interest in obscuring this freedom of theirs: If the public realized that a parent agency was not bound by the advice it solicits, bureaucrats would no longer be able to saddle responsibility for their actions on an advisory body. The same bureaucrats might not hesitate to ignore the recommendations of a commission should they prove inconvenient, however. When the high-profile Council on Structural Reform of the Economy, which was presided over by the chair of Keidanren, actually showed some zeal for deregulation, an official bluntly remarked, "In the end it's only a study group report."[180] Councilors do not appreciate being ignored, needless to say – "Because

---

[175] Upham (1987), p. 171.   [176] Okabe (1969), p. 14.
[177] *Nihon Keizai Shinbun* (8 August 1996).   [178] Okabe (1969), p. 15.
[179] Ōi (1965), p. 56.   [180] Kudo and Kakinuma (1994), p. 21.

decisions are made by the government and ruling parties, even if we debate, it's meaningless," complained a managing director of Keidanren when he withdrew from the Rice Price Council in the middle of deliberations in 1995[181] – but if it is understandable, such frustration reveals a misconception of the limitations of their role. *Shingikai* have no right to make decisions or responsibility to carry them out, and members must understand and consent to that from the start.[182]

It is only natural, after all, to feel that a parent agency that commissions a report should respect it as much as possible, but to require complete compliance with that report could ironically lead to an equally complete loss of freedom for the formally authoritative commission. To force government officials to act on the conclusions of a *shingikai* would give those officials a compelling interest to intervene in the affairs of that *shingikai* in order to ensure outcomes convenient to themselves. And were councilors certain that their recommendations would be implemented, they might become more hesitant in offering creative advice.[183] Recognition of the binding authority of council reports would also aggravate bureaucratic sectionalism and produce chaos in those not uncommon instances when even the best-intentioned councils arrive at contradictory conclusions. Administrative agencies must consider a variety of factors comprehensively, and *shingikai* reports constitute only one of those factors.

Without exaggerating the importance of advisory bodies, many commentators (including the First Rinchō) have suggested that ministries at least spell out precisely why they cannot, or will not, implement specific proposals. Taking this argument to its logical conclusion, one observer reasoned that agencies should officially announce the points of contention and leave the judgment of who is right to public opinion.[184] This procedure would redeem councils as vehicles for the democratization of administration, directly involving the people in bureaucratic policymaking. It would also be hopelessly impractical. Because agencies are loath to admit that they sometimes fail to follow commission recommendations for political reasons, officials could be expected to obscure the points at issue in such cases.[185] Besides, it is inconceivable that citizens would constantly troop to the polls to vote on what would often be abstruse matters of little direct interest to them.

Having submitted a report, a council's work is done, and with the ministries firmly in control of implementation, many reports dealing with controversial questions come to naught. It is not unknown for a bureaucracy to reach a decision without even waiting for a report it has commissioned.[186] Although that is clearly improper, implementation of a given report does not necessarily imply

---

[181] *Nihon Keizai Shinbun* (13 July 1995).   [182] Ogita (1969), p. 47.
[183] E.g., Sugita (1967), p. 90.
[184] Satō C. (1978), p. 3; Katō (1971), p. 56; Sugita (1967), p. 90.
[185] Park (1972), p. 454.   [186] Satō I. (1972), p. 3; Sone et al. (1985), p. 77.

that a parent agency has deferred to a *shingikai*: In making that report, the *shingikai* may itself have deferred to the parent agency, recommending policies that the parent agency had intended to execute from the start. "There- fore, paradoxical as it may sound to those criticizing governments for disregard- ing PAB [i.e., public advisory body] recommendations, such disregard may be the clearest indication that the government indeed appointed the PAB for the stated official purpose of obtaining guidance on the basis of knowledge and experience not available within the administration,"[187] and not to cover its tracks.

That seems to leave *shingikai* poised on the horns of a dilemma: "The minus of a *shingikai's* being used politically is at the same time a plus in being able to find political 'significance'; the flip side of being able to preserve the 'independ- ence' of a *shingikai* is for it to have no political 'significance.'"[188] But independ- ent councils can make a mark, too. Bureaucrats will lend an ear to outside advice when they are unconcerned, undecided, divided over, or eager to avoid an issue. A *shingikai* virtually replaced an agency in making the most difficult and sensi- tive decisions on determining the demand for taxi service and bus routes, with bureaucrats following its recommendation 99 percent of the time.[189] Govern- ment policy is also likely to reflect the advice of commissions that consider highly technical matters, where the expert knowledge of outsiders is indispens- able. A report that successfully adjusts the interests of conflicting groups will have great influence inasmuch as it relieves officials of having to get involved in the confrontation.[190]

Finally, "although a *shingikai* itself is without any administrative rights, when its report is in accord with widely-felt public demands, public opinion strongly pressures government authorities for its adoption and implementation."[191] When the LDP tried to emasculate reforms proposed by the Council on the Election System in 1962, its councilors lobbied officials and party leaders and turned to the public and the press for support, thus preventing opponents of electoral reform from weakening its recommendations further.[192] Over time, *shingikai* members can become more adroit at influencing the public through media coverage of their deliberations, so although it is true that they cannot dictate the direction government should take, they can sometimes hinder poli- cies they strongly oppose.

This discussion has concentrated on commissions' relations with their parent agencies, but how has the emergence of specialized policy *zoku* affected the authority of *shingikai*? Perhaps the most commented-upon case involves the shifting balance of power between the Council on the Tax System (Zeisei Chōsakai, or Zeichō) of MOF and an identically named body within the Policy

[187] Harari (1974), p. 557.   [188] Imagawa (1991), p. 59.   [189] Upham (1994).
[190] Ōi (1965), p. 56; Park (1972), pp. 452, 459; Ishi (1994), p. 6.
[191] Okabe (1969), p. 16.   [192] Park (1972), pp. 460–61.

Affairs Research Council of the LDP. MOF's Zeichō wielded great influence until the early 1970s, but that situation changed with the reduced growth in government revenues and the concomitant emergence of powerful politicians in the party's Zeichō. Although scholars and journalists commonly cite the rise of the latter as an example of the shift in policymaking power from bureaucracies to the LDP, the truth is more complex.

First, the Zeichō was a special case. Given their preoccupation with distributive issues, Japanese politicians have an unusually strong interest in taxes. Second, a division of labor developed between the two bodies. Politicians used their clout to set specific tax rates and confer special breaks on particular industries, but it was MOF's Zeichō that determined the general framework of taxation and comprehensively adjusted conflicting interests. Third, it might actually have worked to the ministry's advantage to have two bodies. While MOF attempted to define policy problems, propose specific solutions, and legitimate its proposals by means of its own Zeichō, it attempted to get its proposals on the political agenda and win the cooperation of politicians by means of the LDP's Zeichō. In fact, the two bodies issued their reports in coordination with one another and often shared MOF's view of the tax system, thus providing the ministry crucial support.[193]

To what extent do bureaucracies manipulate *shingikai*? A first answer would be, less than they used to. Speaking of the various abuses that then characterized commissions, Park wrote in 1972 that "the current practices . . . are so firmly entrenched in the bureaucratic machinery that they will continue to defy meaningful reform attempts."[194] He was too pessimistic. Ministries have, in fact, abolished some of the worst abuses, like overly numerous concurrent appointments, and mitigated others, like the nomination of MPs and incumbent officials as councilors. Reform was due both to outside pressures for reform and to the wrenching structural changes that Japan has undergone since that time (e.g., the shift to slower growth and deficit financing that came in the wake of the oil shocks). Those changes have made agencies more dependent than ever on the introduction of specialist knowledge and the coordination of private interests. Kept bodies and fairy cloaks may still be common, but not as common they were in the past.

Criticisms of the *shingikai* system have never been entirely satisfactory because they have typically drawn on anecdotal or circumstantial evidence (e.g., because a councilor is a bureaucratic OB, he or she necessarily represents bureaucratic interests). The more systematic research of recent years has prompted a reevaluation of commissions. Only now do we have data concerning

---

[193] Takenaka and Ishi (1994); Katō (1994), pp. 93–99.
[194] Park (1972), p. 465.

the perceptions of *shingikai* members themselves, for example. Councilors do not appreciate the fact that parent agencies hold the power of life and death over their recommendations, hence their grumbling. Even so, members generally consider themselves to be making a meaningful contribution to policymaking.

In one survey of consultative (*shimon*) councils, 18 percent of the non-bureaucratic respondents felt "very strongly" that their council was making a serious effort to improve public policymaking, 44 percent felt strongly that it was, and another 26 percent felt so to some extent. Asked to judge their commissions' impact on government policies, half of the respondents thought that they had a very strong (12 percent) or fairly strong influence (38 percent), and only one-quarter believed that they had little (12 percent) or no influence at all (12 percent). Just as bureaucrats sometimes exaggerate the authority of the commissions to which they pretend to defer, councilors sometimes complain of bureaucratic control to account for gaps between their public positions and *shingikai* decisions, including decisions they themselves were persuaded to support over the course of deliberations.[195]

The relationships between Japanese advisory bodies and their parent agencies have varied over time and across policy domains. Although sweeping generalizations are out of place, they are often relationships of communication and accommodation, not domination:

> *Shingikai* outputs result from largely continuous interactions among bureaucrats, officials of various interest organizations, academics, and members of the mass media (and in a small number of cases, Diet members), over the course of which they increase their knowledge of the problems at hand, the constraints under which each of them operates, and the degree to which each is free to define the interests of his or her constituency or to challenge the principles of the professional school he or she is identified with.[196]

Such communication between government and private actors is just as important to effective policymaking as any particular policy tool.

Because bureaucrats frequently play a leading role in policymaking in Japan, it should come as no surprise that they frequently play a leading role in the politics of consultation. The point at issue, though, is not whether *shingikai* operate with pristine independence – they do not – but what light they throw on the coordination of public and private interests in the discrete subsystems responsible for most Japanese policymaking. Only comparative empirical research can answer that question.

Before proceeding to case studies of concrete governmental decisions, a di-

---

[195] Harari (1982), p. 242; (1986), p. 40.
[196] Harari (1986), p. 40.

gression is in order. In the 1980s, two distinctive kinds of commissions participated in the formulation of such important policies that commentators started
speaking of "*shingikai*" or "brain-trust [*burein*] politics." Prime Minister
Nakasone in particular resorted to these advisory bodies to the point where
critics accused him of trying to turn them into a "legislative branch without
suffrage."[197] That is a far cry from "fairy cloaks." What accounted for this
dramatic rise in prominence of consultative councils?

[197] Sugihara (1986), p. 78.

3

Shingikai *in the spotlight*

Before the 1980s, Japanese research on the *shingikai* system peaked twice: around 1964, with the First Rinchō's report, and around 1972, after opposition electoral gains. With private enterprise rationalizing its management during the first period, public administration was perceived to be falling behind, and most commentators stressed councils' potential for introducing expert knowledge into laggard bureaucracies. By the late 1960s, on the other hand, increasing doubts about the desirability of high-speed growth spurred citizens' movements that sought to enhance ordinary people's influence over policymaking. Opposition parties made gains on the local level by offering to institutionalize greater citizen participation, and administrative authorities were compelled to increase their efforts to secure the cooperation of "consumers" of their policies. Although the progressive camp had always emphasized commissions' responsibility to democratize administration, other analysts, too, began giving greater weight to this possibility.[1]

The 1980s witnessed a third surge of interest in advisory bodies. This time, however, the focus shifted from *shingikai* qua auxiliary organs of administration to *shingikai* qua high-level political actors. In the words of one contemporary, "Now the play will change acts. . . . *Shingikai* will leap from the wings to center stage. . . . They have already overstepped the bounds of administration, that is to say, and will commence their march on the level of politics regarding fundamental state policies."[2] Prime Minister Nakasone Yasuhiro (November 1982–October 1987) was largely responsible for this shift. What was noteworthy about the Nakasone Administration was less the number than the kinds of councils he created and the uses to which he put them. Nakasone established several Rinchō-type *shingikai* on the model of the Ad Hoc Commission on Administrative Reform and a variety of "private" advisory bodies that, although outwardly indistinguishable from *shingikai*, were not formally grounded in the National Administrative Organization Act. Both the Rinchō and the private councils were used in ultimately unsuccessful attempts to implement major policy initiatives, the first attacking the subgovernments that had become entrenched during the

---

[1] Kawaguchi H. (1978).   [2] Teshima (1986), p. 38.

years of rapid economic growth and the second promoting a highly conservative ideological agenda on a variety of sensitive issues.[3]

Rinchō politics

Like the early 1960s, the early 1980s had their own Rinchō-type *shingikai*, beginning with the Second Ad Hoc Commission on Administrative Reform (or Second Rinchō), then, based on its model, the Ad Hoc Commission for the Promotion of Administrative Reform, the Committee to Supervise the Rehabilitation of Japan National Railways, and the Ad Hoc Commission on Education. Although grounded in the National Administrative Organization Act, these Rinchō-type *shingikai* represented a major innovation.

Rinchō politics cannot be understood apart from the fiscal crisis that gripped Japan in the wake of the first oil shock. With government revenues booming along with the economy during the 1960s, the LDP was able to play a positive-sum political game, distributing largess without having to make hard choices. Because rapid growth came to be expected as a matter of course and budget discipline grew lax, MOF became increasingly concerned about "fiscal rigidification" (*zaisei kōchok-ka*). As the director of the Budget Bureau explained in 1967:

> The various items which make up the budget gradually come to lose the quality of expansion and contraction, and flexibility declines. Further, the inherent pressures for an item to expand are strong, and we can now see that we are getting into a situation where this cannot be controlled. . . . Then another thing: . . . I think we are now gradually coming to the point where it becomes clear that we cannot return to the high growth of the [late 1950s and early 1960s], and that it is extremely dangerous to expect that possibility. . . . We will have to face the problem of bringing these two trends together.[4]

In 1968, MOF launched a concerted offensive to shake off the inertia that had set in during the period of high-speed growth and regain control over budgetmaking. It failed.

In Japan, as in the United States, fiscal rigidity is largely a product of deep-rooted relationships among interest groups, politicians, and bureaucrats who coalesce in particular policy domains like agriculture and public works to maintain government-derived benefits at the expense of unorganized taxpayers. MOF could expect little help from the governing party, which had difficulty governing itself, let alone riding herd on the ministries in a comprehensive way. The LDP has traditionally courted electoral support by channeling public expenditures to its constituencies, and the expertise and contacts of its increas-

---

[3] Sone (1986b).   [4] Campbell (1977), pp. 241–42.

ingly professionalized and specialized MPs made them nearly unassailable in their respective fiefs. While in some sense strengthening the party's clout, the rise of *zoku* also stimulated the LDP's distributive tendencies to new heights and weakened the party's ability to formulate integrated programs. The party's Policy Affairs Research Council might have served as a vehicle for the coordination of various policies, but its divisions are compartmentalized, each considering its own narrow issue area without much concern for competing interests. Conflicts got bumped up to higher and higher levels of the party until they were resolved in an informal, ad hoc way.

Because the economy defied MOF's expectations and continued to expand, it took the first oil shock in 1973 to bring home the costs of politics as usual. Whereas Japan's GNP grew at an average annual rate of 10.7 percent in the 1960s, it shrank in 1974 and maintained growth of only 3 to 5 percent thereafter. Government revenues slowed just as pump priming seemed in order, America demanded that Japan act as a "locomotive" of the world economy, and spending on welfare took off: Social security expenditures increased ninefold from 1970 to 1982, rocketing from less than 2 percent of national income to more than 16 percent.[5] With the LDP pressuring MOF to abandon its commitment to a balanced budget, the national debt spiraled out of control. In fiscal year 1974, 11.3 percent of general account expenditures were covered by bond issues; by fiscal year 1980, that figure had almost tripled to 33.5 percent for a total of $63 billion, far surpassing the *combined* total of $47 billion for the United States, West Germany, France, Britain, and Italy.[6]

MOF redoubled its efforts to impose new taxes and rein in spending, but the LDP, which was close to losing its Diet majority, failed to provide consistent support. On the one hand, the public in general and big business in particular strenuously opposed raising taxes, and the party suffered in the general election of 1979 after it proposed a consumption tax and strengthened tax enforcement. On the other hand, the beneficiaries of government spending naturally resisted any attempt to curb expenditures. Although the "three k's" – subsidies for rice (*kome*), Japan National Railways (*kokutetsu*), and national health insurance (*kokumin hoken*) – contributed mightily to the government's fiscal hemorrhaging, for example, cuts in the first two threatened to bring corresponding cuts in the rural votes that helped keep the LDP in power, and opposition parties would not countenance reduced welfare spending.

After the LDP finally regained a secure parliamentary majority in June 1980, Prime Minister Suzuki Zenkō elevated administrative reform (*gyōsei kaikaku*, or *gyōkaku*) to his primary goal, vowing to end the sale of deficit bonds (as opposed to investment-oriented "construction" bonds) by 1984. Although spending cuts could be made more palatable if included within a comprehensive attack on "big

---

[5] Okimoto (1989), pp. 190–91.   [6] Noguchi (1982), p. 130; Elliott (1983), p. 765.

government," the public did not trust the government to reform itself, and indeed, "it was difficult for the Diet and administrative organs, which rested atop the vested interests, to promote an administrative reform that would raze their own foundations,"[7] so the mission was entrusted to an independent *shingikai*. With the support of all but the JCP, the Diet in November passed a bill establishing the Second Rinchō, and it was inaugurated in March 1981.

Reviving many of the proposals of MOF's "Break Fiscal Rigidity" campaign, the Second Rinchō addressed a wide array of issues. Among other things, it recommended that the government impose a zero ceiling in fiscal year 1983 and then a minus ceiling through fiscal year 1987 on almost all expenditures except defense and foreign aid and end its dependence on deficit financing by 1984; lower national contributions to the health insurance system, slash subsidies by 10 percent, and put several costly public works projects on hold; freeze public servants' salaries, unify their pension plans, and trim the civil service by 5 percent over five years; streamline the central ministries, their auxiliary organs, and local branch offices; revamp certification and authorization procedures, denationalize public corporations – and not raise taxes. From the outset, the commission's watchwords were "fiscal rehabilitation without new taxation" (*zōzei naki zaisei saiken*). Nakasone vowed to continue the reform process when he replaced Suzuki in October 1982. In order to sustain forward momentum after it disbanded in March 1983, the Second Rinchō recommended the creation of a new body to oversee the implementation of reform, and Nakasone created the Ad Hoc Commission for the Promotion of Administrative Reform (Gyōkakushin) in July 1983 to work directly under him.

Results were apparent even before the commission broke up. The Second Rinchō had proposed that government expenditures be held constant in 1982. They were restrained. Whereas general account expenditures had expanded at an annual rate of about 14 percent until fiscal year 1979, they increased only 1.8 percent in fiscal year 1982, the lowest growth rate since 1955, and the 1983 budget provided for no net increase in spending whatsoever.[8] Commissioners condemned the administrative apparatus as "obese." It went under the knife. In 1982 alone, legislation abolished or revised 355 laws concerning licenses and permits, and the government froze the salaries of civil servants, rejecting the pay hike recommended by the National Personnel Authority for the first time in 33 years. The AMA and PMO were later combined into a Management and Coordination Agency (MCA), reducing the number of central government agencies for the first time in the postwar era.[9]

---

[7] Sone (1986b), p. 149.
[8] Sejima (1983), p. 29; Elliott (1983), pp. 768–69; Curtis (1988), pp. 72–73.
[9] Elliott (1983), p. 777; *Japan Echo* (3 November 1983), p. 26.

The fate of Japan National Railways (JNR) was perhaps the most controversial and far-reaching issue with which the commission grappled. Radical reform was essential – JNR was losing more than $20 million a day, and its cumulative debt exceeded $80 billion in 1983[10] – but politicians opposed the elimination of unprofitable local lines and unions the elimination of jobs. If at first it temporized, the commission finally took the bull by the horns and called for JNR's denationalization. Nakasone established a Committee to Supervise the Rehabilitation of Japan National Railways in June 1983, and did eventually succeed in overcoming stiff resistance to denationalize and break up JNR (and its Sōhyō-affiliated unions). Rinchō recommendations also paved the way for the denationalization of Nippon Telephone and Telegraph (NTT) and the Japan Monopoly Corporation (which sold tobacco and salt).

These were impressive achievements. What accounts for them? The commission had a solid base of support in the business community. Big companies resented the increases in corporate taxes that accompanied increases in government spending and were bitter about what they took to be fiscal irresponsibility on the part of the government at the same time that they were struggling to cut costs in response to the two oil crises.[11] The public, too, naturally preferred the rationalization of administration and the curtailing of public-sector "waste" to the imposition of new taxes. Rinchō Chairman Dokō Toshio, former president of Keidanren and Tōshiba, was practically a national hero: Although one of the most prominent industrialists in the country, he was famous for his austere lifestyle. Besides Dokō, the commission included two businesspeople, two union officials (from Sōhyō and Dōmei), two retired bureaucrats (from MOF and the Ministry of Home Affairs), one journalist, and one academic, all clearly chosen for the balance of groups they would represent and for their extremely high status. The Diet itself approved their nominations.

The Second Rinchō was lent authority by the crisis atmosphere of the time, an atmosphere that the commission consciously fostered. One commissioner later admitted, "We poured out great quantities of material in order that articles on administrative reform would appear in the mass media day after day." For the same reason, the Second Rinchō deliberately produced not one report at the end of its deliberations, but a series of five.[12] Such skillful public relations allowed it to maintain an exceptionally high profile and mobilize public opinion. An "administration reform fever" was produced, a popular consensus that something had to be done to reduce the budget deficit, and because it attracted so much news coverage, people got the impression that the Rinchō could take matters into its own hands, which misconception lent it that much more influence.

[10] *Japan Echo* (1983), p. 26.
[11] S. Vogel (1996).
[12] *Asahi Shinbun* (5 October 1984); Naka (1986).

The commission conducted intensive *nemawashi* with important politicians and bureaucrats and tried to overcome the resistance of interest groups that stood to lose by reform. As a result, opponents never got beyond challenging particular recommendations to mount direct attacks on the Second Rinchō itself. With the conservative coalition – and their tacit allies among private-sector, Dōmei unions – targeting public-sector unions that had been pillars of Sōhyō, administrative reform became entangled with the struggle for leadership in the labor movement.[13] Although they were especially hard hit, and although some labor chiefs and their political allies did assume an antagonistic stance toward the commission, even public-sector unions were granted a measure of indirect influence. Rinchō proposals concerning NTT followed the lines of an agreement informally worked out between the LDP and NTT's union, for example.[14]

Like the Commission on the Constitution but alone among recent *shingikai*, the Second Rinchō reported to the Diet through the prime minister, who was legally obliged to "respect" its findings. Prime Minister Suzuki and Nakasone, his director general of the AMA, were unusually closely involved in the work of the commission. When the Second Rinchō was getting under way, Suzuki publicly staked his career on the success of administrative reform, and he renewed his pledge a year later. Nakasone, on the other hand, saw in administrative reform the key to his succeeding Suzuki as prime minister. Because the whole raison d'être of the AMA was to seek improvements in public administration, the issue highlighted his relatively minor cabinet position. More fundamentally, Nakasone realized that by promoting administrative reform, he could appeal to the business community, whose support he had never enjoyed, and to the urban middle class, which had borne the burden of the LDP's pork-barrel support for farmers and small-business proprietors.

With the cabinet pledging to implement its recommendations unchanged, the commission approached administrative committees like the Fair Trade Commission in its independent decisionmaking authority. Once he became prime minister, Nakasone declared, "The people must all submit to reports presented by the Rinchō just as if they were Supreme Court rulings," and he described its agenda of paring down government as "the greatest housecleaning in the postwar period."[15] The commission was called "the Miyakezaka Mafia" (after the location of its offices), "another government," and "the Privy Council." To its detractors, the Second Rinchō threatened to eclipse the Diet. In the end, however, Nakasone's boast and critics' fears proved equally groundless. The commission passed from the scene, and few of its successes were unqualified.

---

[13] Knoke et al. (1996), pp. 133–34.
[14] Sone et al. (1985), p. 71; Mochizuki (1993).
[15] Japan Communist Party (1986), p. 25; Muramatsu (1983), p. 31.

Large revenue shortfalls in fiscal years 1981 and 1982 prevented the government from achieving its goal of ending the issuance of deficit-financing bonds and drove Suzuki to resign as prime minister; Nakasone announced a "reexamination" of the goal even as he took office in late 1982. The bond dependency ratio of the general account budget decreased very little at first – from 26.2 percent in the initial budget of fiscal year 1981 to 25.0 percent in fiscal year 1984 – and if the rate of growth of public expenditures slowed, the national debt continued to mount, almost doubling between fiscal years 1981 and 1987. The rate of growth of rice subsidies actually *increased* after 1981, and all subsidies still consumed around 30 percent of the budget in fiscal year 1983. In order to placate the opposition parties and get the first reform bill through the Diet, the government granted civil service unions a 5.23 percent wage hike, and personnel cutbacks never went beyond what agencies could achieve through attrition and voluntary departures. Besides reorganizing the AMA, which had a vested interest in reform, the Second Rinchō barely tampered with the administrative apparatus. At least 10,000 rules and regulations survived calls for deregulation, and no fewer than 10,000 businesses still had to obtain government authorizations.[16]

Keidanren strongly backed the administrative reform campaign – indeed, it was pressure from the business community that had called it into existence in the first place – and Rinchō recommendations echoed *zaikai* desires in challenging bureaucratic authority and undermining some of the mainstays of the labor movement. But big business was the commission's only real constituency among economic groups, and once its profits were protected from new taxes, it was less interested in balancing the budget than in expanding the private sector at the expense of the state. If denationalization relieved the government of JNR, a burdensome albatross, it also relieved it of the much needed revenues brought in by the profitable NTT and the Monopoly Corporation.

A cohesive elite consensus never developed in favor of administrative reform, and the commission's ambitions were frustrated by the same subgovernments whose exactions had helped precipitate the fiscal crisis in the first place. The Second Rinchō could not propose a reform without treading on the toes of some such coalition and, in the words of one commissioner, "We learned that the walls of the vested interests are thick indeed."[17] Everyone acknowledged that action was necessary – except in his or her own bailiwick. "Approve the principle, oppose the specifics" (*sōron sansei, kakuron hantai*), as Japanese say. Administrative reform aroused insurmountable opposition within the ministries and LDP as well as among private interests.

---

[16] Katō (1994), pp. 84–85, 138, 145; Namikawa (1987), pp. 121, 124; Sejima (1983), p. 28; Elliott (1983), p. 771. In 1996, there were still 10,760 instances in which a government permit was needed. *The New York Times* (17 November 1996).

[17] Muramatsu (1983), p. 34.

Like their First Rinchō predecessors, Second Rinchō commissioners sat atop a well-developed bureaucracy of their own, one staffed overwhelmingly by officials dispatched from the AMA and the agencies whose reform was under consideration. "Whatever the good intentions of the research assistants, as long as they are temporarily on loan from the ministries proper, they cannot help but listen to what the ministries say," observed one group of commentators of the First Rinchō in 1963. The same was presumably true two decades later, when 57 of the Second Rinchō's 70 full-time research assistants were seconded from central government bureaucracies.[18] The commission based its reports on the recommendations of four committees composed of specialist members and commissioners. Bureaucratic OBs constituted the most numerous group in each of these committees, occupying from almost one-third to fully one-half of the seats – a markedly higher proportion than is found in most *shingikai*. In addition, whereas two-thirds of these OBs held concurrent appointments, not even one-third of any other group's members was assigned to multiple posts.[19]

Retired officials did not always wield their influence en bloc, of course; on most issues, the positions of these OBs varied, just as did the positions of their respective agencies. Even so, it is interesting to note that it was the committee with the fewest retired officials that took the most activist stance and accomplished the most, pushing through the controversial proposals for denationalization of NTT and the Monopoly Corporation. Committee reports were drafted cooperatively by a secretariat composed of officials on loan from the ministries and committee chairs or their proxies. Although businesspeople generally chaired the committees, all of the chairs' proxies were officials, so bureaucratic views were well represented on that level, too.

Exactly what were those views? Jealous of their autonomy and their close links to clienteles, ministries had a conservative interest in the status quo, and they strained to evade the stringent spending guidelines. Rather than challenging Rinchō initiatives outright, officials sought to turn them to their advantage: The same ministries that jointly resisted proposals like the reduction of subsidies were also individually jockeying to expand their jurisdictions under the banner of administrative reform. "Where it is disadvantageous, shelve it, and where the policy is advantageous, try to borrow the authority of the Rinchō," one commissioner later aphorized.[20]

The Second Rinchō knew that it alone could not effect reform, and it was particularly desirous of MOF's support. Only the Budget Bureau had the expertise to monitor agency compliance and, having failed in its own attempts to rein in the ministries and desperate to reduce government expenditures, MOF

[18] Shingikai Kenkyūkai (1963), p. 57; Elliot (1983), p. 772.
[19] Sone et al. (1985), pp. 68, 70.
[20] *Asahi Shinbun* (9 October 1984).

might have seemed a natural ally of the commission. But if the ministry did take advantage of the Second Rinchō to impose austerity and reduce the issuance of deficit bonds, shoring up its authority vis-à-vis the other ministries and the LDP in the process, the two collided over the issue of a tax increase. MOF was uninterested in a structural reform of public finance and the prioritizing of government expenditures, and it wanted to avoid commission intervention in its decisions.[21]

Dissatisfaction with Rinchō politics ran deep within the ruling party itself. LDP politicians were especially irritated by a 5 percent ceiling on new public works spending.[22] One disgruntled member of the construction "tribe" in Nakasone's own faction complained, "For what the Rinchō says to be taken as the golden rule and for what the party says to go unheard is fascist." More generally, LDP leaders were taken aback by Nakasone's desire to short-circuit established channels. The chief of the LDP's Policy Affairs Research Council warned, "because important policies are being decided by means of Rinchō leadership, the foundations of party politics are quaking."[23] Although self-interested and hyperbolic, such reactions were not purely obstructionist. After all, it was the Diet, not the commission, whose members had won a mandate to govern in free elections and who conducted their deliberations publicly. What right had a mere *shingikai* to encroach on parliamentary prerogatives?

Although the Second Rinchō could not move alone on sensitive issues, political leaders had their own agenda. The commission was "a vehicle of prime ministerial politics,"[24] and both Suzuki and Nakasone often found advocacy of a vaguely defined movement to be more expedient than commitment to specific measures. Generally dismissed as a political nonentity who came to power only because Prime Minister Ōhira Masayoshi died in the middle of the 1980 campaign, Suzuki did not exercise decisive leadership. Nakasone, the only major faction leader who had yet to serve as premier, knew better than to run for the office by alienating his fellow Diet representatives while he was director general of the AMA, and his base of support within the party remained weak even after he finally came to power. As Japan came under increasing foreign pressure to expand domestic demand in order to ease trade frictions and rising popular approval for Nakasone stabilized his base within the LDP, his rallying cry gradually shifted from "fiscal rehabilitation without new taxation" to "private-sector vitality" (*minkan katsuryoku*, or *minkatsu*), the mobilization of private initiative and investment for public purposes.

To be fair, it is difficult to imagine *any* LDP leader desiring, let alone attempting, to change a status quo that had maintained conservative pre-

[21] Katō (1994), p. 142.   [22] Ibid., p. 149.
[23] *Asahi Shinbun* (9 October 1984).   [24] Muramatsu (1983), p. 31.

dominance. Because the LDP was a catchall party in a democracy where constituencies expected tangible returns for their votes, it was precisely those pork-barrel programs that offended disinterested analysts as wasteful that were rational and effective from a conservative MP's point of view. If the commission grumbled over private groups' demands for public monies, it did not take the dangerous course of directly attacking the politicians who catered to those demands.

The Second Rinchō never became a quixotic crusade. In the words of one commissioner, "Knowing that our report would be worthless if the government and Diet did not act on it, we decided to limit ourselves to recommendations whose implementation was feasible in Japan's present circumstances."[25] But in pursuit of feasibility, the Second Rinchō sought to reconcile powerful groups and sent its proposals through the regular channels.[26] That was not a formula for sweeping reform. Indeed, the Second Ad Hoc Commission on Administrative Reform actually slighted the reform of administration, or rather equated it with fiscal retrenchment. Because the commission stressed consensus and practicability, it pursued that retrenchment in a way that at best merely palliated, and at worst exacerbated, fundamental dysfunctions of the system.

To have made detailed, hard-nosed evaluations of specific programs and set priorities itself, the Second Rinchō would have had to invade the entrenched fiefdoms of every agency and disturb the established balance among them. Although the commission did make nods in that direction, the task was beyond its limited means. Its main recommendations therefore took the form of uniform guidelines that affected every agency equally, such as the proposals for ceilings on ministries' budget requests and a flat 5 percent cutback on administrative staff. That across-the-board strategy may have been simpler and more acceptable to the bureaucracies, and it did succeed in restraining budget growth in the short term, but "the inherent weakness of this approach even in the ideal case is that program coordination or establishing rational policy priorities across ministerial boundary lines becomes very difficult – policy making is fragmented even more than usual," thus strengthening the subgovernments that had helped swell public spending in the first place.[27]

This overall inability of the Second Rinchō to reform those structures, rules, and processes that originally underlay the bloating of budgets and bureaucracies was as significant as any tally of individual successes. The commission helped cut away the fat of a morbidly obese patient without permanently altering his eating habits; the same policymaking system that had produced costly programs in the past continued to generate pressures for more spending, that is to say.

---

[25] Sejima (1983), p. 29; Naka (1986), p. 76.   [26] Elliott (1983), p. 778.
[27] Campbell (1985), p. 512; Muramatsu (1983), p. 37.

Incremental measures failed to have a marked, immediate effect on the budget deficit, discrediting administrative reform as a means of fiscal rehabilitation, dissipating public enthusiasm for austerity, riling threatened clienteles, and inciting the LDP rank-and-file to rebel after three years to wrest expensive concessions from MOF in 1985. The Diet's passage of a new sales tax three years later buried the principle of "fiscal rehabilitation without new taxation" once and for all.

The Second Rinchō did not quash vested interests to solve the problem of fiscal rigidity. It postponed controversial problems, avoided direct criticisms, resorted to ambiguity, and made concessions when confronted with resistance. Nevertheless, the commission did succeed in putting the critical state of public finances on the political agenda and tiding the government over a difficult period. Rinchō politics helped reestablish LDP dominance by capturing the imagination of the public, weakening the party's political opposition and its union base, and appealing to the urban middle class even as backbenchers appealed to traditional constituencies by portraying themselves as their de-fenders *against* the Second Rinchō.[28] Wielding unprecedented authority for a *shingikai*, it gathered influential persons and possessed a measure of re-presentativeness, leading public opinion and guiding Diet deliberations when it did not overshadow them outright. Perceptions of councils changed thanks to the commission.

Many skeptics now regard the Second Rinchō as a special case. Indeed, it probably would have been impossible to institutionalize Rinchō-style bodies to counter the tight networks of vested interests, and the commission had offspring (including three Ad Hoc Commissions for the Promotion of Administrative Reform, or Gyōkakushin, which operated from 1983 to 1986, 1987 to 1990, and 1990 to 1993, and then an Administrative Reform Committee, or Gyōkakui) but no heirs. If the Committee to Supervise the Rehabilitation of Japan National Railways knew success, it was in a narrow field, and the Ad Hoc Council on Education was an abject failure despite Nakasone's enthusiastic support. Japanese politics has taken a different direction since the early 1980s: Nakasone's successors have acted less independently of the ministries and have been correspondingly more reluctant to establish strong *shingikai* like the Second Rinchō.

The exception proved the rule. Like Nakasone, Prime Minister Hosokawa Morihiro (August 1993–April 1994) had soaring ambitions but a weak base within his own government, so he, too, created independent commissions to advise him on critical problems and appointed the chair of Keidanren, Hiraiwa Gaishi, to lead the most prominent of them, which focused on deregulation of the economy. Although Hosokawa tried to keep out incumbent and retired

---

[28] S. Vogel (1996).

officials, because members of the so-called Hiraiwa Commission had to rely on bureaucrats for information on existing regulations and were under pressure to produce immediate results, their 1993 report essentially reproduced the ministries' own list of measures already targeted for deregulation. To minimize the commission's influence, bureaucrats insisted that it be referred to as a study group (*kenkyūkai*) rather than a committee (*iinkai*) or *shingikai*, and that the cabinet promise only to "refer" (*sankō*) to its recommendations rather than to "respect" (*sonchō*) them.[29]

By 1996, Japan was once again spilling more red ink than any other major industrial country – the annual deficit stood at 7.4 percent of gross domestic product (compared to less than 2 percent in the United States), and the accumulated debt of national and local governments was expected to hit ¥442 trillion ($3.68 trillion) by April 1997 – and the LDP's formation of a single-party administration that year gave a new lease on life to its *zoku* and their pork-barrel projects. In fact, Japan was spending more on public works than the Pentagon was on defense. Hope springs eternal, however. The day after he was formally reelected, Prime Minister Hashimoto Ryūtarō labeled 1997 "Year One" of financial rehabilitation and announced that his first priority would be administrative reform. The centerpiece of his speech was the promise of – another blue-ribbon commission.[30]

Private advisory bodies

Nonstatutory councils go by such names as "roundtable conference" (*kondankai* or *konwakai* – literally, "a gathering for a familiar talk"), "study group" (*kenkyūkai* or *benkyōkai*), or "preliminary conference" (*uchiawasekai*), all of them falling under the catchall "private consultative body" (*shiteki shimon kikan*). For the sake of convenience, this study will refer to them collectively as *kondankai*.

Such bodies are not new. The early 1930s were an especially turbulent period in Japan, and in 1933 the government gathered over 300 prominent thinkers (including leftists) from a variety of disciplines into a Shōwa Study Group to advise Prime Minister Konoe Fumimaro. Originally established as an organization of intellectuals, the Study Group in 1938 established both a Shōwa Comrades' Association to bring together midlevel bureaucrats, business leaders, and politicians to spread the ideas it was developing and a Shōwa Academy to train successors in its methods. It went on to make a total of 30 proposals on various topics (e.g., "To Prevent the Spread of the China Incident," "Essential Points in Renovating Personnel Administration")

---

[29] Ibid., pp. 204–5.
[30] *The Japan Times* (21 January 1997); *The New York Times* (9 November 1996 and 1 March 1997); *The Nikkei Weekly* (11 November 1996).

before its dissolution in 1940. Although it is now largely forgotten, the Shōwa Study Group was one of the largest bodies ever to conduct research on public policy in modern Japanese history.[31]

After the Pacific War, opposition parties charged that Prime Minister Yoshida Shigeru paid greater attention to the recommendations of extralegal councils than to the reports of official *shingikai*, and the number of private commissions established by the cabinet or ministries had already risen to 33 by 1951.[32] Private advisory bodies have been an integral part of the political land-scape since the 1960s. Prime Minister Satō Eisaku had his Roundtables on the Development of Society and the Okinawa Problem, Tanaka Kakuei his Roundtable on Remodeling the Japanese Archipelago, Miki Takeo his Central Policy Research Institute, and Fukuda Takeo his Roundtable to Discuss the Future with the Prime Minister.

When Ōhira came to power at the end of 1978, he inaugurated a staff system designed to bring him the views of well-informed persons on important policy issues. Much of Japan's intelligentsia had been estranged from the conservative establishment during the postwar era, but a rapprochement between scholars and officials developed under Ōhira. His nine policy study groups mobilized more than 200 university scholars, private industry researchers, and elite bu-reaucrats.[33] No postwar administration had ever sought advice on so large a scale, and these study groups were considered the brains of the Ōhira Cabinet. Although private councils drafted such proposals as "A Plan for Pacific Rim Solidarity" and "A Design for Rural Cities," Ōhira did not live to see them. After his death in 1980, scholars who had played a central role in the study groups offered their reports to influential LDP politicians, but they went unread by the new Suzuki Administration. One politician who did take notice, however, was Nakasone, who boasted, "No one's studying Ōhira's politics as much as I am."[34] He was deepening his ties to scholars through the Rinchō commissions and was to rely on their help in preparing for the LDP's 1982 presidential primary. Many of the researchers who had gathered around Ōhira thus gravi-tated to Nakasone.

Kondankai flourished under the new administration. Because the MCA frowns on the establishment of private bodies, ministries do not publish lists of *kondankai*, and no one has ever known precisely how many exist at any one time. According to *Asahi*, however, just the "principal" private advisory bodies con-cerned with the economy numbered 80 in 1984, the existence of 232 private councils was confirmed on the basis of MCA data in 1986, and Tsujinaka Yutaka counted references to 298 different *kondankai* in the press between January 1984 and September 1985. (That figure had risen to 346 by the period of January to

[31] Passin (1975), p. 279; *Mainichi Shinbun* (10 January 1985).   [32] Tsujinaka (1985a), p. 65.
[33] *Asahi Shinbun* (22 October 1984); Tsujinaka (1985a), p. 46.
[34] Naka (1986), p. 75.

September 1995.)[35] A considerable number of them were becoming more formal in their operations, exerting an important influence on policy in such varied fields as telecommunications and long-term land use planning.

Because they sidestep normal legal procedures, the creation of private councils has long invited Diet criticism. The thrust of sponsors' defense has always been that a unified body that submits reports as an organization might fall under the National Administrative Organization Act and thus require legal authorization, but that private commissions are simply administrative gatherings to hear individuals' opinions, and that it would be inappropriate to establish such bodies through formal government directives.[36] The term "private advisory body" is a misnomer, however. Officials have never scrupled to establish *kondankai* by means of cabinet decisions or ministerial ordinances. Although their honoraria may be nominal, participants are remunerated with public funds. Parent agencies themselves usually acknowledge the impropriety of this practice in a back-handed way by not listing these expenditures as individual budget items, as they occasionally did in the past.[37] Parent agencies also provide *kondankai* with secretariats staffed by civil servants.

If sponsors are not obliged to make public the opinions of individuals they happen to consult, they often choose to do so, and any number of private councils have, as councils, submitted reports. When Prime Minister Nakasone's Peace Problem Study Group reexamined the 1976 cabinet decision to limit defense expenditures to 1 percent of GNP, a unified recommendation was forced through despite fierce disagreement among members. The 1986 "Maekawa Report" of the Study Group on Economic Structural Adjustment for International Harmony is one of the most famous and influential proposals ever issued by a Japanese advisory body. "In this way, the private consultative bodies of recent years have already crossed the bounds of what the government calls private conferences or study groups and changed form to become semi-public bodies shouldering part of the official policymaking process," Tsujinaka observed.[38]

The difference between public and private commissions lies not in their operations but in their functions, and some of the latter's functions have been manifestly political. Although Nakasone was determined to break a streak of five short-lived administrations, his prospects were bleak. In Japan's parliamentary system, the sole path to power lay in assuming the presidency of the ruling LDP, but his faction placed a poor fourth in the party after the 1980 election, and he was not known for his skill at brokering interests within the

---

[35] *Asahi Shinbun* (22 October 1984); Sone (1986), p. 151; Tsujinaka (1985b), p. 67; Tsujinaka (1985a), p. 23; Tsujinaka (1996), p. 33.
[36] Hishinuma (1984), p. 40; Sugihara (1986), p. 79.
[37] Wada (1986), p. 35; *Asahi Shinbun* (22 October 1984); Hishinuma (1984), p. 42.
[38] Tsujinaka (1985b), p. 68.

party. When Nakasone finally did become prime minister in 1982, it was only by ignoring severe criticism to entrust important cabinet posts to members of the scandal-tainted Tanaka faction (prompting talk of a "Tanakasone Cabinet"). To make matters worse, the LDP's defeat in the general election of 1983 compelled Nakasone to bring the New Liberal Club (i.e., Party) into his government.[39]

Faced with powerful opposition in both his own party and the Diet, Nakasone had to rely on his own resources. In itself, though, Japan's prime ministry has never provided much of a power base. If Japan's postwar constitution does recognize the prime minister as chief of the cabinet, custom and intraparty competition have required any leader to distribute cabinet posts among LDP factions, thus diluting the authority of the office. The Prime Minister's Office houses a welter of unrelated, extraministerial bodies over which the premier exercises little control. Although the Economic Planning Agency was situated within the PMO, its director general harshly criticized Nakasone's 1985 budget, for example. (Having found it expedient to appoint a political rival as his subordinate, Nakasone also found it expedient to ignore his insubordination.)

Considering his weak base, to have followed the normal procedure of acting with the approval of the LDP's Policy Affairs and Executive Councils would have left Nakasone at the mercy of larger party factions, and his own initiatives would never have seen the light of day. Considering the party discipline of Japanese MPs, there was little chance of Nakasone's drumming up cross-party support in the Diet on a case-by-case basis, either. This was especially true in light of his political agenda. Firmly believing in the need for large-scale policy changes to cope with the new issues facing Japan, he sought to play an unusually innovative and activist role. Nakasone once wrote, "I believe that a Copernican transformation of political principles is demanded," and he called for "a final settlement of accounts of postwar politics" (*sengo seiji no sōkessan*).[40] His plans involved nothing less than a recasting of state administration and finance, the national railways, social security, defense, and education. These ambitious plans were not only broad in scope, but highly ideological in tone. Nakasone had always stood on the conservative fringe of the LDP, and many observers suspected that his ultimate aim was to revise the country's constitution, to complete the "reverse course" that had previously nullified many of the progressive reforms of the Occupation era.

In order to push through his controversial program, Nakasone curtailed discussion within the LDP and Diet, in which he was weak, to appeal for popular support. As he himself explained, "Policies like administrative reform and fiscal rehabilitation are like a glider: without a wind from all the people, they

---

[39] Ibid., p. 69.   [40] Naka (1986), p. 80; *Mainichi Shinbun* (9 January 1985).

will go down. My current politics are certainly stamped in this way."[41] If Nakasone tried to detour party and parliament out of political necessity, he also chose to play the role of a "one-man" (*wanman*) leader as a matter of principle. On trips to the United States after the Pacific War, Nakasone was impressed with the powerful authority and staff of the victor's executive branch, and he admired a "presidential prime minister" like Britain's Margaret Thatcher. Impatient with Japan's parliamentary system, Nakasone had long advocated popular election of Japan's prime minister.

In order to strengthen his hand and extend the life of his administration, Nakasone displayed a degree of leadership rarely seen in Japan, appealing directly to public opinion in three ways. First, because diplomacy is normally a preserve of executive prerogative, he played what was for a Japanese prime minister an uncharacteristically active role on the world stage. Nakasone also bolstered his power base by mustering prominent people from throughout society in the several Rinchō-type *shingikai* that considered major issues of the day. The most convenient way for him to maintain his freedom of action vis-à-vis the LDP and Diet, however, was through frequent recourse to *kondankai*.[42]

Private commissions served Nakasone not in his capacity as head of the cabinet or even the PMO, but as an individual politician. As his assistant cabinet secretary remarked, "It's not the Prime Minister's intention deliberately to appoint advisers to responsible positions because he wants to hear the views of people he considers superior to himself. . . . The Prime Minister is not establishing advisory bodies on impulse, but only when he has elaborated their design before their inauguration. 'I'll decide' is the Prime Minister's favorite phrase."[43] *Kondankai* could reflect Nakasone's positions more forcefully than could the conduct of diplomacy or Rinchō-type *shingikai*: Informal bodies ipso facto lie outside the ambit of legal regulation and were easily subjected to prime ministerial leadership.

Broadly representative advisory bodies were no more likely to endorse a highly conservative "Copernican transformation" of politics than the Diet was, of course. Although he always spoke of appointing private advisory bodies "in order to listen extensively to views from every sphere," their composition belied this claim. The prime minister himself had the final say on who was appointed, and those appointments served two purposes: Nakasone chose members of his personal network in order to guide policy in the direction of his own ideas and mainstream business leaders in order to solidify his connections with a group to which he had never been close.[44]

On the surface, Nakasone's strategy took the form of gathering respected private citizens into an advisory body, then "following" the public opinion

[41] Naka (1986), p. 76.   [42] Tsujinaka (1985b), p. 69.   [43] Naka (1986), p. 77.
[44] *Asahi Shinbun* (5, 7 October 1984); Muroi (1985), p. 29.

generated by their proposals. The prime minister disingenuously portrayed himself as a willing tool of the citizenry: Commissions "suck up the voice of the people, then I implement it. . . . That is the Nakasone Constitution, and I have no choice but to go by whatever the people say."[45] In truth, of course, commissions served as the prime minister's tools, useful levers with which he could attempt to reverse the old maxim *vox populi, vox dei*, to bend people and party to his will. *Kondankai* transmuted the prime minister's personal ideas into official-looking reports that the mass media would publicize – tellingly, journalists' participation in councils expanded in a bound during the Nakasone Administration – with advisers collectively playing the role of a "virtual Nakasone Minister of Propaganda," shaping currents of public opinion to which the prime minister could then appeal.[46] In this way, Nakasone tried simultaneously to restrain the LDP and Diet and to convey the image of an activist administration.

To summarize, Japan's parliamentary democracy formally operates in the following way:

citizenry → Diet → cabinet/administration (← advisory bodies ← citizenry)

Nakasone rescrambled this formula to read:

prime minister → advisory bodies → citizenry → Diet/administration

In 1983, Nakasone remarked, "The LDP *zoku* are too powerful; they're controlling politics. In order to check this, third-party bodies are necessary. If sugar-coated, we'll be able to entangle the opposition parties as well."[47] He was half-right: Within the opposition, only the Kōmeitō was consistently critical of his tactics. More serious discontent was simmering within the LDP, however. In the words of one conservative MP, when Nakasone referred *kondankai* proposals to the Diet, "deliberations were essentially omitted. . . . They ended up as repeat performances [*niban senji* – literally, 'the second brew of tea']."[48] On issues like revision of the tax code, Nakasone was willing to challenge his own party's PARC with ostensibly nonpartisan *kondankai* whose recommendations would more faithfully reflect his personal predilections. This was especially galling to LDP politicians because it threatened to reverse the long-term trend of "party up, government [i.e., officials] down" that was bringing more and more power within their grasp. Nakasone was reportedly warned that if he continued to disturb the conservative mainstream, creating *shingikai* and *kondankai* left and right and moving impetuously to "settle the accounts of postwar politics," retaliation could not be ruled out. "Like Napoleon, who was

[45] *Mainichi Shinbun* (18 January 1985).
[46] Naka (1986), p. 77; Amano (1994), p. 296.
[47] *Asahi Shinbun* (6 October 1984).   [48] Interview with Ōtsubo Ken'ichirō.

born on Corsica, it would be good to graduate quickly from the methods of the outsider," he was advised.[49]

Some of Nakasone's efforts were so heavy-handed as to redound to his disadvantage. When he encountered a storm of criticism in 1984 for testing the principle of separation of church and state by visiting a Shintō shrine dedicated to Japan's war dead in his official capacity as prime minister, Nakasone appointed the Roundtable on the Problem of Cabinet Worship at Yasukuni Shrine. One member of the Roundtable wrote, "At a stage when the members had not in the least settled even the tone of the report, it was reported in the newspaper as if related by the parties involved that it had been decided at the next meeting to put together and submit a report tolerating official visits after attaching conditions. . . . Wouldn't that be inconceivable at a normal *shingikai* or administrative committee?"[50] Conspicuous for Nakasone's intervention and his arbitrary use of its conclusions, the Yasukuni Roundtable became an issue in itself, which was not unusual for private commissions linked to the prime minister.

Nakasone's advisory-body politics was, in essence, an assertion of prime ministerial authority at the expense of parliament. Functions of the Diet, which ideally represents the nation, were increasingly encroached upon by advisory bodies, each of which claimed to be representative in its respective field. "In this way, the *shingikai* that were traditionally to the side of parliament might one by one be given independence as all sorts of 'minor, informal, specialized parliaments.' It is a plan for *shingikai* to become new parliaments [*shin-gikai* – a pun]." Shaken by his own conclusions, the author of these reflections went so far as to suggest that "Fundamentally, we must inquire into [the desirability of] continuing or abolishing the *shingikai* system."[51]

Such alarmism missed the mark. Although high levels of voter support enabled Nakasone to sidestep the LDP's own limit of two two-year terms as party president to remain in power for four years and eight months – longer than anyone since 1972 – his pseudopopulist attempt to concentrate power in the prime ministry failed, and his successors were unwilling or unable to engage in his brand of one-man politics. And yet, *kondankai* have continued to proliferate. Nakasone's deliberately eye-catching advisory-body *politics* diverted attention from more mundane but potentially more profound developments in advisory-body *administration*. Whatever the impression given by press coverage, *kondankai* directly linked to Nakasone and, more generally, those with a strong political nature always occupied an extremely limited fraction of the total. By Tsujinaka's reckoning, only 4 percent of the *kondankai* mentioned in the press between January 1984 and September 1985 operated on the level of the prime

---

[49] *Asahi Shinbun* (9 October 1984).   [50] Sone (1986b), p. 152.
[51] Teshima (1986), p. 43. See also Muroi (1985), p. 35.

minister; 25 percent were attached to cabinet ministers and another 45 percent to bureau chiefs. (This was in sharp contrast to the *shingikai* system, in which 16 percent of all councils were formally established on the level of the prime minister and 84 percent on the level of cabinet minister in 1983.) An even smaller proportion (2 percent) of *kondankai* the subject of whose deliberations could be identified dealt with explicitly political themes.[52]

Tsujinaka found *kondankai* scattered throughout the ministries. Part of the explanation for the spread of private commissions lies in their flexibility. In the words of one ex-bureaucrat, although bodies not based on the National Admin-istrative Organization Act were prima facie illegal in the past, "as a practical problem, because revising or drafting a law [to establish a new *shingikai* legally] may take too long or be very difficult to accomplish, we establish such a body as a de facto organ . . . as an expedient for solving a problem."[53] By enabling the bureaucracy to establish public councils by means of government ordinance, the 1983 revision of the act should have obviated the need for private councils, yet the very next year, *Asahi* declared them to be "in full bloom."[54] Although it was now possible to establish *shingikai* flexibly, the Diet, LDP, and other agencies could still question their memberships or reports. "Because ministries compete with one another, when one considers creating a *shingikai* and others already have *shingikai* with related jobs, they'll say, 'That discussion is our job, not yours. Why is your ministry discussing such a thing?' and will invariably object. Thus, creating a *shingikai* isn't that easy. Ministries can create private advisory bodies without consulting other ministries."[55]

As noted earlier, private advisory bodies make for convenient tools of persua-sion. *Shingikai* may have problems, but their composition and operation are rule-bound; this is not the case with *kondankai*, making them all the more likely to function as kept bodies and fairy cloaks.[56] The use of private panels reduces the transparency of policymaking, for example: Between the end of 1995 and the beginning of 1996, fully 81 percent of the *kondankai* convened opened neither their meetings nor their minutes to the public compared to 51.3 percent of the *shingikai*, and only 60.4 percent of the uncommunicative *kondankai* released summaries of their proceedings compared to 91.5 percent of the *shingikai*.[57] "There was almost no discussion, just explanations of the data by officials. Only about five meetings were held over three months, then a draft of the report appeared, and after the chair conferred [with us about it], I was surprised because it was loudly announced in the newspapers and television with great fanfare," recalled one roundtable member.[58] Agencies sometimes direct such

[52] Tsujinaka (1985b), pp. 70, 72; Tsujinaka (1985a), p. 25.
[53] Sakuma et al. (1972), pp. 37, 38.
[54] *Asahi Shinbun* (22 October 1984); Wada (1986), p. 30.
[55] Interview with Inoguchi Takashi.   [56] Muroi (1985), pp. 32–33.
[57] Sōmuchō (1996); *Nihon Keizai Shinbun* (8 August 1996).
[58] *Asahi Shinbun* (22 October 1984).

public relations against their own *shingikai*. When MOF inaugurated a Management of the National Debt Study Group before consulting a standing commission, one commentator speculated that "because this is a kind of 'theoretical armament' of the bureaucracy whose conclusions will probably be submitted to the Council on the Fiscal System in due time, it can be seen as a means of ensuring their predominance there."[59]

The importance of such ploys should not be exaggerated. First, any legislative proposal requires the endorsement of a *shingikai*, not a *kondankai*, and even if approval is often forthcoming, councilors can, and sometimes do, refuse to go along. Second, it can be argued as a matter of principle that the more councils, the better: "Although there's no way to limit the use of private advisory bodies, I think that if [authorities] want to create them, they should create as many as they like. Wouldn't it be for the best if . . . they all compete, and various views get aired?"[60] Most important, the very fact that ministries feel compelled to prepare for official deliberations, conducting *nemawashi* with interested parties and honing their "theoretical armament" in advance, suggests that *shingikai* now operate more independently than in the past. "Doesn't the recent application of private advisory bodies lie in the flexible absorption of expert knowledge in policy formulation and the manipulation of *shingikai* on that basis? That is, aren't *shingikai* in the process of changing into something that won't act freely for administrative agencies?" the same commentator quoted on the Council on the Fiscal System wondered.[61]

There seems to exist a rough division of labor between *shingikai* and *kondankai*. The largest differences between formal and private councils are the size and level of issues they consider. Formal councils generally deal with large matters, and the level of discussion tends to be high; private ones study new possibilities or foreign countries' experiences, and discussion is informal. The normal process is thus to create a study group at the first stage of policymaking, and if the group's sponsor gets the feeling that the issue is important, that it could lead to a law, then the matter will go to an official *shingikai*.[62]

In this vein, Tsujinaka hypothesized that the fundamental cause for the spread of *kondankai* lies in the profound transformations sweeping Japan: More than half of the bodies he tracked dealt with issues of high technology and post-industrialism, administrative reform and low growth, or internationalization.[63] With the social structure growing more complicated and change accelerating, administration would become unmanageable without the input of private actors, and ministries have established numerous private advisory bodies to collect information, grasp new interest configurations, and draft necessary policies.

[59] Shindo (1983), p. 249.   [60] Interview with Nishio Masaru.
[61] Shindo (1983), p. 249.   [62] Interview with Sone Yasunori.
[63] Tsujinaka (1985a), pp. 45–54; Tsujinaka (1985b), p. 74.

Because administrative reform consolidated many old councils and curtailed the creation of new ones, *shingikai* alone cannot fill the need.

Kondankai have also been of use to ministries in coping with the transformation of their own organizations. Administrative reform and liberalization have curtailed agencies' use of such traditional policy instruments as the granting of licenses, and deficit financing has restrained their budgets. The growing expertise of the LDP has also threatened ministries' prerogatives as its PARC improved its analytical and interest-adjustment capabilities. To regain the initiative in policymaking, it has become more necessary than in the past for bureaucrats to fight with their heads, and they have responded by turning to private commissions to devise new policies. This is especially true of the "regulatory ministries" (*kisei kanchō*) like Construction, Health and Welfare, Posts and Telecommunications, and Transportation, which need to move away from simple regulation and emulate "policy ministries" (*seisaku kanchō*) like MITI and MOF if they are to consolidate their institutional power bases.[64]

Finally, although the establishment of so many private councils on the bureau level might be interpreted as an expression of administrative sectionalism, to the extent that they include a variety of members, *kondankai* also help offset the vertical character of Japanese organizations by distributing information among different departments and enterprises, enhancing the effectiveness of that information, and generally operating as the cores of knowledge networks.[65] In sum, the proliferation of private advisory bodies became especially marked, and remarked upon, during the Nakasone Administration, but their spread throughout the government cannot be accounted for by the machinations of one vulnerable and ambitious politician. Like *shingikai*, they have come to mediate between state and society, and they will continue to do so whoever happens to be prime minister in the future.

Only empirical research can flesh out the politics of consultation and test the relative applicability of different models to Japan. What follows are case studies of specific policy decisions involving three *shingikai*: the Central Labor Standards Council, the Council on the Financial System, and the Rice Price Council.

Why these three? Within the context of domestic policymaking, these examples showcase interesting contrasts. They include a diverse range of important private actors: labor unions, a well-organized economic group firmly opposed to the conservatives; big business, generally ranked as the most powerful interest group; and farmers, considered only a junior partner of the governing coalition but a mainstay of the LDP's electoral support. These *shingikai* dealt with weighty issues that provoked heated conflicts: amendment of the law that regu-

---

[64] Calder (1993), p. 101; Okimoto (1988), p. 322. For MPT's invention of a new activist role for itself, see S. Vogel (1996), Chap. 7.

[65] Tsujinaka (1985a), pp. 45, 56; Tsujinaka (1985b), p. 72; *Asahi Shinbun* (22 October 1984).

lates basic working conditions; the assignment of jurisdiction over profitable new financial futures markets; and the setting of the price of the staple foodstuff. The bureaucratic setting differed in each case: A single bureau was largely able to decide on the revision of labor standards; interbureau disputes over the creation of new financial markets were resolved on the ministry level; and it took the ruling party, in negotiations with two ministries, to set the price of rice.

The political context also differed in each case: Amending the Labor Standards Act ended with a partisan confrontation in the Diet; financial futures never became a subject of serious political debate; and setting the price of rice generated cross-cutting cleavages within the major parties. Finally, these cases also highlight different aspects of the consultation process: the participation of a private advisory body; sectional conflict among the *shingikai* of several bureaucratic agencies; and the involvement of a council that is regarded as little more than a fairy cloak. From the gray of theory, then, to the green of life's growing tree.

4

Amending Japan's labor constitution: Revision of the Labor Standards Act

Described as a "labor constitution," a new Labor Standards Act prepared by Occupation authorities was enacted by Japan in 1947. The act was written with an eye to the working conditions of factory labor prevailing at the time and, with few exceptions, the essentials of the act remained unchanged for four decades. But those conditions did not remain unchanged, of course, and Japan's labor standards became increasingly outdated.

For decades, the Ministry of Labor (MOL) left the reduction of working hours to the independent efforts of labor and management. In 1982, however, without having formulated a plan of its own, MOL commissioned a private advisory body composed of persons of knowledge and experience, the Labor Standards Act Study Group, to reexamine national regulations. Its 1985 report constituted the government's first concrete policy on revison of the act and set the tone for the debate that followed. The superior working conditions of the advanced industrial countries with which Japan would like to be compared and a flurry of government pronouncements raised the specter of foreign pressure (*gaiatsu*) and lent urgency to the issue of working hour reductions. Although MOL was bound by law to consult a formal advisory body, the Central Labor Standards Council, on revision of the act, it was not obliged to follow that *shingikai*'s advice. Nevertheless, the council's public-interest representatives and ministry bureaucrats together mediated between union and employer delegates to arrive at a compromise plan that became the basis for a legislative bill. The Diet passed that bill in 1987, and MOL is now committed to supplementing labor–management efforts to shorten working hours with legislation and government ordinances as well as administrative guidance.

A variety of interested parties did have input, but other interested parties were either neglected or positively excluded. Revision of the Labor Standards Act did favor business, but labor had an undeniable influence over the final outcome. Each side did maintain a fair degree of solidarity, but centralized peak organizations were not comprehensively aggregating interests and negotiating directly with one another. Policymaking did revolve around MOL, but the ministry was careful to address the respective concerns of labor and manage-

116

ment, and politicians freely amended MOL's legislative bill in the Diet. In sum, revision of the Labor Standards Act was a relatively self-contained, bureaucratically led process that involved a limited set of narrowly focused interest groups. It was bureaucratically led because it fell squarely within MOL's jurisdiction and involved policies with few distributive benefits of interest to politicians.

Background

The Labor Standards Act of 1947 represented a great advance over prewar factory laws. Whereas the latter had covered only women and children under 16 and had allowed them to work as much as 11 hours a day, the act applied to all workers and mandated the 8-hour day and 48-hour week for adults, with even stricter limits for children under 18. With the exception of certain industries (e.g., agriculture) and positions (e.g., managers), employees were entitled to a day off each week and to a wage premium of at least 25 percent for overtime and for working on what would normally be a day off.

The act included a number of other provisions affecting working hours. So long as working hours over a four-week period averaged less than 48 hours a week, an employer might make employees work more than 8 hours on a specific day or more than 48 hours in a specific week. Employers, in turn, had to grant six days of paid vacation to any worker who had been employed continuously for one year and reported for work at least 80 percent of the time. Workers continuously employed for two years or more were eligible for an additional day of paid leave for each year after the first up to a maximum of 12 days. Finally, the act looked forward to its own obsolescence: "Working conditions must be such as to satisfy a worker's need to lead a life worthy of a human being. . . . Because the working conditions prescribed by this law are minimum standards, the parties concerned in labor relations are not only forbidden from worsening working conditions, but must on the basis of these standards strive for their improvement."[1]

The average annual working hours of laborers in workplaces of more than 30 employees actually increased with economic growth in the late 1950s, peaking at 2,432 hours in 1960 (see Figure 4-1). Subsequent improvements in labor productivity and increased hiring allowed those hours to contract: Between 1965 and 1975, the proportion of employees who worked no more than 40 hours a week mushroomed from 7.4 to 41.7 percent, and average annual working time reached a low of 2,064 hours in 1975. Regular work hours (i.e., hours on the job outside of overtime) shrank more slowly after that. It was not until 1986 that a majority of employees normally put in no more than 40 hours a week. There

[1] Sōhyō et al., v. 1 (1986), p. i.

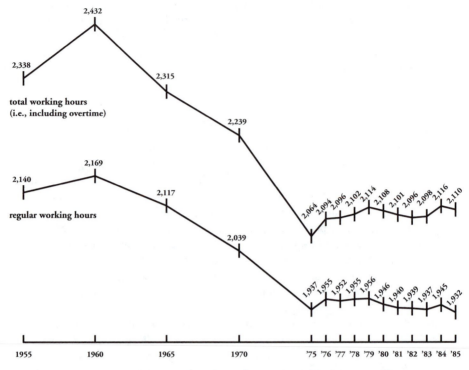

Figure 4–1. Average annual working hours in Japan, 1955–1985 (Sōhyō et al., v. 1, 1986, p. 50).

were several reasons for this blunting of progress. Economic growth decelerated, leading to a softening of the labor market and a sharpening of the struggle over the fruits of heightened labor productivity. And although overtime hours shrank over the years of high-speed growth, they began lengthening again after 1975, offsetting reductions in regular work hours. Between 1976 and 1986, total working time for the average employee remained fairly constant at about 2,100 hours per year.[2]

Japan did not compare favorably with other advanced industrial nations in this regard (see Table 4-1). Although considerably better off than their counterparts in Asia's newly industrializing economies (NIEs), Japanese employees in manufacturing had to work an average of about 200 hours more each year than corresponding Americans or Britons and around 500 hours longer than Frenchmen or Germans.

[2] Hiraga (1987), pp. 4, 6, 11, 12, 208.

Table 4-1. *Average annual working hours in manufacturing, 1985*

	Total hours	Overtime hours	Days of paid leave
South Korea	2,802	—	—
Taiwan	2,472	—	—
Singapore	2,417	—	—
Hong Kong	2,368[a]	—	—
Japan	2,168	229	9
United Kingdom	1,952	161	23
United States	1,924	172	19
West Germany	1,659	83	29
France	1,643	78[a]	26

[a] 1983.

Source: Hiraga (1987), pp. 58–59, 279; Sōhyō et al., v. 1 (1986), p. 53; Shirai (1987a), p. 5.

Two major factors account for these disparities. Because of their "lifetime" employment system, many larger Japanese companies have tended to adjust production by varying overtime hours rather than by hiring and firing, so employees must often put in late hours in return for job security. And although reductions in regular working hours came through an increase in the number of days off more than through a shortening of the workday, Japanese employees still enjoyed fewer weekly and paid vacations than Western workers did.

Like the United States and the United Kingdom,[3] but unlike Germany, France, Italy, and Canada, Japan does not legally limit the hours of overtime that an employer can ask for. There is nothing unusual about putting in ten hours a week of overtime in Japan, and a tremendous amount of after-hours labor goes unreported and uncompensated (so-called *saabisu*, or "complimentary," overtime). In the month of February 1987, 22 percent of MOL's own staff reported that they had worked 50 to 100 hours of overtime, and 10 percent worked over 100 extra hours. At the Labor Standards Bureau itself, 64 percent of the respondents agreed that "if you don't work overtime, you can't complete your normal duties."[4]

The five-day week first appeared in large firms in the early 1960s, spread rapidly in the early 1970s, then spread more slowly with the blunting of economic growth after the mid-1970s. Even in 1986, only 6.2 percent of all firms were granting two-day weekends to 28.2 percent of the workforce every week. Workers took off an average of 10.1 days of national holidays, 4.3 days of New

[3] Brussels ruled in 1996 that the European Union had the right to impose a maximum 48-hour workweek on British companies.
[4] *Nihon Keizai Shinbun* (17 August 1987); *Asahi Shinbun* (6 July 1987).

Year's holiday, 3.3 days of summer vacation, and 8 days paid vacation – only *half* of what they were formally allowed.[5] In a 1987 survey, a paltry 14 percent of the respondents took all of their paid leave, and fully 53 percent reported feeling guilty about taking time off.[6] The managing director of the MITI-affiliated Leisure Promotion Center confessed in 1986 that even within his own organization, whose mission is to encourage long holidays, it was difficult to get workers to take vacations.[7]

Cultural differences undeniably play a part in accounting for these figures. It is not old-fashioned to regard hard work as a virtue in Japan, and a general consensus exists that only through discipline and toil did the country achieve its present prosperity and will it maintain its competitiveness in the future. There is still a strong feeling that an employee belongs to the company, and putting in long hours is considered a sign of corporate loyalty. Furthermore, Japanese men have tended to look to their jobs and workmates for fulfillment and fellowship to a greater degree than do many Westerners and, jealous of their autonomy and their authority over household matters, housewives often feel that "a husband should be healthy and out of the house," as the saying goes.

Nevertheless, there is also an element of calculation involved. The strong preference for income over leisure that workers demonstrated was perfectly reasonable in light of Japan's high price level, undeveloped system of consumer credit, and inadequate pensions. In addition, the country lacked sufficient facilities, whether comfortable homes or convenient golf courses, to make leisure time more attractive. And long working hours do not necessarily involve long hours of work. Because Japanese managers tend to favor people who work long hours when rating personnel, many white-collar workers hesitate to leave the office before everyone else and will often linger in the evening, going through the motions of working at least until their boss has left. The Japanese adage "take annual vacations and miss success" testifies to the same concern.

Whatever the causes of long working hours, they took their toll, particularly on family life. "When you take the company out of Dad, there's nothing left," an official in the Labor Standards Bureau noted.[8] A 1986 survey in one Tokyo suburb revealed that among white-collar couples with stay-at-home wives, the husband typically left the house at 7:39 A.M. and did not return until 9:16 P.M. Teachers at a suburban Osaka junior high school found that 39.1 percent of the students spoke to their father less than ten minutes in an average day, and 12.4 percent did not speak to them at all.[9]

Needless to say, the "Japanese worker" referred to here is a statistical artifact. In truth, working hours varied considerably. In 1986, average annual totals in rural areas exceeded those in cities, ranging from a high of 2,231 in Okinawa to

[5] Hiraga (1987), pp. 13–22.   [6] *Daily Yomiuri* (12 December 1987).
[7] Ibid. (26 September 1987).   [8] *Nihon Keizai Shinbun* (10 January 1987).
[9] *Akahata* (16 August 1987).

a low of 2,071 in Tokyo. By industry, construction racked up 2,276 hours compared to 1,906 in finance and insurance. The most politically significant disparities were among firms of different sizes. Because "lifetime" employment is more common among larger firms, overtime hours actually lengthened with increasing size, but in general, working hours varied inversely with enterprise scale. In 1986, whereas 79.7 percent of laborers in firms with at least 1,000 employees worked no more than 40 hours a week (excluding overtime) and very few (2.4 percent) had to work the legal maximum of 48 hours, only 11.9 percent of laborers in firms with 30 to 99 employees worked no more than 40 hours a week, and 38.8 percent had to work a full 48 hours. And whereas only 7.6 percent of firms with at least 1,000 employees had failed to adopt some form of five-day week, with 35.5 percent always granting a two-day weekend, 55.2 percent of firms with 30 to 99 employees still required a full six-day week, and only 3.1 percent had abandoned it altogether.[10]

The Labor Standards Act Study Group (Rōkiken)

MOL grew concerned about the failure of working hours to decline as early as 1978. The cabinet called for reductions as a means of maintaining and expanding employment opportunities in 1979, and the following year, the ministry issued its first plan, which set a goal of bringing average annual working hours down to 2,000 by 1985 by means of administrative guidance. Lacking any teeth, this plan did not bring results, and MOL became convinced of the need for legislative action.[11] To prepare that action, it turned to the Labor Standards Act Study Group (Rōdō Kijun Hō Kenkyūkai, or Rōkiken).

Established in 1969 as a private advisory body of the minister, the Rōkiken gathered persons of learning and experience to investigate implementation of the act and attendant problems. MOL reconvened the Rōkiken in May 1982 to investigate how enforcement of the act was affected by changes in industrial structure (e.g., the shift to a service economy), the diversification in forms of employment (e.g., an increase in part-time workers), technological innovation (e.g., the spread of electronics), and the aging of the Japanese population. At its first plenary session, the Rōkiken officially chose Ishikawa Kichiemon as its chair and formed three subcommittees to study working hours, labor contracts, and wages. The working hours subcommittee attracted the most public attention and dealt with the most contentious issues. It consisted of six professors of law, one labor economist, and a practicing lawyer: The government clearly looked on revision of the act as a politicolegal, not an economic, issue.

[10] Sōhyō et al., v. 1 (1986), p. 52; Hiraga (1987), pp. 13, 20–22.
[11] Foote (1997).

Neither labor nor management was given a veto over the selection of members, and unions were later to complain that the government had chosen individuals for the "convenience" of their views and had excluded progressive labor scholars. Although MOL bureaucrats blandly explained that "members are chosen on the basis of their previous experience in *shingikai*, *kenkyūkai*, and so on,"[12] connections obviously played a large role. Professor Ishikawa had been in charge of labor studies at the Law Faculty of Tokyo University, the preeminent training ground of Japan's elites, and in that sense he was *the* professor of labor law. Many of the Rōkiken members had studied under him and were his disciples (*deshi*). A member's comments on the formation of the Rōkiken illustrate the personal networks around which Japanese decisionmaking frequently revolves.

> I think Professor Ishikawa was chosen before the Study Group's members, but he didn't have a direct influence on their selection. It's all understood. Professor Hanami Tadashi [i.e., chair of the working hours subcommittee], for example, is a kind of managing director for Professor Ishikawa in that he's one of his senior students, and I think Professor Hanami gave the Ministry of Labor a lot of advice on choosing members. . . . We're a small gang; we know each other very well. . . . People in the Ministry of Labor are aware of that, so there's a sort of virtuous cycle. You know people well and information gets shared, so the Ministry gives us a lot of information, and by doing so this group becomes even more powerfully differentiated from others. When the time comes for the ministry to seek advice, then in a way they're bound to ask us because it's we who have the information.[13]

Members of the working hours subcommittee all considered themselves to be independent, and they self-consciously played the role of representatives of the public interest. The subcommittee conducted original research, eventually collecting thousands of pages of data. Although the Rōkiken lacked money, and although what little money it had went to compensate members for transportation expenses and such, the government pressed companies to submit information. At one point, a Rōkiken member and a ministry bureaucrat spent a month abroad in order to gather statistics and compare various countries' standards. MOL also offered information on its own initiative. Bureaucrats were "presenting reports at the meetings and bringing documents in an effort to convince us. The Ministry of Labor just kept bringing information; I was swamped. To be very blunt, I think that's the whole game," reported one subcommittee member.[14]

MOL was seeking to shorten legal working hours and, given the prevalence of enterprise unions, it assumed that workers would be unable to achieve those

---

[12] Interview with Matsubara Haruki.
[13] Interview with Shimada Haruo.   [14] Ibid.

shorter hours through their own efforts. But the ministry could not ignore the interests of Japanese business, and a simple reduction in labor time would constitute a clear loss for management. It was necessary to compensate employers, to strike a balance, so in a broad sense, the negotiations leading to revision of the Labor Standards Act were to revolve around a trade-off between the shorter hours demanded by workers and the introduction of greater variability in the distribution of working hours demanded by employers. Although the ministry did raise these issues from the start, that is not to say that it controlled subsequent discussions. MOL's goals were rather vague in the early stages of policymaking.

Although the working hours subcommittee usually met about once a month, that increased to once a week as it became busier. A consensus finally jelled after subcommittee members spent an intense three-day retreat hashing over unresolved issues from 9:00 in the morning until 3:00 the following morning. A report emerged by stages. The secretariat would prepare a summary of each set of discussions to serve as a basis for the deliberations that followed. Sometimes these "summaries" included ideas the ministry itself was advancing, but because subcommittee members did not hesitate to argue with bureaucrats over these ideas, the secretariat's rough drafts would be rewritten. This was not an adversarial process of scholar versus bureaucrat, however: MOL officials themselves "often sound like labor economists or sociologists,"[15] and the two sides discussed the issues together, with the report eventually incorporating ideas from both. Decisionmaking was consensual; no votes were taken.

The working hours subcommittee completed its midterm report on 28 August 1984, proposing to "flexibilize" working hours while reducing them. The subcommittee then conducted hearings on its report, consulting 11 labor organizations (e.g., Sōhyō, the Federation of Construction Industry Unions) and 12 employer organizations (e.g., Nikkeiren, the National Federation of Small Business Associations), and the Rōkiken released its final report on 19 December 1985. That report called for legislative action. Intraindustry competition discouraged efforts on the part of individual companies, and the prevalence of enterprise unions limited the scope and power of labor agreements. The latter problem was exacerbated by the low rate of unionization, particularly in small- and medium-sized enterprises: Whereas 64.5 percent of workers in private firms with over 1,000 employees were organized in 1985, that was true of only 28.3 percent of workers in firms with 100 to 999 employees, 6.7 percent of workers in firms with 30 to 99 employees, and a scant 0.5 percent of workers in firms with fewer than 30 employees.[16]

It would be appropriate, the Rōkiken continued, to allocate legal working hours of 45 hours a week among individual days that, in principle, should not

[15] Campbell (1989), p. 13.   [16] Hiraga (1987), p. 209.

exceed 8 hours. Legislation should focus on shortening regular working hours rather than on mandating the five-day week or limiting overtime and day–off labor, in other words, but the wage premium for weekend labor ought to be increased. Because a more effective distribution of working hours would facilitate their reduction, the government should recognize variable hours on as much as a three-month basis when labor and management agreed, and such agreement should also permit the introduction of flextime (i.e., where the individual worker chooses when to begin and end the workday). Paid vacations should be made easier to take, increased to a minimum of ten days a year, and granted to part-time workers in proportion to their hours. Finally, because working hours and annual vacations varied considerably, depending on industry and enterprise scale, it would be necessary to allow small-scale commerce and service businesses to exceed 45 hours a week and to apply new standards in stages to enterprises below a specified size. (This is only a summary of highly detailed proposals that also touched on such subjects as late-night labor, break time, and worker discretion over the timing of paid leaves. For the sake of clarity and brevity, this study passes over these subjects in order to focus on the central issues in dispute.)

One of the advantages of consulting a private advisory body is plausible deniability: Lacking any official status, its report can serve as a useful trial balloon, and if some group vigorously attacks it, then its sponsor can disown any responsibility for it. In this case, negative reaction was not long in coming, but if both camps were critical of the subcommittee's proposals, their reactions were diametrically opposed. While insisting that the reduction of working hours results from improved productivity and independent labor–management negotiations, employers sought the abolition of limits on daily hours and a further extension of the period over which variable hours might be applied. They also argued that shortening weekly hours and lengthening paid vacations would hurt small- and medium-sized enterprises, and that specific industries would have to be exempted from new standards. Employers looked on *kondankai* members as ivory-tower academics ignorant of the real world, and the stubbornness of employers infuriated some *kondankai* members.

The unions were in a delicate situation. They were obliged to champion the interests of less fortunate, unorganized workers, who would benefit from even a marginal reduction in legal working hours and might suffer if strict new standards bankrupted small firms. But because large, modern firms already boasted working conditions superior to those mandated by both existing and proposed legislation, adoption of a 45-hour week could *lower* standards for most of organized labor. Unions opted for a hard line, declaring that the report hewed too closely to the status quo, incorporated important management demands, and ignored international (i.e., more generous Western and specifically Continental European) standards. Concretely, they asserted that working hours ought not to exceed 8 hours a day and 40 hours a week, and that the five-day week should be explicitly required by law. Posing a threat to laborers' health and welfare, variable working hours would have to be strictly limited: The current four-week basis for variable hours should be shortened, not lengthened, and upper limits should be imposed on the flexibilized day. The government must legally cap overtime and day-off labor and increase the wage premium. Employees should receive at least 20 days a year of paid leave whatever their record of attendance. Finally, labor opposed singling out specific industries for special treatment as going against the spirit of the Labor Standards Act.

The Rōkiken was by no means the only government body to grapple with the issue of working hours reduction. The easing of trade frictions had become a paramount policy task, and even as the Study Group was preparing its report, a variety of government bodies began to focus on the problem of achieving working conditions comparable to those of other advanced industrial countries. A veritable avalanche of cabinet decisions, Diet resolutions, and *shingikai* reports called for the curtailment of labor time.

In June 1985, the Central Labor Standards Council raised as a goal for the late 1980s the reduction of the annual average to 2,000 hours. Having decided to expand domestic demand in October, the Cabinet Council on Economic Policy advocated promotion of the five-day week, set a goal of workers' enjoying ten additional days off within five years, and launched a campaign to form a public consensus around the move to a "leisure-creating society." In a December report, the Council on the Economy echoed these calls for a 2,000-hour workyear and an additional ten days off by 1990.

Prime Minister Nakasone appointed a Study Group on Economic Structural Adjustment for International Harmony in October to recommend policies for Japan to pursue in response to its changing position in the world economy and Western complaints of mercantilism. In April 1986, two weeks before his departure for a summit conference in the United States, it submitted the so-called Maekawa Report (named for the Study Group's chair). Recognizing that a continuation of Japan's unprecedentedly large current account surpluses would create a critical situation, the Maekawa Report announced that "there is an urgent need for Japan to implement drastic policies for structural adjustment, and to seek to transform the Japanese economic structure into one oriented toward international coordination."

Foremost among these "drastic" policies was a shift to economic growth driven by domestic demand, and this required a stimulation of private consumption that long hours on the job would hinder. "People should have more free time through reduced working hours, and the active use of paid leaves for longer periods should be encouraged. Total working hours per year in line with the industrialized countries of Europe and North America and early realization of complete [i.e., weekly] five-day weeks should be pursued. . . ."[17] Although it was the product of an ostensibly private advisory body and actually did no more than synthesize a number of policy prescriptions that had already been aired by government agencies, *zaikai*, and *shingikai*, the Maekawa Report received tremendous publicity, the cabinet resolved to adopt its proposals, and other advanced countries treated it as a virtual public promise by the Japanese government.

As the Maekawa Report itself acknowledged, the easing of international economic frictions was only one of a number of long-term developments that needed to be addressed. Less than three weeks after its release, the Council on People's Livelihood recommended the reduction of average annual labor time to 1,800 hours by the beginning of the twenty-first century in order to deal with the aging of the Japanese population. Less than a month later, in May 1986, the Council on the Economy drew on the Maekawa Report to propose that the government investigate revision of the Labor Standards Act, promote the five-day week in the civil service and among financial institutions, and popularize summer vacations of at least a week. MITI's Industrial Structure Council weighed in the following week with a recommendation that annual working hours shrink to less than 1,900 by the end of the century. The cabinet resolved in June that the country must strive for a level of working hours in line with those of the advanced countries of the West. At the end of October, the Office for the Promotion of Economic Structural Adjustment (which was headed by Nakasone himself) made clear its desire to put revision of the Labor Standards Act on the political agenda, and at the end of November, the civil service began experimentally to close government offices every other Saturday.

December was a busy month in 1986. First, the Diet resolved to promote the reduction of working hours through extension of the five-day week in order to maintain and expand long-term employment opportunities. The Council on the Economy then argued that it was necessary to increase workers' free time to boost consumption as well as to ensure long-term employment opportunities, and noted that a more activist policy was needed if the country was to achieve an average working year of 2,000 hours by 1990. Finally, the cabinet agreed to help spread the five-day week and shorten working hours.

In Japanese politics, it sometimes seems as if the likelihood of government action is inversely proportional to the number of public pronouncements made on a given matter. This was not one of those cases. The numbing frequency with which public bodies dealt with the question of working hours reduction from 1985 represented consensus formation, not temporization. The flurry of resolutions and recommendations referred to earlier may not have had many tangible

---

[17] *Japan Economic Almanac 1987*, pp. 248–49

results in itself, but along with the Rōkiken report, it set the stage for the first major overhaul of Japan's labor standards legislation in 40 years. That overhaul was prepared by another council.

The Central Labor Standards Council (Chūkishin)

Article 98 of the Labor Standards Act provided for the creation of a *shingikai* that authorities were required to consult on implementation and revision of the act and the Labor Safety and Hygiene Law, and the Central Labor Standards Council (Chūō Rōdō Kijun Shingikai, or Chūkishin) was duly established on 1 September 1947.

Membership

The Chūkishin is a tripartite commission composed of public-interest, employer, and worker representatives. This kind of tripartism is characteristic of MOL *shingikai*, and all councilors at the time of this narrative were basically satisfied with it. Members' term of office is two years but is renewable. In December 1986, when the Chūkishin submitted its recommendations to MOL, the average union member had served 30.3 months, the average employer 58.6 months, and the average public-interest representative 78.4 months.

The only *official* constraint the minister faces in appointing members is that the council must be composed of 21 members distributed equally among the three groups. Nominations are far from arbitrary, however. Seats are informally allotted among peak associations, industries, unions, and professional organizations, and when the representative of one of these groups resigns, he (a public-interest representative was the sole woman on the council) is replaced by another member from the same group. The ministry does not select interest-group councilors at its own discretion, in other words. A MOL bureaucrat conceded only that private organizations "make recommendations to the minister"; a manager forthrightly asserted that "employers and workers choose their own representatives through their respective trade associations and unions without the ministry having the least influence."[18] The truth is somewhere in between, with each side accommodating the other. If MOL never opposes interest-group nominations, those interest groups never put forward "inappropriate" individuals.

Business was represented by an officer of the National Federation of Small-Business Associations (Chūōkai); an industrialist recommended by the Chamber of Commerce; and five councilors nominated by Nikkeiren: an official of its own and spokespeople for the steel, chemical, textile, and construction indus-

---

[18] Interviews with Matsubara Haruki and Nakai Takeshi.

tries who were suggested by their respective trade associations (see Table 4-2). On the labor side, MOL had the national centers nominate members roughly in proportion to their relative sizes. Four people represented Sōhyō directly, with another councilor representing transport workers at Sōhyō's behest. One member spoke for Dōmei directly, another for a Dōmei-affiliated union, and a third for the small national center Chūritsu Rōren. None of the national centers had a problem with participating in the *shingikai*.

"Interest-group representatives make various self-interested assertions. Who they are matters less than who the public-interest representatives are, those members making their decisions on the basis of an objective assessment of the situation," argued one unionist.[19] How objective were those members? Completely so, in their own eyes. In reply to a written questionnaire, every single union and employer respondent felt that he had been appointed because his position was close to that of a specific private organization. Public-interest representatives, on the other hand, were equally unanimous in attributing their selection to the ministry's trusting their fairness and judgment: Not one felt that he or she had been chosen because his or her position was close to that of an interest group or MOL.

Although significant in themselves, councilors' attitudes tell only part of the story. MOL did not openly consult labor and management, but because the ministry avoided nominating individuals whom the interest groups were likely to oppose, they did wield a "de facto veto" over appointments of public-interest representatives.[20] In 1986, at least two of the seven representatives were generally recognized as having been chosen for their technical expertise, and none of the rest obviously leaned toward one or another of the opposing camps. A union official even ventured that MOL deliberately "chooses people whose positions aren't clear, because somebody with clear positions would be opposed by some group."[21] The consensus among interest-group councilors was that "the public-interest representatives are neutral [vis-à-vis labor and management]. If they have a 'color,' it's that of the government."[22] The interest groups had no problem with the fact that the ministry was unlikely to choose antiestablishment figures. In the words of one unionist:

> I have the feeling that scholars who ordinarily conduct their research from a position of very strong opposition to the government are excluded. But if our opinions differed on fundamentals, if the *shingikai* contained public-interest representatives who opposed the liberal capitalism of Japan, there's no question that conducting the *shingikai* would be very difficult and that discussion among the members wouldn't mesh very well.[23]

[19] Interview with Saiga Shizuya.   [20] Interview with Ishikawa Kichiemon.
[21] Interview with Ōtani Tatsuya.
[22] Interview with Nishikiori Akira.   [23] Interview with Satō Kōichi.

Table 4-2. *Members of the Chūkishin, December 1986*

Public-interest representatives

Kawaguchi Minoru	Professor, Faculty of Law, Keiō University
Nakanishi Masao	Managing Director, Safety and Hygiene Technology Testing Association
Nishikawa Shinhachi	Professor, Faculty of Public Health, Nippon College of Physical Education
Shirai Taishirō[a]	Professor, Faculty of Administration, Hōsei University
Tsuji Ken	Vice President, Japan Institute of Labor
Wada Katsumi	Chair, Employment Information Center
Watanabe Michiko	Attorney

Employer representatives

Gō Ryōtarō	President, Nichien Chemical Engineering
Honda Kazuyuki	Managing Director, Kobe Steelworks
Matsuzaki Yoshinobu	Managing Director, Nikkeiren
Nakai Takeshi	Director, Personnel Department, Mitsui Tōatsu Chemicals
Nibuya Ryū	Senior Managing Director, Mitsubishi Rayon
Nishikiori Akira	Managing Director, National Federation of Small Business Associations (Chūōkai)
Ōmori Takehide	Vice President, Toda Construction

Worker representatives

Endō Yoshikazu	Secretary-General, All-Japan Council of Transport Workers Unions
Hondo Yoshio	Director, Research Bureau, Sōhyō
Okamura Shōzō	Assistant Director, Center for Shorter Working Hours, Sōhyō
Saiga Shizuya	Director, Organization Bureau, Dōmei
Shimizu Eiichi	Director, Center for Shorter Working Hours, Sōhyō
Takagi Tsuyoshi	Director, Industrial Policy Bureau, Japanese Federation of Textile and Garment Workers Unions
Tamura Ken'ichi	Vice President, Chūritsu Rōren

[a] Chair.

Japanese scholars often contend that their tripartism is unique in its use of persons of learning and experience rather than government officials. To some extent, though, this is a distinction without a difference. "Public-interest representatives didn't always yield to the bureaucracy; sometimes they opposed it. [But] without being bureaucrats' proxies, you could say that they were 'understanding.' Bureaucrats were probably trying to make use of the public-interest representatives in order to achieve their own aims," conceded one of those representatives.[24] Without agreeing in every detail, the sincerely held views of public-interest councilors tended to coincide with those of MOL, and they cooperated with it over the course of the Chūkishin's deliberations. That

[24] Interview with Tsuji Ken.

was surely one of the ministry's motivations in appointing those people in the first place.

Some councilors were closer to MOL than others. Wada Katsumi headed the Labor Standards Bureau before he retired, and Nakanishi Masao and Nikkeiren's Matsuzaki Yoshinobu were also ministry OBs. Having joined a MOL-affiliated institute gave Tsuji Ken a slight ministry tinge in the eyes of some. Members were leery of packing councils with ex-bureaucrats, but the OB Wada indignantly defended his participation: "I was appointed as a person of learning and experience concerning the administration of labor standards, *not* as an OB. I never consulted with the Ministry of Labor as an individual. . . . I was only one of seven [public-interest representatives], and my influence was no greater than theirs."[25] While echoing Wada, fellow OB Nakanishi did allow for ulterior motives on the part of MOL:

> I participate as a safety specialist. There's no one else with my technical knowledge. Wada worked for many years in labor administration, and knows all its ins and outs. You can't conduct deliberations without such a man. [But] we may have been appointed because we're close to the ministry's position. After all, having worked there for so long, our opinions aren't very different from those of other administrators.[26]

The labor members were the most ambivalent. Several of them argued that direct bureaucratic involvement was unwelcome outside of the council secretariat, and that qualified persons of learning and experience without administrative experience could have been found. If they were generally wary of bureaucratic attempts to influence *shingikai* deliberations, they were not particularly distrustful of their fellow councilors, however, and they did appreciate the ambiguity of an OB's position. In the words of one union observer:

> There are cases when OBs are no more than proxies for the bureaucracy, but not in the Chūkishin. There *were* instances [in the Chūkishin] of OBs' offering partial criticisms of ministry positions. Incumbent bureaucrats want to control the *shingikai* through OBs, but OBs aren't simply puppets. They've their own ideas. There are senior – junior [*senpai – kōhai*] relationships between retired bureaucrats and incumbents, and seniors guide juniors by means of the *shingikai*.[27]

Matsuzaki's role highlights the fallacy of presuming that OBs necessarily act as willing tools of incumbent bureaucrats. Anything but a MOL stooge, he helped lead the employer camp's charge against revision of the Labor Standards Act.

What about groups that lacked representation on the Chūkishin? Anyone can approach the ministry or lobby Chūkishin members. The council can also invite outside groups to formal hearings when necessary (although members recog-

---

[25] Interview with Wada Katsumi.   [26] Interview with Nakanishi Masao.
[27] Interview with Ōtani Tatsuya.

nized no such necessity on this occasion). Some organizations outside the *shingikai* can transmit their views via organizations included within. Nikkeiren exists precisely in order to represent the interests of employers of any stripe on issues of labor relations. On the labor side, the question of representation was more complex. Communist unions had a voice only to the extent that those unions belonging to Sōhyō could influence that national center's positions, and Sōhyō refrained from nominating Communists because it would have been "inconvenient" for the government.[28] Given that the JCP typically denounces any and all concessions to capital, it might well have been inconvenient to Sōhyō, too. Communists, on the other hand, were aggrieved by their exclusion, and naturally felt discriminated against. Women's groups also felt that their views were inadequately represented by organized labor, but more of that later.

Deliberations

MOL convened the Chūkishin on 11 March 1986. After the Maekawa Report came out in April, the government was fearful of criticism at home and abroad if it failed to produce concrete results. Although the ministry was willing to extend deliberations if necessary, it wanted the Chūkishin's recommendations by December in order to prepare a bill by the time the Diet opened in 1987, so discussions were "sharply squeezed."[29]

The Chūkishin held plenary sessions in May, June, and July. At the last of these, councilors decided that they would henceforth deliberate on working hours and on other issues (e.g., shop rules and retirement compensation) in two subcommittees consisting of five individuals from each of the membership categories. The Working Hours Subcommittee went on to meet seven times in August and September. Because the gap between negotiating positions failed to narrow, it was decided in October that the public-interest representatives would try to adjust their differences by exchanging views with the two sides separately. After 15 separate meetings in October and November, both subcommittees presented reports to a joint session on 3 December, a plenary session unanimously approved those subcommittee reports one week later, and the Chūkishin submitted its proposals to the minister of labor.

Because Professor Ishikawa was chair of the Chūkishin as well as of the Rōkiken, everyone expected him to continue handling revision of the Labor Standards Act, but he thought it improper to chair both the private council that had made the original recommendations and the official council that would act on them, so he prevailed upon his friend Professor Shirai Taishirō to take over. Highly respected by and popular among his colleagues, Professor Shirai, a labor economist, was vice chair of the Central Labor Committee. Although MOL

---

[28] Ibid.   [29] Kawaguchi M. (1987), p. 4.

would have preferred Professor Ishikawa, it knew Professor Shirai well, and his reputation for integrity and balance made him an equally credible candidate. Formally, the Chūkishin was free to choose its own chair, but "the administration lets you know from the start who it wants to be chair. There's some person whom anyone could peg as chair, and that's what he goes on to become."[30] Councilors did not object to this. On the contrary, because *nemawashi* had already confirmed his acceptability to both sides, ministry selection of Professor Shirai simply smoothed the way.

In Japan, a chair's role is best described by the word *matomeru*, which means "to gather," "to complete," or "to settle." The chair's responsibility is to bring discussions to a unified conclusion in accordance with the various participants' opinions without imposing his or her own. Although Professor Shirai is a man of strong convictions, councilors nonetheless did credit him with playing such a mediating role. Leading the public-interest representatives as a group, he would make proposals after he had questioned labor and management members, staking out positions between the two. These positions were never of a sort that would trouble MOL, individuals on both sides pointed out, but Professor Shirai hotly denied acting as the bureaucracy's proxy: "If the ministry thought of framing *shingikai* discussion through the choice of me [as chair], they must have been terribly disappointed, because that's the kind of thing I dislike most."[31]

Professor Shirai had been reluctant to chair the Chūkishin, and it was said that he came to regret having yielded to Professor Ishikawa's entreaties: "He felt like he'd jumped into a minefield."[32] Even before deliberations began, there was disagreement over the *shingikai*'s frame of reference. With the Chūkishin deliberating within the context of a lively policy debate, MOL distributed relevant proposals from other *shingikai* and the cabinet as reference materials at the start, and councilors were particularly influenced by the Maekawa Report. But they did not consider the recommendations of that report to be binding, and because it had extolled the shortening of working hours without going into the attendant costs, its prescriptions had no direct effect on Chūkishin deliberations.

The report of the Rōkiken did, however. MOL instructed the Chūkishin to deliberate "on the basis of" that report, and if councilors felt no obligation to arrive at the same conclusions, they agreed that the Rūkiken report did, in fact, become the basis of their deliberations. With its mutually antagonistic managers and union officials, who lacked the time and expertise to investigate every matter within the *shingikai*'s broad jurisdiction, many councilors conceded that the Chūkishin was less suited to formulating a concrete plan than to adjusting interests in response to one, and the Rōkiken's report was cogent, so "even if

[30] Interview with Nakanishi Masao.
[31] Interview with Shirai Taishiro.
[32] Interviews with Ishikawa Kichiemon and Shimada Haruo.

people wanted to talk about something completely different, they couldn't ignore it. The fact that its details were changed later was less important than its initial framing of the debate."[33] Although employers were opposed to any revision of the Labor Standards Act, they appreciated the report's advocacy of variable working hours. Unions were pressing for still shorter hours and wanted to review the current law in its entirety, but they recognized that there was no alternative to using the Rōkiken's report as a starting point for discussions. To public-interest representatives, it seemed to offer a middle way.

The Chūkishin had no independent secretariat with which to gather information on its own. In the sense of a discrete body of staff, it had no secretariat at all, with any number of lower-ranking bureaucrats from MOL's Labor Standards Bureau serving the *shingikai* on an ad hoc basis. If it was virtually impossible for individual councilors to conduct original research by themselves, organizations did have some resources to fall back on. Nikkeiren formed a special committee for the occasion, trade associations had their own analytical resources, and labor's national centers conducted joint research. But because even a well-organized peak organization like Nikkeiren lacked the means to verify MOL figures, these organizations' research generally consisted of no more than polling their constituencies, so discussions necessarily proceeded on the basis of ministry data. "Private groups can't match the government in information," conceded the Nikkeiren representative. "It's the ministry that can best investigate working hours, and *shingikai* conclusions are based on that data."[34] It should be pointed out, though, that MOL always complied with councilors' requests for information, councilors felt that the information provided was impartial with respect to labor – management disputes, and those disputes focused less on what existing working conditions were than on how to change them.

Finding a mutually acceptable way of changing them proved to be no easy task. One employer representative described a consensual style of decision-making reminiscent of culturalist stereotypes:

> In Japan, labor and management aren't in confrontation, aren't archenemies. Fundamentally, we think we must cooperate. This is extremely difficult for foreigners to understand. . . . There's a fair amount of stiff debate in a *shingikai*, of course, but both labor and management are unhappy if we can't arrive at a settlement, so we make mutual efforts to unite behind something both sides can tolerate.[35]

The intricacies of this high-minded and harmonious method of conflict resolution were difficult for even some Japanese to understand, it seems: Another employer related that "many intransigent positions were taken at the

---

[33] Interview with Shimada Haruo.
[34] Interview with Matsuzaki Yoshinobu.
[35] Interview with Gō Ryōtarō.

shingikai."[36] In fact, labor and management clearly approached one another as antagonists, and even if the Chūkishin could gather their representatives at the same table, its formal meetings were never the locus of actual negotiations. As one employer councilor recalled, "There were just stirring words, formal declarations of positions [*tatemae*] at the *shingikai* bargaining table. The employer and labor sides didn't consult one another directly."[37] Bureaucrats joked that labor and management were "firing canons at each other from opposite sides of the Pacific."[38]

Japanese may often be uncomfortable with face-to-face confrontations, but more than cultural factors were at work. Unionists and employers participated explicitly as representatives of their respective organizations – "I was recommended by Dōmei, so I represent Dōmei's views"[39] was a common attitude – inhibiting the give-and-take of negotiations. One labor councilor described the extent to which his organization got involved in dictating his actions:

> Dōmei created a committee on the Labor Standards Act comprised of members sent from the unions in our national center. I report on the state of deliberations within the *shingikai*, and we debate what position Dōmei is to take. After discussion in this policy committee, we go to the Executive Council to confirm that this is what Dōmei wants for these reasons, then I attend the *shingikai* to state our opinion on what must be done.[40]

Managers, too, would report back to their firms and trade associations and in return receive specific requests for action.

To complicate matters further, the individual interest-group councilor was pulled in different directions. In the words of one employer:

> I speak out in the Chūkishin as an individual member, but behind those statements stands Nikkeiren, so I refrain from voicing completely personal opinions. Because a Nikkeiren representative is the same as an employer representative, in a broad sense it is correct to say that I'm participating as an employer representative. At the same time, though, because I also have to consider the national standpoint, which must bring together different opinions, when the employer side's position isn't reflected 100 percent, I'm afflicted with doubts over what to do.[41]

This dilemma was especially acute for another employer representative, whose remarks on the subject were not for attribution:

---

[36] Interview with Ogawa Yasuichi.
[37] Interview with Nishikiori Akira.
[38] Interview with Nozaki Kazuaki.
[39] Interview with Takagi Tsuyoshi.
[40] Interview with Satō Kōichi.
[41] Interview with Ogawa Yasuichi.

I've a position that must be presented in my capacity as an interest representative, and an opinion as an individual expert. There are inevitably two. On those occasions when they're the same, there's no problem. When they're different. . . . Although as an expert I want working hours to be like those in the West, I was told by my organization to oppose [the reduction of working hours] to the bitter end, so I strongly resisted the government in the *shingikai*. It was extremely painful for me. Even if my organization is opposed, society must advance. You can't stop progress. I didn't tell anyone in my organization that I was pushing for 46 hours [a week instead of 48]. No one knows. Opposition would inevitably have emerged, so I didn't disclose the contents of *shingikai* deliberations. I could have approached the LDP to take effective action, but I didn't. I couldn't swallow business's demands whole.

As these remarks suggest, councilors did enjoy some freedom of maneuver and sometimes strayed from the instructions of their constituencies. To facilitate negotiations, deliberations were closed to the public. Besides Chūkishin members and staff, the national centers Sōhyō, Dōmei, and Chūritsu Rōren and the management organizations Nikkeiren, the National Federation of Small Business Associations, and the Tokyo Chamber of Commerce were each permitted to send one observer to the *shingikai*. Otherwise, few people received permission to attend. Outside organizations that would have liked to pressure, or at least monitor, councilors were naturally displeased. An advocate of the rights of women workers complained:

In the end, of course, they release the labor and management opinions, but on what data were deliberations based? What were the points at issue? What was asserted by whom? We've no idea at all. We don't know what was said by union members, the so-called "labor representatives." Although we brought lists of demands, we don't know whether they even got to *shingikai* members. . . . Because we don't know what they're saying behind closed doors, we can't apply pressure. . . . A *shingikai* is meaningless if it doesn't reflect popular opinion.[42]

Although the closure of deliberations thus shielded councilors from outside pressure to some extent, it did not suffice, and in the end private mediation became necessary. Besides the separate, official *shingikai* sessions that public-interest representatives held with groups of labor and management councilors, there were also smaller, more intimate meetings, usually on an individual basis, where councilors could reveal their true intentions. MOL was in close contact with all of the participants, and bureaucrats played an active role in brokering a compromise agreement. Several councilors were careful to distinguish between public-interest representatives' "adjustment" (*chōsei*) of conflict-

---

[42] Interview with Konno Hisako.

ing interests and officials' "root-binding" (*nemawashi*). "We public-interest representatives don't conduct *nemawashi* – that's for bureaucrats. We have our own
opinion, and the bureaucrats conduct *nemawashi* on the basis of that," insisted
one councilor.[43]

Public-interest representatives sought to bridge the conflicting positions of
labor and management; conversely, the two sides actively courted their support.
One union councilor compared their role to that of "a sumo referee dispensing
wisdom" and went on to explain that "we must win public-interest representatives' understanding of [i.e., sympathy for] labor's position. . . . If public-
interest representatives tell us that our assertions are wrong, even if we force the
issue, the *shingikai* won't go in that direction."[44] Nozaki Kazuaki, director
general of MOL's Human Resources Development Bureau, described the
nemawashi process as follows:

> The first stage involved listening patiently to the demands of labor and
> management. The public-interest representatives and the Ministry of
> Labor analyzed, evaluated what the other representatives said. In this way,
> the public-interest representatives' first plan was put together. With this in
> hand, I'd visit [other] members at their offices and sound them out without
> revealing the plan, trying to fathom their unexpressed intentions. Although
> *nemawashi* is an extremely vague expression, you come to understand that
> "this employer member will yield for us on this in the end, but is adamant
> about that." Once you understand one side, you go to the other.[45]

The distinction between public-interest councilors' "adjustment" of conflicting interests and MOL's "root-binding" was largely artificial, however. As the
executors of labor policy, ministry officials were unlikely to restrict themselves
to serving as the passive foot soldiers of a group of outsiders. After all, they, too,
consider themselves to be representatives of the public interest, and in a survey
of central government bureaucrats, more respondents in MOL than in any other
ministry replied that an ability to negotiate was the most important qualification
for advancement (85 percent versus an average of 70.5 percent).[46] Ministry
bureaucrats themselves would sometimes suggest possible compromises, compromises that the interested parties did not feel free to dismiss out of hand. In
the words of the same union representative quoted earlier, "The ministry lets
you know that it wants things done *this* way, and if the labor side wants to be
understood, it will cooperate as much as possible."[47]

The distinction to be made between the respective functions of public-
interest representatives and ministry bureaucrats is not between substantive

[43] Interview with Kawaguchi Minoru.
[44] Interview with Satō Kōichi.
[45] Interview with Nozaki Kazuaki.
[46] Muramatsu (1981b), pp. 75–76.
[47] Interview with Satō Kōichi.

"adjustment" and persuasive "root-binding," but between interest adjustment carried on aboveboard (*omote*) and behind the scenes (*ura*).[48] Drawing on theatrical terminology, one of the public-interest representatives characterized MOL as the "mastermind" (*kuromaku* – literally, "black curtain" from behind which wires are pulled) of the labor-management agreement: "the government cunningly rotated the stage from behind without appearing in front."[49]

This is not to say that MOL was heavy-handed in its intervention. "They might tell us, 'On the basis of this information, you should conclude something along the lines of so and so,' but they weren't put out by our not doing so."[50] No councilor complained of having been pressured individually, and councilors interested in staying on were always reappointed to the *shingikai*. Rather than objecting to MOL's involvement in deliberations, some Chūkishin members may have actively sought it. In the words of one (OB) member,

> The Labor Standards administration is responsible for enforcement [of the act], and it's they who're most knowledgeable about the current situation. Because they're ultimately responsible for revision [of the act], it's only natural that the *shingikai* should ask how they want the law changed. The administration *couldn't* take the role of a spectator: their opinion was asked. And there was a desire in the *shingikai* to accommodate the ministry as much as possible.[51]

Even so, MOL was in no position to dominate the Chūkishin, if only because its own goals were none too clear. The ministry occupies an ambiguous position. On the one hand, MOL was originally established as a service ministry for workers, and because most LDP politicians have been hostile to the ministry, its officials have been more insulated from outside pressures than many of their colleagues.[52] On the other hand, though, its ostensible role as a mediator requires MOL to maintain relationships with employers as well as unions. Bureaucrats differed among themselves, and to the extent that a ministry position ever emerged, it did so in stages over the course of *shingikai* deliberations. There is no question that MOL wanted to adapt the Labor Standards Act to changes in the Japanese economy, reduce working hours, and accomplish this with the least inconvenience to business and itself, but its plans did not extend to the particulars of a legislative bill. It would not be much of an exaggeration to say that MOL had advanced the Rōkiken report as a basis for discussion because it was there: It offered a concrete plan of action, and although it is true that the plan was in no way contrary to bureaucratic thinking, the ministry was not committed to its every detail. Many of those details were to be altered

---

[48] Interviews with Tamura Ken'ichi and Tsuji Ken.
[49] Interview with Tsuji Ken.
[50] Interview with Gō Ryōtarō.
[51] Interview with Wada Katsumi.
[52] Garon and Mochizuki (1993), p. 157; Campbell (1989), p. 13.

by the Chūkishin's proposal, which then became the new government position.

Because MOL was most afraid that the wrangling between labor and management would scuttle revision of the act, the secretariat's primary goal was to help formulate a plan agreeable to everyone, so the proposals it made on its own initiative invariably took into account the positions of the interested parties. "Even if you say that the Ministry of Labor is realizing its goals, it sizes up the employers' situation and unions' way of thinking rather than having ministry bureaucrats' ideas come out one-sidedly," observed a Nikkeiren official. "The ministry plan will pass a significant percentage of the time because, to the extent they can compromise, the views of interest parties are adopted, too."[53]

The relationship of bureaucrats to public-interest councilors was marked by cooperation, not jealous competition. "It wasn't a matter of one or the other being on top. There were many points on which the two groups concurred."[54] And when they did not concur, they conferred. "The ministry was always discussing its views with us public-interest representatives. If we didn't like the bureaucrats' stand, they'd change it, and if bureaucrats thought our opinion was unreasonable, *we'd* change it. Both sides were gradually amending their views."[55] As one official explained, public-interest councilors and MOL bureaucrats formulated the *shingikai*'s final recommendations together:

> It would be a mistake to think that the public-interest representatives had to accept a plan foisted on them by the ministry. After the ministry would draft a plan, we [officials] told the public-interest representatives to amend it, to seek out labor and management views, or to ask for the opinions of legal specialists. A first plan, second plan, third plan – they were revised any number of times by the public-interest representatives. It's fair to say that there were large differences between the first plan considered and the one eventually produced by the public-interest representatives.[56]

What were the contents of that plan?

The report

When asked to evaluate the sources of interest-group power, a group of American state legislators mentioned group size and electoral influence most often, followed by organization and leadership, financial resources, importance of issues, lobbying skill, information, influence over public opinion, and group prestige (in that order).[57] In response to a written questionnaire, Chūkishin

---

[53] Interview with Ogawa Yasuichi.   [54] Interview with Nakai Takeshi.
[55] Interview with Kawaguchi Minoru.   [56] Interview with Nozaki Kazuaki.
[57] Kenneth Janda et al., *Legislative Politics in Indiana* (Bloomington: Indiana University Press, 1961).

Table 4-3. *Characteristics of parent organizations and Chūkishin deliberations*

To what extent do you think each of the following attributes of councilors' parent organizations influence advisory body deliberations?

No influence whatsoever 1 2 3 4 5 Extremely strong influence	($n = 17$)
1 Technical information presented	3.38
2 Ability to affect public opinion	3.35
3 Degree to which affected by the council's reprot	3.19
4 Ability to affect the ministries	3.0
5 Percent of the total eligible population represented	2.94
Ability to affect the Diet	2.94
6 Number of members	2.82
7 Prestige	2.71
8 Lobbying skill	2.25
9 Economic resources	1.44
To what extent does the principle of balance influence these deliberations?	3.5

members also ranked the influence of such factors on their deliberations (Table 4-3). In sharp contrast to the American results, councilors strongly emphasized the influence of technical information and a group's ability to affect public opinion, but they attributed the greatest significance to the principle of "balance" (*baransu*), or even-handedness. Accordingly, the Chūkishin's recommendations were the result of neither money politics nor principled debates; they involved a series of balances struck between the conflicting claims of labor and management.

It might be least confusing to discuss the content and outcomes of negotiations thematically, issue by issue, so legal working hours, variable workdays, overtime labor, and paid vacations are each dealt with in turn.

Legal working hours. That the Labor Standards Act expressly designate the 8-hour day and 40-hour week as legal maximums was the unions' key demand. Although they appreciated the fact that the government was finally taking the initiative in pushing for revision of the act, they resented the government's previous inactivity. "From our point of view, not to have revised the act by this late date is outrageous," protested one unionist.[58] Even now, labor felt, it was the shift to a service economy, the need to stimulate domestic demand, and the threat of foreign pressure that spurred MOL to action, not a desire to shorten working hours per se.

---

[58] Interview with Hondo Yoshio.

One union organization suggested taking advantage of the situation and making use of *shingikai* to bring international pressure to bear.[59] Within the Chūkishin, labor representatives did emphasize how the reduction of working hours had a diplomatic aspect in that Japan faced criticism from abroad for "social dumping," for failing to observe fair standards of international competition. Conversely, to meet union demands would be to meet International Labor Organization (ILO) standards[60] and advance international cooperation. "Foreign pressure was a major argument for the necessity of reducing working hours," asserted one union councilor.[61]

Employers, on the other hand, attributed foreign criticism to ignorance of Japan's unique employment system. Although anxious about trade frictions, they discounted the international ramifications of Japanese working conditions and did not feel obliged to follow ILO conventions that Japan and most other advanced industrial countries had never formally ratified. If business representatives felt no *direct* pressure from overseas, the Democratic Party's victory in America's 1986 congressional election exerted a subtle influence nonetheless. Nikkeiren's Matsuzaki stated publicly that "even if such pending problems as autos, rice, and beef catch fire, they won't have an effect on the debate over time reductions," but another employer councilor was concerned that there was "a possibility that [the United States] will come to take aim at as basic an issue as working hours."[62]

Whether or not foreign pressure was uppermost in councilors' minds, international comparisons clearly influenced both sides. Although major corporations had already achieved working hours comparable to those of their Western counterparts, a rapid reduction of legal working hours would raise the costs of small- and medium-sized companies facing competition from the NIEs, where working hours were longer (see Table 4-1) and wages were no more than a quarter of Japan's. If reductions preceded the rationalization and modernization of those smaller firms, an increasing number of them would shift production overseas, furthering deindustrialization and aggravating unemployment, employers warned. Undaunted, unions pointed out that the NIEs could not compare to Japan in labor productivity, and they sought conditions on a par with those of America and Britain. "Employers were thinking 70 percent of the Asian NIEs and 30 percent of the advanced countries; we [unions] were thinking 30 percent of the NIEs and 70 percent of the advanced countries."[63]

---

[59] Foote (1997).
[60] In 1919, when the fledgling ILO began to set nonbinding standards for working conditions, its very first convention called for the 8-hour day and 48-hour week in industry. Convention #30 (1930) extended these maximums to commercial establishments and office work, and the widespread unemployment of the Great Depression prompted advocacy of the 40-hour week in Convention #47 (1935).
[61] Interview with Hondo Yoshio.
[62] *Nihon Keizai Shinbun* (12 November 1986).   [63] Interview with Takagi Tsuyoshi.

Some labor councilors did concede that the unfairness of disparities within Japan was a more serious problem than disparities among nations, that the reduction of working hours was fundamentally a domestic problem. As one public-interest representative explained, "It's a fact that foreign pressure was one inducement for the government to act, but it's also true that we felt that we had to move in the direction of shorter hours anyway, even without foreign pressure."[64] Employers, too, realized that reductions were inevitable, if undesirable, acknowledging that the question was not whether to reduce labor time, but how and how much.

As for how, labor and management clashed over the necessity of writing new standards into law. "We recognized a need to improve the actual situation, not to change the law," an employer councilor noted. "Although legal working hours there are still 48 hours a week, Germans now work 38.5 hours [on average]. On that analogy, isn't our law all right?"[65] Because no objective basis exists for setting working hours, their reduction is a problem of how to distribute the fruits of productivity, and it would be unreasonable to enforce uniform reductions by law, regardless of performance. It would also be ineffective. Shortening legal working hours would simply increase overtime, hiking companies' costs without having the desired effect. Finally, employers time and again made an appeal to principle: Labor relations are best left to agreements independently arrived at by labor and management.

Such a laissez-faire stance was totally unacceptable to the unions, which demanded that the 40-hour workweek be written into law. Revision of the Labor Standards Act might in itself be insufficient – unions were all in favor of revising labor–management agreements, too – but it was necessary. Unlike West Germany, a much smaller percentage of the Japanese workforce was unionized, and given their narrow scope, labor agreements failed to equalize working conditions. Public opinion favored labor's position. When the PMO conducted a poll during *shingikai* deliberations in July 1986, over 70 percent of respondents with an opinion thought that revision of the act would be necessary if working hours were to be reduced.[66] More important, the Chūkishin's public-interest councilors also sided with labor, and the *shingikai*'s report supported legal revision despite management resistance.

Whether the law should expressly mention the 40-hour week was the "highest mountain" to scale in reaching a settlement.[67] Whereas the Rōkiken had suggested reducing legal working hours to 45 hours a week, the Chūkishin ultimately recommended shrinking the legal workweek to 46 hours "for the time being" and to 44 hours "as soon as possible." The 40-hour week was to be explicitly acknowledged, but only as a "goal" to be achieved at some unspecified

[64] Interview with Watanabe Michiko.
[65] Interview with Gō Ryōtarō.
[66] Hiraga (1987), p. 211.   [67] Kawaguchi M. (1987), p. 5.

time in the future. Small- and medium-sized enterprises should enjoy an indefinitely long grace period before having to observe the new standards, the *shingikai* concluded. Since the Rōkiken report had appeared in December 1985, the background to the debate had shifted: The Maekawa Report and other calls to action had appeared, rapid appreciation of the yen in the wake of the Plaza Accord had lent urgency to the expansion of domestic demand, and international criticism had mounted. "If it had been last year, a 45-hour week probably would have been the limit. Western pressure on Japan became a favorable wind behind working-hour reductions," explained a MOL staffer.[68]

There were several reasons for implementing the reduction in stages, however. First, whereas the 45-hour week seemed like a half-measure, a dead end, an average 46-hour week could easily be implemented by providing a two-day weekend once a month and an average 44-hour week by providing a two-day weekend twice a month. Second, the timing of revision was inauspicious in that many small- and medium-sized firms were already struggling with rapid appreciation of the yen and intensified competition from the NIEs. During the "high-yen [*endaka*] slump," they were incapable of raising either productivity or prices in order to absorb the increased costs that would accompany time reductions. Without a grace period, they would face an unenviable choice between penal sanctions and going under. Widespread bankruptcies among smaller firms would inevitably lead to increased unemployment, and because a disproportionate number of older workers and women worked in the kinds of companies suffering from the downturn, the victims would be those people least likely to find work elsewhere.

Although union representatives granted that concessions to small business might be necessary, they unsuccessfully sought to restrict them. Labor councilors favored limiting the grace period to businesses with fewer than 100 workers or, better yet, distinguishing among different industries rather than among enterprises of different size. Unions were more upset with the ambiguity surrounding the grace period's duration than with its scope, however. If it turned out to be too lengthy, revision of the act would degenerate into a formal exercise, and there was a danger of its perpetuating overlong working hours rather than correcting them.

The real ambiguity at the heart of the Chūkishin's recommendations was the lack of a timetable for achieving the 40-hour week. The Labor Standards Act was a means of ratifying rather than forcing change in the eyes of many (nonlabor) councilors, and it seemed meaningless to write into law what would have been an arbitrary schedule when no one could accurately predict future business trends and their effect on working conditions. More than even the employers, perhaps, Professor Shirai was unyielding on this point:

---

[68] *Mainichi Shinbun* (1 March 1987).

If conditions of long working hours become established over a lengthy period, even if you ignore that situation and resolve on a hasty time reduction by law, that law will have no effect. A social consensus on that law's propriety will be insufficiently formed, and if there are many violators, it will be impossible to expose and punish them all. . . . Legal working hours are by nature standardizations of improvements in actual working hours made through the independent efforts of the concerned workers and employers or through the guidance of labor administration after those improved levels have spread to a reasonable degree. Rightfully, they must chase after actual conditions.[69]

This attitude, that law should ratify social change rather than force it, is common in Japan.[70]

Such principles aside, drafting a precise timetable for working hour reductions was not an option for the Chūkishin. If it had been extremely difficult to establish the simple "goal" of a 40-hour week, it was downright impossible for labor and management to agree on specific dates. While making allowances for the difficulties involved, unions fought to move to a 44-hour week by government ordinance immediately and to realize the 40-hour week within a designated period, like five or six years. Employers, on the other hand, were thinking of some time in the twenty-first century, and there was no neutral basis on which the public-interest councilors could choose some intervening date. Only at the very last meeting of the *shingikai* did the labor representatives reluctantly agree to the report's nebulous formula.

In retrospect, management resistance to the reduction of legal working hours takes on the aura of a rear-guard action – a successful rear-guard action. As one employer councilor explained, "Of course we confronted the unions, but it's in the nature of things for working hours to decrease, so changing the act was inevitable. The main point for management was *when* working hours were to be reduced, the timing of the move. . . . In that sense, we don't consider revision of the act a defeat."[71] No one else considered it a defeat for management, either. In truth, the attention of employer representatives was focused elsewhere. "The inclusion of provisions on flexibility was more important to us than the reduction of working hours by law. Our feeling was, let's acknowledge the legislation of shorter working hours if in return we get an end to the traditional way of thinking about a uniform eight-hour day."[72] That is exactly what they got.

Variable working hours. The government must abolish outworn limits on the length of the workday and permit labor–management agreements that would

[69] Shirai (1987a), p. 3.
[70] Upham (1987), pp. 152, 208.
[71] Interview with Nibuya Ryū.
[72] Interview with Gō Ryōtarō.

average working hours over long periods of time, employers argued. In comparative perspective, that demand was unexceptional. Various Western countries sanction the flexible distribution of working hours and accord a fair degree of freedom to the private parties concerned. Even a year-long system is provided for in the United States, Canada, and France, and Britain leaves the regulation of working hours entirely to labor–management agreements.[73]

The Rōkiken report had justified variability with the argument that reductions in working hours could be expected from a more effective distribution of labor time, and some of the public-interest and even union councilors appear to have shared that hope. Management naturally encouraged that hope, but it demanded greater flexibility in order to cut costs, not hours. "You can't expect a decrease in regular working hours," one employer warned. "It's overtime that will decrease, and with a decrease in overtime, there's the possibility of reducing costs through a drop in the wage premium [i.e., overtime compensation] we'll have to pay."[74]

At Japanese companies, bonuses typically account for a significant fraction of total compensation but are not taken into account in calculating overtime compensation, so the effective wage premium for most workers is well under 20 percent.[75] Nevertheless, reductions in overtime pay promised employers no small savings. According to MOL statistics, an estimated 39.49 million workers earned a total of ¥10.58 trillion ($75.6 billion) in overtime compensation in 1985. Under a three-month variable system that would average 40 hours a week, the mean monthly overtime of a full-time worker would fall from 14.8 to 4.4 hours and his or her extra monthly earnings from ¥22,332 ($160) to ¥6,589 ($47). In large firms whose workweeks were already 40 hours or less, variable hours could reduce overtime – and overtime compensation – without having any effect whatsoever on employees' total working hours. If all "constant" overtime (i.e., extra labor time that does not vary with business conditions) were included in variable working hour schemes, corporate Japan would save an estimated ¥8 trillion ($57.1 billion).[76] Employers felt that these savings at the worker's expense were necessary to cope with the cost increases that would accompany reductions in working hours. Labor begged to differ.

The Rōkiken had suggested recognition of a three-month system of variable hours where labor agreed to it. Just as employer councilors resisted to the end reduction of the legal workweek to 40 hours and finally delayed its implementation, labor councilors resisted to the end management demands for the widespread and unlimited adoption of variable working hours and finally succeeded

---

[73] Although a 1996 ruling of the European Court of Justice mandated a maximum 48-hour week unless employers and unions agree otherwise, Britain's Conservative government rejected the ruling. *The New York Times* (14 November 1996).
[74] Interview with Nibuya Ryū.
[75] Foote (1997).   [76] *Akahata* (22 April 1987); *Akahata* (9 August 1987).

in attaching the preconditions of labor agreement, ministry regulation, and an average workweek of 40 hours (44 hours for small- and medium-sized enterprises). The transaction was never explicit, but these two concessions were, in effect, made in return for one another.

Overtime labor. Whereas management opposed any hourly limits on overtime or an increase in the wage premium, unions pointed to the major contribution overtime made to Japan's long working hours. Although one of the charms of variable working hours for management was its promise to *reduce* overtime, there remained the danger that variable working hours could at least occasionally be *combined* with overtime, and unions demanded legal limitations. The Rōkiken had emphasized achievement of the five-day week over reductions in overtime and spoke vaguely of increasing the wage premium for weekend labor. In its final recommendations, the Chūkishin, too, left the reduction of overtime and holiday labor to the independent efforts of labor and management, and agreed only to "investigate" limitations on annual overtime hours.

Union demands were never much discussed, labor councilors' having agreed to postpone deliberation on overtime. There were several reasons for unions' tractability. Just as in the timing of working hour reductions, Professor Shirai strongly opposed regulating overtime and holiday labor or hiking the wage premium because actual conditions had yet to advance much beyond the law, and in 1986, 83 percent of all firms paid no more than the 25 percent wage premium laid down four decades before.[77] It was the unions that he blamed for this: "Because labor unions have the right to engage in collective bargaining and to strike, it goes without saying that these are matters that should be standardized after they are won independently. But as everyone knows, the past record of our country's unions on this point . . . is meager."[78]

Why was unions' record so "meager"? Both working hour reductions and an increase in the wage premium promised to raise employers' costs, and unions gave precedence to the former. More important was the effect that regulation of overtime would have on *workers'* finances. Employer councilors argued:

> Demands for upper limits on overtime were no more than a pretense [*tatemae*]. For the individual, a reduction in overtime means a reduction in income – it would be a problem. It's not just a matter of workers' being *forced* to do overtime. And it would be unfair for the wage premium to get too high. Although some jobs allow for a lot of overtime, for good pay, that's a cause for jealousy among workers without such opportunities.[79]

[77] Sōhyō et al., v. 1 (1986), p. 55.
[78] Shirai (1987a), p. 10.
[79] Interview with Nakai Takeshi.

Labor councilors admitted that unions were not united on the issue. There was even some debate as to whether increasing the wage premium might not lead workers to *increase* the hours of overtime that they worked.

Paid vacations. Management asserted that an increase beyond the current six days of paid leave would hamper the supervision of personnel and impose a one-sided cost increase without guaranteeing a compensatory improvement in productivity. The expansion of vacation time should await workers' taking advantage of more of the days to which they were already entitled. An ILO convention from 1970 had recommended a minimum of three full workweeks of paid vacation, however, and unions demanded that any employee who had worked continuously for at least a year should be eligible for 20 days' paid leave. Labor councilors had to acknowledge workers' low rate of vacation-taking but pointed out that the average concealed significant generational differences. Young people do take nearly all the vacations to which they are entitled, so an increase in the minimum would enhance workers' leisure opportunities in the future, they reasoned.

The Rōkiken had proposed hiking the minimum from six days to ten and prorating the vacations of part-time workers. Because other councilors simply did not take labor's aggressive demands seriously, unions had no choice but to yield in favor of the Rōkiken's compromise, with the Chūkishin adding only that small- and medium-sized enterprises should enjoy a "reasonable" grace period in moving to the higher standards.

On 10 December 1986, at its final plenary session, the Chūkishin presented its proposals to Minister of Labor Hirai Takayuki. No member had opposed adoption of the report just outlined. This lack of open resistance should not be mistaken for unanimous support: Both sides were dissatisfied. Nevertheless, neither labor nor management felt it had much to gain by blocking passage of the compromise proposals. They had each won concessions on the points of greatest concern to them: the reduction of legal working hours and the introduction of greater flexibility in the distribution of those hours. Revision of the Labor Standards Act and the consequent realization of those gains would be impossible if the *shingikai* failed to unite behind a single set of recommendations, and the Chūkishin's proposals went to the limit of what a tripartite body could agree upon.

Coercion as well as calculation was involved. Japanese often obscure this by falling back on culturalist language in their descriptions of conflict resolution. In the words of the employer representative whose small-business constituency had opposed – and would continue to oppose – change most vehemently, "While it was possible for me to resist, that would have destroyed harmony. Although my organization objected, it was inevitable that we'd agree in the end."

Agree passively, but agree. In this way, a consensus was achieved. It's very difficult for Westerners to comprehend."[80] What these remarks only hint at, and what more dewy-eyed accounts of Japanese decisionmaking overlook entirely, is that opponents of an ostensible compromise face censure for intransigence and that acquiescence must not be confused with support.

Because the public-interest councilors were apparently selfless, and because their compromise proposal provided a (temporary) means of achieving the norm of consensus, rejecting their proposal would have been portrayed as a selfish embrace of conflict. Further, although there was no legal bar to the Chūkishin's submitting majority and minority reports, or even three separate reports from the *shingikai*'s three sides, Professor Shirai stubbornly insisted on a unified set of recommendations, arguing that a divided report would both delay and disrupt revision of the law. Interest-group representatives complied willy-nilly. MOL's Nozaki, who helped guide deliberations to a conclusion, observed that "employers were loath to write the 40-hour week into law. They were opposed to the end of the end. The worst case would have been if they'd walked out and destroyed everything, but then they'd have incurred criticism by the public. It would have been very risky for either labor or management" to have refused to yield.[81] Nikkeiren's Matsuzaki concurred: "Neither employers nor labor really agreed with the final proposals, but with the mass media announcing the public-interest representatives' plan, we couldn't raise objections. Although both sides were put out, people said that we tacitly approved."[82] To some extent, it was thus consensus formation by intimidation that won formal interest-group approval of the compromise plan.

The road to parliament

The reception this plan received made abundantly clear just how grudging participants' approval had been. Taking the same diametrically opposed positions they had staked out during *shingikai* deliberations, both sides publicly denounced crucial aspects of the Chūkishin's compromise plan. Rather than signifying a final resolution, agreement had only advanced debate from the confines of an advisory body to a wider, more public arena where the battle could be joined once again. The employer councilors were especially vocal in their criticism; it was sometimes difficult to recognize in them the *shingikai* members who had just approved the recommendations they now decried.

Press reaction to the council's recommendations was swift and reproachful. The left-leaning *Asahi Shinbun* detected "a deep coloring" of management influence in the proposals and felt that the *shingikai* was "crying wine and selling

---

[80] Interview with Nishikiori Akira.
[81] Interview with Nozaki Kazuaki.
[82] Interview with Matsuzaki Yoshinobu.

vinegar." The *Nihon Keizai Shinbun*, Japan's *Wall Street Journal*, was not much more forgiving. Although it lauded the Chūkishin's "bold proposals," should Japan procrastinate in moving beyond the provisional goal of a 46-hour week, "we cannot say that the revisions will have had much meaning."[83] From the start, the press had emphasized the international angle. Behind the council's report lay foreign criticism of Japanese as "worker bees living in rabbit hutches" (sic) and the need for the country to live up to the commitments it had made in the Maekawa Report. The reduction of working hours would serve as the "trump card" of the domestic demand expansion that would end economic frictions.[84] Government officials did nothing to discourage this interpretation. "From the perspective of [Japan's] international status as an advanced country, time reduction is a task that cannot be avoided," proclaimed MOL's Nozaki. Even the employer councilors of the Chūkishin, who in private conversations minimized the weight of such considerations, seconded these notions with public statements like "We must think of Japan's international station."[85] In this case, as in so many others, it was easier to exaggerate the role of foreign pressure in forcing change than to address openly the domestic issues that really lay at the root of the controversy, and management representatives could use an excuse to justify their concessions.

Labor won an unexpected boost when the LDP's Working Hours Problem Subcommittee won approval from PARC's Labor Division on 11 December for a proposal to set working hours at 46 hours a week "at present," consider shifting to 44 hours three years after amending the Labor Standards Act, and realize the 40-hour week within ten years. "In light of the current of the times, this is an objective that must be achieved, that can be achieved," Chairman Niwa announced.[86] The Working Hours Problem Subcommittee suggested that MOL use administrative guidance to ensure that the reduction in legal working hours be accompanied by a reduction in actual working hours. (It was reported that same day that MOL was strengthening its administrative guidance to limit overtime to 50 hours a month, and that it would set an upper limit to total annual hours, too.[87]) Most surprisingly, the LDP subcommittee also recommended that small- and medium-sized enterprises observe the new standards without the benefit of a grace period. "Whenever you draw a distinction, differentials never shrink," Chairman Niwa argued. "We won't hesitate to yank along small- and medium-sized enterprises on time reductions. We cannot agree to the establishment of exceptions to the rule."[88]

[83] *Asahi Shinbun* (11 December 1986); *Nihon Keizai Shinbun* (11 December 1986).
[84] *Asahi Shinbun* (30 November 1986); *Yomiuri Shinbun* (5 August 1986).
[85] *Nihon Keizai Shinbun* (12 November 1986); *Nihon Keizai Shinbun* (11 December 1986); *Sankei Shinbun* (11 December 1986).
[86] *Asahi Shinbun* (12 December 1986).
[87] *Nihon Keizai Shinbun* (11 December 1986).
[88] *Asahi Shinbun* (12 December 1986); *Nihon Keizai Shinbun* (12 December 1986).

The LDP has generally refrained from intervening in industrial relations and, as measured by MOL's declining budget share over the years of LDP rule, the weight of labor policy was becoming lighter and lighter at the national level.[89] What accounts for these apparent concessions to unions from the party of its opponents?

Even before MOL's labor standards bureau chief submitted the Rōkiken's report to the Chūkishin, he had consulted with the chair of the PARC Labor Division, Ōtsubo Ken'ichirō. Ōtsubo's committee could have taken up the report before the council began deliberating, but it was decided to consult the *shingikai* first, and the PARC's Labor Division did no more than receive progress reports on the course of Chūkishin deliberations and organize a study group (including ministry officials) without taking a position of its own. Conservative MPs could not contact the *shingikai* without opposition parties' demanding the right to discuss matters with the council themselves, and any expression of party views prior to the emergence of a detailed plan would have opened the LDP to charges of meddling.

Ōtsubo supported revision of the act, and he was not alone. Although some people refer offhandedly to a "social and labor affairs tribe" (*sharō zoku*), it is not comparable to the construction or agriculture tribe: Including problems of labor relations, social welfare, and medical care, its purview is very diverse, and conservative MPs shared almost no interest relation with unions, which were the mainstay of the opposition parties. Nevertheless, there were some conservative representatives (like former MOL or Health and Welfare bureaucrats) who were attentive to labor problems and had "pipes" to moderate union organizations, and the LDP did meet periodically with labor leaders to exchange views. Although the national centers never negotiated directly with the party on working hours, the LDP was well aware of their thinking.

There was no denying that working conditions in Japan were inferior to those prevailing in the West. "When you start comparing economic statistics, Japan isn't advanced, so there was always a latent body of opinion within the LDP, too, that something had to be done about this," explained Ōtsubo.[90] But "the LDP was caught between a rock and a hard place."[91] On the one hand, the cabinet had supported working hour reductions to maintain and expand employment opportunities as early as 1979, even some conservative politicians felt that employers were being "extremely disagreeable" over the revision of labor standards,[92] and MPs from cities with modern industries approved of shorter hours. On the other hand, small- and medium-sized enterprises were violently opposed, and they had many friends within the party.

[89] Knoke et al. (1996), p. 54.
[90] Interview with Ōtsubo Ken'ichirō.
[91] Interview with Takagi Tsuyoshi.
[92] Interview with Wada Katsumi.

The small-business sector had negotiated a "social contract" with conservative politicians during the first half of the 1950s. An important swing constituency, "small-business associations exchanged their political power (the ability to mobilize voters) for governmental policies that would compensate for their weaknesses in the marketplace."[93] To expand its base of organizational networks, the LDP passed laws promoting the formation of small-business associations, and pressure from those associations brought such payoffs as subsidies, noncollateralized loans, regulation of predatory behavior by large firms, and lax law enforcement that permitted tax evasion and labor abuses.[94] Big business and MITI acquiesced in these distributive politics because they helped maintain LDP dominance and did not substantially deflect the course of industrial policy. Although under fire, this social contract survived into the 1980s. LDP policies maintained the sector in the face of massive economic restructuring, and small-business holders were, along with farmers, the party's most vigorous supporters. Despite having half the population of the United States, Japan had about the same number of small-scale enterprises in the early 1980s, and although small-business proprietors accounted for only 12.4 percent of the total electorate, they made up 28.4 percent of the party's membership in 1981.[95]

PARC's Working Hours Subcommittee met six times, attracting 30 or 40 more MPs than its official membership of about 20. "At the last meeting or two, those in favor and those opposed were shouting. The debate was so fierce that desks were overturned and ashtrays sent flying," related one observer.[96] Because the social and labor affairs tribe clusters there, PARC's Labor Division inevitably tends to reflect its views, and the subcommittee ultimately pushed through its plan despite its many opponents. The Labor Division is only one of many in PARC, however; all committee decisions must be approved by the LDP's Policy and Executive Councils; and the higher echelons of the party did not share the Labor Division's enthusiasm for speedy, uniform reductions in working hours. Although the party was eventually to make concessions that actually went beyond the Chūkishin's recommendations, it was not about to tip its hand by pressuring MOL to amend the council's proposals before Diet deliberations had even begun.

On 7 February 1987, MOL submitted to the Chūkishin the outline of a legislative bill for revision of the Labor Standards Act. It differed from the council's December proposals in details alone. Whereas PARC's Labor Division had endorsed uniform enforcement of the new standards, for example, the bill instead followed the Chūkishin's original recommendation in allowing for the exemption of enterprises in industries or of a scale to be decreed by MOL. Far more significant, even though two of the bill's main provisions stipulated that

---

[93] Garon and Mochizuki (1993), p. 146.
[94] Allinson (1993b), p. 44. See Calder (1988).
[95] Inoguchi (1990), pp. 206, 208–9.   [96] Interview with Nozaki Kazuaki.

"employers are forbidden to make their employees work more than 40 hours a week . . . [or] more than eight hours a day every day of the week" (illustrating the new priority given to regulation of the workweek over the workday), a supplementary provision of the bill added the qualification that "for the time being, working hours will be set by decree and shortened by stages, taking into consideration workers' welfare, trends in working hours, and other conditions."[97] In apparent violation of Article 27 of the Japanese constitution, which stipulates that standards for hours and other working conditions "shall be fixed by law," the bill nowhere indicated what provisional hours the decrees would set.

MOL's legislative bill thus left the transition to the 40-hour week more obscure than ever. In an article entitled "Japanese-Style Deliberateness Will No Longer Be Honored," the *Yomiuri Shinbun* warned of the dangers of equivocation:

> Here is a method of repainting a sign for Western countries in the main provision, parrying their criticisms of "overwork," when actually taking into consideration [in the supplementary provisions] the small- and medium-sized enterprises that are lagging in time reduction. . . . We can praise the outstanding resourcefulness of Japanese bureaucrats and their distinction between outward- and inward-directed faces, but this method will not be admissible forever.[98]

A member of the Chūkishin, on the other hand, emphasized the domestic, rather than the international, expediency of obscurity: "Right from the start, managers were saying that [working hour reductions] must not be decided by law, so as much as possible, it was left unclear to gain their approval."[99] MOL itself was not of one mind over whether to link time reductions to improvements in productivity or to try and expedite the process.[100] Another suggested explanation for MOL's recourse to ordinances was that with labor and management deadlocked, it was necessary for the ministry to take the initiative. Or perhaps MOL simply wanted to avoid being constrained in its enforcement of the act: Because it is typically bureaucrats rather than politicians who take the lead in lawmaking, it is *generally* the case that Japanese legislation leaves a great deal of room for administrative discretion.

In any event, the Chūkishin held a plenary session on 21 February to deliberate on the outline of MOL's bill. To soften labor opposition, the ministry disclosed that it anticipated an immediate 40- to 50-hour reduction in average annual working hours on the basis of its bill, intended to limit overtime to less than the prevailing (nonstatutory) standard of 50 hours a month through the use

---

[97] Hiraga (1987), pp. 164–69.
[98] *Yomiuri Shinbun* (13 February 1987).
[99] Interview with Endō Yoshikazu.
[100] *Mainichi Shinbun* (1 March 1987).

of increased administrative guidance, and would be vigilant in monitoring firms' use of variable working hours. Union representatives would have preferred the law to have been more specific, but they did not want to jeopardize their gains and were counting on being able to review implementation of the new standards at a later date. Although both employer and labor councilors attached short commentaries to the report that essentially repeated their earlier reservations, the council unanimously approved MOL's outline on 28 February 1987.

Nevertheless, voices began to be heard even within the LDP that the ministry was too conservative in refusing to commit itself to a clear schedule, and these voices became a chorus as talk of working hour reductions picked up in the spring. Under the same Maekawa Haruo, the Council on the Economy's Special Committee on Economic Restructuring issued what was to become known as the New Maekawa Report on 14 May. In order to stimulate consumption and ease trade frictions, it recommended the reduction of working hours to 1,800 a year "as soon as possible, and no later than the end of the century" through five-day workweeks and the granting of 20 days' annual paid vacation. That same month, the Cabinet Council on Economic Policy decided to reduce working hours by spreading the five-day week through early revision of the Labor Standards Act, promotion of independent labor–management efforts, and the granting of two-day weekends to civil servants every other week. By this time, even the Construction Committees of both houses of the Diet were resolving to increase leisure time. Because shorter working hours were expected to contribute to the expansion of domestic demand and the reduction of trade frictions, Prime Minister Nakasone promised early legislation of the five-day week when he attended the G-7 economic summit in June. At a news conference held for the foreign press, Nakasone acknowledged that "if Japan has a flaw, it's that working hours are long and vacations are few,"[101] and he pointed to the proposed revision of the Labor Standards Act as evidence of his determination to rectify these shortcomings.

Bows to the foreign audience notwithstanding, policymakers had neglected a sizable domestic constituency that was less concerned with the reduction of working hours than with the introduction of greater variability to those that remained. If men worried about loss of income, women feared that they would no longer be able to hold down full-time jobs at all. In the past, the act had limited women workers' overtime to 2 hours a day, 6 hours a week, and 150 hours a year. Ironically, the Equal Employment Opportunity Act of 1985 actually worsened women's working conditions by ending the limitation on daily overtime, changing the weekly limit to a maximum of 24 hours over four weeks

---

[101] *Tōkyō Shinbun* (5 June 1987, evening).

(for women outside manufacturing), and abolishing all limitations for certain managerial and professional positions. With the loosening of regulations, many businesses began to demand more overtime of their female employees, trying to sift out those women who could work "like a man" from those who could not.

Working mothers in particular were at risk. Two-thirds of working women were married and more than 60 percent of them were raising children,[102] and they were hard pressed to juggle both job and family responsibilities. Estimated to do only one-half to one-third as much housework as their Western counterparts, Japanese men were not much help: According to MOL statistics from 1981, working men spent 7 minutes a day on housework and child care to working women's 2 hours and 36 minutes, and 5 minutes on shopping to women's 29 minutes.[103] Day-care centers normally closed at 5:00 P.M., and the only alternatives were "baby hotels" or "baby salons" to which national standards for day care did not apply. With flexibilization and the extension of regular hours, though, working mothers would not be able to leave early without having their pay docked, and they would naturally be the first targets for dismissal should layoffs become necessary. Increasing numbers of women who already had trouble working as regular employees were becoming part-timers (classified as anyone who averages fewer than 35 hours a week) or temps, sometimes going back to work at the same companies for half their previous wages and without such benefits as unemployment and health insurance or a formal system of retirement allowances. In 1987, 70 percent of Japan's part-time workers were women.[104]

These were all bread-and-butter issues for the more than one-third of the Japanese workforce that women constituted, and their opposition to variable working hours was strenuous, but problems peculiar to women had never been a major subject of discussion at the Chūkishin, and both the *shingikai* and MOL were startled by the vehemence of their reaction. Although the unions were responsible for representing the interests of women workers in the council, the labor delegation included no women: Female union officials were rare, and only 6.7 percent of all *shingikai* members were women in 1988.[105] "Male Japanese workers aren't grappling with the problems of women workers very enthusiastically," observed the public-interest representative Watanabe, the only female councilor, and even she did not consider herself to be a representative of women in particular, preferring to consider the interests of "men and women together, as human beings."[106]

---

[102] *Daily Yomiuri* (11 July 1988); *Mainichi Shinbun* (26 May 1987).
[103] *Akahata* (11 June 1987).
[104] *Daily Yomiuri* (13 October 1987).
[105] *Japan Times Weekly Overseas Edition* (2 August 1989). By 1995, that figure had risen to 13.1, more than twice the 6.1 percent of Diet seats that women representatives occupied (Nakanishi, 1995).
[106] Interview with Watanabe Michiko.

Some labor councilors pled guilty. "We had strict orders from the Women's Bureau [of Sōhyō], and we raised the issue [of variable working hours], but only weakly. There was insufficient consideration of, and sympathy for, the situation faced by women workers," confessed one unionist.[107] Employer councilors, on the other hand, evinced little interest in the issue and tended to attribute women's opposition to variable working hours to a lack of understanding and union obstructionism:

> During the deliberation process, I received stacks of postcards against [variable working hours]. They were all from women. But they were high-school teachers, staffers in local governments – people whose occupations had scarcely any relation to variable hours. I don't understand why they should have been opposed. It wasn't a matter of those individuals being opposed. Because their organizations were against it, they were made to send [those postcards] by their unions. When I met such people, spoke with them, asked them if they were really opposed, they'd say, "I don't know."[108]

Some women knew. The labor lawyer Nakajima Michiko gained some prominence as a result of her outspoken attacks on managers' proposal to dispense with the eight-hour day:

> It is equivalent to our approaching the day when if you work, you must not bear or raise children, and if you want to bear children, you must quit and become a part-timer.
>   Life is led from day to day. . . . If we ignore this and decide working hours on the basis of the firm's convenience alone, women who shoulder the responsibility for life will not be able to work, families will not be able to eat together, fathers and children will never be able to see each other – what on earth will happen?
>   . . . Are the screams of women and children totally inaudible to the Ministry of Labor and *shingikai* that prepare legislation? . . . If my opinion is wrong, or there is no need to worry, by all means answer me.[109]

Nakajima's appeal did not go unanswered: MOL's Nozaki offered a reply. Variable working hours were not being introduced for the first time: The law already provided for a four-week system that 10 percent of large-scale enterprises had adopted without the dire consequences feared by women. Besides, companies could implement the new system only if labor agreed and if workweeks averaged no more than 40 hours (44 hours in small- and medium-sized establishments), two preconditions never required in the past. It was already normal for the workday and workweek to be flexibilized in foreign

---

[107] Interview with Shimizu Eiichi.
[108] Interview with Gō Ryōtarō.
[109] *Yomiuri Shinbun* (19 March 1987).

countries like America and France, and MOL could be trusted to forestall any abuses.[110]

Nozaki's arguments were accurate, reasonable – and irrelevant. He acknowledged that revisions of the act were "a little difficult to understand"; for MOL bureaucrats, so were the concerns of working women, it seems. They continued to treat women's protests as the result of a misunderstanding. At a question-and-answer session held for women's representatives at the end of May, officials asserted that it was "inconceivable" that employers would take advantage of the three-month system to extend the workday excessively; to the women, this betrayed "a total ignorance of workplace realties, or weakmindedness in the face of such knowledge." The bureaucrats pointed out that the Labor Standards Act already recognized 30 minutes of the morning and afternoon as child-rearing time that people could use to take children to and from day-care facilities; the women's representatives pointed out that these periods were insufficient. Because the introduction of variable hours required labor agreement, it would be impossible for workers' interests to suffer, MOL argued; labor and management were not equally matched, the women countered. The women's representatives got the impression that "the content of [the ministry's] answers was not such as a woman would understand from the actual experience of working on the job."[111]

Meanwhile, the mainstream of the labor movement continued to press its claims. On 21 June, Sōhyō, Dōmei, Chūritsu Rōren, Shinsanbetsu, and Zenmin Rōkyō compiled a joint set of goals that included starting reduction of the legal workweek from 44 hours a week, moving to 40 hours within three years, and setting a midterm goal of achieving 1,800 average annual working hours by 1993. Unions were unusually successful in cooperating with one another during this period. Organized labor played a major role in the broad-based and ultimately victorious campaign to block imposition of a sales tax, and private-sector unions were preparing to inaugurate Rengō, the new, inclusive national center. Since the Chūkishin had issued its report, increased foreign pressure for the expansion of domestic demand and the New Maekawa Report had bolstered labor's case.

The government showed unions unwonted attention. When the secretaries general of the five labor organizations met with Minister of Labor Hirai on the afternoon of 30 June to present their demands, he assured them that MOL's and the New Maekawa Report's ways of thinking were "basically the same" and that he would deal with their proposals "constructively." Hirai hosted a two-hour meeting that evening between the union leaders and Prime Minister Nakasone, the first such meeting since November 1985. Even so, when Nakasone acknowledged that "the reduction of working hours isn't something that must be left entirely to the labor and management of individual enterprises: if it does not

---

[110] Ibid. (27 March 1987).
[111] *Fujin Shinbun* (10 June 1987).

advance by means of government leadership to a certain extent, the path will be very difficult to open," he glossed over the distinction between legislation and administrative guidance, and controversial topics were not addressed during the meeting.[112]

Momentum continued to build nonetheless. The five labor organizations called on employees around the country to gather at their workplaces on the day that the government was to explain its bill to the Diet. That was unprecedented, the first time that they had all raised a common goal and called for simultaneous workplace meetings, and unions were enthusiastic. "Shortening working hours is the voice of heaven," Sōhyō's secretary general warned at a 30 July rally. "If Japan does not resolutely promote time reductions, it will be isolated in international society."[113] Five mass media unions set out to ensure just that. They hit upon a novel tactic: appealing to international public opinion by taking out advertisements in the main newspapers of America, Britain, Germany, France, and Italy that condemned the proposed revisions of the act. The first advertisement occupied a half page of *The New York Times* on 20 August:

> WHO SAID "YOU'VE COME A LONG WAY, BABY"? We haven't really. . . . We believe that [Japan's] long hours . . . constitute one of the major causes behind the current trade imbalance between Japan and the U.S., and we fear that this new legislation may well worsen the situation. . . . We call for international solidarity to rectify the labor policy of the Japanese Government so that we will have NO MORE UNFAIR COMPETITION and a solution to the Japan – U.S. trade imbalance.[114]

Although the fact that unions were openly inviting foreign pressure attracted notice in Japan, it is unlikely that this ploy had much effect on the domestic debate.

On the eve of Diet deliberations, a host of official reports and estimates appeared both inside and outside Japan that underlined the potential benefits of reduced working hours. Even as the "high-yen recession" was raising concern over unemployment, the Organization for Economic Cooperation and Development (OECD) released a statement on 1 July emphasizing that "in order to direct advantages arising from the technical revolution towards the improvement of employment, [Japan] must accelerate time reductions." The Economic Planning Agency (EPA) seconded that conclusion, estimating that every 1 percent reduction in working hours would bring a 0.43 percent increase in employment.[115]

Other EPA calculations showed that the reduction of working hours would increase employment opportunities for the elderly in particular. The agency

---

[112] *Asahi Shinbun* and *Tōkyō Shinbun* (1 July 1987).
[113] *Mainichi Shinbun* (31 July 1987).
[114] *The New York Times* (20 August 1987).
[115] *Asahi Shinbun* (2 July 1987).

announced on 15 July that employment opportunities for senior citizens would rise by 14.7 percent if the average salaried worker in Japan were to work 1,800 hours a year instead of the prevailing 2,100.[116] With Japan graying demographically, such an improvement was much to be desired. Even as the fraction of the population over 65 years of age rose from 7.9 percent in 1975 to 10.1 percent in 1985 (and was projected to soar to 21.1 percent by the year 2015), job opportunities for senior citizens were declining, with the employment rate for men aged 60 to 64 dropping 9.9 percent between 1968 and 1988.[117]

Two days after the release of the OECD statement, it was reported that the Management and Coordination Agency had decided to aim for the introduction of a five-day week every other week for national civil servants in fiscal year 1987. Less than two weeks later, the National Personnel Authority (NPA) resolved to press for full-scale implementation of that system. The government had started implementation on an experimental basis in November 1986, and by April 1987, 89.4 percent of all civil servants were enjoying alternate Saturdays off. The NPA reported that implementation of the shorter workweek was progressing more quickly than had been expected.[118] After the NPA officially submitted its recommendations on 6 August, all four of the major dailies praised the government initiative. Perhaps buoyed by this show of support, the NPA decided to embark on a wholesale reexamination of the working hours of national civil servants, and it announced plans to inaugurate a new private advisory body to draw up a concrete plan of action.

The torrent of EPA statistics continued unabated. On 4 August, the agency released a report that estimated that a complete shift to the five-day week by all workers would boost consumption by an estimated ¥1.7 trillion ($12.1 billion) and GNP by 0.5 percent. By this time, though, attention had shifted from speculative econometrics to backroom politics.

Diet passage

MOL submitted its bill to revise the Labor Standards Act on 9 March 1987, but because the Diet was embroiled in debate over the introduction of a new sales tax and the abolition of popular, tax-exempt *maruyū* savings accounts, it never had a chance to consider the bill, which was carried over to a special session held during the summer. Working hour reductions continued to take a back seat to tax reform, however, and with the LDP and opposition parties engaged in a sterile, head-on confrontation, all legislation ground to a halt. MOL's bill was in limbo, and at one point looked as if it might be dropped.

The government was willing to amend its proposal, especially in return for an end to the opposition's obstructionist tactics. Reasoning that "the reduc-

---

[116] *Daily Yomiuri* (16 July 1987).
[117] Hiraga (1987), p. 203; *Japan Times Weekly Overseas Edition* (5 August 1989).
[118] *Nihon Keizai Shinbun* (4 July 1987); *Sankei Shinbun* (16 July 1987); *Daily Yomiuri* (19 July 1987).

tion of hours is the trend of the times, so the government will have no choice,"[119] Sōhyō gave priority to defending *maruyū*, and the JSP agreed not to make a deal linking *maruyū* to the Labor Standards Act. Dōmei, on the other hand, considered even the government's bill an advance and was eager to revise the act during the current Diet session. Whether a tacit trade-off was involved or the national center simply decided that continued resistance was futile, Dōmei made a 180-degree turn and announced that it would support ending *maruyū*. Dōmei's defection induced the DSP to defect, too, shattering opposition unity, hastening the normalization of Diet deliberations, and allowing the LDP to move ahead without having to ride roughshod over the parliamentary minority. (The tax issue was eventually settled when the LDP, JSP, Kōmeitō, and DSP agreed to a package that combined abolition of *maruyū* with income tax cuts.)

The Standing Committee on Social and Labor Affairs of the lower house began deliberations on the government bill on 25 August. Two days later, all of the major opposition parties except the Communists submitted a joint set of demands for amendments to the bill. On the whole, these demands were identical to the joint goals previously set forth by the five labor organizations and, indeed, the opposition parties had sought and won approval for their proposals at a 31 July meeting with the unions. The scheduled end of the Diet session was fast approaching. Whether or not amendments of the act would "board the last bus" of eleventh-hour legislation depended on the government and LDP's reaching an accommodation with the opposition. The LDP had an additional incentive to compromise in its desire to win an extension of the Diet session that would allow it to attend to other legislative business like revision of the Foreign Exchange Act.

The opposition parties had submitted their demands not to the full committee but to its governing body, or *rijikai*. This directorate, which is a formal Diet institution, is composed of representatives from all of the major parties in rough proportion to their parliamentary strength (at that time, five from the LDP and one each from the JSP, Kōmeitō, DSP, and JCP). Its essential function is to gather both government and opposition parties in order to discuss committee operations – what sorts of deliberations to conduct on which bills in what order, and so on – but it can also serve as a locus for negotiations. Directorates meet behind closed doors, so it is often the case that seeming antagonists will cooperate in stage-managing the public proceedings of Diet committees.

At a 1 September meeting of the directorate of the Committee on Social and Labor Affairs, the LDP expressed its willingness to amend MOL's bill on three points: The ministry would have the power to set (unspecified) upper limits to daily hours, weekly hours, and number of workdays in a row under the three-

---

[119] *Mainichi Shinbun* (18 August 1987).

month system of variable hours; employers would have to report to the government any labor agreements concerning variable hours; and the administration
would investigate implementation of the new regulations and the progress of
working hour reductions after three years and take whatever measures were
necessary. The LDP also proposed a supplemental resolution that recommended future consideration of another increase in paid vacations that would
"refer to" ILO standards and strengthened administrative guidance to promote
the reduction of working hours among small- and medium-sized firms and
prevent employers from obstructing the taking of vacations.

In addition to these tangible concessions, Minister of Labor Hirai offered oral
assurances on issues untouched by the LDP plan. The country would move to
a legal workweek of 46 hours immediately, and to 44 hours in as little as three
years after implementation of the revisions, which was scheduled for 1 April
1988. "We will exert ourselves to the utmost to realize the 40-hour week as early
as possible in the first half of the 1990s," he promised.[120] This ambiguous
expression was devised by the committee directorate in order to satisfy both
sides. The opposition understood it to mean that MOL might meet the labor
movement's target of 1993; the LDP was unwilling to commit itself to any date
before 1995. In any event, the transition period was being compressed. Although the amended bill did not explicitly cap the workday at ten hours, as
unions demanded, "it's common sense that the upper limit for one day's working hours is about ten hours," continued Hirai.[121]

The JCP took this opportunity to burnish its credentials as the only true
defender of working-class interests, submitting its own set of amendments that
would immediately establish a 40-hour, five-day week, delete all provisions
concerning variable working hours, raise to 20 the minimum number of days of
paid vacation, and so on. This amounted to a whole new bill, of course. When
it finally came to a vote that day, the government's bill and the amendments
sponsored by the LDP were both adopted with the support of the LDP,
Kōmeitō, and DSP. The JSP continued to have reservations about such issues
as the obscurity of the transition to the 40-hour week and the lack of regulations
concerning variable working hours, but Socialists did not vote for the Communists' amendments. The supplementary resolution of the LDP passed unanimously, with even the Communists joining in. Two days later, the lower house
passed both the bill and the attached amendments and sent them to the upper
house.

In the lower house, in addition to their written demands, the opposition had
orally proposed special protections for expectant and nursing mothers. No
action was taken at the time. Although the LDP felt that protesting voices

[120] *Asahi Shinbun* (1 September 1987, evening).
[121] *Mainichi Shinbun* (2 September 1987).

"were primarily those of radical leaders of women workers and were atypical,"[122] the party now submitted amendments that met the opposition's demands. On 17 September, the government's bill and the LDP-sponsored amendments passed the Standing Committee on Social and Labor Affairs of the upper house with the support of the LDP, Kōmeitō, and DSP, the Communists' proposals were overwhelmingly voted down, and a set of supplementary resolutions similar to those of the lower house breezed through without opposition. Both houses of the Diet passed the government bill and the successful amendments the very next day.

Epilogue

When the Chūkishin first presented its proposals, Labor Standards Bureau Chief Hiraga declared that "after forty years, this is a turning point in labor legislation."[123] On the same day, an academic referred to those same proposals as "a half-baked, complicated wonder."[124] They were both right.

A common criticism was that the revisions of the act represented nothing more than a ratification of the status quo. In the short term, at least, that was demonstrably true. Given the many small- and medium-sized enterprises in Japan, 84.8 percent of all workers were exempted from the new 46-hour week from the start. Of the remaining workers, 94.7 percent *already* enjoyed workweeks of 46 hours or less, and a few industries like construction and transportation were exempted from immediate application of the standards, so the new regulations that were to be enforced "for the time being" had almost no effect whatsoever on actual working hours.[125] Both the staggered implementation of the new standards and the extensions granted smaller businesses and specific industries were probably inevitable, but for most workers, amendment of Japan's "labor constitution" seemed anticlimactic. "It's like having a delicious-looking rice cake held out of one's reach and being told, 'There's a rice cake. Isn't that good?'" lamented one union official.[126]

Emphasizing the issue of international adjustment, MOL mounted new campaigns for working-hour reductions. In 1988, the government launched a program called Economic Management Within a Global Context to realize the 40-hour workweek and shrink the average workyear to 1,800 hours by the end of 1992. When that failed, the Employment Council, a MOL *shingikai*, submitted a new five-year plan called Sharing a Better Quality of Life Around the Globe to achieve the same goals by encouraging the spread of the five-day workweek

---

[122] Interview with Ōtsubo Ken'ichirō.
[123] *Yomiuri Shinbun* (11 December 1986).
[124] *Asahi Shinbun* (11 December 1986).
[125] *Akahata* (28 March 1987).
[126] *Tōkyō Shinbun* (11 December 1986).

and the full use of paid vacation days. The government declared the 1990s to be the decade in which Japan would finally become a "lifestyle superpower" (*seikatsu taikoku*), and in 1992 it mandated a five-day, 40-hour workweek for more than 1 million civil servants. (Officialdom did not set much of an example, however: The bureaucratic author of the plan to make Japan a lifestyle super-power boasted that he himself had never taken off more than five consecutive days of work.[127]) In a related development, all schools began taking off one Saturday per month in the fall of 1992.

Smaller businesses continued to lag, complaining that competitive pressures forbade them from unilaterally shortening their hours. To address that concern, MOL approached the Chūkishin in October 1991 to propose new legislation that would permit local labor standards offices to establish stiffer, binding standards for working hours reduction in a given industry or region when a substantial number of its workers or employers petitioned for them. Although labor welcomed the proposal – it actually echoed a union demand from 1987 – management did not, and it was revised so that the ministry could issue only "guidelines," not standards, employers need only "make efforts" to meet the guidelines, and only employers could initiate the process. Despite unions' out-rage at these changes, the labor members of the Chūkishin acquiesced, and the Diet passed the Law of Ad Hoc Measures to Promote Reductions in Working Hours in June 1992.[128]

Meanwhile, MOL had once again asked the Rōkiken to review needed revi-sions to the Labor Standards Act in July 1991, and in December 1992 the Chūkishin once again submitted a similar set of recommendations in the wake of the private body. The government was to reduce the legal workweek to 40 hours effective April 1994. Although labor opposed any exceptions, business sought an extension of the 46-hour exemption for small- and medium-sized businesses for at least two years beyond its scheduled expiration date of 31 March 1993. After the Chūkishin settled on a compromise that would continue the exception at either the 44- or 42-hour level, business appealed to its political allies, and MOL reportedly promised LDP leaders that it would extend the existing 46-hour exemption for most businesses with fewer than 100 employees. When the Chūkishin subsequently considered this extension in March 1993, its labor councilors refused to participate in what they called "an unprincipled hearing in which the conclusion has been predetermined, without any prior consultation of the Chūkishin" and walked out in protest. While themselves criticizing MOL, public-interest representatives accepted a one-year extension of the 46-hour exemption as an "emergency measure," the Diet passed a bill containing the new provisions, and it became law on 1 July 1993.[129]

---

[127] *The Wall Street Journal* (2 October 1992).
[128] Foote (1997).   [129] Ibid.

At the time of this writing (early 1997), the government goal is a 40-hour workweek for companies with 30 or more employees and an annual average of 1,800 working hours by March 1997. Those goals do not look achievable. Working hours have been declining, however, and as was the case before 1987, economic conditions rather than legal standards deserve most of the credit. Although an acute labor shortage during the boom of the late 1980s made it difficult for workers to get away from their jobs, that same shortage compelled management to cut working hours to attract employees, and if companies were becoming reconciled to the idea of cutting hours when they were struggling to meet demand, they actually began to like the idea when the overheated "bubble economy" burst and sales slumped in the early 1990s.

MOL estimated that blue-collar manufacturing workers in Japan put in 1,960 hours in 1994, while the comparable American figure had *risen* to about 2,004 hours. The Japanese average exaggerated the decline by including part-time labor, which had soared, and excluding complimentary overtime, which had probably increased, too, but progress is real. Japan's prolonged slowdown aside, there has been a longer-term shift to a shorter workweek and more vacations. Between 1985 and 1993, the proportion of laborers in firms with 30 or more regular employees who worked no more than 40 scheduled hours each week rose from 48.0 to 70.1 percent, and the proportion who received two days off every week shot up from 27.1 to 52.9 percent. Japanese workers are taking a growing fraction of their vacation days (56.1 percent in 1993), and the government has been increasing the number of holidays. There were already 14 national holidays in Japan, compared with 10 in the United States, and Japan added another 1 in 1996.[130]

"I'd like the setting forth of the 40-hour week to become the occasion for changing people's way of thinking about working hours," Labor Standards Bureau Chief Hiraga grandly proclaimed when the Chūkishin submitted its recommendations in 1987,[131] and he was undoubtedly correct in stressing the values that motivate behavior as well as the laws that constrain it. Even before revision of the Labor Standards Act, a wide variety of survey data pointed to attitudinal changes that augur Japan's gradually becoming a more leisure-oriented society.

The proportion of Japanese who lent the greatest significance in their life to leisure rose from 13.8 percent in 1974 to 29.0 percent in 1986, at which point it ranked first in people's hearts, before their dwellings, food, consumer durables, and clothing. When asked how they chose among different job offers, the first answer of male university graduates in the mid-1980s was that they looked for a

---

[130] *The New York Times* (29 April 1995); Management and Coordination Agency, *Japan Statistical Yearbook, 1996*, pp. 124, 125; The Japan Institute of Labour (1996), pp. 40–45.
[131] *Yomiuri Shinbun* (11 December 1986).

five-day workweek. Faced with a hypothetical choice between a shorter workweek and a pay raise, 47 percent of the respondents to a 1992 survey of newly hired employees preferred shorter hours versus only 28 percent who opted for higher pay. Soon after several Japanese politicians derided American workers as lazy in 1992, another survey found that 11 percent of Japanese did not like or want to work, compared with only 4 percent of Americans.[132]

As the word *yutori* – time (or room or money) to spare – has come into vogue in recent years, so has *karōshi* – death from overwork. Attention to this problem arises from a heightened consciousness, rather than a heightened incidence, of it. Survivors of *karōshi* victims have started to demand that it be recognized as grounds for worker compensation, and in a 1992 case against Mitsui, not only did the company cooperate and pay compensation, it also took steps to prevent similar occurrences, declaring that it would assess general managers by how well they set overtime hours, kept subordinates healthy, and encouraged workers to take vacations.

Not all recent developments have been favorable to the reduction of working hours. In 1991 the Supreme Court upheld the firing of an employee who refused overtime on a single occasion, and in 1992 it ruled that employers can make their employees work as needed even if they have vacation time coming to them. Nevertheless, the self-sacrificing work ethic that has characterized Japanese appears to be less an immutable cultural trait than a reaction against poverty, war, and occupation – experiences that today's young do not share.[133] Koreans have already taken to deriding Japanese as "the lazy Asians."

Whether they pointed to MOL's frequent recourse to advisory bodies, the prevalence there of tripartite membership, or the real influence of public-interest representatives, many Chūkishin members appeared to take pride in the way it and other ministry councils are run. "Ministry of Labor *shingikai* are probably those whose opinions are most respected" by their parent agencies, speculated one councilor.[134] What follows is a case study in which the significance of *shingikai* deliberations was more ambiguous.

[132] Hiraga (1987), pp. 202–6; Shirai (1987b), p. 19; *Japan Digest* (16 April 1992); *The Wall Street Journal* (20 February 1992).
[133] Johnson (1982), p. 307.
[134] Interview with Watanabe Michiko.

5

Regulating the invisible giant: The introduction of financial futures markets

The invention of financial futures created an industry so hot that its growth chart looked like "the path of a homesick angel."[1] Given the unusual nature of futures, however, it developed into an "invisible giant" that traded in seemingly "nonexistent" goods.[2]

Beginning in 1985, MOF gradually expanded the opportunities for trading financial futures in response to the prompting of private industry. In the ensuing struggle between bankers and stockbrokers over control of the new markets, MOF's Banking, Securities, and International Finance Bureaus lined up behind their regulatory constituencies, and that support was reflected in the reports of their respective *shingikai*. Neither the third-party councilors in those *shingikai* nor individual bureaus made much effort to mediate between the two sides, so a compromise had to be hammered out at the ministry level. Given their lack of financial expertise and fear of alienating either of the business antagonists, politicians stayed on the sidelines and instead rubber-stamped MOF's proposed settlement. In 1988, Japan's government finally authorized the establishment of financial futures markets comparable to those of other advanced industrial economies.

Only business interests had input into the policymaking process, but those interests were divided into squabbling banking, securities, and insurance circles. MOF was thoroughly in charge of the introduction of new futures markets, but it was mediating among private actors more than asserting independent interests of its own. Those private actors were diverse, but MOF slighted several other concerned parties that attempted to press their claims. Each industrial sector has its own trade association, but they did not serve as vehicles for bargaining across sectors or with the state. In sum, the introduction of new futures markets was a relatively self-contained, bureaucratically led process that involved a limited set of narrowly focused interest groups. It was bureaucratically led because MOF enjoys a comprehensive mandate over the financial industry, and emphasizing the distributive nature of the issue would have cost LDP politicians by forcing them to choose sides between supporters.

[1] *The New York Times* (29 November 1992).
[2] *Nihon Keizai Shinbun* (26 May 1988).

Background

Futures are contracts to buy or sell physical or financial commodities (e.g., pork bellies or bonds) at a specified price, date, and place. Unlike the trading of actual goods, or "spots," where buyers take physical delivery of something and settle accounts for the entire amount of the contract, if the parties concerned engage in "offset" or "counter-trading" (i.e., the repurchase or resale of the contract) before the scheduled date of delivery, futures can be liquidated through payment of only the difference between the value of the original contract and that of the offsetting contract. Suppose a Japanese company contracted to buy 1 million U.S. dollars in six months at ¥100 to the dollar. If the dollar rose to ¥105 and the company was able to sell its futures contract at the prevailing rate before the date of delivery, it would earn ¥5 per dollar, or a total of ¥5 million (ignoring transaction costs). Conversely, if the dollar fell to ¥95 and it chose to sell the contract, it would incur a loss of ¥5 million. After six months, it could also purchase the million dollars for ¥100 million in accordance with the contract, of course.

Because most transactions are settled on the margin, futures can be traded even where no spot good exists. Stock price index futures, for example, are agreements to pay or be paid a sum reflecting the difference between the level of a particular index at a future time and the level of that index at the time of the original contract. It is impossible to take delivery of an index, needless to say. When traded in tandem with corresponding spot goods, futures provide a cheap and effective means of avoiding risk, a kind of insurance. Investors can offset the capital losses that would accompany a decline in the stock market by short-selling stock price index futures. By reducing investment risks and expanding markets to include new participants and a wider range of instruments, futures exchanges serve as a kind of financial infrastructure, energizing the spot markets they complement.

Futures do more than hedge risks – they can also be used to arbitrage price discrepancies or to speculate – and there are other ways to hedge risks, of course. Forward contracts are similar to futures in that they provide for transactions at a future date but, as in spot trades, the parties involved liquidate contracts in their entirety when they mature rather than settling accounts on the margin. Options confer the *right* to buy a specified quantity of some good at a set price within a fixed period of time, but the owner of an option can always abdicate that right should the transaction prove unprofitable. Forward contracts were already legal at the time of the events to be described, and the Japanese government typically lumped options together with futures in its deliberations, so whatever will be said of futures applies equally to options unless otherwise noted.

Ironically, the original birthplace of futures trading was Japan itself. In

1730, Osaka's Dōjima commercial center organized a futures exchange for rice contracts with all the modern features: a clearinghouse, a membership system, expiration dates, margin requirements, and the ability to square a position before a contract's expiration.[3] Market crashes before the Pacific War led Japanese regulators to distrust the speculative aspect of financial futures trading, and Occupation authorities eliminated it altogether in an attempt to reduce the volatility of securities markets, but as market fluctuations and attendant uncertainty increased in the wake of the first oil crisis and the shift to floating exchange rates, trading in financial futures began to spread elsewhere in the first half of the 1970s and grew explosively in the decade that followed.

Because American law distinguishes between futures and spots without distinguishing among different kinds of futures, the Commodity Futures Trading Commission supervises all futures trading in a unified manner. With its vertically split administration (*tatewari gyōsei*), Japan, on the other hand, divides regulatory responsibility among several ministries. Whether the transaction involves spots or futures, MITI is responsible for fibers and precious metals and the Ministry of Agriculture, Forestry, and Fisheries for grains. All trading in financial instruments falls within the jurisdiction of MOF, and this study focuses exclusively on debates surrounding the introduction of financial futures.

Specializing in negotiable instruments, it was the securities industry that took the initiative in Japan. Having observed firsthand the innovations sweeping America, leading stockbrokers returned from an inspection visit to propose the inauguration of financial futures trading in 1981. A few years later, as the deregulation of interest rates picked up speed, Japanese authorities began to examine the introduction of financial futures as a means of hedging against interest-rate fluctuation. After MOF's Securities Exchange Council recommended the establishment of a market in Japanese government bond futures in a December 1984 report, the Diet amended the Securities Exchange Act, and the Tokyo Stock Exchange (TSE) initiated trading in ten-year government bond futures in October 1985.

When trading began, the TSE expected a daily volume of about ¥100 billion. It reached several *trillion* yen, with total volume skyrocketing to about ¥940 trillion ($6.7 trillion) in 1986. In its first full year of operation, the Japanese market had already outstripped the Chicago Board of Trade, which until then had been the world's largest market in (long-term U.S. Treasury) bond futures. This spectacular growth continued in 1987: By November, total annual volume had ballooned to more than twice the turnover of the previous 12 months. With trading on Japan's government bond market increasingly lively, hedging

---

[3] Itō (1992), p. 30.

and speculation by means of futures gained currency, as it were.[4] In light of this success, financiers began demanding authorization to trade other futures instruments.

A bitter conflict was brewing over the opening of new markets, however. In essence, "rather than a problem of futures, this was a problem of the banking industry versus the securities industry."[5] Like the "wall" erected by America's Banking ("Glass-Steagall") Act of 1933, after which Occupation authorities modeled the legislation, Article 65 of the Securities Exchange Act of 1948 interposed a "fence" (*kakine*) between the banking and securities industries in Japan. Globally, that is the exception rather than the rule. Germany and France do not legally separate banking and securities brokering, Britain liberalized its financial markets with the "Big Bang" of October 1986, and even the United States is gradually breaking down the barriers raised by Glass-Steagall. With Japan, too, considering liberalization, a study group of MOF's Council on the Financial System concluded two years of deliberation in November 1987 by calling for a review of the existing system.

Banks in particular sought to breach the fence in financial futures markets, both to bolster short-term profits and to set a long-term precedent for the lowering of barriers in spot markets. Acting as agents for customers' buy and sell orders, securities houses earned futures trading commissions of ¥37.9 billion ($271 million) in the six months of October 1986 to March 1987, an amount that exceeded the total for the previous year. Although they accounted for fully one-third of the volume in government bond futures, not a penny of those commissions went to banks because they could trade only for their own accounts.[6] (In all that follows, it is essential to keep in mind the distinction between trading for one's own account and brokering, that is, getting paid to act as an agent for others.) When the market was inaugurated, banks obtained special memberships enabling them to trade government bond futures on the TSE, and they anticipated that MOF would also grant them a "#2 license" to broker the instruments when the ministry reviewed the operation of the new market after a year. The TSE rebuffed banks' demands, however, arguing that the prevailing system functioned satisfactorily without them.

Banks had little choice but to try to enter the securities business at this time: Their share of the financial services market was declining. As a result of a process of "disintermediation," many of the large Japanese corporations that had been banks' best customers no longer depended on loans; they had become more profitable, and with improved access to securities markets (including overseas Euromarkets), they could often raise money more cheaply by issuing stocks or bonds. On the other side of the ledger, banks were losing individual

[4] *Yomiuri Shinbun* (8 September 1987); *Nihon Keizai Shinbun* (28 December 1987).
[5] Interview with Kanda Hideki.
[6] *Asahi Shinbun* (11 September 1987).

deposits to the postal savings system. Regulatory changes gave an added impetus to banks' search for new lines of business. The liberalization of interest rates threatened further hemorrhaging of bank profits, and with the abolition of tax-exempt *maruyū* savings accounts in 1987 (see Chapter 4), savers faced a 20 percent levy on all interest earnings. Banks were extremely anxious about whether and whither the ¥300 trillion ($2.14 trillion) parked in their *maruyū* might move. Not all depositors would turn to securities, but banks would suffer if they could not service those who did.

The securities industry argued that the spots and futures of any particular financial instrument ought to be traded in the same market. Stock and bond futures ought therefore to be listed exclusively on stock exchanges and brokered by stockbrokers alone. In addition to being a matter of principle, it would be risky for depositors if banks were to become the nucleus of futures trading.[7] The banking industry brushed aside stockbrokers' solicitude for its clients as unnecessary, considering its positive record in bond futures trading, and derided the "principle" of uniting spots and futures as nonsense. Fearful of being left behind once again, the industry's trade association, the National Federation of Bankers Associations (Zenkoku Ginkō Kyōkai Rengōkai, or Zenginkyō), outlined an alternative scheme in a February 1987 report: Because the increasing need for hedges against risk necessitated the introduction of instruments in addition to government bond futures, a new, comprehensive market ought to be established on the basis of a single law that would govern all financial futures trading.

Zenginkyō's report enumerated the merits of this scheme. Trading techniques are identical whatever the object, and the enactment of separate legislation for each futures instrument would only waste time, reduce the market's ability to cope flexibly with users' needs, and pose the danger of contradictory regulation, so a unified legal system was clearly desirable. The trading of all financial futures in one comprehensive market separate from the markets in corresponding spot goods would also facilitate the settling of accounts with the many foreign exchanges that had already adopted such a format, reduce the impact of fluctuations in any one instrument, lighten economic burdens like deposits, and permit arbitrage among different kinds of futures. Although Zenginkyō focused specifically on the need to create futures markets in foreign currencies and interest rates, fields familiar to banks, it was eager for its proposed exchange eventually to list stock and bond futures, too.

As in the battle over revision of the Labor Standards Act, each side cited international considerations only when and to the extent that they bolstered its

---

[7] The security industry's argument was ironic given that the rhetoric of "depositor protection" typically disguises MOF *protection* of the banking industry. See Rosenbluth (1993), p. 124.

case. Banks tried to improve the chances of their belated bid to enter futures trading by campaigning under the banners of liberalization and internationalization, and the international context did seem to favor their plan. If domestic futures trading attracted investment from abroad, that would deepen all the country's financial markets and solidify Tokyo's place as an international financial center equal to New York and London. A failure to establish futures exchanges on a par with those overseas, on the other hand, might lead to the "hollowing out" (*kudō-ka*) of domestic financial markets as Japanese investors turned to more up-to-date exchanges abroad.

The securities industry attacked the contention that futures were handled in a unified manner overseas. Although it is true that spot and futures markets are separated in the United States, America does not have a unified futures market. In Chicago, the Mercantile Exchange may handle the Standard & Poor's 500 stock price index, currency contracts, and three-month Eurodollar deposits, but it is the Board of Trade that lists 20-year U.S. Treasury bonds, the most popular American futures instrument. With the right technical apparatus, having several exchanges need not pose a problem. There was really no pressing need for a comprehensive market, in other words.

The cast of actors

Because politicians' involvement in the contest remained peripheral, there are three main protagonists to this story: the securities industry, the banking industry, and MOF. Relations within and among them had a profound influence on the struggles they waged with one another.

The securities industry

Although all stockbrokers recognized the need for new futures markets, they differed in their plans to take advantage of them. Nomura, Daiwa, Nikkō, and Yamaichi – the "Big Four" – dealt in a wide variety of instruments that could be hedged and served many clients who wanted to participate in futures trading. Smaller companies had fewer such needs and clients. The interests of stockbrokers are aggregated by both the TSE and a trade association, the Securities Dealers Association of Japan (Nihon Shōkengyō Kyōkai). The Big Four annually take turns chairing the association, and the association typically serves as a mouthpiece for the Big Four. "The underlying assumption of the organization was that the large companies got their way on crucial matters but were prepared to support small companies in matters not so important to themselves."[8] On this occasion, although the association did not play a very active role, it did make

---

[8] Horne (1985), p. 102.

efforts on behalf of smaller securities houses that were not represented in *shingikai*.[9]

The banking industry

Not only did MOF rigidly partition the securities and banking industries, it compartmentalized the banking industry itself. In 1989, there were 3 long-term credit banks, 7 trust banks, 12 city banks, approximately 130 regional banks, 448 credit cooperatives, 456 credit associations, and the agricultural cooperatives.[10] Although boundary lines began to blur with liberalization, MOF traditionally confined each of these institutions to its own specialized niche and prevented them from competing with one another. The rule has been "everything is regulated, and regulation is protection."[11] The giant city banks operated extensive branch networks and were active overseas, but they could make only short-term loans. Long-term credit banks, on the other hand, were not allowed to accept individual deposits. Only trust banks could manage trusts and pension funds, and so on.

Different categories of banks naturally have distinct interests, and they have independent trade associations. These more specialized associations gather under the umbrella of Zenginkyō, whose chair annually rotates among four city banks headquartered in Tokyo: Daiichi Kangyō, Fuji, Mitsubishi (now Bank of Tokyo-Mitsubishi), and Mitsui (now Sakura). Although Zenginkyō attempts to represent the entire banking industry in its disputes with outsiders, unity is often difficult to achieve on so general a level. Zenginkyō took the lead in preparing for a new exchange, establishing a Financial Futures Special Subcommittee composed of representatives of city banks, long-term credit banks, trust banks, and regional banks. As one newspaper reported, though, "the advent of financial futures markets looks like it will become an occasion for the opening of new gaps among banks."[12] Only city banks showed much zest for futures trading; regional banks had yet to study the issue, and smaller retail banks lacked the skills necessary to enter the new markets. They offered no active resistance to the plans of city banks, however.

The LDP

It was precisely because the LDP was close to the contestants that it sat out the battle. Although city banks tended to look to MOF more than to the LDP and to relate to the party on an organizational rather than a personal level, they were always one of the biggest financial supporters of the conservatives.

[9] Interview with Itatani Masanori.   [10] Rosenbluth (1989), p. 24.
[11] Interview with Minaguchi Kōichi.   [12] *Mainichi Shinbun* (23 March 1988).

A large proportion of campaign contributions are never disclosed, but along with the steel and electric power industries, banking was one of the funding mainstays (*gosanke*, or "three honorable houses") of the LDP, consistently accounting for about 20 percent of industry's publicly reported political contributions.[13]

Even though the securities industry naturally strives to have its views reflected in MOF policy as much as possible, it has sometimes tried to reverse ministry decisions through the good offices of its allies in the Diet. Going back to the end of the Occupation period, when it needed help to fend off banks' assaults on Article 65, the smaller securities industry has also cultivated its political connections, but instead of supporting the LDP and the conservative status quo as a whole, it has sought particularistic, distributive benefits for itself by funding individual factions and politicians. This has been especially true since 1975, when, as an unintended consequence of campaign financing reform, limitations on direct corporate donations increased the importance of stock manipulation as a source of funds.[14] Stockbrokers demonstrated their political clout at the time of these events when Prime Minister Nakasone, Minister of Finance Miyazawa Kiichi, and Governor Sumita Satoshi of the Bank of Japan all addressed the National Securities Convention in October 1987.

As Rosenbluth has pointed out, because the party sat on both sides of the fence, the LDP strongly preferred to delegate to MOF the balancing of banks' and securities houses' interests and, conversely, MOF's individual bureaus and private actors had an equally strong preference for resolving their differences among themselves. A bureaucratically led bargain – the "preemptive equilibration" of conflicts of interest – was preferred to overt politicization by everyone concerned because "it allows the bureaucracy to retain its procedural integrity, the competing groups to obtain a resolution at less cost than would be required in all-out lobbying, and the politicians to retain the usual, uninterrupted flow of campaign contributions from both sides in the dispute."[15]

MOF

In the introduction of new futures instruments, MOF was the key government actor. Three of its seven bureaus regulate private-sector finance: the Banking, Securities, and International Finance bureaus. It is often said that MOF is "all bureaus, no ministry," with each bureau defending its particular regulatory constituency. That is too simple a picture of the relations between regulators and regulated and among the regulators themselves, but there is a measure of truth to it.

The different bureaus cannot simply act as advocates for their charges. MOF

[13] Rosenbluth (1989), p. 35.   [14] Calder (1993), pp. 239–41.
[15] Rosenbluth (1989), pp. 26–27, 8; Rosenbluth (1993), p. 126.

officials are widely regarded as the most select elite in Japan, and they take seriously their duty to rise above particularistic squabbles. Furthermore, the relationships of banks and security houses to their eponymous bureaus are not exclusive. It is more accurate to think of each agency's jurisdiction in terms of the laws it administers (e.g., the Securities Bureau and the Securities Exchange Act) rather than in terms of a specific set of financial institutions whose operations it supervises. Because banks had received special licenses to deal in government bonds, there was nothing unusual about banks approaching the Securities Bureau, for example. Most important, the bureaus have no alternative to reining in their respective sectors' selfish tendencies and working toward compromises if they are to protect MOF's own unity. Ministry personnel policies are thus designed to facilitate interbureau coordination.

> Perhaps most important is the rotation of personnel, generally every two years. A Banking Bureau official this year may be in the Securities Bureau the next. . . . [In addition,] once in the ministry, bureaucrats still face fierce competition for the highest administrative positions. . . . Bureaucrats who push too hard for sectional interests at the expense of the MOF's integrity can expect to be bypassed for important positions.[16]

That said, it remains true that with its extremely broad jurisdiction – combining many of the powers of America's Treasury Department, Federal Reserve Bank, Internal Revenue Service, Office of Management and Budget, and Securities and Exchange Commission, among others – MOF has been preoccupied with issues of internal coordination. The ministerial secretariat, which is the primary body responsible for coordination, has actually shrunk over time, so by the late 1980s, MOF had the smallest secretariat (relatively speaking) of any major government organization in Japan. Although career tracks are designed to unify the ministry, officials at the highest levels are less and less able to control the organizations under them, if only because of their transience, and each bureau's private-sector constituency joins it in defending its autonomy.[17]

In confrontations between the two industries, the Banking Bureau thus tends to support banks and the Securities Bureau securities houses. In light of their different jurisdictions, it is natural that they often disagree, and a certain rivalry exists between the two. The Banking Bureau is older, larger, and more prestigious than the Securities Bureau. Although the Securities Exchange Act gave stockbrokers a virtual monopoly in the underwriting and trading of stocks and (nongovernment) bonds, MOF long encouraged the indirect financing of industry through bank loans, so the banking industry was more powerful economically, and with it the Banking Bureau.

Companies have relied to an increasing degree on direct financing through the issuing of equities. As banks have been losing their dominant role and the

---

[16] Rosenbluth (1989), pp. 19–20.   [17] Calder (1993), pp. 94–98.

securities industry has achieved rough parity in political influence, a measure of power has shifted from the Banking to the Securities Bureau within MOF, too. "For the first time, the Securities Bureau has become a cheerful place to work," a financial scholar observed in 1988.[18] Even so, the director of the Banking Bureau still ranks above the director of the Securities Bureau, and "because the Banking Bureau is stronger, there has long been a tendency for the Securities Bureau to prove its existence by asserting the views of the securities industry forcefully."[19] In a joking reference to MOF's Tokyo location, the Securities Bureau has been dubbed "the Toranomon branch of Nomura Securities."

The International Finance Bureau was also a party to any decision on expanding futures trading. Japan's growing role in the international economy has been reflected in the growing status of that bureau. In this case, it would regulate the participation of domestic institutions in foreign futures markets and share with the Banking and Securities Bureaus the oversight of foreign institutions' participation in Japan's domestic markets. The introduction of currency futures was of particular concern to the International Finance Bureau because the handling of foreign exchange is entirely within its jurisdiction.

"There was a pretense [*tatemae*] that the International Finance Bureau was neutral, but in fact, it acted as a rooting section for the Banking Bureau."[20] First, because the established doctrine of "exchange bank-ism" (*tamegin-shugi*) forbade security houses from handling foreign exchange, banks constituted the Bureau's primary regulatory constituency. Second, the bureau followed banks in preferring a comprehensive, independent futures exchange because that would more closely resemble overseas markets and thus ease participation for foreigners, who constitute another of the bureau's clients. (Incidentally, the chief of the International Finance Bureau at this time had been an attaché in Washington, and was well versed in American finance.)

On this occasion, then, although there may have been differences over details, each bureau broadly supported its main regulatory constituency on what form futures markets should take. The Securities Bureau leaned toward stockbrokers' argument that the direct participants in any futures market should be limited to participants in the corresponding spot market, the Banking and International Finance Bureaus toward banks' argument that they should have the same rights as securities firms vis-à-vis financial futures. These preferences came to be expressed in reports of the bureaus' *shingikai*. Although officially it is the minister who consults ministry councils, MOF's *shingikai* in reality function as auxiliary bodies of their respective parent agencies. The Securities Bureau has its Securities Exchange Council (Shōken Torihiki Shingikai, or Shōtorishin),

[18] Interview with Rōyama Shōichi.
[19] Interview with Sugita Ryōki.
[20] Ibid.

the Banking Bureau its Council on the Financial System, and the International Finance Bureau its Foreign Exchange Council.

As noted earlier, MOF had consulted the Shōtorishin in 1984 before authorizing the introduction of government bond futures. The Shōtorishin set the ball rolling again in 1987 when it recommended the expansion of domestic markets to include other financial futures.

The Securities Exchange Council

In the hyperbolic words of a scholar, trading in stock price index futures was "the demand of the current age." Price volatility was growing with the liberalization and internationalization of capital markets, and stockholding was becoming more concentrated in the hands of institutional investors: By the end of September 1987, the stockholdings of trust banks had climbed to more than ¥46 trillion ($329 billion) and those of life insurance companies to almost ¥31 trillion ($221 billion).[21] Some means of hedging the risks that accompanied those vast investments was becoming essential. Foreign investors were buying Japanese stocks to diversify their portfolios, and they naturally wanted to protect their investments with Japanese stock price index futures, too.

In order to investigate the creation of new futures markets, the Shōtorishin established a Special Subcommittee on Futures. With representatives from all of the most interested parties, there was no obvious imbalance in the composition of the subcommittee. It comprised 15 members: 3 from security houses, 1 from the TSE, 3 from banks, 1 from the Bank of Japan, 1 from institutional investors, 1 from industry, 1 from the mass media, 3 academics, and the chair of the parent Shōtorishin (see Table 5-1).

The Shōtorishin entrusted its chair with the selection of subcommittee members but, after having been consulted, the chair simply obtained the approval of the rest of the *shingikai* for the choices of the Securities Bureau. When asked about the role of interest groups, a bureaucrat in the secretariat replied that "they've no influence over the selection of members. MOF chooses them freely."[22] That was an exaggeration, however. "There's a sort of custom to the mode of selection. In each industry, the enterprise that chairs the trade association takes responsibility for relations with MOF, and the top person responsible for MOF comes forward as a member. The Securities Bureau doesn't choose them – they come forward naturally."[23] The subcommittee thus included members from Mitsubishi, the city bank then chairing Zenginkyō; Sumitomo Trust, which led the trust banks' trade association at that time; the Industrial Bank of Japan, as a representative of long-term credit banks; and Daiwa, in its capacity

---

[21] *Nihon Keizai Shinbun* (28 December 1987).
[22] Interview with Moriya Manabu.
[23] Interview with Rōyama Shōichi.

Table 5-1. *Members of the subcommittees considering financial futures*

	Shōtorishin	Gaitameshin	Kinseichō
Banks			
City banks	Hirano Tsuruo (Managing Director, Mitsubishi Bank)	Nakamura Taizō (Managing Director, Mitsui Bank)	Suematsu Ken'ichi (Vice President, Mitsui Bank)
Trust banks	Nishiyama Hiroichi (Managing Director, Sumitomo Trust)	Okawa Susumu (Managing Director, Yasuda Trust)	Tachikawa Masami (Managing Director, Yasuda Trust)
Industrial Bank of Japan	Sugishita Masaaki (Director)	Ishihara Hideo (Managing Director)	Nishimura Masao (Managing Director)
Exchange bank		Umemoto Fumio (Managing Director, Bank of Tokyo)	
Securities houses			
Nomura	Sakamaki Hideo (Managing Director)	Yamada Morimasa (Managing Director)	Mizuguchi Hiroichi (Vice President)
Daiwa	Okumoto Eiichirō (Vice President)	Nobuchika Masahiro (Managing Director)	Nakatsuka Yukio (Managing Director)
Other	Katō Saiichi (President, Okasan Securities)	Kaneko Tarō[a] (President, Marusan Securities)	
TSE	Satō Mitsuo[a] (Managing Director, Tokyo Stock Exchange)		
Bank of Japan	Wakatsuki Mikio (General Affairs Bureau Chief)	Tanji Makoto (Foreign Bureau Chief)	Aoki Akira (Director)
Institutional investors			
Insurance	Utsunomiya Ichirō (Managing Director, Meiji Life)	Shidara Katsu (Managing Director, Nippon Life)	Hirose Tokutarō (Vice President, Nippon Life)
Nōrin Chūkin Bank		Takashima Hiroshi (Managing Director)	Arai Jōji (Managing Director)
Industry	Sakamoto Akihira (Managing Director, Tōray)	Imai Takashi (Managing Director, Nippon Steel)	Miyauchi Yasuo (Vice President, Hitachi Manufacturing)
		Sugita Keiichi (Managing Director, Mitsui Trading)	
Academe			
Law		Egashira Kenjirō (Tokyo U.)	Kanzaki Katsurō (Kobe U.)
		Kanda Hideki (Tokyo U.)	

Table 5-1. *(cont.)*

	Shōtorishin	Gaitameshin	Kinseichō
Economics	Kurasawa Motonari (Yokohama Natl. U.) Rōyama Shōichi[b] (Osaka U.)	Iida Tsuneo[b] (Nagoya U.)	Horiuchi Akiyoshi (Tokyo U.) Wakasugi Yoshiaki (Tokyo U.)
Mass media			
Nikkei Shinbun	Takei Teruyoshi (editorial writer)	Suzuki Takashi (Managing Director)	Sugita Ryōki (Economics Bureau Chief)
NHK	Ōyama Hiroto (commentator)		
Other	Tanimura Hiroshi[a] (Chair, Foundation for the Promotion of Capital Markets)	Watanabe Kiichi[a] (Governor, Small- and Medium-Sized Business Finance Corp.)	Kondō Michitaka[ab] (Chair, Hakuhōdō Advertising) Tsuno Osamu (Division Chief, Cabinet Legislation Bur.)

[a] OB (all from MOF).   [b] Subcommittee chair.

as chair of the Securities Dealers Association. The inclusion of Nomura was *de rigueur* by virtue of its commanding size, whether it happened to be chairing the Securities Dealers Association or not. Okasan Securities, on the other hand, came as a representative of smaller brokerage houses.

Bureaucrats did select the persons of learning and experience. Because Japanese finance has traditionally revolved around banks, though, few scholars were experts on the stock market, which limited the choice of academics. As for the journalist, a Securities Bureau staffer explained that the ministry could learn the sentiments of the industrial world at large through a business reporter. The inclusion of a journalist also had an intrinsic value: At MOF, "it's thought to be extremely important what sort of views are held by the press [itself]. They're chosen as members [of *shingikai*] in most cases."[24]

Two Finance OBs participated, Tanimura Hiroshi and Satō Mitsuo. After reaching the pinnacle of the bureaucratic hierarchy as administrative vice minister, Tanimura left the ministry in 1968 to chair the Fair Trade Commission for three years. Serving ex officio as chair of the Shōtorishin, he was more of an observer than a disputant. Satō had risen to become director of the Customs and

[24] Ibid.

Tariff Bureau before retiring in 1986 to become a director of the TSE. "OBs sometimes use incumbent MOF people for the sake of their current jobs, and sometimes you have just the reverse," according to one subcommittee member.[25] Because Japanese lacked experience with futures instruments, ministry OBs were not necessarily more knowledgeable than other councilors.

The Securities Bureau chose as subcommittee chair Professor Rōyama Shōichi, an Osaka University economist who had become familiar with futures trading through research in the United States and was known outside academic circles. "Formally, he was chosen by the members. Actually, the government came to us and said, 'We'd like you to make it this person, please.' "[26]

The subcommittee held its first meeting in January 1987 and went on to meet six more times. Although the Securities Bureau imposed no specific time limit, there was a desire to wrap up deliberations before a scheduled reshuffling of MOF personnel disrupted administrative operations. The ministry supplied all of the data, without the subcommittee's undertaking any research of its own. "At first, it was exclusively explanations by the MOF secretariat in response to members' questions. The committee was formalized, like the Diet, with questions usually submitted in advance."[27] They were not permitted to act as proxies or to speak, but subordinates would accompany corporate representatives.

"While there was a to and fro between the interest groups outside of meetings and a search for points of compromise, MOF thought that the different views probably wouldn't come together at this *shingikai*."[28] MOF was right. There was little give-and-take at subcommittee meetings between councilors and officials or among the councilors themselves. Outside of the representatives of the banking and securities industries, members were basically disinterested, but unlike their counterparts in MOL's Chūkishin, these members did not attempt to mediate between the antagonists. Rather than debating, councilors simply stated their respective views at the final session.

After the conclusion of deliberations, the subcommittee's secretariat drafted a plan in cooperation with the chair. Although one official insisted that the secretariat only "arranged" the views expressed by members, he did admit that "there was a need for adjustments when too foolhardy an opinion was offered."[29] In accordance with the custom of adopting reports unanimously, officials consulted each councilor individually in order to amend their plan as necessary in advance of the final session. Banks paid especially close attention to bureaucrats' drafts, forcing officials to clarify extremely detailed points. The Securities Bureau is thought to have discussed its plans with the Banking and International Finance Bureaus, too.

The times demanded additional methods of risk management, the report noted, and with active futures and option trading on the world's other principal

[25] Interview with Takei Teruyoshi.   [26] Ibid.   [27] Interview with Kurasawa Motonari.
[28] Interview with Takei Teruyoshi.   [29] Interview with Moriya Manabu.

markets, Japan's capital market would become a less competitive market if it failed to follow suit. The early introduction of stock price index futures and stock options was therefore a "very urgent" task.[30] Because index futures are based on stock prices set in the spot market and are intimately connected with spot trading through hedging and arbitrage, it was "extremely important" to coordinate spot and futures markets. With their abundant know-how in the operation of securities markets, including bond futures, stock exchanges were the appropriate site for index futures trading. Although the subcommittee acknowledged the desirability of permitting the participation of a wide range of institutions in order to increase the depth of the market, it recommended limiting direct participation to firms authorized to broker stock spots – to securities houses, that is.

Some newspapers characterized the Shōtorishin's recommendations as a "rollback" of the banking industry's plans, and there was no denying their pro-stockbroker slant, but "there was a feeling [among councilors] that this report was inevitable."[31] Why?

"It's because it's the Securities Exchange Council," explained one banker. "The banking industry's views are listened to, but nothing more."[32] This explanation is too simple. The fact is, the banks' view was the minority view; they were alone in advocating a comprehensive market. Although third parties did not necessarily agree with every aspect of the securities industry's position, they did not strongly oppose it, either. The banking industry was handicapped in making its case because it was lagging in its research and preparations. Whereas the TSE's market in government bond futures had been in operation for years, Zenginkyō proposed the creation of a new exchange only after the subcommittee had begun its deliberations. "The banking side's ideas of what to do about futures were sometimes a little late in coming," admitted one banker.[33]

There clearly was an element of truth to the charge of bias, however. The Securities Bureau had framed the subcommittee's deliberations in a way favorable to stockbrokers by limiting its terms of reference to the introduction of "securities futures" alone. "That was our intention from the start," remarked Professor Rōyama.

> We invented the phrase "securities futures" [shōken sakimono, as opposed to the more general "financial futures," kin'yū sakimono], and by the use of that word, it was decided that these futures were commodities derived from securities and should be listed on stock exchanges. We discussed the matter in those terms. When I jokingly asked Mr. Kitamura, who was the bureau chief at the time, whether we should include everything, currency and

---

[30] Shōken Torihiki Shingikai (1987), pp. 1–2.
[31] Interview with Kurasawa Motonari.
[32] Interview with Hayakawa Yoshio.
[33] Interview with Tachikawa Masami.

short-term interest futures, too, in subcommittee discussions, he replied, "That would be terribly troublesome."[34]

The appointment of Professor Rōyama as chair also influenced the content of the report. One councilor characterized the chair as "simply a program director" who planned the progress of deliberations without controlling them,[35] and a bureaucrat on the subcommittee's secretariat repeated the standard line: "Because the chair is in the position of bringing deliberations to a conclusion, his function is to let members state their views, to arrange those views, and to draft a report without forcing his own opinion."[36] Other observers demurred. Even if he refrained from pressing his views at subcommittee meetings, Professor Rōyama was an "opinion leader,"[37] and his opinions were clearly consonant with those of the securities industry. Professor Rōyama had previously chaired a group conducting research on stock futures for the Osaka Stock Exchange. One stockbroker spoke admiringly of how Professor Rōyama authoritatively buttressed his industry's case: "Although MOF's Securities Bureau was distressed when it started this *shingikai*, they ended up with a report that reflected Professor Rōyama's views very strongly. If you look at the membership composition [of the subcommittee], there were bank people, too, but there wasn't anyone who had a theory that outdid Professor Rōyama's."[38]

Representatives of the banking industry approved the report in the end. That is not to say that they approved *of* the report, but for all its partiality toward the securities industry, the report did make a few face-saving concessions to banks. Stockbrokers' initial demands had been even more one-sided: They had argued not simply that securities futures ought to be handled separately from other financial futures, but that the creation of other financial futures might cause problems.[39] And the very last line of the report acknowledged that "at the time of these deliberations, a fraction of the members held the view that the establishment of a comprehensive futures market for financial commodities is necessary."[40] The banks behind this "fraction" knew that they would get a second chance to debate these questions in the *shingikai* of the Banking and International Finance Bureaus, forums sure to be more receptive to their arguments.

The plenary Shōtorishin approved the subcommittee's draft without deliberating on it at length or altering it in any substantive way and submitted the report to Minister of Finance Miyazawa on 20 May 1987.

Although Tokyo had taken the lead on bond futures, Osaka introduced the first stock price index, the "Kabusaki [stock future] 50," on 9 June 1987. This

---

[34] Interview with Rōyama Shōichi.   [35] Interview with Takei Teruyoshi.
[36] Interview with Moriya Manabu.   [37] Interview with Hayakawa Yoshio.
[38] Interview with Kikuichi Mamoru.   [39] Interview with Tachi Ryūichirō.
[40] Shōken Torihiki Shingikai (1987), p. 15.

instrument combined the 50 most representative stocks of the Nikkei 225 index into a package whose price averaged those of its component shares, and the trading mechanism was similar to that of the TSE's government bond futures market. Because the government had yet to authorize trading in stock price indices, this was not a true futures contract: In the absence of an offsetting trade, the contract had to be settled by physical delivery of the actual package of stocks. It did help investors hedge their positions against market fluctuations, however.

Japanese investors in the new Kabusaki 50 had lessons to learn. Although the market opened with a bang, it declined continuously thereafter, and in July, domestic investors suffered losses (*aburage o sarawareta* – literally, "had their fried bean curd snatched") at the hands of the veteran foreign traders Morgan Stanley and Salomon Brothers. Although American securities houses had embraced risky new strategies after deregulation in the mid-1970s, Japanese stockbrokers had been content to rake in huge profits on small-investor orders under the government-sanctioned system of fixed commissions, and they now lamented their inexperience: "Even if we understand the theory, when it comes to practice, our limbs don't move."[41] Despite such early reverses, volume quadrupled when the tax on exchanges was cut at the end of September, and by December, average daily turnover had swollen to about ¥182 billion ($1.3 billion), or twice the volume of spot transactions on the Osaka Stock Exchange's first and second sections.[42]

Even as it was considering the expansion of futures markets at home, MOF began relaxing its restrictions on Japanese participation in markets overseas. On 19 May, the day before the Shōtorishin submitted its report, the International Finance Bureau decided to remove its ban on domestic financial institutions' and institutional investors' trading on foreign futures exchanges. In the past, they had worked through their foreign branches or other companies on the spot; now, banks, securities houses, insurance companies, and investment trust companies could participate directly in foreign markets from their head offices in Japan. Although MOF initially limited the liberalization to financial institutions' trading for their own accounts, it took only a few weeks before the ministry decided to permit financial institutions to act as agents for other investors.[43]

MOF was following a familiar pattern in granting financial institutions greater latitude overseas as a prelude to liberalizing markets at home. Providing access to financial futures markets abroad gave large investors a way to hedge their burgeoning foreign-currency assets against the risks posed by exchange- and interest-rate fluctuations. The ministry also faced American pressure. It was

[41] *Mainichi Shinbun* (24 March 1988).   [42] *Yomiuri Shinbun* (23 January 1988).
[43] *Nikkan Kōgyō Shinbun* (8 June 1987).

important to the U.S. government that American financial investments remain attractive to Japanese: Japanese brokerage firms had bought more than one-third of the U.S. bonds and notes sold at several Treasury auctions held in 1986 to finance the federal deficit. Finally, by means of a phased approach, MOF hoped to avoid costly mistakes.[44]

The easing of regulation precipitated yet another intersectoral confrontation, however: It was open to question whether banks and securities houses should share this business equally, or whether different instruments should be allotted to one or the other. There was no fence between banks and securities houses in futures markets overseas. Even in America, where, just as in Japan, regulations separated the spot operations of the two, both banks and securities firms could broker trades in futures markets. But when the story circulated at the end of July that MOF had decided that both could broker trades overseas, stockbrokers offered strong opposition, prompting a leading official of the Securities Bureau to deny that the issue had been settled. Brokerage houses asserted that the Securities Exchange Act ought to apply to foreign as well as to domestic securities futures: Banks were not authorized to act as agents at home, and neither should they be allowed to act as agents overseas.

Long-term U.S. government bond ("T-bond") futures became the focus of conflict. Because Japanese institutional investors had huge holdings in these bonds, there was little question that this futures instrument would be in great demand. Rumors began spreading that the TSE would start trading T-bond futures in the fall of 1988. That would enable securities houses to buy and sell America's principal financial futures instrument domestically whether or not they brokered orders abroad, and they would naturally come to monopolize commissions. In order to allay securities industry resistance, banks had announced that their proposed comprehensive financial futures market would begin with currency and short-term interest futures and would not attempt to list stock and domestic bond futures until it was well under way, but they were unwilling to forgo T-bond futures without a fight. Dealing in T-bonds would give substance to bankers' notion of a "comprehensive" market free from the regulations that partitioned spot transactions among banks and stockbrokers. More to the point, in the words of one banker, "it will be difficult to maintain a new futures market with just currency and interest [instruments]; it's no exaggeration to say that our success or failure depends on T-bond futures."[45]

Banks were hard pressed and in sore need of support. They got it in the form of a favorable *shingikai* report.

---

[44] Semkow (1989), pp. 41–42.
[45] *Nikkei Kin'yū Shinbun* (30 November 1987).

The Council on the Financial System and the Foreign Exchange Council

The Banking Bureau's Council on the Financial System (Kin'yū Seido Chōsakai, or Kinseichō) established a Financial Futures Subcommittee on 14 July 1987, and the International Finance Bureau's Foreign Exchange Council (Gaikoku Kawasetō Shingikai, or Gaitameshin: *tame* is an alternative reading of the first character of the word *kawase*) followed suit on 30 July. At the first meeting of the Gaitameshin's subcommittee on 31 August, its secretariat explained the status quo; the secretariat of the Kinseichō's subcommittee did so the next day. In its September and October sessions, the Gaitameshin's subcommittee heard witnesses from Citibank, the Chicago Mercantile Exchange, Daiichi Life, and Mitsubishi Trading Company speak on financial futures markets overseas and on the organization of a Japanese exchange. Similarly, the Kinseichō's subcommittee questioned officials from Mitsui Bank, Goldman Sachs, and the TSE. The two subcommittees thereupon decided to combine their operations, and joint meetings were held on 28 October and 6 November.

Why was there a need for further deliberations when the Shōtorishin had already considered the problem? If further deliberations were necessary, why were two subcommittees established instead of one? And once two independent subcommittees had been established, why did they combine?

Although security houses did, in fact, assert that there was no need to discuss the matter further, there were several reasons for renewing deliberations. First, the Shōtorishin had taken a very narrow approach, leaving various questions unresolved. Reflecting their parent bodies' jurisdictions, the Securities Bureau's Shōtorishin had dealt with securities futures, the Banking Bureau's Kinseichō was to examine any domestic futures markets in which banks might participate, and the International Finance Bureau's Gaitameshin was to investigate the liberalization of futures trading by Japanese firms overseas and the creation of a market for currency futures at home.

More to the point, perhaps, "because the views of the Shōtorishin were extremely one-sided in reflecting the views of the securities industry, there were many people who decided that its report wasn't necessarily in the interests of all Japanese."[46] In addition to disgruntled bankers seeking to overturn the recommendations of the Shōtorishin, officials of the Banking and International Finance Bureaus wanted to ensure that they, too, would have a say in the regulation of new futures markets. Banks could have used either the Kinseichō or the Gaitameshin to revive their proposal, but neither the Banking Bureau nor the International Finance Bureau could rely on an advisory body of the other to

---

[46] Interview with Sugita Ryōki.

represent its own standpoint adequately, so they initially had an incentive to consult their respective *shingikai* independently. Conversely, recognizing that they cannot pursue liberalization without one another's cooperation, officials from one MOF bureau have even been known to *request* that another bureau's council discuss a matter of mutual concern.[47]

Although the Kinseichō's and Gaitameshin's inquiries did differ somewhat at first, there was obviously considerable overlap in their deliberations. Combining the subcommittees enabled their parent bureaus to coordinate their views in advance. Given that the Securities Bureau had already acted on its own, two reports on the same subject would be less troublesome for MOF to reconcile than three. There may also have been a more self-interested motive for combining the subcommittees: "acting in tandem, the two provided a more powerful check on the influence of the Shōtorishin."[48]

Membership composition

The chairs of the Kinseichō and Gaitameshin nominated the councilors of their respective subcommittees on the basis of their parent bureaus' recommendations. "It's really MOF's business to choose," asserted one chair. "The members of the *shingikai* weren't consulted."[49] That is not to say that the ministry selected councilors with a free hand – far from it. Although an official of the International Finance Bureau asserted that "there's never any pressure from interest groups,"[50] just as in the case of the Shōtorishin, once the parent agencies had determined which industries would participate, informal rules described by councilors as "customary" and "natural" determined which corporations would represent them:

> First they choose the representatives of financial institutions. This has become a vested right. If it's a city bank, it's typically a manager from the bank chairing Zenginkyō. If it's a long-term credit bank, it's the Industrial Bank of Japan [the largest and most prestigious member of the group]. If it's a trust bank, it's the bank chairing the trust banks' association. The chair of the Securities Dealers Association comes. As for insurance companies, Nippon Life has been going recently because it chairs the Life Insurance Industry Association's Financial Affairs Committee. In general, it's all decided.[51]

Thus, both the Banking and International Finance Bureaus independently appointed officials of Mitsui Bank, Yasuda Trust, the Industrial Bank of Japan, Daiwa Securities, and Nippon Life to sit on their subcommittees (see Table

[47] S. Vogel (1994), p. 226.   [48] Interview with Sugita Ryōki.
[49] Interview with Kaizuka Keimei.
[50] Interview with Kitagawa Hiroyasu.
[51] Interview with Deguchi Haruaki and Kajio Akihiko.

5-1). Both bureaus also invited representatives from the Nōrin Chūkin Bank (the central bank of the agricultural cooperatives), securities industry leader Nomura, and a director of the TSE. Rounding out the list of members from financial institutions, the International Finance Bureau appointed a delegate from the Bank of Tokyo, which specialized in international transactions, and the president of Marusan Securities, a smaller brokerage house. Interests like smaller banks that had yet to show an active interest in futures were not invited to participate.

Speaking for nonfinancial industries that were likely to use futures were three councilors from major corporations. Those companies, too, were chosen for their representativeness. Keidanren recommended a vice president of Hitachi Manufacturing, for example. "Hitachi does all kinds of things – household goods, computers, communication equipment – . . . [so] we're like the Japanese economy in miniature, and our view represents the view of Japan's industrial circles."[52] Similar considerations surely lay behind the inclusion of Mitsui Trading and Nippon Steel. Despite the bids both sides made for their support, these potential corporate customers were basically neutral vis-à-vis the fence problem. Although favoring the creation of new futures instruments with which they could hedge their risks, "we've no interest whatsoever in whether only the securities industry or only the banking industry handles them."[53]

None of the persons of learning and experience had strong ties to the concerned parties. "In Japan, there's very little cooperation between industry and academe, and because such a [futures] system is rather new, scholars weren't biased. They spoke from the perspective of their specialized fields."[54] That is not to suggest that MOF officials selected these neutral members on the basis of purely technocratic considerations, however.

> Persons of learning and experience have no direct interest, so MOF doesn't *have* to make them members, but once they're serving as members, there's no way to control them. In other words, from MOF's point of view, it's neutral representatives who're the most frightening. In this sort of case, officials will listen to gossip, and try someone out on a council where it won't matter in order to see how he looks. After a personal connection has been established, they'll put him on an important council.[55]

Out of a total of 34 members, the joint subcommittee included 4 OBs, all from MOF. The chair of the Kinseichō's subcommittee, Kondō Michitaka, had been director of the Banking Bureau and served as a link to the parent *shingikai*, to which he belonged. In the Gaitameshin's subcommittee, Watanabe Kiichi had served in MOF from 1950 to 1983, finishing his bureaucratic career as a finance

[52] Interview with Miyauchi Yasuo.
[53] Interview with Imai Takashi.
[54] Interview with Satō Masayuki.
[55] Interview with Deguchi Haruaki and Kajio Akihiko.

secretary (*zaimukan*). At the time he joined the joint subcommittee, he was governor of a government bank. The other two OBs, Satō Mitsuo and Kaneko Tarō, offer a study in contrasts.

Satō, who spent 31 years in MOF before retiring as director of the Customs and Tariff Bureau to become a director of the TSE in 1986, had the unique distinction of getting appointed to all three *shingikai* subcommittees deliberating on financial futures. He had dealt with banks when serving on the Bank of Japan's Policy Committee but had also served in, and considered himself closer to, MOF's Securities Bureau. Another member of the joint subcommittee went further, describing Satō as a "representative of the interests of the Securities Bureau": "The Securities Bureau will say something excessive, then Mr. Satō will say something excessive at the Banking Bureau's *shingikai*. Although the Banking Bureau frowns on this, the Securities Bureau's behind him, and if he didn't say excessive things, the Securities Bureau would no longer recommend him."[56]

His tie to the ministry having attenuated, Kaneko, the president of Marusan Securities, offered a very different example. He entered MOF in 1949, moved to the Environment Agency in 1975, and retired in 1981 after having become its director. In his own eyes, Kaneko participated as a disinterested individual. "I'm not trying in the least to represent some government office or industry, and I'm not closer to MOF than other stockbrokers just because I'm an OB. On the contrary, I'm more distant [in my views]. The position of the Big Four differs little from that of the Securities Bureau, but mine is just the opposite. I'm of the opinion that [trading in] futures is premature."[57]

Individuals with ministry backgrounds do enjoy certain advantages. Because they are knowledgeable about Japan's financial system, "Finance OBs can do without staff. Because they've got experience, it's not a great burden. It's thus easier for an OB to become a member than for a non-OB." Even the author of these remarks warned against exaggerating the influence of individuals, however. "The strength of a person's voice was determined by the strength of his company [there were no women councilors] rather than by him personally."[58] Most councilors agreed that the role of OBs was no different from that of other members.

Retired bureaucrats aside, the joint subcommittee included three active officials, two from the Bank of Japan and one from the Cabinet Legislation Bureau. The Bank of Japan was neutral vis-à-vis banks and securities companies, but it naturally had an interest in how futures trading would influence monetary policy, for which it is responsible. The Cabinet Legislation Bureau, on the other hand, is responsible for drafting laws, and it attended the subcommittee in order

[56] Ibid.
[57] Interview with Kaneko Tarō.
[58] Interview with Itatani Masanori.

to determine at an early date what sort of bills would be necessary to provide for new futures instruments.

Councilors resisted any suggestion of close ties with the administration. In response to a written questionnaire, not a single respondent felt that he had been selected because his standpoint was close to that of the ministry, that his greatest responsibility was to the appointing authority, or that his role as a councilor was to represent an administrative agency. Significantly, neither did any member feel that his job was to mediate between conflicting interests, more of which later.

In sum, there is no evidence that the Banking and International Finance Bureaus selected *Japanese* councilors in a particularly manipulative or unrepresentative way – but the creation of new futures markets did raise the issue of *foreign* participation in *shingikai*. International linkages had multiplied, and foreign dealers encouraged the movement to create futures markets in Japan. It was with the support of America's Futures Industry Association (FIA) that 50 Japanese banks, securities houses, trading companies, and commodity traders began to organize a futures-dealing trade association in the summer of 1987. They modeled it on the American organization and even took the name FIA Japan. Underlining the international significance of developments in Japan, the chair of America's FIA traveled to Japan in August to confer with the heads of both MOF and MITI.

Foreigners were more than simply helpful. For Tokyo to be recognized as an international futures market, foreign brokers were indispensable, both for their know-how and for their clienteles. Most crucially, though, Japanese traders wanted to attract the participation of American speculators. In order for a futures market to perform properly, it is necessary for investors to differ over where the market is headed, but it was open to question whether there were enough Japanese investors willing to play the role of risk taker. Japanese traders were mostly "salaryman" employees of financial institutions, and unlike an individual investor who might be willing to speculate boldly, they tended to follow the pack.

Foreign futures brokers started coming to Tokyo in May, when MOF began lifting its prohibitions on Japanese firms' overseas dealings, and by the end of the year, almost all of the major concerns had opened representative offices. And yet, not one foreign organization was represented in either the Shōtorishin's, Kinseichō's, or Gaitameshin's subcommittee in spite of their indisputable interest in the proceedings. Because *shingikai* members are technically public servants, foreign nationals were at the time considered ineligible for membership, but this rule need not have excluded Japanese employees of foreign firms.

This issue had already become a source of friction. In order to provide foreign companies with the same window on policymaking enjoyed by their domestic competitors, the U.S. government in 1984 requested the inclusion of their

Japanese executives on such bodies as MITI's Industrial Structure Council. The Japanese reaction was violent. "One high official was quoted as saying our [i.e., American] proposal was akin to Japan demanding seats on the U.S. National Security Council. It was repeatedly said that we wanted to put foreigners who could not speak Japanese on the council. In fact, our proposal concerned only the possibility that Japanese citizens working in the Japanese subsidiaries of foreign companies have the same rights as other Japanese."[59] Ultimately, a few Japanese executives of foreign companies did begin sitting on *shingikai*, but not on those in question here. Although the subcommittees called foreigners as witnesses, it is questionable whether this form of participation carried much weight in *shingikai* deliberations.

With finance growing more international every day, many members of the joint subcommittee felt that the inclusion of representatives from foreign firms would one day be natural, even essential. Other members had reservations, however. Foreign firms did not rank among the largest companies in Japan's financial industry; did they really deserve a place on *shingikai*?[60] Would foreigners even know how to take advantage of the opportunity if MOF granted them such recognition? "Although Japanese have a knack for reading each other's thoughts [literally, "for understanding 'ah' and 'unh'"], foreign companies don't even have their head offices in Tokyo. They don't know what MOF's saying."[61]

They had yet to learn how to listen. *Shingikai* offer one route of access to MOF, but private corporations also maintain contact with ministry officials on a daily basis through special MOF liaisons (*Ōkurashō-tan* or *Mofu-tan*, from *Ōkurashō no tantōsha*, "the person in charge of [relations with] MOF") or, more picturesquely, "hallway swallows" (*rōka tonbi*, from their always flitting about the corridors of the ministry). The continuous, informal communication nurtured by these employees and the formal representation provided by *shingikai* complement one another.

> They're both important. Even if there's daily contact, it's often the case that an interest will be ignored if it doesn't speak out at *shingikai*. And even if an interest participates in *shingikai*, there'll be a tendency for its remarks to be misdirected if it isn't sending over "hallway swallows" every day. The balance between activity within the *shingikai* and the daily activity of the MOF-liaison is critical, but [the latter] costs a tremendous amount of money, and foreign firms aren't trying to do it. At first sight, it seems like a waste of time to send over a top man. . . . [Foreign firms] aren't familiar with the policymaking process of the Japanese government.[62]

[59] Prestowitz (1988), pp. 120–21.
[60] Interview with Horiuchi Akiyoshi.
[61] Interview with Deguchi Haruaki and Kajio Akihiko.
[62] Interview with Rōyama Shōichi.

Until foreign firms do manage to insinuate themselves into the entire communication networks of which *shingikai* are only a part, council membership may indeed be of little use to them.

Deliberations

Any new legislation would have to be prepared by the middle of March 1988 if the next ordinary Diet session was to act on futures, and because of various procedural formalities, the real deadline was January, so MOF was aiming for a settlement by year-end. Before the two specialist subcommittees had even begun their deliberations, newspapers reported that they would have to submit their recommendations in November. Although the subcommittees' parent bureaus did not explicitly set such a schedule, councilors understood that they faced a general deadline.

Nevertheless, their respective frames of reference were quite broad. Although the Kinseichō's subcommittee was to focus on the domestic market and the Gaitameshin's on international linkages, their parent bureaus decided that "it was all right to investigate anything to do with futures. There were no limits."[63] By not explicitly excluding securities futures, with which the Shōtorishin had already dealt, the Banking and International Financial Bureaus may have been implicitly inviting their *shingikai* to reconsider that body's report.

Formally, it was the subcommittee members who chose their own chairs, but in reality they simply agreed to the candidates put forward by their parent bureaus. The chair of the Kinseichō's subcommittee was Kondō Michitaka, chair of the advertising firm Hakuhōdō; the chair of the Gaitameshin's subcommittee was Iida Tsuneo, an economist from Nagoya University. Although Kondō was probably selected because he belonged to the Kinseichō (and perhaps because he was a Banking Bureau OB), Iida claimed to have no idea why he was chosen. The International Finance Bureau's reason for choosing him is not difficult to discern, however. Because the city of Nagoya had wanted to start trading in futures and options, it had joined Osaka in sending a fact-finding group to Britain and the United States several years earlier. Iida had been one of the Nagoya representatives, just as Professor Rōyama, chair of the Shōtorishin, had been one of the Osaka representatives.

Unlike Professor Rōyama, though, neither Professor Iida nor Kondō (who alternated in presiding over the joint meetings) exerted much substantive influence over subcommittee deliberations. Although they were responsible for conducting meetings smoothly and attempting to bring opposing views together, "the chairs never settled matters on their own authority."[64] In Professor Iida's own words, "I was just calling on people when a hand went up, so I was scarcely

---

[63] Interview with Kitagawa Hiroyasu.   [64] Interview with Satō Masayuki.

playing an active role." Ironically, that may have been for the best as far as the International Finance Bureau, which appointed him, was concerned: Personally, Professor Iida thought that futures trading was "extremely undesirable because of the 'money game' [i.e., speculation]."[65]

Because members coordinated their schedules in advance, almost everyone would attend meetings; sending proxies was forbidden. A considerable number of nonmembers did show up at meetings, though, perhaps twice as many as the councilors themselves. Behind corporate representatives would sit the subordinates who actually conducted investigations for their industries. They would not speak at the *shingikai*, but these subordinates would follow deliberations, discuss strategy after meetings, and go to MOF to press their industry's claims directly. While the subcommittees were in session, minutes of the proceedings would circulate among banks, securities houses, and other corporations, which could then approach councilors if they had an opinion to register. The Kinseichō's and Gaitameshin's subcommittees were closed to the public, however.

Delegates from the private sector had all attained the rank of at least managing director and, needless to say, companies sent people with expertise in the issues under discussion. Financial corporations have research organs of their own, and MOF itself depends on these firms for cooperation in gathering data. Of the 16 respondents to a written questionnaire, 14 joint subcommittee members felt that their possession of expertise had something to do with their having been selected councilors; only 2 (both representatives from nonfinancial businesses) felt that they had no special knowledge or experience relevant to the subject at hand.

Nevertheless, when asked whether he depended on MOF for information, even an official of a multinational like Daiwa had to reply that "it would be a lie to say no. We needed to supplement insufficiencies in our data, and . . . we couldn't help but rely on the ministry."[66] Persons of learning and experience lacked any staff whatsoever to brief them. The bureaucratic secretariat invariably responded to councilors' queries, though. On a scale of 1 ("do not use at all") to 5 ("use a great deal"), subcommittee members assessed their own knowledge at an average of 3.56, and data provided by the ministry at 4.31. The *shingikai* did not conduct research itself. Although there was talk of the Gaitameshin's subcommittee going overseas to examine the operations of other futures exchanges, money was never budgeted for such a field survey.[67]

One newspaper described the process of joining the two councils as "fitting together by rubbing."[68] Members reported no appreciable friction between the

[65] Interview with Iida Tsuneo.   [66] Interview with Satō Masayuki.
[67] Interview with Kitagawa Hiroyasu.
[68] *Nihon Keizai Shinbun* (25 October 1987).

subcommittees as solidary entities, however. Regardless of where members were originally appointed, it was banker versus stockbroker, not subcommittee versus subcommittee. "Speakers didn't make clear to which subcommittee they belonged. They participated as individuals representing an interest, and weren't the least bit concerned with which *shingikai*'s view they were representing"; "it felt like one council."[69]

Despite a pretense of individuality, there is no question that MOF chose most members on the understanding that they would speak for particular constituencies. One member asserted that "it's forbidden to appear too much in the guise of an interest representative at *shingikai*," but that same member went on succinctly to note, "I am not the individual Miyauchi. I'm not even the representative of Hitachi Manufacturing. Everyone is participating as the representative of his industry."[70] It is interesting to observe that one of the few exceptions to this rule was Kaneko, the ministry OB. He probably had the self-confidence to speak his mind precisely because he was a retired official. "I may speak as an individual, but that's rare. The representatives of the Big Four don't speak as individuals."[71] Kaneko was right. As an executive of Nomura Securities explained, "even if you have views as an individual, when they're different from the views of the organization to which you belong, you won't state them at the *shingikai*."[72]

Except for the maverick Kaneko, councilors from the securities industry presented a united front. The positions of Daiwa, Nomura, and the TSE never differed on fundamentals, and smaller brokerage firms simply did not count: "Because you're a representative of the securities industry, you state views in a way that adequately reflects the wishes of the securities industry, but what you say doesn't reflect *everyone's* opinion."[73] Mitsui Bank conducted *nemawashi* through Zenginkyō to define and unite that industry's more diverse views in advance of *shingikai* meetings. (Whichever city bank serves as chair in a given year will perform many of the functions of Zenginkyō, which lacks much of a formal organization of its own.) "We went as representatives of the interests of all banks, from large to small," one Mitsui official declared.[74] That was not entirely true. Although there clearly was a basic understanding on what bank members would say at the *shingikai*, "they united around the standpoint of big banks. Had the subcommittees included representatives of small- and medium-sized banks, we may not have seen such unity. The views of those people from small- and medium-sized banks whom we called as witnesses were very conservative."[75]

---

[69] Interviews with Ōyama Hiroto and Iida Tsuneo.
[70] Interview with Miyauchi Yasuo.   [71] Interview with Kaneko Tarō.
[72] Interview with Itatani Masanori.   [73] Ibid.
[74] Interview with Yahagi Mitsuaki.
[75] Interview with Horiuchi Akiyoshi.

Table 5-2. *Characteristics of parent organizations and joint subcommittee deliberations*

To what extent do you think each of the following attributes of councilors' parent organizations influence advisory body deliberations?

No influence whatsoever 1 2 3 4 5 Extremely strong influence	(*n* = 16)
1 Degree to which affected by council's report	3.75
2 Ability to affect the ministries	3.67
3 Ability to affect public opinion	3.44
4 Technical information presented	3.25
5 Ability to affect the Diet	3.0
Percent of the total eligible group represented	3.0
Lobbying skill	3.0
6 Number of members	2.5
7 Prestige	2.33
8 Economic resources	1.6
To what extent does the principle of balance influence these deliberations?	3.93

Curiously, there were extreme differences of opinion among participants over the nature of deliberations. On the one hand, several councilors reported that discussions were temperate. "Representatives of industry cautiously observed the situation and didn't speak much themselves. They were looking for material in preparation for when they'd apply pressure on MOF from behind the scenes later," observed one scholar.[76] Other members painted a much stormier picture, describing arguments that were "dreadfully heated," "vehement."[77]

In response to a written questionnaire, members of the joint subcommittee reported that the principle of balance, the degree to which the interests represented would be affected by council recommendations, and those interests' ability to affect the ministries were the factors having the greatest influence on deliberations (see Table 5-2). Just as in MOL's Chūkishin, councilors minimized the importance of organizational strength in general and economic resources in particular. Assessments varied little by member category, although representatives of corporations other than banks and security houses gave extra emphasis to groups' lobbying skills and prestige, and scholars downgraded the significance of organizations' ability to influence the Diet.

[76] Ibid.
[77] Interviews with Miyauchi Yasuo and Kanzaki Katsurō.

The report

In September, a ministry official said, "As for what form [a settlement] will take, we're leaving everything to the committees."[78] Actually, MOF tried to arrive at an intraministerial settlement *before* the two councils started drafting a report, and it was disclosed in mid-October that the ministry was moving toward a compromise plan of its own. A revised Securities Exchange Act would allow stockbrokers to trade futures in the financial instruments that stock exchanges already listed, a new Futures Trading Act would permit transactions by banks and perhaps securities houses in other domestic and foreign futures instruments, and banks and stockbrokers would "ride together" abroad. Although this was in line with stockbrokers' demand for linking spot and futures markets domestically, the plan allotted American T-bonds to the banks' exchange.[79]

There was some tentative support for this plan within the securities industry, but Takeuchi Michio, TSE chair (and a former MOF vice minister), refused to relinquish the exchange's claim to T-bonds, and industry leader Nomura Securities rejected the plan. Banks, on the other hand, felt it was stockbrokers whom the plan favored. Although securities firms would be able to take advantage of active markets in currency and interest futures abroad, the opportunities opened to banks in overseas exchanges would not compare with the trading in Japanese government bond futures in domestic stock exchanges that would remain closed to them. MOF was thus unable to adjust the conflicting interests in advance of the joint subcommittee.

The two councils put together a common report on 26 November. This joint report looked very different from the Shōtorishin's (see Table 5-3). The Shōtorishin had focused on domestic securities markets, but the joint report noted how Japan could profit from the experience of countries that had already developed futures markets.

> The first characteristic of financial futures transactions in foreign countries is that there are comprehensive markets where it is possible to trade a wide variety of financial futures. . . . The second characteristic is that such comprehensive financial futures trading is conducted on the basis of a uniform regulatory system. . . . At a time when the integration of markets among various countries is progressing, . . . it is essential to create a framework that has as much as possible in common with financial futures markets overseas.[80]

The joint report thus implicitly recommended that a comprehensive exchange should handle the bond and stock price index futures that stock

---

[78] *Nikkan Kōgyō Shinbun* (1 September 1987).   [79] *Kin'yū Keizai Shinbun* (12 October 1987).
[80] Kin'yū Seido Chōsakai and Gaikoku Kawasetō Shingikai (1987), pp. 4, 7.

Table 5-3. *A comparison of the two reports on financial futures*

	Shōtorishin	Kinseichō and Gaitameshin
Goal	In light of the liberalization and internationalization of financial markets, to provide a means of hedging investments	Same
Legal basis	Revise the Securities Exchange Act	Enact a new Financial Futures Act
Futures to be listed	Securities futures alone	As wide a range of instruments as possible
Site of trading	Existing stock exchanges	A new, comprehensive financial futures exchange independent of existing stock exchanges
Direct participants	Limited to securities firms	As wide a range of actors as possible
Relation to spot markets	Unified operation of the two markets is necessary: futures must be handled by the brokers who handle the corresponding spot goods	It is unnecessary to unite the two markets

Source: *Nihon Keizai Shinbun* (27 November 1987).

exchanges claimed for themselves. As for access to the new market, the report distinguished between those participants who would trade for themselves alone and those who could also act as trustees for others, but the thrust of the proposal was that "it is desirable to make the scope of direct participation in financial futures markets as wide as possible."[81] A uniform set of regulations should govern brokering both at home and abroad. In short, the government should completely remove the fence between banks and stockbrokers in futures.

The press observed how the report "reflected" the banking industry's assertions, was "partial to banks," or was even "modeled on" Zenginkyō's February proposal.[82] Bureaucrats of the Banking and International Finance Bureaus rejected these assessments. "Such descriptions are journalistic," complained one official. "It wasn't a matter of making a model of something. It's often the case that each industry['s trade association] acts as a go-between. After various discussions within each industry, a consensus is born and submitted in the form of a written request. Sometimes we ignore these requests, sometimes we expand on them."[83] Most subcommittee members, on the other

---

[81] Ibid., pp. 11, 12.
[82] *Nihon Keizai Shinbun* (18 November 1987); *Asahi Shinbun* (18 November 1987); *Nikkei Kōshasai Jōhō* (9 November 1987).
[83] Interview with Koyama Yoshiaki.

hand, echoed the press's "journalistic" assessments. Councilors were not constantly referring to Zenginkyō's plan at meetings, and it was not adopted unamended, but "the fundamental current of discussion was extremely similar"; "it wasn't a matter of starting with a clean slate."[84] Just as the banking industry had violently opposed the way the Shōtorishin's proposals reflected stockbrokers' demands, it was now the turn of the securities industry to attack the joint report as one-sided.

Why was the report of the Kinseichō's and Gaitameshin's subcommittees so favorable to banks? Officials of the Banking and International Finance Bureaus attributed the disparities in the reports to timing: "After the Shōtorishin report, everyone started studying futures trading in America and elsewhere, and the idea that Japan, too, should handle futures more comprehensively gradually started to gain strength."[85] It is true that the banking industry was better prepared to press its case for the separation of spots and futures in the fall than it had been in the spring, but the most significant financial event of the intervening months was unquestionably the stock market crash of 19 October, which *undermined* confidence in the American model that the joint report ended up endorsing.

One councilor pointed to the influence of foreign actors: "In order to cope with foreign pressure, MOF wanted to make it a more general system. And even in the absence of foreign pressure, they wanted to demonstrate that Japan can change."[86] Private interests overseas clearly were interested in the early establishment of futures markets in Japan, and America's Treasury Department was said to have supported demands for the liberalization and internationalization of Japanese futures markets in its ongoing discussions with MOF.

Foreign pressure did not play a major role in shaping the contents of the joint report, however. Such pressure was probably most intense when MOF was liberalizing the overseas trading of Japanese and was presumably motivated by a desire for increased Japanese investment on foreign exchanges. At home, Japanese were spontaneously seeking out the views of foreign actors without having to be pushed. "Rather than foreign pressure, we actively approached people at places like Chicago's Board of Trade and the Mercantile Exchange," reported a Banking Bureau official.[87] Although foreign traders did plan to use any new Japanese futures markets, they had no pressing need for them. "Even without a Japanese futures market, [foreigners] can already hedge their risks here through forward contracts, and they can trade in futures overseas. A futures market is being created because of strong demands from the *domestic* financial industry in order to maintain Japan as a financial center."[88] The main impetus for change came from within Japan, and it was exclusively Japanese

---

[84] Interviews with Satō Mitsuo and Ōyama Hiroto.
[85] Interview with Kikuta Yutaka.   [86] Interview with Horiuchi Akiyoshi.
[87] Interview with Koyama Yoshiaki.   [88] Interview with Tachi Ryūichirō.

actors who determined the course of that change. Foreigners were concerned with their access to Japanese futures markets, not with precisely what form those markets took.

Some councilors suggested that the membership compositions of the respective councils had determined their conclusions. A bank executive's remark was typical: "At the Shōtorishin, because securities companies were more numerous, even if we voiced our views, we were in the minority. At the Kinseichō, it was the opposite."[89] And yet, a quick glance at Table 5-1 reveals that the membership compositions of all the special futures subcommittees were quite similar, and certainly not different enough to account for diametrically opposed reports. It flies against reason to think that MOF bureaus would try to influence their *shingikai* in so crude a way. "When interests are violently opposed, it's difficult to choose members in a way advantageous to one side. If the ministry did that, they wouldn't be able to expect cooperation after passage of a law."[90] In truth, the exact ratios of banker versus stockbroker members mattered little. "If we decided by majority vote, it might have some significance, but because we don't run *shingikai* by majority vote, it's not all that meaningful whether the representation is fair." The author of these remarks asserted that "compromise, rule by consensus, are presupposed."[91] That consensus was not readily forthcoming, however.

Although the views of the antagonists "traced parallel lines" in the joint subcommittee,[92] as in the Shōtorishin, neutral members did not attempt to mediate. As one scholar recalled, "it was impossible to mediate the confrontation, so I didn't think I'd try. We [persons of learning and experience] are sometimes expected to do that, but. . . ."[93] Why should it have been impossible for neutral members to mediate? "There was a feeling that 'this is a banking industry *shingikai*,' so everyone thought from the start that it would be impossible to gather views and have the *shingikai* mediate the confrontation."[94] "This is a banking industry *shingikai*": To most subcommittee members, the difference in parent bureaus was reason enough to expect different reports. Whereas the Securities Bureau had managed the Shōtorishin in the interests of the securities industry, the Banking and International Finance Bureaus managed the Kinseichō and the Gaitameshin in the interests of the banking industry. In the metaphor of a stockbroker in the joint subcommittee, "it was disadvantageous for us to clash at an away stadium [literally, 'a neighboring sumo ring']."[95]

One member took a cynical view of the entire process, arguing that ministry consultation and coercion of private interests allowed it to "have the conclusion from the start":

[89] Interview with Yahagi Mitsuaki.   [90] Interview with Egashira Kenjirō.
[91] Interview with Ōyama Hiroto.   [92] Interview with Arai Jōji.
[93] Interview with Kanda Hideki.   [94] Interview with Satō Mitsui.
[95] Interview with Itatani Masanori.

In order that views in line with the ministry's come out during deliberations, there'll be *nemawashi* before the *shingikai* is in session, and a detailed
adjustment will be carried out. You'll understand in advance that MOF's
idea is A, and when MOF's idea is A, even if the representative's idea is B,
it's difficult to say B. If a representative voices an opinion that isn't in line
with MOF's, they'll take revenge later.[96]

So extreme a view is out of place in this instance, if only because there was no
consensus among the different MOF bureaus. The Banking and International
Finance Bureaus could not very well punish stockbrokers for taking a position
supported by the Securities Bureau, and stockbrokers are not bashful about
enlisting that bureau's aid.

One member described the canvassing of councilors by the Banking and
International Finance Bureaus:

They had an objective: it was necessary to establish a futures market soon.
Security companies had stolen a march and created stock price index
futures on the Osaka Stock Exchange. This coup troubled them, and they
were in a hurry. Two or three days before the *shingikai* met, officials would
come and visit to conduct *nemawashi*. "We want to do it this way, and we'd
like your cooperation." Some people cooperated, some didn't.[97]

Even this account is open to misinterpretation in that the subcommittees'
recommendations clearly did represent the majority opinion. Neutral members
in the joint subcommittee had their own reasons for favoring the banks' position.
"From the user's point of view, there's no question that having one [futures]
market is more convenient. . . . With one route, there'd be more depth to the
market," observed a trading company official.[98] "I had the impression that the
way of thinking advocated by Zenginkyō was more reasonable. The assertions of
the security companies were too domestically oriented," argued another disinterested councilor.[99] This time, it was representatives of the securities industry
who stood alone.

Although the chairs entrusted the drafting of the report to the secretariat, it
could not write something at odds with the proceedings of the subcommittees,
particularly when the confrontation between interested parties had been so
sharp. "At the *shingikai*, various views came out freely, briskly. Bureaucrats
listened to these views because they foretold what each representative would
demand later."[100] Staffers met councilors at their homes, one by one, to solicit
their opinions of prepared drafts, and the secretariat amended those drafts
where necessary to defuse objections. Every group of members requested some

[96] Interview with Deguchi Haruaki and Kajio Akihiko.
[97] Interview with Ōyama Hiroto.
[98] *Nikkei Kin'yū Shinbun* (22 January 1988).
[99] Interview with Sugita Ryōki.
[100] Interview with Horiuchi Akiyoshi.

modifications but, predictably, the securities industry offered the greatest resistance to the first plan. Without ever explicitly labeling them as such ("An opinion was advanced that . . ."), the final report acknowledged stockbrokers' contentions often enough to trace the outlines of a minority report. (Academics have argued that reports should name the authors of the views they cite; MOF opposed such a move.)

Bureaucrats will not present a final draft that is likely to be changed in any major way, so "it's extremely rare to voice opposition to a report at the *shingikai* itself. In the end, everyone can't help but say 'okay.'"[101] An official of the Securities Dealers Association condemned the joint committee's way of settling its report as "a little highhanded."[102] "Banks' assertions are treated as orthodox, and securities firms' assertions as additional points of view. You can't say that's fair," grumbled one councilor.[103] The representatives of the securities industry nevertheless refrained from blocking passage of the report, and the joint subcommittee approved it unanimously. "Several members couldn't individually consent to the report. Although they still opposed it, perhaps, they put their names down and acknowledged it. That's one form of consensus formation," Chairman Iida noted without a trace of irony.[104]

Although stockbrokers once again criticized the joint report at plenary sessions of the Kinseichō and the Gaitameshin, theirs was a minority opinion; other councilors had only minor reservations. With negotiations already completed at the subcommittee level, the two *shingikai* did not conduct substantive debates. Plenary sessions of the Kinseichō and the Gaitameshin approved the joint report on 4 December and 8 December, respectively.

The final settlement

As a bureaucrat in MOF's Banking Bureau commented at the time, "the submission of the [joint] report isn't the end, it's the beginning."[105] Because the joint report had targeted as wide a set of financial instruments as possible instead of limiting itself to currency and interest futures, a collision with the TSE was unavoidable. There was also the issue of how to harmonize a new, unified Financial Futures Act with those provisions of the Securities Exchange Act that already provided the legal basis for trading in bond futures. There was no alternative to the concerned parties' somehow coming to an understanding: Everyone agreed that it was necessary to introduce financial futures to Japan. MOF's Securities, Banking, and International Finance Bureaus groped for an acceptable compromise. For one newspaper, it would be "a showplace of administrative authorities' ability to reconcile" conflicting interests.[106]

---

[101] Interview with Yahagi Mitsuaki.   [102] Interview with Kikuichi Mamoru.
[103] *Nikkei Kōshasai Jōhō* (9 November 1987).   [104] Interview with Iida Tsuneo.
[105] *Nikkei Kin'yū Shinbun* (30 November 1987).   [106] Ibid.

Buoyed by the joint report, banks began preparing a new, comprehensive financial futures exchange. Although they also planned to list T-bond and, ultimately, stock and Japanese government bond futures, their exchange would begin with the yen–dollar exchange rate and the interest rates on short-term Euroyen and Eurodollar deposits. Stockbrokers, on the other hand, anticipated that their standpoint would prevail in the administrative adjustment to come. After all, stock exchanges were already handling Japanese government bond futures and were readying stock price index futures for the summer of 1988. The securities industry hoped to create another fait accompli before the banks' exchange saw the light of day.

Interested parties continued to press their views on MOF bureaucrats after the *shingikai* submitted their reports. An executive of the Securities Dealers Association spoke of the "intense appeals" the association made at this time.[107] Bankers approached officials in the Securities Bureau, and stockbrokers approached officials in the Banking and International Finance Bureaus. Everyone downplayed the effect of industry lobbying on intraministerial negotiations, however.

As an OB councilor explained, the esprit de corp of MOF limits the influence of extragovernmental actors:

> MOF people are terribly proud; they don't in the least consider themselves to be servants of industry. Government officials dislike private interests' trying to apply pressure. They compose reports by looking into the interests of the respective industries, but in the end, the Securities, Banking, and International Finance Bureaus all want to decide what to do by themselves, apart from industry. I think that kind of great pride among bureaucrats is a decisive difference between Japan and America.[108]

Incumbent officials held forth on their idealistic sense of mission. "If the issue were decided by power relations alone, the system would be distorted," declared one bureaucrat. "We don't listen to loud voices alone, but to soft ones, too. We take pride in thinking of the greatest happiness of the greatest number."[109] They routinely minimized the role of private actors in the final negotiations. "We already grasped [industries'] wishes," noted the Banking Bureau official in charge of reaching a settlement. "Compared to lobbying in America, the influence of approaches by industry was fairly slight."[110] A banker echoed this assessment: "In previous stages, like at the *shingikai*, we told the Banking Bureau that we'd like to have them negotiate along such and such lines. After a certain point, we're just repeating the same thing. Basically, the banking industry has no choice but to rely on coordination by the Banking Bureau."[111]

[107] Interview with Kikuichi Mamoru.   [108] Interview with Satō Mitsuo.
[109] Interview with Kikuta Yutaka.   [110] Interview with Koyama Yoshiaki.
[111] Interview with Kimura Hajime.

Although a Banking Bureau official complained at the end of November that "we don't have any idea what kind of bill will result"[112] and MOF failed to meet its self-imposed year-end deadline, the broad outlines of a settlement began to emerge. It was obvious from the start that banks would have to retreat from the comprehensive market they envisioned. First, the stubborn facts were that stock exchanges already listed bond futures, and the Kabusaki 50 being traded in Osaka represented a concrete step on the road to stock price index futures. Second, "no one had prepared their theoretical armament more thoroughly than the Securities Bureau."[113] Most important, a truly comprehensive financial futures law would have to supersede those portions of the existing Securities Exchange Act relating to securities futures, yet stockbrokers were unalterably opposed to so inclusive a law, and there was support even within the Banking Bureau for a more flexible approach that would divide markets between a new Financial Futures Act and the old Securities Exchange Act. Although the banks' new exchange would have the legal potential to trade a wide range of financial commodities in the future, it would initially confine itself to things like currency futures and short-term interest instruments, thus avoiding competition with stock exchanges. Where to trade T-bonds remained a sticking point, however.

Intraministerial negotiations moved up and down the bureaucratic ladder. While in close contact with their superiors, the responsible section chiefs (*kachō*) at the Securities, Banking, and International Finance Bureaus talked to one another continuously behind the scenes. "Those at the top will give instructions and decide in the end, but when they themselves talk, negotiations are already largely completed. In Japan, it's the section chief level that moves," observed a Banking Bureau official of that rank.[114]

On 12 January 1988, the three MOF bureaus finally reached an agreement. The government would revise the Securities Exchange Act so that stock exchanges could list the futures of all securities, including T-bonds, and enact a Financial Futures Trading Act in order to establish a separate exchange for all other futures instruments. Participation in both markets would be as wide as possible. MOF would allow domestic and foreign securities houses to broker the trading of all instruments listed on the new Financial Futures Exchange except for currency spot options. Correspondingly, banks would be permitted to broker the trading of all of the new instruments listed on stock exchanges except for stock price indices and stock spot options. The same rules would apply to overseas markets. Foreign dealers who specialized in futures trading alone could handle all of the instruments listed on either domestic exchange. The ministry

[112] *Nikkan Kōgyō Shinbun* (30 November 1987).
[113] Interview with Rōyama Shōichi.
[114] Interview with Koyama Yoshiaki.

Table 5-4. *The scope of permissible dealing in futures markets*

Futures instrument	Domestic banks	Domestic stockbrokers	Foreign futures specialists
Interest rates	O[a]	O	O
Currencies	O	O	O
Domestic government bonds	O	O	O
Foreign government bonds	O	O	O
Stock price indices	X	O	O
Stock spot options	X	O	O
Currency spot options	O	X	O

[a] O = permitted; X = forbidden.
Source: Adapted from *Nihon Keizai Shinbun* (13 January 1988).

had chosen to follow a third path, one between those of the two antagonists (see Table 5-4).

Seen in perspective, this settlement was typical of MOF's long-term strategy for liberalization. As Steven Vogel has concluded, "By the mid-1980s, ministry officials were convinced that they would have to desegment the financial system over time to produce stronger financial institutions and more efficient markets. But the MoF view of the public interest bears a strong preference for stability, even at the expense of efficiency." In concrete terms, "the ministry operated a tacit barter system between the banks and the securities houses" to protect financial institutions from failure.[115] In this case, too, banks and securities houses would share both gains and pains, with MOF compensating each sector in one area for business it might lose in another. Predictably, though, their reactions to each facet of the compromise were diametrically opposed.

If securities houses approved of the plan's linking spots and futures, banks were miffed at the rejection of their comprehensive market, and they raised the specter of foreign displeasure. In the words of a director at one of the city banks, "Without paying attention to international considerations, the Tokyo market is unfortunately moving in the wrong direction. . . . Because this ruling recognizes two exchanges, which is peculiar in light of the world trend, it won't be accepted internationally, and could thus hamper development of the Tokyo market."[116] Although MOF had decided to allow foreign futures specialists to broker the trading of all instruments, including the stock price indices barred to bankers, out of precisely such "international considerations," that did not prevent bankers from complaining of "reverse discrimination"

[115] S. Vogel (1994), pp. 238, 225. Cf. S. Vogel (1996), p. 199.
[116] *Nikkei Kin'yū Shinbun* (13 January 1988).

against themselves. (This was not the first time that MOF granted greater power to foreign firms than to their domestic counterparts. It had previously permitted foreign commercial banks with trust departments to engage in trust banking and securities affiliates of foreign commercial and universal banks to apply for Japanese securities licenses while denying those opportunities to domestic commercial banks.[117])

Regarding stock price indices, bankers called attention to how American banks could broker their futures through subsidiaries and how banks themselves could trade them in Britain. But in line with a long-standing policy, the International Finance Bureau also withheld the right of stockbrokers to trade in spot currency options. Chairman Tabuchi Setsuya of the Securities Dealers Association charged MOF with having been "swayed too much by exchange bank-ism" and wondered whether continued adherence to this practice, peculiar to Japan, would not invite a "queer feeling" abroad.[118] Options perform the same functions as futures, and investors often use the two together to limit risks; what rationale could there be for permitting securities firms to trade one and not the other? Because MOF would now permit stockbrokers to broker currency futures, bankers, on the other hand, feared that the ministry compromise had *destroyed* their exclusive jurisdiction over foreign exchange.

One banker characterized these aspects of the settlement as a "minus barter: if you do this, then you can't do that."[119] There were at least two reasons for this arrangement. Dealing in foreign currencies is lucrative for exchange banks; stock price indices promised to be a rewarding new line of business for securities houses. Continued regulation of those market niches thus amounted to continued protection of each industry's profitability. "The ministry is striking a balance here. Overall, everyone's a loser, but everyone's a winner."[120] In addition, a more thorough liberalization would have required the immediate abolition of Article 65 of the Securities Exchange Act and a major overhaul of the Foreign Exchange and Trade Control Act, a regulatory revolution of whose benefits MOF was skeptical.

Concerning the disposition of bond futures, one stockbroker confessed, "I don't know who gained."[121] The trading of Japanese government and American T-bond futures would be conducted on stock exchanges and regulated by the Securities Bureau. Thus limited to currency and short-term interest futures, the volume of transactions on their financial futures exchange would be too small to cover overhead costs, bankers fretted. And yet, MOF had promised to grant banks #2 licenses recognizing their right to broker domestic and foreign bond futures. Although banks would not be allowed to broker these futures on the

[117] Semkow (1989), pp. 55–56.   [118] *Nihon Keizai Shinbun* (13 January 1988).
[119] Interview with Kimura Hajime.   [120] Interview with Kanda Hideki.
[121] *Nikkei Kin'yū Shinbun* (13 January 1988).

TSE until securities houses began brokering financial futures on the banks' new exchange, this concession almost wrecked the entire arrangement.

Stockbrokers were outraged. "The #2 license is sacred ground for the securities industry," a stockbroker had asserted before the ministry settlement. "If they broach that, we'll be stabbing at each other."[122] One bond newsletter reported that Chairman Takeuchi of the TSE had asked the chief of the Banking Bureau to "please stop sticking your hand in other people's pockets."[123] After it was learned that banks would, indeed, be receiving #2 licenses, the Securities Dealers Association's Tabuchi lamented, "We in the securities industry insisted it was premature, but the Ministry of Finance wouldn't do us the favor of acknowledging that. Because banks' branch networks are rather large, the securities industry's share [of business] will be eaten up, leading to terrible losses."[124] There was thus a feeling among stockbrokers that banks had taken profit over fame (*na o sutete, mi o totta* – literally, "thrown away the name and taken the fruit"). Some stockbrokers had conjectured from the start that banks' advocacy of a comprehensive exchange that could list bond futures was no more than a ploy to jolt the TSE and obtain #2 licenses. Bankers, meanwhile, resented having to barter away the listing of government bond futures in order to gain the brokerage rights to which they felt they had been entitled all along.

MOF officials bridled at reports that they had presided over a merely expedient "barter." One bureaucrat conceded that

> you can definitely say that we had to make adjustments among interest groups, but we decided after considering various factors: whether the system will move smoothly this way, whether the futures markets will be able to go on to grow internationally, how to protect investors. We take a more comprehensive view. When you just conduct barter transactions, the system will be distorted, so we're careful on that point.[125]

Another, higher-ranking official was downright indignant. "As the person in charge, my only impression is of having done what had to be done. If securities futures were to be listed on the stock exchange, then it was natural to let banks act as agents. There was nothing that could be defined as 'barter.' It's deplorable to be capable of only that sort of point of view."[126] Most other observers were less fastidious. Asked whether the listing of T-bonds on stock exchanges had, in effect, been bartered for #2 licenses, Professor Rōyama replied, "Yes, exactly. In Japan, barter's rarely explicit. Those who're involved all know, but it isn't made public."[127]

[122] Ibid. (28 December 1987).   [123] *Nikkei Kōshasai Jōhō* (18 January 1988).
[124] *Nikkei Kin'yū Shinbun* (14 January 1988).
[125] Interview with Kikuta Yutaka.
[126] Interview with Koyama Yoshiaki.
[127] Interview with Rōyama Shōichi.

Despite the Securities and Banking Bureaus' having compromised, the securities and banking industries continued to drag their feet. At a meeting with Deputy Director Matsuno Masahiko of the Securities Bureau on the eve of MOF's announcement of its plan, four brokerage house vice presidents went so far as to suggest that they would rather see the futures issue deferred than accept the ministry's compromise. Matsuno was reportedly "purple with rage" at this display of defiance.[128] Banks were dissatisfied with the compromise plan for reasons of their own. After having already consulted three *shingikai* on the same problem, MOF was ready to go to any length to avoid an inconclusive outcome, and industry opposition was contained though intense *nemawashi*. (Although they acknowledged the lack of support for their final settlement among interested parties, MOF officials belittled reports like this: "It's wrong to understand relations between industry and MOF, and within MOF, in terms of yellow journalistic phrases like 'intense *nemawashi*.'"[129])

"Following the course of past financial administration, this adjustment plan adds the claims of the banking and securities industries and divides by two, which has not always delineated the best form that the market should take for the future," sniffed *Nihon Keizai Shinbun*. In criticizing MOF, the newspaper had actually pinpointed the practicality of the plan. "I don't think there's anyone who's 100 percent satisfied, but MOF has settled the debate skillfully for us," commented a director of the TSE. "Although I can't say that I'm 100 percent satisfied in light of the comprehensive market that we were insisting on, as a realistic policy, there was no choice but to start in a way like this," conceded a banker. Although *Nihon Keizai Shinbun* had predicted that "it is unavoidable that some kind of demands for improvement will come from foreign traders sooner or later," even foreigners expressed relief that the bickering and dickering were over and that Japan would finally move ahead. According to Morgan Futures's top man in Tokyo, "Whenever you start to debate, a considerable amount of time gets eaten up. Because the introduction of futures is a pressing problem, better this settlement than being particular forever and ever and delaying matters."[130]

MOF's compromise settled the fence problem of banks versus securities houses in the sphere of financial futures. The ministry plan seemed to have given consideration to the interests of all of the concerned parties, including foreign companies. That impression is misleading. Life insurance companies, which are neither fish nor fowl in this field, were left hanging by a settlement that focused on the head-on collision of bankers and stockbrokers, and regional interests had been slighted by the geocentric Tokyo establishment.

[128] *Nikkei Kin'yū Shinbun* (13 January 1988).
[129] Interview with Kikuta Yutaka.
[130] *Nihon Keizai Shinbun* (13 January 1988); *Nikkei Kin'yū Shinbun* (14, 15 January 1988).

Given their vast assets, life insurance companies wanted futures markets with as wide a range of instruments and as many ways of hedging risk as possible. Although that inclined them toward the banking industry's point of view, they were more interested in acquiring the right to deal for themselves and in the early establishment of futures markets than they were in the exact form those markets took.

Banks were not unanimous in their support of insurance companies' claims, but they themselves had called for a market that would allow as broad participation as possible and they were willing to accept foreign dealers, so it was difficult to refuse. Besides, as large institutional investors, insurance companies would become important players on the fledgling futures exchange. The TSE was less anxious about its volume of transactions, so stockbrokers' reaction to the advances of the insurance industry was cool. Securities houses considered it imposition enough that they had to deal with banks, and they asked where the Insurance Industry Act provided for insurance companies' handling instruments like government bond futures. "Japan's life insurance companies have gotten too big. They're trying to do everything," an official of the Securities Dealers Association complained.[131]

The Shōtorishin's 1984 and 1987 reports had concluded that direct participation in securities futures trading could be expanded beyond securities firms, but only to those financial institutions authorized to broker the corresponding spots. Neither report had clarified the scope of membership for firms that would trade only for themselves. Insurance companies had taken a back seat at the Shōtorishin's subcommittee in 1987. "At first, they weren't interested. Although they spoke if pressed, they didn't actively try to represent the standpoint of institutional investors. Only gradually did they begin to recognize the importance" of the issue.[132] Officials of MOF's Securities Bureau defended their having focused their attention elsewhere: "Each industry has its respective desires, and we can't adopt all of them. We have to make adjustments. The requests of life insurance companies were cut during those adjustments. They weren't completely ignored, however. We discussed them. . . . Because there are stages [to the policymaking process], it's not as if we'll never do anything for them in the future."[133]

Even at the Kinseichō and Gaitameshin's joint subcommittee, life insurance companies "cast a faint shadow"; "speaking infrequently, they weren't conspicuous."[134] Although insurance companies were relatively slow to grasp the opportunities and dangers posed by financial liberalization, they did echo banks' demands and insisted from the start that they wanted to be included as full members of any new financial futures exchange, something denied them by the

[131] Interview with Kikuichi Mamoru.   [132] Interview with Rōyama Shōichi.
[133] Interview with Moriya Manabu.
[134] Interviews with Minaguchi Kōichi and Kanda Hideki.

TSE. According to one banker, the insurance industry supported banks in the joint subcommittee in order to ensure their becoming members in the banks' exchange, and banks called for a "broad range" of participants out of consideration for insurance companies.[135] The report of the joint subcommittee explicitly approved of direct participation in futures markets by firms that would trade only for themselves as well as by those that would broker trades.

There was reason for the insurance industry to hope: When the government lifted its prohibition on trading for one's own account in overseas futures markets, it treated banks, securities houses, investment trusts, *and* insurance companies equally. Yet MOF's final settlement referred only to "financial institutions" (*kin'yū kikan*), "securities companies," and "investors," without ever specifying whether life insurance companies were included with banks among "financial institutions." When questioned, the ministry bluntly explained that the question was still open.[136] Insurance companies felt as if they had been dealt out.

Insurance companies are not supervised by an independent bureau, but by the Banking Bureau, and the Banking Bureau, needless to say, concentrates on banks. It did not establish an Insurance Department until 1965, and that one department employed only a small fraction of the bureau's officials. Although a Coordination Division is responsible for adjusting the interests of the various constituencies of the bureau, officials dealing with insurance are regarded as junior to banking officials of comparable rank, and in Japan, the seniority of an agency's chief determines its power. "In principle [*tatemae*], banks and insurers are equal. In reality [*honne*], banks are more powerful. And this power relation is reflected in the voices that reach administration."[137]

Shingikai thus play an important role. "Because there are no superiors or inferiors among [council] members, we insurance companies can state our views as equals there," noted one insurance official. But even this exception proved the rule: "When the representative of an industry isn't included in the Kinseichō, it means that it's not yet respectable [*ichininmae* – literally, 'hasn't reached adulthood']," and the insurance industry was not included until 1987. If the insurance industry was generally satisfied with the report of the joint subcommittee, MOF still had to reconcile this report with that of the Shōtorishin, and discussions focused on the conflicting claims of banks and stockbrokers. "When the Banking and Security Bureaus go at it, the Banking Bureau moves with the majority view, and the Insurance Department represents a minority. It was a bitter contest for insurance companies."[138]

They petitioned MOF. Although the ministry settlement had not explicitly allowed for life insurance companies to act as brokers, neither had it closed the

---

[135] Interview with Kimura Hajime.
[136] *Nikkei Kin'yū Shinbun* (13 January 1988).
[137] Interview with Deguchi Haruaki and Kajio Akihiko.   [138] Ibid.

door to their trading on the new exchange for their own accounts, which was all the companies were requesting. Their petition emphasized three points: It was necessary to diversify the participants and to deepen the market for the futures exchange to function, it was fitting that insurance companies participate directly in their capacity as large institutional investors, and MOF had already approved of their trading financial futures overseas. The ministry promised to conduct a "forward-looking" investigation of the insurance companies' request, and Zenginkyō eventually decided to let both life and indemnity insurance companies trade for their own accounts on its new exchange.

Japan's *Wirtschaftswunder* has resulted in the decline of regional centers and an ever greater concentration of business activity in Tokyo. As the port for Kyoto, Japan's old imperial capital, Osaka was long Japan's commercial capital, but between 1955 and 1984, Osaka prefecture's share of national industrial output fell from 12.6 to 8.4 percent.[139] Although each of the three main Osaka-based banks – Sumitomo, Sanwa, and Daiwa – had a presence in the capital and was in daily contact with MOF, they did not take turns chairing Zenginkyō. Tokyo was also far and away the leader among Japan's eight stock exchanges: in 1987, Tokyo handled fully 83.6 percent of the total volume of stock transactions and Osaka only 11.8 percent.[140] Osaka may have ranked fourth in the world in market capitalization (after Tokyo, New York, and London), but it could not hope to compete with the capital in the spot market, so, like Chicago before it, "Japan's second city [was] fighting for respectability in the nation's booming markets by campaigning to become the center of futures trading."[141]

MOF discussions revolved around what sort of futures markets to establish, not where to locate them. Neither the Securities, Banking, nor International Finance Bureaus invited any Osaka businesspeople to their special subcommittees on futures. "My choice as a representative of the Kansai area [i.e., the Osaka-Kyoto-Kobe region] wasn't explicit, but it had that connotation," observed Professor Rōyama, a Kansai native. Even so, "I don't think it would go well if we included a Kansai representative. If the chair of the Osaka Stock Exchange were to enter, there'd be confusion because of the inclusion of the chair of the Tokyo Stock Exchange, too, and nothing would get settled. There's certainly conflict during discussions, but it's necessary to improve things as much as possible without thrusting [conflict] to the surface."[142] And yet, one of the main rationales for creating a *shingikai* is precisely to provide a forum for all of the most interested parties to gather and thrash out a mutually acceptable course of action.

[139] Semkow (1989), p. 50.
[140] *Yomiuri Shinbun* (23 January 1988).
[141] *The Asian Wall Street Journal* (17–18 June 1988).
[142] Interview with Rōyama Shōichi.

Professor Rōyama offered another explanation for the absence of Osaka representatives when he noted that "unfortunately, the number one reason for the decline of the Kansai area is that there isn't anyone to speak out on the national stage."[143] Characterizing it as an effect rather than a cause, an executive at Nippon Life amplified on that observation.

> It's not bias [on MOF's part]. It's said that in finance, what's important are the three poles: Tokyo, London, and New York. With the revolution in technology, you can use any market at all, but the location of people who make policy decisions is of decisive importance. In recent years, people who make decisions have increasingly gathered in Tokyo, and firms based in Tokyo have an overwhelming advantage. You'd do better to think that there are no [major] financial institutions based in Osaka, no [major] institutions that can make financial decisions there. They're all based in Tokyo.[144]

The Shōtorishin's report touched on Kansai economic interests in only one passage, where it simply noted that the Osaka Stock Exchange planned to introduce index futures trading, and some subcommittee members had opposed the inclusion of any express reference to Osaka at all.[145] The Kinseichō and Gaitameshin's joint report vaguely recommended that "regarding the location of a financial futures exchange, it is necessary to plan to cope in an appropriate way by considering comprehensively a variety of conditions such as the desire for an exchange expressed by several regions and the fact that effective competition has developed among a number of separate exchanges in America."[146]

Osaka had gotten off to a running start when it introduced its Kabusaki 50 in June 1987. With the prospect of the Diet's revising the Securities Exchange Act in early 1988 to permit the trading of real stock price indices, the Osaka Stock Exchange made plans to introduce an instrument based on the *Nihon Keizai Shinbun*'s Nikkei 225 index, which averaged the prices of 225 selected stocks. Unwilling to relinquish this new market, the TSE began preparing TOPIX (from the English Tokyo Stock Price Index), which would reflect movements in the aggregate market value of all 1,117 shares listed on the exchange's first section.

MAFF and MITI, which regulate commodity futures, "were worried that MOF might try to get a word in,"[147] so MOF consulted them. Because its plans dealt with financial futures alone, which everyone acknowledged to be within

---

[143] Ibid.   [144] Interview with Deguchi Haruaki and Kajio Akihiko.
[145] Interview with Rōyama Shōichi.
[146] Kin'yū Seido Chōsakai and Gaikoku Kawaseto Shingikai, p. 13.
[147] Interview with Kikuta Yutaka.

MOF's exclusive jurisdiction and which promised, if anything, to stimulate trading in MAFF's and MITI's commodities futures, no turf battles developed. At least one interesting problem did arise in the course of drafting legislation, however. Because the purchasers of futures are typically betting on general market trends, it was necessary to undertake a serious investigation into whether the new instruments would violate those articles of the penal code relating to gambling. Like horse and bicycle racing before it, futures trading was exempted from those regulations.

It has been argued that public opinion encouraged liberalization. "Resentment by the public is an important factor in this process," one MOF official asserted. "Individuals think financial companies are gaining extra profits because the Government protects them."[148] In this case, at least, although the mass media took a lively interest in the debate between banks and security houses, the general public did not. The problem was too technical, too far removed from the lives of most people. "Public opinion scarcely comprehends it."[149]

In truth, politicians were not much better. "In America this could be handled by legislation introduced by a congressional representative, but there's practically no Japanese MP who really understands financial matters like a [Senator William] Proxmire. Most politicians with MOF experience were budget or tax people; people who oversee the banking and securities industries don't become politicians."[150] And once the Banking and Securities Bureaus had achieved a "preemptive equilibration" of the conflict, the interested parties did not appeal for party intervention to challenge the agreement. Bureaucracies can never afford to take politicians for granted, however, so officials conducted talks with ruling party and opposition MPs in order to obviate any Diet modification of the ministry's bills. Such prior consultation has an intrinsic as well as an instrumental value. In the words of the Banking Bureau's point man on futures, "because politicians are in contact with fine grassroots, they offer extremely good advice. For example, because they'd heard from people who'd been defrauded by means of financial futures, some of them wanted to have preventive measures devised, and such views were included in the bill."[151] Politicians did not concern themselves with any issues other than investor protection, though, and no real resistance to MOF's proposals developed.

On 15 March 1988, the LDP's Executive Council approved the revision of the Securities Exchange Act and the passage of a new Financial Futures Trading Act. Cabinet approval followed three days later. On 28 March, MOF submitted its bills to the Diet, which immediately referred them to the Finance Committee of the lower house. The committee, and then a plenary session of the house, passed the measures on 13 May, sending them on to the Finance Committee of

[148] *The New York Times* (1 December 1989).
[149] Interview with Minaguchi Kōichi.
[150] Interview with Rōyama Shōichi.   [151] Interview with Koyama Yoshiaki.

the upper house. That committee approved the two bills on 24 May, and the upper house passed them the next day. "By means of these [laws], the age of financial futures will finally arrive in Japan, too," one newspaper proclaimed grandly.[152]

Epilogue

Both the Tokyo and Osaka Stock Exchanges launched stock price index trading on 3 September 1988. Surpassing the most optimistic projections, the combined value of the two exchanges' contracts was around ¥5 trillion ($36 billion), 8.2 times the value of the day's spot contracts on the TSE's first section and 5.5 times the average daily trading value of the Chicago Mercantile Exchange, the world's leading stock futures market.[153] Another surprise was the strong showing of Osaka, which garnered two-thirds of the first day's trading. Trading in both contracts eased after that initial explosion of orders, but investors found the downside protection afforded by futures increasingly attractive after the stock market began a long decline at the of start of 1990. In addition, given that stock futures were cheaper and more convenient to sell than their underlying stocks, many individual as well institutional investors found that they could manage their equity holdings through futures trading alone.[154]

Osaka continued to gain at Tokyo's expense and, just as in the United States after 1987's "Black Monday," critics began blaming derivatives like futures for the stock market's slide. "It's not the numerous financial scandals plaguing Japan, they say, or tight money, lower corporate earnings, Japan's negative economic reports or a bear market now [i.e., 1992] in its third year: trading in Tokyo has been falling off because individuals are uncertain about the influence of futures," *The Wall Street Journal* noted sarcastically.[155] The attack focused on Osaka's Nikkei 225 index. Especially large and savvy investors could manipulate the index by making large trades in thinly traded issues and then capture the momentary price gaps that resulted between Nikkei 225 futures and a basket of their underlying stocks, and critics asserted that such index arbitrage depressed spot prices by increasing stock market volatility and driving away small investors.

Defenders of Nikkei 225 futures countered that it provided a hedge against losses, thus reducing the pressure to sell shares and *stabilizing* the market. If Osaka was profiting at Tokyo's expense, they continued, it was because its market was more liquid and the commissions Osaka charged to trade its stock price index futures were only one-eighth of those Tokyo charged to trade stocks.

---

[152] *Mainichi Shinbun* (26 May 1988).
[153] *Nihon Keizai Shinbun* (4 September 1988).
[154] Semkow (1989), p. 44.
[155] *The Wall Street Journal* (31 March 1992).

Whatever the merits of the opposing arguments, MOF sought to make stock trading more attractive and boost TSE volume by imposing higher commissions, tighter margin requirements (i.e., the down payment an investor must make to initiate a trade), and shorter hours on the Osaka futures market in April 1992.

Japan's mushrooming futures markets were no longer a purely domestic concern, however: The hike in commissions brought a strong letter of protest from the chairs of several U.S. congressional committees who objected to "efforts by Japanese securities regulators to place unfair restrictions" on trading activities in which foreign firms had a competitive edge.[156] Although ministry officials denied that that was their intent, foreign futures traders were, in fact, being singled out for special blame. Nomura and Nikkō were often more active in index arbitrage than any foreign firm, but negative reports in the local press focused on the likes of Goldman Sachs, Morgan Stanley, and Salomon Brothers and, indeed, their know-how and profitability stood out at a time when most Japanese firms had not yet learned how to exploit the new markets and were operating in the red. Initially courted, foreign securities firms thus came to be scapegoated, and yet another source of bilateral friction was born.

If that was not enough, MOF also made a futile attempt to extend its grasp beyond Japan's borders when its curbing of domestic futures trading drove investors overseas. Trading of Nikkei 225 futures on the Singapore International Monetary Exchange (SIMEX) skyrocketed 364 percent from 1991 to 1992.[157] Finance Ministry and TSE officials thereupon pressured SIMEX, too, to dampen trading in Nikkei 225 futures, but the exchange demurred. Similar trouble was brewing in the United States. At the end of 1991, TSE Deputy President Satō had defended futures contracts: "They are useful to the entire community in providing hedging opportunities." Less than a year later, though, when visiting officials repeatedly asked him what kind of Japanese stock derivatives the TSE would sanction on the American Stock Exchange, he snapped, "No new derivatives!"[158]

These problems were not resolved until MOF finally overhauled the Nikkei 225 in 1993. In order to reduce volatility and make arbitrage more difficult, the new index was broadened and market capital rather than price weighted. In a departure from MOF's previous hostility to futures trading, margin requirements were gradually to be cut in half, and ministry officials announced that they would no longer stand in the way of foreign exchanges' listing of Nikkei index futures.

Given the heated disputes over stock price index futures, it is easy to overlook Japan's other futures instruments. By 1988, the trading of Japanese bond futures

---

[156] Ibid.   [157] *The Daily Japan Digest* (7 January 1993).
[158] *Japan Times Weekly International Edition* (25 November–1 December 1991); *The Wall Street Journal* (19 October 1992).

had grown to the point where it far exceeded the trading of the actual bonds, and it expanded all the more after the TSE began listing futures in 20-year government bonds in July 1988. Banks were already dealing in government bond futures on the TSE as special participants, but in June 1989, 220 banks finally won #2 licenses to broker customers' orders, and on 1 December the TSE started trading T-bond futures. Contrary to the high expectations that had surrounded them, Tokyo's T-bond market had a monthly turnover of around $12 billion in 1991 – only 1.2 percent of the aggregate turnover of Japanese government bond futures. The new market found little favor with investors because it was forbidden to deal in spot U.S. bonds and cross-market settlements with the Chicago Board of Trade were unavailable.[159]

The Financial Futures Trading Act was enacted on 31 May 1988 and came into effect on 27 March 1989. Listing three-month Euroyen and Eurodollar interest rate futures and yen–dollar currency futures, the Tokyo International Financial Futures Exchange (TIFFE) started operating on 30 June. Trading volume for the three products (primarily the yen interest rate futures) quickly rose from 43,728 contracts in June to 2,037,044 contracts in December. Of the 165 general members in March 1990, 33 were insurance companies.[160]

Both the Kinseichō and Shōtorishin continued to deliberate on ways to liberalize Japan's capital markets, and both continued to examine the issues primarily from the perspectives of the banking and securities industries, respectively. MOF prepared legislative bills after receiving the final recommendations of the two councils in 1991. Deliberations on financial liberalization had lasted for more than five years, but in 1992 the Diet finally approved the first major revision of Japan's financial system since the Occupation had raised the fence between the banking and securities businesses. Beginning in 1993, city banks, long-term credit banks, trust banks, and securities firms would be permitted to enter (some of) one another's businesses by means of wholly-owned subsidiaries in a phased process that let the industries with fewer branches and less capital move first. MOF left many barriers in place in order to continue protecting the core business of each industry, however, and backed off from its commitment to reduce government intervention. Bureaucrats seized on the stock market crash that began in 1990 and a series of scandals to reaffirm their traditional stance that financial management should not be left to the market alone.

Because much of MOF's power derives from the wide jurisdiction that enables it to broker deals among its varied regulatory constituencies, the ministry has beaten back repeated attempts to narrow that jurisdiction. When it was revealed in 1991 that Japanese securities firms had compensated their top corporate clients for losses suffered during the crash, critics proposed the creation of

---

[159] Foundation for Advanced Information and Research (1991), p. 221.
[160] Ibid., pp. 237, 214.

an independent watchdog agency on the grounds that the ministry's close ties to securities firms prevented it from serving as an effective regulator. MOF did create a new Securities Exchange Surveillance Commission in 1992 – as an agency attached to the ministry and staffed almost entirely from within its own ranks. Given the intense criticism of the ministry's intimate relationship with its regulatory constituents, however, MOF did decide to exclude all retired ministry officials, corporate executives, and representatives of the banking and insurance industries from the Shōtorishin. Except for the head of the Securities Dealers Association, a director from the Bank of Japan, and the chair of the TSE (who at the time was, in fact, a Finance OB), the council was henceforth to be composed entirely of academics to ensure the "neutrality and transparency" of its deliberations.[161]

When MOF recommended using taxpayers' money to absorb losses at seven bankrupt *jūsen* mortgage lenders at the start of 1996, public censure of the ministry rose to a fever pitch once it became clear that MOF itself had exacerbated the problem through a combination of lax oversight, bad judgment, and deliberate efforts to protect the ministry OBs who ran many of the firms. In the past, most politicians were more interested in preserving or cultivating relationships with the ministry than in reforming it. This time, however, the LDP and two small allies agreed at the end of 1996 to merge MOF's Banking and Security Bureaus and to establish a new independent agency to take over the ministry's task of inspecting and supervising financial institutions by fiscal year 1998.

Prime Minister Hashimoto also called for a financial "Big Bang," a Tokyo equivalent of London's 1986 reform, that would remove barriers between market segments, allow new financial products and services to be introduced more freely, liberalize transaction fees, and harmonize the legal system with global standards by the year 2001. (Under the leadership of activist bureau chiefs, the Shōtorishin and Gaitameshin helped draft these proposals.) On paper, at least, this initiative is radical and comprehensive; it is *not* designed, "as was typical in the past, to make piecemeal, step by step adjustments calibrated to balance concessions between competing domestic and foreign interests, while preserving MOF prerogatives and power."[162] Even many ministry officials have come to fear for MOF's future if the financial industry is not reformed.

The *shingikai* described in this chapter clearly did play a part in the representation and eventual mediation of different private interests. The following chapter deals with an open clash of interests that has been repeatedly censured and suppressed in a *shingikai* whose influence is anything but clear.

---

[161] *The Daily Japan Digest* (17 October 1991).   [162] Radin (1997).

6

The god that fell: Reducing the price of rice

"God is rice," explained a Japanese theologian trying to transpose Western religion into his own cultural context.[1] Rice planting and harvesting rituals are central to Shintō, the country's indigenous religion. On a more mundane level, rice is far and away the single most important crop in Japan and the staple foodstuff. In 1985, rice was grown on 44 percent of the total area under cultivation by 84 percent of Japan's farmers, and 1987's harvest was worth ¥3.23 trillion ($23.1 billion), or almost one-third of the total value of the country's agricultural output.[2] Of special significance to this study, "rice agriculture constitutes the institutional core in terms of jurisdiction, budget share, constituency base, numbers of assigned bureaucrats, institutional legitimacy, and reason for being" for both the Ministry of Agriculture, Forestry, and Fisheries (MAFF) and agricultural cooperatives.[3]

Mounting farm budget deficits, domestic criticism of high prices, and foreign demands for the liberalization of imports combined to pose "the greatest crisis in 2,000 years for the Land of Vigorous Rice Plants [an elegant, ancient name for Japan]," in the hyperbolic words of one agriculture *zoku*.[4] After the government postponed reductions in 1985 and 1986, a price cut could no longer be deferred. When organized agriculture tacitly accepted that fact, its LDP allies negotiated the size of the cut with MAFF and MOF without waiting for MAFF to consult its Rice Price Council, presenting the *shingikai* with a fait accompli. Although the cut was narrowed as a result, the government did finally succeed in reducing its purchase price of rice for only the third time in the postwar era and the first time in 31 years.

Farmers were a mainstay of the conservative coalition, but neither Marxist nor ruling triad models explain why Japanese business long shouldered a mountainous burden of state support for farmers or why that support finally declined. Cultivators are tightly organized in cooperatives whose peak association participates directly in agricultural policymaking and administration, but it is neither monopolistic nor fully in control of its constituency. A multiplicity of economic,

---

[1] *Japan Times Weekly International Edition* (13–19 May 1991), p. 9.
[2] George (1988), p. A5; Ministry of Agriculture, Forestry, and Fisheries (1990), pp. 85, 176.
[3] Bullock (1995), p. 9.   [4] *Yomiuri Shinbun* (25 June 1987).

political, and bureaucratic organizations took an interest in agricultural pricing, but few of those organizations were attentive to its details or enjoyed effective power. The concerned ministries were attentive and powerful, but it was the LDP that had the last word. In sum, setting the price of rice was a relatively self-contained, politician-led process that involved a limited set of narrowly focused interest groups. It was politician led because no one bureaucracy had exclusive jurisdiction over the issue, and the price of rice is a textbook example of a distributive policy whose electoral significance makes its politicization attractive.

Background

Japan's government has regulated the rice economy since at least 1600, but it took previous trends to their logical conclusion with the Food Control Act of 1942, which asserted the government's right to purchase and ration all rice at prices of its own choosing. The same market advanced enough to give the world its first futures contracts two centuries earlier had been marched back into the past. Because the Food Control System (*shokuryō kanri seido*) was established to ease severe shortages, it initially protected consumers at the expense of producers, with the government paying and charging below-market prices during the Pacific War and Occupation. Once agricultural production recovered, however, rather than abolish Food Control, politicians transformed it into a form of welfare support for farmers. Notwithstanding the market distortions that resulted – massive burdens on consumers and the public treasury, surpluses, stockpiles, crop diversion and acreage reduction schemes, and growing disparities between domestic and foreign prices – both farmers and conservative politicians found continued regulation advantageous.

Organized agriculture realized that it had more to gain from political maneuvering within a regulatory regime than from the free play of markets. Because labor productivity almost always rises more quickly in manufacturing, the living standards of farmers tend not to keep pace with those of city dwellers, but the relative economic decline of agriculture actually led to heightened political influence for farmers in Japan, as in other advanced industrial democracies, by uniting them behind state support for their incomes.

That Japanese farmers would press for government aid was inevitable; that the government would yield to that pressure was not. Nor does the Japanese economy's long-term structural transformation account for the ebb and flow of government support. Calder's theory of crisis and compensation highlights the other side of the equation, the pressures of electoral politics. "In periods of political crisis, appeals to the countryside may be crucial for ruling conservative elites. The support of urban constituencies is frequently cast into doubt at such times and is difficult to systematically mobilize. . . . Accordingly, crisis often induces compensation for agriculture. . . ." Given that rice was far and away the most widely cultivated crop, conservatives turned to hikes in the government's purchase price as the most efficient means of bolstering farm income and their own rural support base. Unlike other policy domains characterized by a dynamic of crisis and compensation, however, because these surges of compensation were not always followed by retrenchment, "the cumulative result was a strong upward ratcheting effect on agricultural support levels."[5]

Although the government's producer price rose rapidly from 1949 to 1953, it actually fell 6.3 percent in 1954 and fell again, if only 0.9 percent, in 1956. But growing opposition strength at the end of the 1950s and the Security Treaty crisis of 1960 kindled real fear in the LDP, so from 1961 the government began to compensate rice farmers in accordance with a new "cost of production-income supplement" (seisanhi shotoku hoshō) formula designed to close the income gap between farmers and urban workers and increase the production of rice. It succeeded all too well in both respects.

With producer prices[6] doubling between 1960 and 1968 and redoubling from 1971 to 1977, the Japanese producer price spurted to nearly four times the world price by the mid-1970s. Thus, if the income and savings of the average farmer's household were 91.4 and 112.5 percent of a nonfarm worker's in 1960, those figures had risen to 127.9 and 228.5 percent, respectively, by 1986.[7] In comparative terms, although the labor productivity of Japanese agriculture was less than one-tenth that of the United States, the average Japanese farm household earned 19 percent more than its American counterpart in 1984, and exchange rate shifts significantly widened that disparity in the late 1980s.[8]

With prices high and sales guaranteed, Food Control promoted both inefficiency *and* overproduction. Economies of scale were precluded: Occupation reforms had broken up large landholdings and restricted the amount of land any individual could own, and tax laws discouraged farmers from leaving or converting their land. As a consequence, Japanese farm households cultivated an average of only 0.9 hectare of paddy in the mid-1980s compared with an average American rice farm of 114 hectares – a ratio of 130 to 1.[9] Nevertheless, because politics required that the compensation for farm and factory labor be roughly equivalent, the government purchase price rose along with wages regardless of farmers' productivity, and because the cost formula was based on the expenses

---

[5] Calder (1988), pp. 234, 225.

[6] To be precise, the Japanese government distinguished among five gradations of rice quality, each with its own price, but this study refers only to the "standard price" calculated by the cost of production-income supplement formula.

[7] Because farm households tend to be larger, their per capita income was still lower than that of worker households.

[8] Donnelly (1984), p. 354; Takeuchi (1987), p. 27; Calder (1988), p. 242.

[9] *Sankei Shinbun* (28 June 1987); MAFF, "Japan's Agricultural Review," vol. 15 (March 1987), p. 5 .

of almost all producers, even small-scale farmers could expect to recover their costs.

Farm households were able to stay on the land even as they came to earn most of their income off of it. If only about one-third of all farmers lived in part-time farm households that derived most of their income from nonagricultural pursuits before 1960, more than two-thirds of all farmers fell into that category by 1980. Agricultural income fell from 50.2 percent of total household income in 1960 to 15.8 percent in 1984, and income from rice in particular came not to exceed 5 percent of the average farm household's total annual income.[10]

Growing rice thus evolved from a normal vocation into a risk-free way for rural households to supplement their earnings and take advantage of the extremely low taxation of farmland, but falling demand led to repeated surpluses. Although imports were required until 1965, MAFF began encouraging small-scale, part-time farmers to leave agriculture, or at least shift from rice to crops for which demand was increasing, from the early 1960s, and in 1971, the ministry instituted a paddy diversion program, setting acreage reduction targets and subsidizing farmers who switched to other crops. Given its limited success, MAFF went a step further and introduced land diversion quotas in 1978, and the government sank close to ¥3 trillion into "production adjustment" between 1978 and 1987.

In order to reduce government purchases, introduce a measure of market discipline to prices, and reflect consumer preferences more accurately, the Diet established a semicontrolled (*jishu ryūtsū*) market in 1969. Although monitored and regulated by MAFF, semicontrolled rice bypassed the Food Control bureaucracy, flowing directly from the cooperative movement's marketing arm, Zennō, to rice wholesalers. If the government had formerly compelled farmers to sell it their rice, quotas soon limited how much MAFF was willing to buy. The government's producer price still served as a yardstick, but the price of semicontrolled rice was decided at national negotiations between marketing and wholesalers' organizations. There also existed a black market outside of state control. As government support for agriculture was gradually reduced, the advantage of selling rice to the government was also reduced, and selling on the black market enabled farmers to defy acreage limitations. In 1987, government rice amounted to 3.65 million tons, semicontrolled rice to 2.75 million tons, rice for brewing to 650,000 tons, and black market rice to an estimated 3.15 million tons – a full 30 percent of national demand.[11]

Price supports imposed a severe financial burden on the national treasury, especially after 1970, when the producer price came to exceed the consumer

---

[10] MAFF (1990), p. 3; Curtis (1988), p. 55; Zenchū (1987), p. 5; *Asahi Shinbun* (26 June 1987).
[11] *Yomiuri Shinbun* (18 June 1987); *Tōkyō Shinbun* (23 June 1987); *Yomiuri Shinbun* (29 October 1987).

price.[12] Thanks to this "reverse margin" (*gyakuzaya*), the government lost money on every sack of rice it sold, and recurring deficits in the Food Control Special Account had to be covered by funds from the general accounts budget. Given the need to trim expenditures, a marked downward pressure on the producer price developed, permitting the government to slow, then reverse, the growth in agricultural supports. From 1976, the producer price began to fall every year in real terms, and by keeping increases in the government's purchase price smaller than increases in its sale price, MAFF succeeded in reducing the reverse margin and nearly halving the deficits in its Domestic Rice Control Account by 1986.[13]

Although agricultural spending as a proportion of government expenditures had returned almost to the level of 1949, Japan had only ameliorated, not eliminated, its farm problem. Japan's 1986 producer rice price was generally estimated to be 5.6 times the U.S. government's target price and perhaps a dozen times the Thai price, agricultural expenditures' share of the national budget was still several times that of most other advanced industrial nations, and the government lost ¥3,691 ($26.36) every time it sold the standard measure of 60 kilograms of rice (see Figure 6-1).

The financial burdens on the government were enormous. Along with the national railroad (*kokutetsu*) and national health insurance (*kenpo*), subsidies for rice (*kome*) produced one of the so-called three k deficits that left the government awash in red ink in the 1980s. In fiscal year 1987, the price reverse margin cost the government ¥48.9 billion ($349 million) and operating expenses another ¥213.8 billion ($1.53 billion), with the total Domestic Rice Control Account deficit amounting to ¥380.5 billion ($2.72 billion). When expenditures for agricultural base maintenance, grants for crop diversion, bounties for high-quality rice, and subsidies for the semicontrolled distribution system are included, the rice-related budget reached ¥1.3 trillion ($9.29 billion). In concrete terms, that amounted to a burden of more than ¥10,000 ($71) on every Japanese man, woman, and child, or the lavishing of ¥45 in tax money on the production of every ¥100 of rice. Because the domestic price of rice greatly exceeded the international price, adding opportunity costs to tax expenditures swelled the total to around ¥5 trillion ($35.71 billion), and even that figure does not include subsidies paid by local governments.[14]

Japanese agricultural policy had fallen into a vicious cycle: Because high prices encouraged gluts, the government reduced farming acreage without encouraging consolidation, but that hindered the improvement of productivity,

---

[12] To be precise, whereas "purchase" (*kaiire*) or "producer" (*seisansha*) price refers to the price that the government pays farmers, "sale" (*uriwatashi*) or "consumer" (*shōhisha*) price refers not to the price paid by consumers, but to the price at which the government sells to authorized distributors.

[13] George (1988), p. A31.   [14] *Sankei Shinbun* (28 June 1987); *Sankei Shinbun* (1 July 1987).

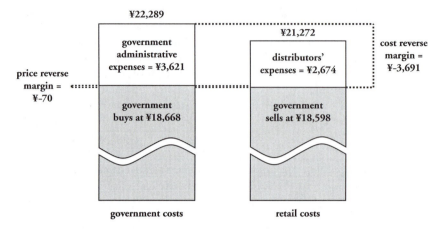

Figure 6-1.   The rice price structure, 1986. (Source: *Sankei Shinbun*, 28 June 1987.)

making price maintenance all the more necessary. Prospects for the future were not bright, either. With supply continuing to exceed demand, another surplus was in the making in the mid-1980s.

That the situation had become unsustainable was obvious, and so were the economically rational solutions: Cut price supports and import rice from abroad. MAFF estimated that every 1 percent cut in the rice price would lighten its financial burden by ¥13.5 billion ($96 million), and one scholar calculated that if the government removed *all* rice controls and ended forcible acreage reduction, supply and demand would balance at around ¥12,000 per 60 kilogram – more than 35 percent below the 1986 producer price.[15] Given the large price disparities, the importation of even limited quantities of rice would have had a noticeable effect: If Japan bought American rice at one-fifth of its domestic price, then supplying 10 percent of the country's demands with imports would bring an 8 percent drop in the domestic price.[16] And because the proceeds from rice cultivation no longer exceeded 5 percent of the average farmer's total income, farm incomes would shrink a minuscule 0.5 percent even if the rice price fell 10 percent.

The cast of actors

The economically rational need not be politically rational, however. Producers, politicians, and public officials all had vested interests in the status quo, and

[15] *Sankei Shinbun* (22 June 1987); *Asahi Shinbun* (26 June 1987).
[16] *Tōkyō Shinbun* (19 June 1987, evening).

neither consumers nor the United States, the likely beneficiaries of reform, was pressing hard for change.

The agricultural cooperatives (Nōkyō)

Virtually all rice growers belong to the Federation of Agricultural Cooperative Associations (Nōgyō Kyōdō Kumiai Rengōkai, or Nōkyō), which is the single largest voluntary association in Japan. In 1986, close to 4,300 multipurpose cooperatives boasted a total of 8.1 million members and almost 300,000 employees.[17] Nōkyō's peak organization is the Central Union of Agricultural Cooperatives (Zenkoku Nōgyō Kyōdō Kumiai Chūōkai, or Zenchū), which is responsible for unifying and representing the political interests of member farmers.

Nōkyō is on a par with the largest private enterprises in Japan: In the late 1980s, it handled more savings and pension funds than any commercial bank or insurance company, had a bigger turnover than Nippon Telegraph and Telephone (the largest corporation listed on the stock exchange), and ranked second only to the government as the country's biggest employer. In 1986, the total volumes of cooperatives' supply and marketing businesses were ¥5.2 trillion ($37.1 billion) and ¥6.7 trillion ($47.9 billion), respectively, and the balances of their loans, long-term insurance, and savings accounts were ¥12.2 trillion ($87.1 billion), ¥21.2 trillion ($151.4 billion), and ¥37.1 trillion ($265 billion), respectively.[18]

Nōkyō has a tremendous stake in Food Control. In the mid-1980s, cooperatives handled 95.2 percent of all rice sold to the government. Although the marketing commissions, storage fees, and interest subsidies that it earns from rice under the Food Control System account for a shrinking fraction of its operations, Nōkyō still earned at least ¥110 billion ($786 million) from that business in 1985.[19] Government payments for rice go directly to the Agricultural Cooperative Bank (Nōrin Chūkin), helping to make it the world's eighth largest non-American financial institution in terms of deposits that year and providing Nōkyō with sizable funds for its other economic operations.[20]

In certain respects, change posed a greater threat to Nōkyō than to many of the farmers it represented. Although the proceeds from rice cultivation had fallen to a small percentage of the average farmer's income, Nōkyō would lose commissions on the sale of rice and funds for its credit enterprises if the producer price were to drop. Whether farmers and the association that ostensibly served them always shared interests was thus open to question. Producers could already sell their rice at a higher price to black market wholesalers than to

[17] Zenchū (1987), p. 20.   [18] Ibid., p. 20.
[19] George (1988), pp. A7–A8, A10.
[20] Calder (1988), p. 231; Donnelly (1977), p. 154.

Nōkyō, and with farmers (especially part-time farmers) relying on Nōkyō for most of their inputs, lack of competition permitted it to charge exorbitant prices. In 1987, fertilizer, agricultural chemicals, and machinery were respectively 7, 8, and 17 times more expensive in Japan than in California.[21]

Prewar agriculture was conspicuous for its top-down state corporatism. If postwar reforms failed to empower the individual farmer, the balance of power nevertheless did change fundamentally as a result of Nōkyō's clout vis-à-vis the LDP.

The LDP

Mainichi Shinbun estimated in 1987 that about 60 percent of all LDP Diet representatives were tied to agriculture and argued that "the structure of the LDP is such that it could not exist if it were abandoned by farming communities."[22] That was an exaggeration. Although shrinkage of the primary sector and of the LDP's electoral support proceeded pari passu until the late 1970s, the party then rebounded despite continued urbanization. The LDP preempted opposition policies, taking the initiative on issues like pollution and welfare, and as it succeeded in making inroads into formerly hostile groups like the urban middle class and young adults, the share of total LDP support accounted for by farmers fell from 29 percent in 1965 to only 13 percent in 1985, at which point even industrial workers accounted for a larger share of party support.[23] The LDP became a broad-based, catchall party that had to balance the conflicting interests of a wide variety of constituencies.

That said, it cannot be denied that Japanese farmers have wielded disproportionate influence. Until the redistricting of 1994, the reapportionment of seats badly lagged urbanization, so rural voters long enjoyed overrepresentation in the Diet. (Japan still does not acknowledge the principle of one person, one vote. In 1994, the Tokyo High Court ruled that population differences between electoral districts should be no greater than – in other words, could be as great as – 2 to 1 under the new system.) Farmers were always the LDP's most reliable supporters, and conservative electoral success continued to vary directly with the rural hue of a district. The LDP may have succeeded in broadening its appeal, but its new constituencies were unreliable: The party identity of "floating" urban supporters tends to be weaker and their election turnout lower than farmers'.[24] Nōkyō, on the other hand, can be counted on to use its considerable organizational and financial resources to back sympathetic candidates – whether or not they run in agricultural districts – and cooperatives often form the backbone of a politician's individual support group (*kōenkai*). That was especially significant

[21] *Asahi Shinbun* (30 June 1987).
[22] *Mainichi Shinbun* (1 July 1987). See also *Asahi Shinbun* (28 June 1987).
[23] Komari (1991), p. 31.   [24] Okimoto (1989), p. 193.

in light of the LDP's weak to nonexistent grassroots party organization and the outsized influence that accrued to blocs of voters who voted in a predictable fashion in Japan's multimember electoral districts.

With so many of its members thus holding a stake in the outcome, the LDP held extensive intraparty discussions before entering into rice price negotiations with the government. The first official party organ to deal with the price was the Comprehensive Agricultural Policy Commission, which would form a Subcommittee on Basic Agricultural Policy to conduct actual deliberations. The commission would then hold joint sessions with PARC's Agriculture and Forestry Division, but because the two bodies together embraced almost two-thirds of the party's total Diet delegation, they would select a smaller Rice Price Committee to decide the LDP's position on the producer price.[25] It was the leaders of these formal committees, commonly referred to as the "agricultural gang of eight," who held real power and conducted negotiations. In any given year, the most influential members of this group were the "three key agricultural officials" (*nōrin san'yaku*): the chairs of the commission, the division, and the committee.

The LDP's farm *zoku* were divided into several groups that cut across intraparty factions. In the late 1960s, the most influential of them began to accept the need for crop diversion and heightened efficiency, and they widened their focus beyond rice to become known as the Comprehensive Agricultural Policy faction. The most powerful *zoku*, including the agriculture *san'yaku*, belonged to this group, and because they aspired to leadership positions within the party, they could not afford to be too uncompromising. In opposition to the "regular army" of the Comprehensive Agricultural Policy faction, those MPs who were closest to Nōkyō and still fought for rice price increases to the bitter end belonged to one of two "guerrilla units": the Diet Representatives' Conference for the Promotion of Rural Communities or the Association for the Reform of Japanese Agricultural Policy, nicknamed the "Viet Cong" and the "Apache," respectively. Although great, the influence of the LDP's agricultural *zoku* should not be exaggerated. Like any other representatives, *zoku* must work through official party organs, and in order to rise to a leadership position within the party, an MP cannot be identified with a single interest.[26] With the deepening of the crisis in farm policy in the 1980s, even the guerrilla units began to moderate their demands.

After intraparty differences were reconciled, the LDP would enter into final negotiations with the government. The party would be represented by its secretary general, the chairs of PARC and the Executive Council, and the agriculture

---

[25] George (1988), pp. A20–A21.
[26] Cf. Katō (1994) on the incentives for more secure representatives to balance the servicing of special interests with a concern for general policies in order to increase their reputation and promote their influence within the party.

san'yaku, the government by the ministers of agriculture and finance and the chief cabinet secretary (who acts as the prime minister's chief of staff and liaison to the ministries). Although the prime minister would not participate directly in these negotiations, he had to endorse the outcome. Party leaders may have owed their positions to the support of individual backbenchers and to their continued reelection, but as leaders, they were also responsible for the party's long-term prospects, and they had an incentive to rein in the short-sighted demands that grew out of backbenchers' focus on the next election.[27] Whatever their previous stands might have been, LDP politicians generally opposed large price increases once they entered the cabinet.

Although the government tried to maintain the fiction that the prices it set were determined objectively, calculations were anything but automatic. The cost of production–income supplement formula "structured the debate, but its specific application was open to interpretation and disagreement. . . . Within the technical boundaries of the [formula] there was room to adjust, tinker, twist, and modify."[28] In order to burnish their credentials as champions of rural interests, agriculture *zoku* would each year insist on an upward revision of whatever price MAFF recommended, and ministry officials would take this "political addition" (*seiji kasan*) into account when they formulated their recommendation. Given that the upper limit of the producer rice price was reportedly negotiated in advance, the decisionmaking process that went on before the public eye was reduced to little more than political theater staged for farmers' benefit to ensure that LDP representatives won credit for wresting concessions from the niggardly ministries.[29]

The ministries

Given its jurisdiction over government expenditures, MOF participates in all price negotiations, and its objective is straightforward: to act as a brake on the Food Control System. The program threatens any number of ministry goals. Because the rice price is decided outside of the normal budget-making process and because financial aspects of Food Control frequently conflict with the ministry's fiscal policies, it encroaches on MOF's power and autonomy. Because the program is not constrained by the incremental politics that govern other allocations, it upsets budgetary "balance." And because Food Control deficits are higher than what MOF considers sound or fair, it violates the ministry's sense of national priorities and fiscal responsibility.[30]

With farmers and LDP backbenchers trying to increase the price of rice by narrowing the issue to costs of production and urban wage levels and MOF

---

[27] Ramseyer and Rosenbluth (1993), pp. 193–94.
[28] Donnelly (1977), p. 149.   [29] George (1988), pp. A24–A25.
[30] Donnelly (1977), pp. 151, 158–59; Donnelly (1984), p. 346.

trying to prevent increases by placing the issue in the broadest context of budget deficits and general price levels, MAFF, like political leaders, is caught in the middle. Both its role and its ability to play that role are often misunderstood, however.

Although MAFF is generally regarded as a clientele ministry whose role is to represent the interests of farmers, the two sides do not necessarily see eye to eye. "When you speak of 'interests,' there are two kinds. . . . Even when we agree on long-term interests, when it comes to short-term interests, whether to raise or to lower this year's [rice] price, for example, the ministry doesn't necessarily represent the interests of farmers," conceded one Food Agency official.[31] MAFF cannot secure the future viability of Japanese agriculture without nods to economic rationality that estrange it from its agricultural clientele, and ministry officials have developed models of "structural reform" that permit them, in the words of Skocpol and Finegold, "to make policy *for*, rather than just *with*, the farmers and their organizations."[32]

On a more mundane level, ministry officials, like their colleagues in Nōkyō, have a personal stake in the existing administration of agriculture, whatever its value to individual cultivators. Were Food Control abolished, the Food Agency, the core of the ministry, would lose its raison d'être and thousands of people would lose their jobs. And whether it contributed to a deficit or not, every yen of Food Control expenditures is a yen that someone owes to MAFF. The ministry might fight to maintain as much state spending on agriculture as possible, but for whose benefit? "The MAFF dislikes budgetary cuts because they lower its status and power as a ministry in a system where bureaucratic power is very much derived from the power to dispense subsidies."[33] In some ways, however, MAFF's organizational interests diverge from those of Nōkyō, let alone individual farmers. Huge Food Control deficits and domestic–foreign price gaps divert funds from other programs and embarrass the ministry, which must at least seem to balance the interests of consumers against those of producers.

If fully 95 percent of surveyed bureaucrats credited MAFF with either "extreme" or "considerable" influence over agricultural policy, a retired ministry official once observed that "the LDP and Zenchū have a clear stage in the rice price campaign . . . [while] MAFF has the role of getting thrashed."[34] These contradictory perceptions arise because the Food Control System constitutes a double-edged sword. MAFF's ability to offer subsidies – and in the mid-1980s, subsidies comprised about 60 percent of its annual budget[35] – gives it clout

---

[31] Interview with Baba Kumao.
[32] Skocpol and Finegold (1982), pp. 274–75.
[33] George (1988), p. A34. See Campbell (1977) for the 1960s and early 1970s.
[34] Muramatsu (1981), p. 233; *Yomiuri Shinbun* (20 June 1987).
[35] Donnelly (1984), p. 345.

vis-à-vis farmers. Those same subsidies, however, invite the intervention of farmers' political allies. Agricultural policymaking thus displays a balance of power. In the words of one MAFF official, "If we don't pass the LDP's Agriculture [PARC] Division, we can't settle important policy. Thus, how we're going to get past the Agriculture Division is what we're most anxious about beforehand. But that isn't to say that the LDP can make us submit to everything they say when they make unreasonable demands."[36]

When setting the price of rice, MAFF is required by law to consult the Rice Price Council (Beika Shingikai, or Beishin), a trilateral body that includes producer, consumer, and public-interest representatives. Its workings will be described later.

Consumers

Food processors have (weakly) opposed the Food Control System for raising the prices of their inputs, and given its interest in restraining wage demands and avoiding international friction, the broader business community has issued (muffled) calls for deregulation. Keidanren's position in early 1987 was that the government should permit imports of rice for use as a raw material and that "flexible responses are called for" regarding rice for home consumption.[37] Nevertheless, the potential benefits of liberalization to business were not worth the costs of a frontal assault on its conservative ally Nōkyō, and this is one policy domain where the LDP consistently slighted business in favor of an economically less central yet more needy – and far more numerous – electoral constituency. But what of the largest electoral constituency of all, the mass of individual consumers?

In 1986, about 6.8 percent of all voters lived in households that marketed rice, and another 4.5 percent lived in households that grew but did not market the crop.[38] But if close to nine out of ten Japanese voters were strictly consumers, they had precious little influence over pricing decisions. The reasons for this are familiar to any student of interest-group theory. The organizability of producers, who were relatively homogeneous, narrowly focused, and enjoyed concentrated benefits, actually increased as the farm sector declined, whereas the cost of agricultural supports was diffused over a growing mass of consumers, who had no collective identity, experienced high rice prices only as part of more general issues like inflation, and had every incentive to free-ride on any movement to oppose supports. In addition, "the separation of consumer and producer prices institutionalized the absence of 'countervailing power' which might have held prices down."[39] Under the circumstances, no party openly identified itself

[36] Interview with Baba Kumao.   [37] Calder (1988), p. 272.
[38] George (1988), p. A14.
[39] Donnelly (1984), pp. 342–43; Donnelly (1977), p. 151.

with the interests of urban consumers in the mid-1980s. Freed from the cross-pressures and responsibilities of government, opposition parties attempted to exploit the issue to partisan advantage by fiercely criticizing the LDP – for its penny pinching rather than for its profligacy.

There were consumer organizations appealing for reform or abolition of Food Control and the liberalization of rice imports, but they were in the minority. A survey conducted in June 1987, right in the middle of the price-setting process, found that the public was not terribly dissatisfied with the status quo. If 53.4 percent of the respondents thought that the price of rice in Japan was high, only 14 percent felt that it must be cut substantially, and although 49.7 percent of respondents agreed that Food Control had to be reformed to a certain extent, 31.8 percent described it as necessary, and a mere 13 percent wanted it abolished.[40]

The most compelling reason for this complacency was that the price of rice is actually of little economic significance to consumers. The average annual consumption of rice among urban households steadily declined by two-thirds from a peak of 118.3 kilograms in 1962 to 41.6 kilograms (about two and a half bowls per person per day) in 1986, at which point Japanese actually ate more dairy products than rice. Although rice accounted for 13.3 percent of the average nonfarm household's consumption expenditures in 1955, as demand fell and incomes rose, it came to account for a trifling 2.2 percent of the total in 1986, a smaller fraction than that spent on meat.[41] As rice's share of the family budget shrank, so did concern for its price. Thus, a director of the Housewives' League could matter-of-factly note, "debate over whether rice is expensive or cheap is not important to consumers."[42]

The United States

There is a larger international dimension to Japan's rice policy than to its policies on labor standards or financial futures. The high domestic prices required by Food Control could not be maintained without excluding imports, and the United States objected to this state of affairs. Trade in agricultural goods reversed the general pattern of bilateral trade, with the protectionist demands of uncompetitive *Japanese* producers failing to halt the seemingly inexorable growth of *U.S.* exports. Because growth in productivity outpaced growth in domestic demand, American farmers had little choice but to seek foreign markets, and in spite of its protectionism, Japan had already become their largest single customer and remained one of their best prospects for future growth.[43]

[40] *Tōkyō Shinbun* (24 June 1987).
[41] Ibid. (30 June 1987); *The Washington Post* (23 January 1993); MAFF (1990), p. 20.
[42] *Sankei Shinbun* (30 June 1987).   [43] Paarlberg (1990), pp. 133, 136.

Why would America provoke its best customer? Rice is a crop of little economic significance to the United States, where it accounts for less than 1 percent of total agricultural output and is cultivated on only one-half of 1 percent of all farms by a mere 11,400 producers. Besides, there was no guarantee of how much liberalization of the Japanese market would benefit American growers: Given production costs that were about twice as high, U.S. rice was not competitive with Thai rice. Nevertheless, the global market in rice is comparatively thin and about half of the U.S. crop was exported in 1987, so if American output accounted for only 1.3 percent of total world production, it still exported 18.9 percent of the rice traded internationally. In addition, Japan's ban on rice imports served as a symbol of its closed markets during a period of massive Japanese trade surpluses and, more important, perhaps, making an exception for Japan would have undercut the firm U.S. stand against the European Community's protectionist Common Agriculture Policy at the Uruguay Round of the GATT talks.[44] (It should be noted that the United States itself imposed quantitative restrictions on imports of farm products like sugar, peanuts, and beef, and its exports of rice resulted in part from large subsidies, which totaled $1.02 billion, or $90,000 per farmer, in 1987.[45])

America's repeated assertion was straightforward: Japanese consumers were being robbed of the freedom to choose cheap, tasty California rice. From the Japanese perspective, the situation was far more complicated. Food Control benefited a powerful voting bloc, and if Americans routinely dismissed the idea as a mere rationalization for protectionism, Japanese insisted on the need to maintain foodstuff security. Although the economic argument for self-sufficiency in rice was logically specious – Japan could have enhanced its security through cheaper, less trade-distorting strategies like stockpiling, diversification of external sources, cultivation of long-term supply relationships, and maintenance of adequate capacity, and real security would have had to involve many more foodstuffs than rice alone – it did resonate with the public.[46]

Japanese had painful memories of the starvation that had accompanied the end of the Pacific War and its immediate aftermath. More recently, the vulnerability that came with dependence on imports had been brought home by the oil shocks of the 1970s. The largest net importer of agricultural products in the world since 1984, Japan maintained an overall self-sufficiency rate of only 70 percent in the mid-1980s and relied on imports for almost half its calories. Japan was already the least self-sufficient of the larger advanced industrial countries, and its ability to feed itself continued to decline over time.[47] As for the security of American supplies, it was the United States that had forced Japanese housewives to stand in line in front of tofu stores when the Nixon

[44] Komari (1991), pp. 17, 19.   [45] *The Daily Yomiuri* (31 October 1988).
[46] Komari (1991), pp. 7–8.   [47] MAFF (1986), pp. 8, 11, 12.

Administration forbade the export of soybeans in 1973 and the United States that publicly fretted about the potential dangers of *its* growing dependence on *Japan*.

One of the LDP's agriculture *san'yaku* gave special emphasis to the international context of Japan's decision in 1987: "This year's rice price won't be as simple as it has been until now. . . . Starting with the United States, every country in the world will be paying attention."[48] Both American bluster and Japanese hand wringing were exaggerated, however. Impassioned rhetoric (deliberately?) obscured the fact that in agricultural trade, neither government embraced the more extreme demands of its constituents, and conflicts between the two countries were managed. Too many groups had too large an interest in keeping the trade relationship on an even keel.

Run-up to a showdown

In 1984, in order to supplement extremely tight supplies, Japan imported about $70 million worth of rice from South Korea, ostensibly as repayment in kind for previous agricultural assistance.[49] Even under these circumstances, an enraged Nōkyō appealed to farmer unity and attempted to interrupt rice shipments. Although there had been four bad harvests in a row from 1980 to 1983, the shortage was also due to the government's attempt to economize by limiting stockpiles, and Nōkyō regarded the shortage as a policy failure. The government should disregard expense in the pursuit of an adequate domestic supply of foodstuffs, the cooperatives argued. Nōkyō had overreached, however: It attracted growing criticism, and public support for opening the rice market dates from this time.

In 1985, although the price formula called for a 2.6 percent drop, government–LDP negotiations deferred a cut. In 1986, for the first time in 20 years, the producer price of wheat was reduced (1.1 percent), and for the first time in 30 years, the government submitted a plan to cut the producer price of rice. The state's finances had worsened, demands for the liberalization of rice imports were rising overseas, and thanks to a decline in production costs due to appreciation of the yen, the existing formula called for a drop of 6.6 percent. The LDP ruled that out as unacceptable but decided that a cut of about half that size was inevitable. "In order to ease a sudden change," the calculation formula was altered, and MAFF submitted to the Beishin a plan to reduce the producer price by 3.8 percent.

Although the Beishin was splitting fifty-fifty over the cut, the rice lobby broke out in revolt against the government. Zenchū debated whether to call for maintenance of the status quo or an *increase* in the price of rice and finally opted for

---

[48] *Tōkyō Shinbun* (25 June 1987).   [49] Calder (1988), pp. 231–32.

the former, obscuring its concession by demanding something "at or above the current price." With election campaigns for both houses of the Diet coinciding with the price campaign, the LDP's rice *zoku* duly followed suit. In the end, Prime Minister Nakasone abandoned any attempt to cut the producer price, but the government and the LDP exchanged a written memorandum pledging to decide the 1987 price in accordance with the 1986 formula; there would be no tinkering with the method of calculation and no political addition, in other words.

The farm lobby's victory proved to be Pyrrhic. There was a glut of semicontrolled rice at the time of the decision, so while that came down in price, government rice did not, inviting such a heated backlash among consumers that even the agricultural gang of eight acknowledged that the LDP had gone too far in maintaining the status quo. MCA Director General Tamaki Kazuo, who had resisted *zoku* pressure, characterized Nōkyō as "a cancer in the Food Control System" and launched an investigation of the organization's operations. Nakasone criticized Nōkyō, too, remarking: "I put Tamaki up to his remarks. . . . Nōkyō must reform itself."[50] This clash deepened Nōkyō's isolation and weakened its spirit.

The imbroglio over the 1986 price decision gave fresh impetus to American demands for the liberalization of imports. The American Rice Millers Association insisted that the closing of Japan's rice market constituted an unfair trade practice in violation of Section 301 of the Trade Act and brought the case before the Office of the U.S. Trade Representative (USTR). Although the USTR rejected the rice industry's case in October, arguing that the matter ought to be handled multilaterally at the Uruguay Round of the GATT talks, it did promise to reexamine the problem after a year if Japan was not "forthcoming" on the issue and intimated that it would accept the suit if it were renewed. Zenchū reacted violently, insisting that the liberalization of rice imports would inevitably lead to the ruin of Japanese farmers. MAFF, too, vetoed imports, asserting that GATT recognized the legitimacy of Japan's restrictions. The American industry's action nevertheless galvanized Japanese debate on Food Control and its costs, diplomatic as well as financial, and the possible effects of price decisions on U.S.-Japan relations could no longer be ignored.

Whatever the government's intransigence vis-à-vis foreigners, its policies were losing ground at home. *Shingikai* reports reflected and reinforced the shift. Even before the rice price drama had been played out, the New Maekawa Report of April 1986 had called for agricultural policies befitting an "age of internationalization," including the encouragement of "core" (that is, larger-scale, full-time) farmers, greater reliance on the market, and the reduction of domestic–foreign price disparities. Before disbanding in June, the Ad Hoc

[50] *Asahi Shinbun* (28 June 1987).

Council for the Promotion of Administrative Reform advised the government to focus its policies on core farmers and to cut both the producer and consumer rice prices.

In the wake of the 1986 price decision, the prime minister's Agricultural Policy Council released a long-term "vision" report in November that recommended an increase in semicontrolled rice; the fostering of core farmers and the enhancement of productivity through an increase in the circulation and concentration of agricultural land; the setting of prices that would reflect the production costs of core farmers and movements in supply and demand, lighten the financial burden on the government, and "earn people's consent and understanding"; and the improvement of market access for foreign producers. Encouraged by this report, MAFF subsequently axed the prices of livestock products and wheat.

Nakasone wanted the LDP to appeal to independent urban voters, and he feared that if the government simply maintained the status quo, it would invite a backlash from them. The time seemed ripe for a reform of agricultural policy: There was a feeling that the party had fulfilled its obligation to rural voters in 1986, the LDP's overwhelming victory in the simultaneous Diet elections of that year gave some hope that the party could overcome any opposition from the farm lobby, and Nakasone's success in privatizing the national railway over stiff resistance had won him public support and bolstered his self-confidence. When the LDP suffered unexpected defeats in the spring of 1987 in a Diet by-election and in regional elections, however, the consensus was that these losses stemmed in part from farmers' mistrust of reform. Nakasone thus refrained from open criticism of agricultural policy. As someone close to the prime minister remarked, "The wise policy is to advance gradually without goading rural communities."[51]

MAFF was even more meticulous than usual in its preparations. After successfully reducing livestock prices, the ministry started sending up trial balloons in April, with the mass media reporting that the government had hardened its resolve to cut the producer price of rice 6 to 8 percent. On the economic front, a rollback would reduce the deficit of the Food Control rice account, allow for the lowering of the consumer price to draw down government stockpiles, and promote a shift by producers to other crops. On the political front, scaling down the domestic-foreign price gap would placate Japanese consumers while permitting continued protection of farmers. Circumstances favored the government. On account of three straight years of bumper crops, falling commodity prices and interest rates, rising productivity, sluggish wage increases, and the failure to reduce the price in 1986, the accepted formula pointed to a sizable cut in the producer price.

[51] Ibid.

Never far from officials' minds, international pressures once again moved to the fore at this time. Due to economic friction, the second summit conference between President Ronald Reagan and Prime Minister Nakasone started on 1 May in an atmosphere of crisis. Only a week before, Congress had begun full-scale hearings on a trade bill. In light of the lack of improvement in America's current account balance, criticism of Japan had intensified, and the House of Representatives was debating the Gephardt Amendment, which demanded a sharp reduction in trade surpluses like Japan's. Immediately before Nakasone's arrival, Reagan himself called attention to the fact that Japanese consumers were paying ten times the international price of rice and publicly resolved to pressure Japan on the liberalization of rice imports.

On 13 May, an OECD meeting of cabinet ministers issued a communiqué spelling out America's, Japan's, and Germany's responsibilities for maintaining growth and correcting trade imbalances, and for the first time, the organization took a stand on the sensitive issue of liberalizing agricultural trade. Although Japan succeeded in having its security concerns addressed – the OECD recognized "noneconomic aspects such as maintaining stability of supply of foodstuffs" – the communiqué unambiguously called for the staged curtailment of protectionism and greater application of the market principle.[52]

That very day, Zenchū opened its Central Headquarters Committee to Establish Policy on Rice Paddy Agriculture (hereafter "Central Headquarters Committee"), and for the first time in its history, Zenchū agreed the next day on a "demand" that tacitly accepted a price cut. As early as March, a Zenchū official had publicly agreed that "the producers' rice price should eventually be lowered."[53] By the organization's own estimate, the price ought to *rise* 2.66 percent in 1987, but it called on the government to set "an appropriate price that will guarantee continued rice production and [farmers'] income." Sakurai Makoto, the Zenchū managing director in charge of rice policy, admitted at a press conference that productions costs had dropped substantially, Zenchū's ideal was out of reach, and it was necessary to win consumers' support. In the face of a growing chorus of criticism at home as well as abroad, Zenchū feared it might discredit Food Control if it stonewalled change and reasoned that it could maximize its ability to minimize a cut by acknowledging that cut's inevitability and focusing its efforts on amending the price calculation formula.

Zenchū was still obliged to submit its proposal to its constituent cooperatives before a formal demand could be made, and the national executive was vulnerable: It was asking farmers to accept a drop in income when the "high-yen slump" had already narrowed job opportunities and the government was strengthening its acreage reduction program. Many local cooperatives felt that their headquarters was weak-kneed, and there was a strong movement on the

---

[52] *Mainichi Shinbun* (14 May 1987).   [53] George (1988), p. A39n.

prefectural level to demand that the government at least maintain the status quo. It was on account of this, to avoid a split in the organization as well as to forestall public criticism, that the executive had formulated so vague a demand. The highest ranks of Zenchū's leadership anticipated trouble nonetheless, and its chair announced on 14 May that he planned to retire. Although he cited health reasons, inside sources reported that his intention was to sacrifice himself for the sake of the organization.

Upon his return from the OECD meeting, Minister of Agriculture Katō Mutsuki told a Diet committee on 16 May that he was satisfied with the way the communiqué reflected Japan's concern with foodstuff security, but he warned that "if we don't drastically raise productivity and shrink the domestic-foreign price gap, I have the feeling we won't be able to resist criticism from abroad." Although he promised to implement the Agricultural Policy Council's report faithfully, to reexamine the prices of farm goods in general and of rice in particular, he declared that "Japan's future agricultural policy will not be carried out under duress from overseas. It must be handled as Japan's own problem."[54]

Katō's remarks were misleading: Japan's political leadership was employing the threat of *gaiatsu* to parry *domestic* criticism. Editorial opinion was unanimous in calling for lower prices. *Nihon Keizai Shinbun* advocated breaking away from the rigidity of a government rice price that never declined. "Rice may be the root and trunk of Japanese agriculture, but just because that is true does not mean that we can set it aside for special treatment. After all, rice, too, is a commodity."[55] Even an agricultural trade paper run by Nōkyō observed, "It goes without saying that we will not be able to win wide support from all classes of people if we indiscriminately demand the price we want on the basis of some pretexts and a lot of excuses."[56]

On 21 May, MAFF opened the Beishin's Rice Price Roundtable (Beika Kondankai) to deliberate on the factors to be considered in calculating a price. The ministry proposed using the cost of production-income supplement formula in 1987, too, and with all members approving, a reduction in the producer price became a certainty for the first time. There was a hitch, however. In order to reduce the original recommendation of a 6.6 percent cut to 3.8 percent, the formula had been altered in 1986 to factor in the average harvest per unit area of the preceding five years rather than the previous three. But even the amended formula called for a cut that was unacceptably high at a time when rural areas were suffering from a recession. MAFF asked the roundtable to examine ways of constricting the range of the drop and members obliged, stating that "in order to soften the influence of fluctuations in harvest size, stabilization of the price is

---

[54] *Yomiuri Shinbun* (16 May 1987); *Nihon Keizai Shinbun* (16 May 1987, evening).
[55] *Nihon Keizai Shinbun* (13 May 1987).
[56] *Nihon Nōgyō Shinbun* (16 May 1987).

inevitable."[57] The Beishin would accept a trimming of the recommended price cut, in other words.

Trade in agricultural goods was one of the chief items on the agenda at the Venice Economic Summit of 8 June through 10 June. In the end, the summit reaffirmed its commitment to the agreement on agriculture set out in the OECD ministerial communiqué of 13 May. As the world's largest net importer of foodstuffs, Japan had always absolved itself of any blame for agricultural trade friction, but it now had to acknowledge that importing countries also bore responsibilities, and there was no denying that it maintained a high-cost agricultural sector through extremely protectionist policies. The Japanese government promised to make greater efforts to open its markets.

Meanwhile, cooperatives had been debating Zenchū's plan. June 12 was a long, hot day that farmers faced with a mixture of dissatisfaction and resignation as Zenchū finally gathered its prefectural representatives in Tokyo to make a formal decision. In a sharp departure from its usual practice, Zenchū's executive did not plan to make an explicit demand. Until 1985, it had always demanded a specific price, and if in 1986 Zenchū requested only that the price not be changed, the preamble of its declaration had included calculations that pointed to a 6.24 percent price hike. Zenchū's own calculations yielded a price hike of 2.66 percent for 1987, but that figure was tucked away in an appendix of reference materials rather than presented as a demand. As they had in May, Zenchū officials suggested requesting that the government "decide the price in such a way as to guarantee continued production and [farmers'] income."

If Zenchū was, in fact, swallowing a price reduction, it could not say so publicly for fear of undermining the solidarity of the rice lobby. Although many prefectural representatives argued that Zenchū should clearly state how much it wanted in the text of its demand, or at least include an estimated price in the preamble, 39 of the 47 prefectural central committees ultimately supported the executive's plan (5 wanted to demand "more than at present," and 3 held out for a specific price hike). Zenchū had tacitly accepted a cut.

After presenting Minister of Agriculture Katō with Zenchū's demand, Managing Director Sakurai held a press conference in which he strained to avoid clarifying what his organization had deliberately obfuscated. When asked to explain Zenchū's position, he responded, "I'm not going to say a single word about approving a cut in the price of rice. . . . We're not demanding something more or something less. . . . The Western way of thinking, simply giving a logical explanation, won't do. I expect I'll be understood by Japanese," he asserted, his voice raised in anger. As it happens, "his reply was unclear to some Japanese, too," one newspaper reported; another characterized the press conference as "a Zen dialogue." The chief of Zenchū's Rice Paddy Agriculture Section

[57] Ibid. (22 May 1987); *Nihon Keizai Shinbun* (22 May 1987).

was somewhat more forthcoming. If at first he toed the party line – "I can't say whether Zenchū requested a raise, the status quo, or a cut" – when reporters persisted, he pled, "Please make allowances for our distress. . . . Naturally, we can't say 'drop the price.'"[58]

Farmers' acquiescence had not come cheap. In return for swallowing a price reduction, Zenchū now intended to throw all its strength into narrowing the cut through the introduction of "measures to ease a sudden change." With regard to the price calculation formula, Zenchū sought changes in the farmers surveyed, the evaluation of land capital, remuneration for family labor, the distribution of the fruits of improvements in productivity, and the interest credited to self-capitalization. Zenchū further requested more government planning for the future, a reduction of costs through land improvements and subsidization of the expansion of scale, maintenance of distribution facilities, expansion of the demand for rice, and controls on the prices of producer inputs.[59]

With an eye to the upcoming struggle, Zenchū planned mass meetings and special movements throughout the country to press its demands. The largest of these gathered 7,000 people in Niigata Prefecture on 15 June. Zenchū could not have been entirely pleased with what it had wrought, however. In addition to staging symposiums to win consumer sympathy and drum up resistance to American demands, farmers expressed irritation at the prospect of a price drop, criticizing the national organization for having been too lenient and not having specified an explicit price target. Although Zenchū's Tokyo headquarters was festooned with outsized banners as always, instead of exhorting supporters to "Achieve the Rice Price Demand," as they often had in the past, 1987's appeals were the more defensive "Our Own Foodstuffs by Our Own Hands" and "Oppose Liberalization!"

A one-shot calculation

As the struggle over the 1987 producer price began in earnest, MOF staked out one extreme, releasing a report designed to forestall tinkering with the price formula by recapitulating all of the arguments in favor of a price reduction. If the formula used in the past were applied, falling production costs would justify a 12 to 13 percent price cut, and the introduction of a coefficient to smooth out fluctuations in harvest size shrank that cut only to 10 percent. Despite the 30 percent of all rice paddies lying fallow, the prevailing price inevitably led to overproduction, and Japan was hard pressed internationally to weaken its extreme protectionism and strengthen competitiveness. At ¥6.9 million ($49,000), the average farming household's annual income was close to 30 percent better

---

[58] *Yomiuri Shinbun* (13, 18 June 1987); *Nihon Keizai Shinbun* (16 June 1987); *Asahi Shinbun* (7 July 1987, evening).
[59] *Nihon Nōgyō Shinbun* (13 June 1987).

than the average worker's in 1985, and because a raise in compensation was already included in the current calculation formula, trimming the price cut would widen this disparity further. The Food Control Special Account deficit stood at ¥380 billion ($2.7 billion) in 1986, and when other subsidies were included, that ballooned to ¥1.2 trillion ($8.57 billion) of taxes lavished on rice. Every 1 percent cut in the producer price would lighten the government's financial burden by ¥11 billion ($79 million). In conclusion, "there are not sufficient grounds for a constriction of the range of a price cut."[60]

Staking out the middle ground, MAFF questioned MOF's tactics. According to one MAFF official, "whenever MOF tries to restrain Nōkyō and the LDP and proposes a completely unrealizable policy of substantial cuts, it backfires." A more politicized ministry, MAFF was more attuned to political realities. From early on, in fact, it had instructed regional agricultural bureaus and foodstuff offices to report on local Nōkyō and Diet representative movements.[61] MAFF itself was ambivalent, however. Because it sought to make up for the cancellation of the 1986 price cut and hoped to reduce the domestic-foreign price gap and its own embarrassing deficits, MAFF would have preferred a drop of 9 to 10 percent, but the ministry decided to aim for a cut of around 6 percent as more realistic.

At the other extreme, conservative politicians were naturally doubtful about the expediency of reducing the incomes of some of their most reliable supporters, and LDP losses in local elections heightened their concern. Although there was no question that a proposed sales tax had also alienated voters, the setback was attributed to the stalled economies of rural communities, and a sudden change in agricultural policy might invite an even more severe backlash. If the LDP and Zenchū acknowledged that a drop in the price of rice was inevitable, they would fain constrict a cut to 3 or 4 percent and drew the line at 5.

In return for maintenance of the status quo in 1986, the party had promised not to make a political addition in 1987. In making that commitment, most rice MPs had focused entirely on the decision at hand, with no thought of the morrow, but if some Diet representatives were now ready to renege – in the words of one *zoku*'s staffer, "There hasn't been a time when a political decision was more necessary than now"[62] – they were in the minority. Because it could not resort to a political addition, the rice lobby aimed at a "one-shot calculation": The Beishin could be counted on to approve a recommendation that had solid support from the government, so the LDP would take a hand in determining that recommendation through negotiations with MAFF and MOF *prior to* the Beishin's 1 July opening. The party had already adopted this strategy of

[60] *Nihon Keizai Shinbun* (18 June 1987).
[61] *Asahi Shinbun* (25 June 1987).
[62] *Nihon Nōgyō Shinbun* (12 June 1987).

prior adjustment and successfully avoided explicit political additions when setting the 1987 prices of livestock and wheat.

History had come full circle: The LDP had originally resorted to political additions in order to *avoid* prior adjustments. In 1961, Beishin deliberations were delayed by negotiations that had already, in effect, determined the price of rice. After the council submitted its irrelevant report, its chair and five other neutral members resigned in protest. Following this incident, even if party-government negotiations continued to take place before the Beishin was consulted, the LDP waited until after the council had made its report to press for political additions in order to forestall unnecessary flak.[63]

On 16 June, the LDP opened its Comprehensive Policy Committee and the committee's Basic Policy Subcommittee and heard reports from MAFF and agricultural organizations. The following day, precisely because a majority of the subcommittee acknowledged that a price reduction was inevitable and that a political addition was not in the cards, MPs made every effort to constrict the range of the cut recommended by the government to the Beishin and to include compensatory countermeasures in a supplementary budget. After the subcommittee meeting closed, an LDP agriculture *zoku* exclaimed, "Without being swayed by inflexibly rational economic theory, now's the time to demonstrate our power as politicians. A cut in the price of rice? The liberalization of rice imports? Inconceivable!"[64] By coincidence, Senator Lloyd Bentsen that very day submitted a trade bill that took Japan to task as a "hostile trading nation" and would have mandated retaliatory measures.

On 22 June, MAFF announced that, when calculated by the (modified) 1986 formula, the producer price ought to fall 9.8 percent. Although there had been little discussion at its first sessions, the Basic Policy Subcommittee now spat fire. Conservative politicians lambasted the ministry for trying to sway public opinion by broadcasting its projections to the mass media and demanded that it withdraw the offensive figure. MAFF lamely defended itself by explaining that 9.8 percent was only an estimate and that, of course, "public opinion" (i.e., LDP pressure) would also be reflected in its formal recommendation. Even so, Chairman Okawara Taiichirō announced that deliberations would move forward without any commitment to the 9.8 percent figure, reconfirming that the price of rice was something to be negotiated between the government and the party and that the party was ready to alter the calculation formula in order to reduce the cut.

A preliminary session of the Beishin opened on 24 June in order to let MAFF explain the situation and answer questions. Although neutral and consumer councilors were willing to support MAFF's −9.8 percent estimate if it accurately reflected the current economic environment, even they thought that such

[63] Donnelly (1977), pp. 171–73.
[64] *Yomiuri Shinbun* (20 June 1987).

a cut might be too large. When a neutral member pointed out that a political addition had overturned the Beishin's proposal the year before, Minister of Agriculture Katō apologized and promised that it would not happen again. Katō had already publicly stated, "We don't want to set a rice price that fosters popular distrust in politics to the extent it did last year. Our goal is by all means to have a one-shot decision without a political addition."[65] What he failed to acknowledge was that this method called into question the raison d'être of the Beishin. As *Mainichi* editorialized, if the producer price were decided through political negotiations in advance of *shingikai* deliberations,

> there would be no meaning to the Beishin's deliberations. . . . If the government determines the rice price on political grounds after having received expert advice [from the Agricultural Policy Council and the New Maekawa Report], one can only say that that will incur all the more mistrust in politics. For that reason, we have a request to make of the Beishin. If the submitted rice price is a price that, for all intents and purposes, has already been decided, rather than simply replying yes or no, propose your own idea. We want action taken to raise the Beishin's authority.[66]

In the past, party bosses and the minister of agriculture had often held secret conferences on the price of rice before and after the Beishin met. On the evening of the Prior Beishin, the LDP's gang of eight and the minister gathered at a restaurant in the Akasaka district, the traditional setting for backroom politicking. Although it is unclear what transpired at that meeting, Chairman Kondō Motoji of PARC's Agriculture and Forestry Division later made it quite clear that he wanted the government and LDP to agree on a price before consulting the *shingikai*. On 25 June, he said that he wanted to unify the government and party positions "even if we [have to] stay up all night on the 29th and 30th" of June.[67]

With the opening of the Prior Beishin, internal party debate shifted from the Basic Policy Subcommittee to the Rice Price Committee. There, one MP after another attacked the American call for market opening, requested reconsideration of the price formula, and proposed urgent countermeasures for the improvement of rice production and the promotion of rural communities. The cabinet agreed on 30 June to include in its 1987 supplementary budget a ¥192.8 billion ($1.34 billion) set of measures that contained funds for land improvement, irrigation drainage, storage facilities, and so on. In addition to softening farmers' dissatisfaction with a reduced rice price, this money was meant to answer the criticism that the ¥6 trillion ($42.86 billion) that the government had already budgeted for domestic demand expansion was focused primarily on cities.[68]

---

[65] Ibid. (20 June 1987).   [66] *Mainichi Shinbun* (25 June 1987).
[67] *Yomiuri Shinbun* (26 June 1987).   [68] *Tōkyō Shinbun* (1 July 1987).

Meanwhile, Zenchū's Central Headquarters Committee discussed its demands with MAFF officials on 25 June. Zenchū vehemently opposed the ministry's −9.8 percent estimate, calling attention to how, for the first time in its history, Nōkyō had suppressed internal unrest and approved a cut before the price struggle had even begun. Zenchū insisted that the government reexamine its formula. Minister of Agriculture Katō repeated the necessity of adopting a price policy that could earn the people's "understanding, consent, and support." On a more conciliatory note, he added, "We're determined not to open the rice market. We're determined to defend the foundations of Food Control."[69] When representatives of the opposition parties met Katō, they insisted, as always, that the producer price be decided in accordance with the cooperatives' demand, but for the first time they did not seek a price increase, instead proposing maintenance of the status quo.

The 26 June meeting of the LDP's Rice Price Committee once again took up the subjects of amending the calculation formula and adopting government measures to compensate for the coming drop in price. Because the cut would represent a major transition, it would be necessary to prepare farmers; perhaps the price should be left unchanged for three years, it was suggested. At its 29 June meeting, the committee continued these discussions and finally entrusted negotiations with the government to Comprehensive Agricultural Policy Commission Chairman Niwa Hyōsuke, Agriculture and Forestry Division Chairman Kondō Motoji, and its own Chairman Okawara Taiichirō, the LDP's agriculture san'yaku.

As for the party's diehard zoku, the Viet Cong held an urgent meeting on 29 June and unanimously resolved that "significant cuts in the rice price will disrupt our nation's rice agriculture, so we absolutely cannot approve."[70] The next morning, the Apaches, too, had a general meeting where they confirmed their opposition to a substantial reduction in the price of rice and demanded that the price ultimately be determined by the party. In truth, though, the guerrilla corps lacked drive. In order to maintain the status quo in 1986, they had gone to such extremes that the reformist faction within Zenchū itself had been vexed; "We were dragged by the Apaches," they complained.[71] In 1987, by contrast, when the Viet Cong had scheduled meetings for 11 and 24 June, fewer than 20 of its 200 members showed up. The resolution passed at the emergency meeting held on 29 June included no demand for maintenance of the status quo, let alone a price hike. Compared to 1986, when the movement had an explicit goal, the situation was more ambiguous now: Although Zenchū recognized the need to stage a retreat, there were cooperatives that refused to concede defeat, so it was taboo to discuss the scope of the impending cut.

[69] *Nihon Nōgyō Shinbun* (26 June 1987).
[70] *Sankei Shinbun* (30 June 1987); *Nihon Keizai Shinbun* (30 June 1987).
[71] *Sankei Shinbun* (1 July 1987).

Zenchū's ambivalence precluded a coherent strategy and infuriated its own partisans. When MPs did not act, Zenchū would complain, but when they consulted Zenchū on its objectives, the response would be "'take care of us somehow or other,' with no figure coming out," lamented one rice *zoku*. "If you push, they run away, and if you pull, they come chasing after you. I can't for the life of me understand Nōkyō's stance." Rice *zoku* feared that they themselves would suffer because of Zenchū's passive stance. In order to attract farmers' votes, MPs wanted to stage a drama, but "if there's no goal, there's no way to inject passion." As one newspaper observed, although "known for their close unity, a draft is blowing between Zenchū and rice Diet members this year."[72]

The Apaches resolutely opposed a price reduction, threatening to go to opponents' electoral districts to spread rumors that they had favored a substantial cut. They were isolated within the party, however. PARC Chairman Itō Masayoshi branded as "irresponsible" the Apache call to scrap the 1986 party-government agreement. Even the Viet Cong deserted them. When MAFF's −9.8 percent estimate was leaked to the media, the Viet Cong made a fuss at an intra-LDP conference ("Fire the man responsible!"), but they demonstrated some flexibility, backing the agriculture *san'yaku*. Most rice *zoku* privately acknowledged that the price would drop. Rather than the extremists, it was the more broad-minded *zoku* in the Comprehensive Agricultural Policy faction who took center stage, and in the words of one of their leaders, "production without consumption is impossible" – the price of rice would have to come down.[73]

Party-government negotiations began on the morning of 30 June with the LDP's agriculture *san'yaku* informally discussing the government's recommendation with MAFF and MOF officials. They also met the LDP's three party leaders (also called *san'yaku*) – Secretary General Takeshita Noboru, Executive Council Chairman Abe Shintarō, and PARC Chairman Itō – at party headquarters. The Rice Price Committee opened at 3:00 P.M., 8:00 P.M., 11:40 P.M., 5:25 A.M., and 11:00 A.M. but quickly adjourned each time because of the large disparity between the LDP's and the government's positions. "The extreme right supports the status quo and the extreme left a 9.8 percent cut, but you can't very well add them and divide by two to arrive at 4.9 percent, can you," remarked one member.[74] Negotiations between the party *san'yaku*, the agriculture *san'yaku*, and the ministries continued throughout the night. Prime Minister Nakasone kept abreast of developments but deliberately stayed out of the fray.

[72] Ibid.; *Nihon Keizai Shinbun* (30 June 1987).
[73] *Yomiuri Shinbun* (5 July 1987); *Sankei Shinbun* (1 July 1987).
[74] *Nihon Keizai Shinbun* (1 July 1987, evening).

The ministries' opening bid was for a 9.8 percent cut, but that was obviously a nonstarter, and they quickly pared it down to 7.6 percent. The LDP argued yet again that farmers would be dealt a double blow if the rice price were lowered at the same time that acreage reduction policies were being reinforced, and that the adverse effect on regional economies would be large. The government, in turn, asserted that an unreasonably large constriction of the drop would invite the people's mistrust, fail to convince the neutral and consumer members who constituted a majority of the Beishin, and fly in the face of Japan's international obligation to reduce agricultural protectionism. MOF was apparently aiming at a cut of about 7 percent, MAFF 6 percent, and the LDP and Zenchū 5 percent. The battle was waged in 0.1 percent increments worth ¥1.1 billion ($7.9 million).

As the rice price was being decided without them, Beishin members had nothing to do but ponder their role and meditate on their feelings of impotence and anger. After Chairman Nakano Kazuhito gave his opening remarks on the morning of 1 July, Food Agency Director General Gotō made apologies for the absence of the minister, who was still busy engaging in political negotiations, and the *shingikai* recessed after just five minutes. When it reopened in the afternoon, because the government's proposal had yet to be settled, the Beishin was unable to begin real deliberations, and at 3:40 Chairman Nakano suggested recessing until the next morning. Irritated at uselessly spinning their wheels, councilors agreed. At a press conference after the meeting, Chairman Nakano said that it was "regrettable" that the Beishin had not been consulted despite its having convened, and that determining the government's proposal through prior political negotiations called into question the significance of the *shingikai*.

Those political negotiations approached a dénouement as the agriculture *san'yaku*, the party *san'yaku*, and, representing the government, Chief Cabinet Secretary Gotōda, Minister of Finance Miyazawa, and Minister of Agriculture Katō gathered for a summit conference at LDP headquarters at 4:00 P.M. An acrimonious debate raged for two and a half hours. The government side suggested a price cut of 6.5 percent and, when that was rejected, presented 6.2 percent as its final offer, insisting that this was the largest reduction of the original 9.8 percent estimate that could be explained "rationally" (i.e., without openly acknowledging its political nature). Arguing that the rice lobby would not settle for anything above the 5 percent level, the party went no higher than 5.9 percent. "Isn't that the same as Zenchū's claim?" Gotōda asked. "Must we listen to what Zenchū says two years running?"[75]

Minister of Agriculture Katō, who at one point had threatened to resign, agreed to compromise if Miyazawa would. Gotōda got Miyazawa's consent,

[75] *Yomiuri Shinbun* (5 July 1987).

then sought the prime minister's approval. Nakasone added 0.05 percent to the party offer for a final settlement of −5.95 percent. (The government–LDP agreement also included measures to stimulate rice cultivation and rural communities and a pledge to hold fast to the fundamentals of Food Control and the policy of domestic self-sufficiency in rice.) If technically at the 5 percent level, saving the face of the party, it rounded off to 6 percent, saving the face of the government. Many rice MPs were unconvinced, but a 7:30 meeting of the Rice Price Committee approved the plan, finally ending negotiations that had extended over 24 hours.

If politicians could finally catch up on their sleep, bureaucrats still had a busy night ahead of them. The scope of the contemplated price cut had changed time and again. As a deputy of PARC Chairman Itō admitted, "considering the rice price calculation factors, a purely reasonable estimate went [only] as far as 6.2 percent. The 6 percent level was broken out of consideration for the feelings of farmers."[76] When a 5.95 percent cut was finally settled on, MOF and MAFF were completely at a loss as to how the existing price formula could possibly justify the figure. Thus began a flurry of activity, with bureaucrats belatedly tinkering with the formula to make the agreed-upon price look plausible. To take one example, the 1986 standard for interest had been Nōkyō's rate on annual time deposits for the preceding year; in 1987, it was changed to Nōkyō's average rate for the last five years.

The government blandly claimed that it had simply reexamined its price formula and arrived at a figure that was within the scope of a rational calculation. When asked afterward how they had arrived at the various prices proposed during negotiations, officials conceded that "the figure changes depending on the way one factors in the variables. It wasn't something based on exact calculations." *Yomiuri* put it less charitably: "Depending on its inclination, the Food Agency can change the calculation factors any way at all. They can find reasons for whatever scope of cut is decided at government–LDP negotiations prior to the Beishin."[77]

After the figures were appropriately juggled, all that was necessary was for the Beishin publicly to lend its imprimatur to the settlement the party and government had privately worked out.

The Rice Price Council

Established on 2 August 1949 by the same legislation that created the Ministry of Agriculture and Forestry, the Beishin is designed to assemble a diverse range of interest groups along with nonpartisan experts.

[76] *Asahi Shinbun* (2 July 1987).
[77] *Nihon Keizai Shinbun* (3 July 1987); *Yomiuri Shinbun* (4 July 1987).

Membership composition

The council's members are appointed by the minister of agriculture, without the Diet's playing any role. There is no need: Whatever the Beishin's report, its recommendations can be overturned by party negotiations with the government.

Initially, politicians were themselves included as councilors. Although the First Rinchō had called on the government to respect the separation of powers and partisan strife exacerbated the Beishin's natural divisiveness, the government did not move until the council failed to agree on any recommendations whatsoever for two years. In 1968, Prime Minister Satō removed not only politicians but, for good measure, the representatives of producer and consumer groups, too. Composed of nine journalists, seven academics, and six former government officials, this "neutral Beishin" was able to recommend unprecedented reforms like the establishment of the market in semicontrolled rice and the crop diversion program. Whereas producers and consumers returned to the Beishin (in reduced numbers) the following year, politicians did not.[78]

Although all Beishin councilors have been regarded as persons of learning and experience since that time, the *shingikai* consistently includes 5 producer members, 5 consumer members, and (usually) 15 neutral members, with seats allotted to the same set of parent organizations year after year (see Table 6-1). The five-member producer delegation, for example, always includes individuals from Nōkyō (in 1987, from Zenchū and Zennō); the National Chamber of Agriculture, a government-subsidized association of locally elected committees that helps carry out official policies; the All-Japan Federation of Farmers Unions, which is more leftist and militant than other farm groups; and an individual rice farmer who does not represent any particular organization. "To have one person each from Zenchū, the National Federation of Agricultural Cooperatives, and so on sitting on the producer side has become traditional. It's a tacit restriction [on MAFF's appointive authority]. It may not be official, but it's self-evident."[79]

Actually, MAFF does wield some influence over the choice of interest-group representatives. According to one producer councilor, "Because organizations do recommend specific people, there've been times when the government has asked them to choose someone else because an individual wasn't welcome to the government. Although that sort of thing goes on behind the scenes rather than publicly, it happens often."[80] A consumer councilor told a similar story. "The government will ask an organization to please send a member to the Beishin. As in any *shingikai*, it won't order an organization to send X; it's a principle that the organization itself decides whom to send. But you can't say the government

[78] Donnelly (1977), p. 191; Donnelly (1984), p. 356.   [79] Interview with Ara Kenjirō.
[80] Interview with Tanimoto Takashi.

Table 6-1. *Members of the Beishin, July 1987*

Producer representatives	
Ikeda Hitoshi	Executive Director (*senmu riji*), National Chamber of Agriculture
Ishikawa Shōhei	Managing Director (*kaichō riji*), National Federation of Agricultural Cooperatives
Kunigo Yoshifusa	Vice Chair (*fuku kaichō*), Central Union of Agricultural Cooperatives (Zenchū)
Nishimura Fukuji	Private farmer
Tanimoto Takashi	General Secretary (*shokichō*), All-Japan Federation of Farmers Unions
Consumer representatives	
Hayashi Iku	Professor, Faculty of Domestic Science, Mukogawa Women's University
Katsube Kiichi	Counselor (*san'yō*), Japanese Consumers Cooperative Union
Ōkawa Nobuo	Director (*riji*), National Federation of Food Industry Cooperatives
Ōtomo Yofu	Chair (*kaichō*), Regional Women's Organization Liaison Conference
Wada Masae	Vice Chair (*fuku kaichō*), Housewives League
Public-interest representatives	
Ara Kenjirō	Professor, Hitotsubashi University
Isobe Norio	President (*shachō*), Hakuhōdō Advertising
Kagayama Kunio	Chair (*rijichō*), Agriculture, Forestry, and Fishery Research and Development Association
Kishi Yasuhiko	Editorial writer, *Nihon Keizai Shinbun*
Masamoto Hideo	Vice Chair (*fuku kaichō*), National Association of Towns and Villages
Miyawaki Nagasada	Executive Director (*senmu riji*), Japan Economic Research Institute
Miyazaki Isamu	Chair (*rijichō*), Daiwa Securities Research Institute
Mizuno Masaichi	Professor, Nagoya University
Mochida Keizō	Professor, Faculty of Economics, Wakō University
Nakamura Yasuhiko	News commentator, NHK
Nakano Kazuhito[a]	Chair (*kaichō*), Japan Grain Inspection Association
Namiki Masayoshi	Chair (*rijichō*), Food and Agriculture Policy Research Center
Sawabe Mamoru	Chair (*rijichō*), Japan Racing Association
Yamazaki Kōu	Professor, Faculty of Agriculture, University of Tokyo

[a] Chair.

never suggests, 'If you don't mind, we'd like you to send X.'"[81] MAFF's influence is limited, however. There is an ex officio quality to much of the interest-group representation: The chair of Zenchū normally sits on the Beishin, for example. "Rather than interest groups' 'choosing' [their representatives], it's better to think in terms of someone's *automatically* becoming a member," noted one neutral councilor.[82]

If the ministry does choose neutral members directly, without explicitly consulting the concerned parties, there is plainly an established framework for selecting most of those councilors, too. The Beishin typically includes four

[81] Interview with Wada Masae.   [82] Interview with Kishi Yasuhiko.

university professors, a couple of journalists, several representatives from government-tied economic research organizations, and one or two local government officials. Interest groups do not normally meddle in MAFF's selection of neutral councilors, but the ministry presumably takes interest-group preferences into account without being asked to. "Before it becomes a matter of [interest groups'] rejecting a neutral member, MAFF acts so as not to choose someone who would be rejected."[83]

Although the ministry maintains that the Beishin's membership composition is what it is because MAFF wants a fair and objective report, this contention strikes many people as disingenuous. Professional qualifications often play a distinctly secondary role in the selection of councilors. An agronomist surmised, "I was chosen because I'm an expert in the techniques of rice plant cultivation. My predecessor was a[nother] Tokyo University Faculty of Agriculture professor, an expert in the techniques of rice plant cultivation. If I were to quit, I think that another expert in the techniques of rice plant cultivation would be chosen." But he was the only technical expert included in the Beishin, and even he acknowledged, "my closest friend is currently MOF's chief of the Budget Bureau. There's that connection."[84]

Some neutral members naturally lean one way or another. In the words of the councilor from the National Town and Village Association:

> Although there are both producers and consumers among our residents, because agriculture now faces such a harsh situation, we must speak for farmers. It's we small-town mayors and heads of villages who are in contact with farmers at the lower levels, and it's very trying to be put in the position of a mayor who has to say "Don't grow rice" in spite of the availability of good paddy fields. There are hardly any other crops with which to make money in place of rice, so one can't help but oppose price cuts and acreage reduction. I'm a neutral member, and I don't necessarily act in concert with producer representatives, but because we directly reflect the voice of farmers, I'm somewhat different from a purely neutral member.[85]

Similarly, the representative from the National Federation of Food Industry Cooperatives observed of his own organization: "We collect the product and distribute it to consumers, so we have the same kind of relationship to both producers and consumers. . . . I'm considered a consumer representative, but I'm completely neutral."[86] A neutral councilor wondered aloud whether another "consumer" group deserved that label: "The Housewives League and local women's consumer leagues clearly take a stand in support of consumers, but in the past, because farmers' women's associations were included as subordinate organizations and some consumer cooperatives were tied directly to agricultural

---

[83] Ibid.   [84] Interview with Yamazaki Kōu.
[85] Interview with Masamoto Hideo.   [86] Interview with Ōkawa Nobuo.

cooperatives, there were also times when they did *not* take the consumer's side."[87]

There is other evidence to suggest that producers have the upper hand vis-à-vis consumers. Although councilors are routinely reappointed every year, producer representatives tend to serve longer, for example. As of June 1987, producer members of the Beishin had served an average of 92 months (63.5 months when an outlier who had sat on the *shingikai* for more than 17 years is excluded), neutral members an average of 45.4 months, and consumer members an average of 32 months. (On average, bureaucratic OBs had served only slightly longer than other members, 54.7 months to 51.5.)

In light of the traditional producer bias of the Beishin, which was itself a function of ministry choices, MAFF now makes it a point to include advocates of reform. As one councilor explained: "When you include many people who're knowledgeable about agriculture, it's inevitable that many will lean toward agriculture [i.e., the policy positions of farmers]. The ministry thus includes people with different positions in order to check such thinking."[88] The balance that MAFF seeks is not all-inclusive, however; there are limits to the diversity of opinion it formally acknowledges through its appointments. "You could say, perhaps, that the government chooses members from the range of people who can talk together," noted one councilor. "There aren't any of the sort of members who would cry out 'No!' from the start, in direct opposition to national policies."[89] That is a charitable way of portraying the situation: The real question for most observers – and many Beishin councilors themselves – is whether the government is really interested in *any* position other than its own.

With public-interest members, who constitute a majority of councilors, appointed at MAFF's discretion, "the [Beishin's] composition is such that the ministry can obtain reports along the lines of its own inclinations," complained one producer representative.[90] A consumer councilor echoed this opinion: "The responsibility for appointing [neutral] members belongs to the minister of agriculture, and because he appoints people who cooperate, the Beishin can't help but become a council that complies with [ministry] policy."[91] Even a ministry OB admitted that officials "don't choose people whose views are that different from their own. They choose people who understand [i.e., sympathize]. There's a feeling that the margin [of decision] is settled right from the start."[92]

It is especially noteworthy in this regard that in 1987, 7 of the Beishin's 14 neutral members were OBs, 5 from MAFF and 1 apiece from MOF and the Economic Planning Agency. (The number and distribution of OBs has remained fairly constant over time.) Chairman Nakano and Sawabe both joined the Beishin after retiring from the position of administrative vice minister (*jimu*

---

[87] Interview with Miyawaki Nagasada.   [88] Interview with Kishi Yasuhiko.
[89] Interview with Wada Masae.   [90] Interview with Tanimoto Takashi.
[91] Interview with Ōno Shōji.   [92] Interview with Mochida Keizō.

jikan) of MAFF. Kagayama, Mochida, and Namiki had not advanced quite as far in the ministry before leaving, but Isobe and Miyazaki had also reached the level of administrative vice minister at MOF and the EPA before stepping down. In truth, MOF had what amounted to two representatives: In addition to its OB, another neutral member reported that he was recommended by MOF to sit on the Beishin because he was a member of that ministry's Council on the Financial System.[93]

Bureaucratic OBs made no attempt to disguise their close ties to their parent agencies. "Officially, I don't speak for MOF, but am included as a person of learning and experience, . . . yet my thoughts are the same as the ministry's even without my asking what they're thinking."[94] "If we weren't OBs, we wouldn't be here. . . . It's not as if anything they [i.e., incumbent officials] say is OK, but there's agreement on a basic line."[95]

Other councilors were ambivalent about this contingent of retired officials. Although charging that OBs were too numerous, had disproportionate influence, and tended to support current office holders, they also acknowledged that OBs had necessary expertise, spoke candidly, and participated actively. This ambivalence was captured in the remarks of one neutral councilor:

> The character of the *shingikai* is largely ordained by the appointment of bureaucratic OBs, I think. The more OBs that are included, the easier it is for the government's proposal to pass. . . . [Nevertheless,] even among the OBs, views vary with the individual, so I don't think that they represent [only] government policies, and because government policies do change over time, the current government's thinking and OBs' thinking aren't necessarily in accord. There are occasions when they protest the current government's line.[96]

Even if OBs do reflect the positions of their parent agencies, it remains the case that in the Beishin, OBs come from different agencies with different perspectives. And as noted by one councilor in a revealing comment, "If we really did make decisions, then it'd be strange not to do it with pure people, without including OBs as members, but then the *shingikai* doesn't set the price of rice."[97]

Deliberations

Although the entire Food Control System falls within its purview, "the Beishin is a *shingikai* to set prices," as one MAFF official observed succinctly. "It's a *shingikai* that deals with a limited matter, and opens [only] when the govern-

---

[93] Interview with Mizuno Masaichi.   [94] Interview with Katō Takashi.
[95] Interview with Mochida Keizō.   [96] Interview with Yamazaki Kōu.
[97] Interview with Masamoto Hideo.

ment's deciding the prices at which to buy and sell rice and wheat."[98] Although
the Beishin can submit recommendations (*kengi* or *ikensho*) at its own discretion,
it rarely does, and some councilors did not even acknowledge that possibility.
"The Beishin issues reports in response to inquiries received from the government," one member asserted. "If it's not asked, it can't report. Discussions are
conducted within a set framework, in other words."[99] And that framework could
not be more straightforward. "The government's inquiry is a simple thing: it's
just a question of what about a price like *this*?"[100] In response to that question,
councilors might suggest slightly increasing or decreasing the proposed change,
but they will not offer an entirely different price of their own.

The Beishin meets at regular intervals, considering the government's purchase price for wheat in June, its purchase price for rice in July, and its sale
prices for both wheat and rice in December. As noted earlier, the Beishin also
holds a prior (*jizen*) session a month before its regular July meeting to discuss
broader issues surrounding the rice price, and it may hold extraordinary sessions, too. The Beishin sometimes establishes subcommittees, usually to
reexamine the government's price-setting formulas, and those subcommittees
may include bureaucratic experts or scholars in addition to regular councilors.
Even so, they are few and far between (there are no standing committees), they
tend to be dominated by Ministry of Agriculture OBs,[101] and their reports must
be approved by plenary sessions of the *shingikai*.

Only councilors and government officials participate in Beishin deliberations.
Although the *shingikai* can invite outsiders as witnesses, they are not credited
with much influence, so interested parties are reduced to working through, or
on, councilors. Actually, for "interested parties," read "producers": "Postcards
come to my home from individual farmers, and petitions from producers'
groups. About a thousand pieces of mail come," reported one neutral member.
"Sometimes, producers will come visit my home. . . . Consumers never approach me; I haven't experienced that even once."[102] It is interesting to note that
producer organizations do not apply the same pressure on consumer councilors
– given the latter's sympathetic stance, they feel no need to[103] – and consumer
groups make little attempt to influence *shingikai* deliberations other than
through their appointed representatives. Politicians do not approach councilors,
either. "*Zoku* approach the government administration, the minister of agriculture, the prime minister, but not the Beishin. Neither do they work on
[*shingikai*] members individually."[104] Why would they? "Because LDP representatives think that they themselves decide [the price of rice], they don't in the

[98] Interview with Baba Kumao.   [99] Interview with Kishi Yasuhiko.
[100] Interview with Miyazaki Isamu.
[101] Interview with Miyawaki Nagasada.
[102] Interview with Yamazaki Kōu.   [103] Interview with Ōkawa Nobuo.
[104] Interview with Nakamura Yasuhiko.

least make an issue of the *shingikai*. There's no need to pressure it. Rather, Beishin members are working on the LDP."[105]

Although the proceedings of the Beishin were originally intended to be private, that principle was gradually relaxed until, in 1957, the *shingikai* admitted not only journalists, but also rank-and-file members of interest groups. Primarily farmers, these outsiders disrupted deliberations and encouraged many councilors, particularly the politicians then included, to play to the audience, so proceedings were once again closed to the public in 1962. Downplaying considerations of freedom of information or transparency, almost all members defended closed deliberations as a sine qua non of frank discussion. "There's no problem as to the points at issue or what kind of discussions take place because the secretariat or the chair provides that kind of information to the public. Because it would hinder smooth discussion to reveal each member's statements, [however,] . . . there are no announcements of members' names. If that were open to the public, we'd no longer be able to speak."[106]

The one councilor who did criticize closed hearings offered an openly self-serving alternative. "We producers take the position that the price of rice should be set in the Diet. Unlike the Beishin, which is closed to the public, that would clarify for the people exactly how the price is decided. But an even better method would be to decide the price at [direct] negotiations between producer organizations and the government."[107] Minutes of council deliberations are produced, if not published, and reporters' clubs receive detailed information on what is said in camera.

The Beishin is attached to the Food Agency, whose Planning Section serves as its secretariat. The transportation expenses and small honoraria that MAFF pays are listed among the agency's conference expenditures; the Beishin has no budget of its own. It should come as no surprise, then, that the Beishin conducts no research of its own. Nōkyō technical staff conduct their own independent surveys, and producer members are in a position to verify or challenge the data provided by MAFF, digit by digit. Although councilors from research institutions and bureaucratic OBs do have subordinates and analytical resources to fall back on, most neutral members depend entirely upon information provided by the government, and although consumer members have organizations behind them, because groups like the Housewives League or the Federation of Consumer Cooperatives are not focused exclusively on agriculture, they have limited expertise.

Be that as it may, councilors freely make requests of MAFF, and when they do, the Beishin's secretariat conscientiously presents the data they seek. Members affirm that the ministry has never refused a request, although there have

[105] Interview with Katō Takashi.   [106] Interview with Miyazaki Isamu.
[107] Interview with Tanimoto Takashi.

been occasions when it has taken time to compile the desired information. As for MAFF's integrity, one OB councilor remarked that "bureaucrats' views may not be woven into the data, but they'll bring as much data supportive of their own aims as possible. That's natural. While we can trust the information presented, there's also information that doesn't come out, of course."[108] Although most other members did not have the impression that MAFF hides troublesome information, one councilor did make the interesting observation that "MAFF has no reason to hide data from the Beishin because it [now] wants to lower the price as much as possible."[109]

"The secretariat doesn't influence the Beishin," one neutral member maintained. "It performs calculations, provides data, and makes explanations, but it does these things only at the behest of the Beishin."[110] Surprisingly (or predictably, perhaps), it was retired officials who most insistently asserted the reverse, arguing that the secretariat *does* try to lead the council toward conclusions favored by MAFF. A Finance OB warned that "at a glance, it seems that the ministry is not in the least involved. . . . MAFF's hidden, not at all visible."[111] But as an Agriculture OB explained, "The Food Agency is usually in the background, trying to manipulate things. . . . After making their [price] proposal, [officials] have to leave management of the Beishin to its chair, . . . but before that, they're conducting *nemawashi*. It's called 'prior explanation' [*jizen setsumei*]. They explain that they're considering moving in such and such a direction."[112] A neutral councilor gave an account of this process: "MAFF officials invariably come to my home to make explanations. They come from MOF, too. Because it wants to lower the price of rice, MOF in particular applies intense pressure. Although I don't think that pressure's effective, when people convey their opinions or data, it's helpful in arriving at a decision."[113] Further, during deliberations themselves, despite the pretense that it was Chairman Nakano who set the Beishin's schedule, it was actually the ministry.

As in other *shingikai*, councilors tend not to participate as individuals. "Formally, it's the responsibility of the individual, but because one becomes a member through the recommendation of one's organization . . . , there's a stronger coloring of organizational than individual representation. Everyone recognizes that as the de facto situation," explained a consumer member.[114] A bureaucratic OB was more emphatic: "Representatives are 200 percent bound to their organizations."[115] On each side, interest-group councilors confer with their respective parent organizations and with one another. "Everyone consults with his own camp on a plan that's basically settled," the consumer councilor noted.

[108] Interview with Mochida Keizō.   [109] Interview with Kishi Yasuhiko.
[110] Interview with Miyawaki Nagasada.   [111] Interview with Katō Takashi.
[112] Interview with Mochida Keizō.   [113] Interview with Yamazaki Kōu.
[114] Interview with Katsube Kin'ichi.   [115] Interview with Sawabe Mamoru.

"We often get together before the *shingikai*. Members of the consumer side call a MAFF section chief and gather in the form of a study group to coordinate our views. Of course, producers do it even earlier on."[116]

The self-images of interest-group representatives were more similar to those of one another than to those of neutral members. Most councilors, including OBs, explained that they had been appointed because MAFF trusted their fairness and judgment. Whereas a number of producer and consumer members felt the same way, an equal number felt that they had been chosen by virtue of their ties to specific private groups. Unlike the councilors interviewed in the previous two case studies, a couple of Beishin members even reported that they owed their seats to the fact that they were close to the appointing authorities. Whereas most councilors thought that their greatest responsibility was to those persons who would be affected by the policies under consideration or to no one in particular, half of the producer and consumer members who responded to a written questionnaire felt most responsible to the organizations they represented. Finally, whereas neutral councilors conceived of their role as the application of expert knowledge to technical problems, almost all producer and consumer members saw themselves as open advocates for interest groups.

Interest-group representatives report on the state of council deliberations to their organizations, and they often receive clear instructions from those parent bodies. One consumer member reported, "We have various discussions at the board of directors of the Housewives League, for example. We stage diverse movements, learn the general ways of thinking, views, and requests of our members concerning rice . . . , and my remarks [at the Beishin] will be based on those. When [a session] is over, I'll naturally report at the next meeting of the board of directors that I said this about that."[117] Producer members will go so far as to read aloud statements prepared by their organizations.[118] More surprising, what is true of interest-group representatives is no less true of some of the neutral members. As one OB councilor noted, "We say 'neutral' members, but there's generally some sort of a parent organization. You're recommended by MOF or the Economic Planning Agency[, for example]. It's certain that [such members] are being told from behind something like 'Please stand firm on this point. Please help us on that point.'"[119]

Even if councilors did not report back to their parent organizations, their statements would appear in the Beishin's minutes, and even if they did choose to speak as individuals, their remarks would tend to reflect the thinking of the groups from which they hail. Nevertheless, it would be a mistake to credit councilors with no freedom whatsoever. Representing so mobilized a constitu-

---

[116] Interview with Katsube Kin'ichi.   [117] Interview with Wada Masae.
[118] Interview with Namiki Masayoshi.   [119] Interview with Mochida Keizō.

Table 6-2. *Characteristics of parent organizations and Beishin deliberations*

To what extent do you think each of the following attributes of councilors' parent organizations influence advisory body deliberations?

No influence whatsoever 1 2 3 4 5 Extremely strong influence	$(n = 19)$
1 Number of members	3.58
Ability to affect the Diet	3.58
2 Ability to affect the ministries	3.37
3 Percentage of the total eligible group represented	3.31
4 Degree to which affected by council's report	3.26
5 Lobbying skill	3.21
Ability to affect public opinion	3.21
6 Technical information presented	3.11
7 Prestige	2.84
8 Economic resources	1.89
To what extent does the principle of balance influence these deliberations?	3.06

ency, producer members are generally considered to be the least flexible, but as one of those members himself noted, "Because it's open to question whether it would be good to raise the price of rice as much as we're told to from below, or because there's no choice but to lower it a little, there are occasions when we can't listen to 100 percent of what's said below even if we *are* producer representatives. At such times, a member's individual way of thinking enters into the picture a little. It would be bad if that weren't so."[120]

When councilors were asked how various attributes of parent organizations influenced Beishin deliberations, there was a consensus that size and ability to affect the Diet carried the greatest weight, and that prestige and economic resources carried the least (see Table 6-2). Although councilors' evaluations did not differ dramatically, it is surprising to note that producer representatives regarded a group's ability to affect the Diet and its inclusiveness as much less influential, and technical information as much more, than did other members. Farm organizations are strong in all these respects, but it is their political heft rather than their technical expertise that is usually stressed. In another unusual contrast, whereas other neutral members emphasized the degree to which a group would be affected by a Beishin report, Ministry of Agriculture OBs downplayed that factor. Finally, no group of councilors attached much importance to the principle of balance, which has been ascribed great influence over other spending decisions in Japan.[121]

---

[120] Interview with Ikeda Hitoshi.
[121] Campbell (1975).

The Beishin is not a scene of heated confrontation between producer and consumer councilors or even between interest-group representatives and neutral members. Although it would be typical of Japanese policymaking, little discussion takes place among councilors at other venues, either. "Several of us consumer members sometimes go out and exchange views, and we also have producers approaching us outside of the *shingikai*, wanting to be understood. But you don't have Beishin members debating someplace outside of the *shingikai*."[122] Rather than a panel discussion featuring spirited debate among members, "the *shingikai* is a one-way street – just between the *government* and members."[123]

Several councilors attributed this pattern of discussion to the restraining influence of cultural norms of harmony and consensus. One councilor made the stock comparison between contentious Americans and nonconfrontational Japanese: "It's extraordinarily different from America, I think. In Japan, because emotional problems come to the fore whenever a conflict is directly debated, it's often impossible to remain composed. . . . In Japan, the appropriate way is to do things calmly . . . so that when the committee adjourns, something emotional won't remain."[124] Although such appeals to culture are not irrelevant, other, more straightforward forces are also at work.

The reactive modus operandi of the Beishin does little to encourage discussion among members: Because MAFF asks the council to approve a specific proposal of its own, it is only natural for members to spend most of their time questioning officials about that proposal. "Once the government has set forth its policy on the formula for calculating the price of rice or on the prices to factor into the formula when making a calculation, we want those decisions explained. . . . It's a matter of the government's submitting a problem and our responding."[125] Besides, with the Beishin ultimately carrying little weight in the overall decisionmaking process, councilors cherish few illusions as to the influence of their debates.

The Beishin cannot reconcile conflicting interests because neither its chair nor its neutral members are in a position to mediate. Formally, councilors choose their chair themselves. Actually, MAFF carefully stage-manages his selection (the chair has always been a man), consulting more senior councilors in advance to pave the way for someone they trust. "Ministry officials conduct *nemawashi* and generally win approval for the proposition that 'the next chair should be someone like X.' An elderly [i.e., respected] person generally nominates X at that point, members say, 'That's fine,' and everyone claps. No one is opposed, not one person, because they were all consulted in advance."[126]

---

[122] Interview with Wada Masae.   [123] Interview with Ara Kenjirō.
[124] Interview with Yamazaki Kōu.   [125] Interview with Wada Masae.
[126] Interview with Mochida Keizō.

"If the chair opposed MAFF, the *shingikai* couldn't operate, could it?" one member asked. "To avoid that, they make chair someone who can work harmoniously with MAFF,"[127] and officialdom trusts no one so much as one of its own. Of the ten people who served as chair between 1949 and 1987, seven were bureaucratic OBs (six from MAFF and one from the EPA). The other three chaired the Beishin for only 2 of those 38 years, in 1967 and 1968, when the controversy over agricultural policy came to a climax.[128] As noted earlier, the chair of the Beishin in 1987, Nakano Kazuhito, had served as administrative vice minister of MAFF, the highest nonpolitical position in the ministry, before retiring in 1975. He joined the Beishin just a year later and began chairing it in 1984.

The chair has authority in that it is he who manages meetings, decides whether or not the *shingikai* will deliberate on some point, and represents the Beishin vis-à-vis MAFF and the LDP. But the chair simply officiates; it is impossible for him to ignore councilors' positions or to try to change them, to force proceedings in a particular direction. "The chair never states his own opinion. He brings together everybody's views without himself speaking at the committee. . . . His role revolves around presiding or expediting."[129]

Public-interest councilors on the Beishin tend to have a narrow conception of their role. "MAFF and the LDP adjust differences; neutral members do not," observed one. "Neutral members just state their opinions."[130] What are those opinions? Unlike the persons of learning and experience who stood between employers and unions in MOL's Chūkishin, many of the Beishin's neutral councilors are anything but neutral in the sense of disinterested. Rather than attempting to mediate between consumers and producers from some position in the center, they tend, as a group, to coalesce around another position entirely – the government's. In the words of a producer councilor:

> In the past, the consumer side stood in sharp confrontation with the producer side, but more recently, consumer representatives have embraced the more positive idea that we must maintain rice cultivation in Japan, that Japan would suffer if rice farming disappeared. Thus, producer and consumer representatives are usually in accord. It's *neutral* members who have the strongest opinions on cutting the price of rice. It's wrong to think that neutral members stand between producer and consumer representatives and referee.[131]

It is often pointed out that councilors draft their own reports. "Only in the Beishin do members themselves write reports," boasted one member. "In al-

[127] Interview with Katō Takashi.
[128] Sone et al. (1985), p. 92.
[129] Interview with Yamazaki Kōu.
[130] Interview with Miyazaki Isamu.
[131] Interview with Tanimoto Takashi.

most all other *shingikai*, they just submit a government-drafted plan for deliberation."[132] That is largely a distinction without a difference, however. There
are five mediators or go-betweens (*sewanin*) who are chosen by each group of
councilors to work with the chair and his deputy. Although the Beishin does
entrust the writing of the report to this subcommittee, it is the (numerous)
Ministry of Agriculture OBs among them who do most of the work, and the go-
betweens work with officials in composing a draft.

The Beishin does not adopt reports by voting. Under a majoritarian principle,
it would be a foregone conclusion that the formally neutral councilors, who
occupy 15 seats out of 25, would decide. Instead, go-betweens and officials
engage in *nemawashi*. "They take an original plan to each member, and when
someone says, 'This is no good. Why did you write this?' they bring it back,
adjust it, then take it around again. . . . As a result, if everyone says that it's all
right, because there's been previous agreement, that's the end."[133] In such cases,
each councilor will express at a plenary session of the Beishin his or her opinion
of a plan that has already been settled on.

Despite such nods to the norm of consensus, previous agreement is sometimes unattainable, however. Drafters of a report will make use of the extremely
subtle turns of phrase to which Japanese lends itself to obscure the fact that
members' opinions are almost never truly unified, but even so, when confrontations are severe, discussions follow parallel lines and a unified report becomes
impossible. In that event, majority and minority opinions – or even producer,
consumer, and neutral-member reports – are submitted side by side without
settling anything, and it is not unheard of for councilors to throw up their hands
and submit no report whatsoever. Between 1969 and 1984, the Beishin submitted a divided report or no report at all far more often than not, and what unified
reports it did submit often came at the price of ambiguity, permitting different
groups to interpret the result in different ways.

All things considered, is it fair to characterize the Beishin as a kept body
of the government? Paradoxically, the *shingikai* might be *too* divided to be
conquered.

> The council cannot reflect the predominant views of the government be-
> cause of its [diverse] composition and because agencies of the government
> are frequently divided. More often the council has served as a platform for
> partisan members to articulate their views before an attentive press. If the
> council has sometimes not been able to play a decisive role it is not so much
> because it lacks legal authority as because it lacks the political ability to
> bring all the conflicting interest together, balance them, and arrive at a
> compromise.[134]

[132] Interview with Ikeda Hitoshi.
[133] Interview with Mochida Keizō.
[134] Donnelly (1977), p. 158.

In sum, if the Beishin does not mediate among private interests, neither can it be counted on to authorize government plans effectively.

The report

Minister of Agriculture Katō presented the government's recommendation to the Beishin on the morning of 2 July. Many councilors found government revisions of the price calculation formula to be incomprehensible and unconvincing. Neutral and consumer members were dubious about compensating farmers for interest for the use of their own capital, for rent for the use of their own land, and particularly for such "administrative planning labor" as bookkeeping, technical training, or the coordination of teamwork. Whereas other costs were calculated on the basis of all producers' experience, administrative planning labor was to be calculated by surveying farmers with at least 1.5 hectares (i.e., larger farmers), and because MAFF's most recent data on administrative planning labor were two decades old, it would be necessary to rely on data provided by producers themselves.[135]

(There was nothing new about these artifices or the resistance they provoked. Cooperatives had been arguing since the mid-1960s that agricultural production involves planning, study, the learning of new skills, and proper administrative organization in addition to physical labor, and that the price of rice should take this managerial process into account. In response to the more extreme of these arguments, one newspaper had predicted that rice farmers would next demand compensation for time spent sleeping if it included dreams about labor in the fields.[136])

On the morning of 3 July, every member of the Beishin except the chair expressed himself or herself in turn. Because they had been unable to resolve their differences, the final report included two distinct opinions. The five producer representatives appreciated the "improvements" in the calculation formula but opposed the government's price recommendation on the grounds that the cut was still too large. Despite their own dissatisfactions, all 18 of the consumer and neutral members supported MAFF's recommendation. According to the majority opinion: "Although there remain problems with the method of calculation, considering such factors as the harsh domestic and foreign environments for rice, a supply and demand situation that requires a substantial reinforcement of crop diversion, and the need to show concern [for farmers] and ease a sudden change, a majority of the members either approves of the government's estimate or regards it as inevitable."[137] July 3 also saw the LDP formally

[135] Takeuchi (1987), p. 29; *Yomiuri Shinbun* (4 July 1987).
[136] Donnelly (1977), pp. 178, 190.
[137] *Tōkyō Shinbun* (4 July 1987).

approve the final settlement at an Executive Council meeting, and the government officially set the new producer price of rice at a cabinet meeting the following day.

The settlement pleased no one. Looking on the bright side, Prime Minister Nakasone admitted, "We can't speak of a perfect score of 100, but it is significant to have made the first cut in 31 years." If that cut naturally irked Zenchū and if the JSP went so far as to describe it as an "extremely dangerous decision," most observers echoed Nakasone. "The collapse of the myth that 'the producer price of rice does not go down' is highly significant," one newspaper editorialized.[138]

Even those who lauded the drop in the producer price were unanimous in condemning the price-setting process, however. Although it was anything but unprecedented, everyone denounced the way the decision had been politicized. The secretary general of the Housewives League complained that "more than how many percent the producer price will fall, the problem is that politics is emerging across the board," and a producer representative within the Beishin conceded that "LDP interference is inevitable up to a point, but strong interference like this is disturbing." Politicization ruled out any objective rationalization of the price. "We can no longer say that there exists a price calculation that can be debated seriously," *Asahi* lamented. "There is no limit to the ways of computing costs."[139]

A bureaucrat noted how "the rice price calculation loses its meaning when decided this way. In order to become more logical and rational, we'd like to request improvement of the Beishin." But whether the LDP constricted the scope of a cut initially recommended by the government or subsequently made a political addition, its purpose, of course, was precisely to circumvent the Beishin. "With the government and LDP continuing to negotiate behind closed doors," a spokesperson for the opposition Kōmeitō pointed out, the decision had "stripped the Beishin of its function."[140]

The Beishin's seeming irrelevance riled no one as much as its members. At the start of its 2 July session, Chairman Nakano had confronted Minister of Agriculture Katō with an exceptional request: "I want the Beishin to be respected."[141] Afterward, councilors complained openly that the legislative branch was illegally interfering with the administrative branch, that a Beishin whose deliberations follow prior political negotiations was meaningless, and that more than the calculation formula, it was the entire price-setting process that required examination.

[138] *Sankei Shinbun* (3 July 1987); *Nihon Nōgyō Shinbun* (5 July 1987); *Yomiuri Shinbun* (5 July 1987); *Tōkyō Shinbun* (6 July 1987).
[139] *Mainichi Shinbun* (1 July 1987); *Asahi Shinbun* (4 July 1987); *Asahi Shinbun* (3 July 1987).
[140] *Sankei Shinbun* (3 July 1987); *Yomiuri Shinbun* (5, 3 July 1987).
[141] *Sankei Shinbun* (3 July 1987).

Setting the consumer price of rice

Because most backbenchers were willing to let the cabinet bear responsibility for the decision, "the consumer price was never determined in the context of massive political mobilization, an obdurate and demanding LDP, and the general hoopla and disarray that surrounded the setting of producer prices."[142]

Although it was not scheduled to be dealt with officially until a December meeting of the Beishin, MAFF officials suggested the possibility of lowering the 1987 consumer rice price from the very start of the decisionmaking process in April. Minister of Agriculture Katō himself spotlighted the issue at a press conference on 16 June when he mentioned that the consumer rice price ought to drop in tandem with the producer price. EPA Chief Kondō seconded this opinion several days later: "With the yen high and crude oil cheap, production costs are falling, and it's necessary to pass this on to consumers. The consumer rice price must naturally be lowered."[143] The idea was anything but "natural" – if such a cut were realized, it would be only the second time since the inauguration of the Food Control System in 1942 – but MAFF had just succeeded in linking cuts in the producer and consumer prices of wheat, and various arguments could be marshaled in favor of reducing the consumer price of rice, too.

Expensive rice fueled dissatisfaction with Food Control at home and provided the United States with ammunition for its campaign against protectionism. Cheaper rice, on the other hand, would help unify public opinion behind the government's refusal to open the market. Lowering the price would also expand rice consumption in general and facilitate the disposal of MAFF's 1.5-million-ton stockpile of 1986 rice (to say nothing of the 400,000 tons stored by producer organizations) in particular. Not least, if the two price cuts were linked, the popularity of a reduction in the consumer price would help blunt the efforts of the farm lobby to constrict the cut in the producer price.

"There'll be a considerable [financial] loss," Katō acknowledged, "but we want to make every effort, and will carry out a [consumer price] cut even if we spill blood." The blood spilt would be bureaucrats': MOF disapproved. "We must not confuse the decision on the producer price with the issue of the consumer price," a MOF official publicly cautioned.[144] Whereas MAFF wanted to lower the government's buying and selling prices by the same amount, MOF was intent not only on liquidating the price reverse margin of 0.4 percent, but also on shrinking the larger cost reverse margin (which included administrative expenses) of 19.8 percent. The proceeds of a producer price cut ought to be

[142] Donnelly (1977), p. 190.
[143] *Nihon Keizai Shinbun* (19 June 1987).
[144] Ibid. (17 June 1987); *Nihon Keizai Shinbun* (19 June 1987).

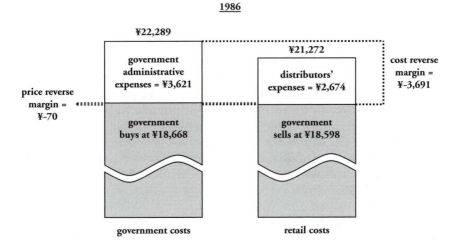

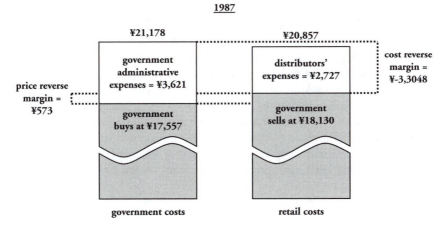

Figure 6-2.   The rice price structure, 1986 vs. 1987. (Source: *Sankei Shinbun*, 28 June 1987, and *Yomiuri Shinbun*, 29 October 1987.)

devoted to trimming the Food Control deficit, it argued, and MOF wanted to link a drop in the producer price with a *hike* in the consumer price.

Of the 23 Beishin members (excluding the chair), a majority of 12 argued that the consumer price should fall and a minority of only 2 recommended caution, so an appendix to the July report demanded that "a cut in the producer price must be reflected in the consumer price." It is interesting to note that Zenchū was pleased with this result: "For a reduction in the producer price to go straight into the pocket of MOF would be unsatisfactory. Better to restore it to consumers and earn some sympathy for the Food Control System."[145]

No sooner was the producer price settled than the ministries began preparing for a cut in the consumer price. MOF opposed lowering the consumer price as much as the producer price – the Food Control Special Account was already close to ¥400 billion ($2.86 billion) in the red, and that was sure to grow with a rice surplus of 2 million tons forecast – so MAFF aimed at a total cut of 3 to 4 percent. In October, the ministry recommended reducing the price of rice by a weighted average of 3.5 percent: In order to promote the sale of rice left over from 1986, the price of new rice would fall by 2.5 percent to ¥18,130 per 60 kilograms, and the price of old rice by 5.5 percent to a more attractive ¥17,580. Although some councilors advocated a larger cut, a majority of the Beishin agreed with MAFF's recommendation or regarded it as inevitable when it reported on 28 October.

The price reverse margin had been liquidated: For the first time in 25 years, the price at which the government bought rice no longer exceeded the price at which it sold it. A cost reverse margin remained, however: When administrative expenses were included, the government still lost money on every bushel of rice it sold (see Figure 6-2). Under pressure from MOF, the government ended up passing on to consumers only 80 percent of the ¥65 billion ($464 million) it had saved by reducing the producer price; the remainder went toward defraying the Food Control deficit. In more concrete terms, the new consumer price would save the average household all of ¥152 ($1.09) a month. Thus, although the move was hailed as a bold decision on the part of the government, and "'the first postwar cut reflected in the retail price'[146] has a wonderful ring to it, there is also a feeling that it is the merest nothing [literally, 'a sparrow's tear']," noted one newspaper.[147] In addition, with the government now selling rice at a higher price than it was paying for it, diverting rice to the black market became that much more attractive to producers.

Epilogue

"The significance of the 1987 producer rice price decision should not be overestimated," one Western political scientist cautioned shortly thereafter. "It should be interpreted in the context of price shifts occurring for more than a decade." Yet given that the producer rice price had dropped for the first time in 31 years, even this analyst described the 1987 price campaign as "an historical turning point."[148] The Japanese perception was less restrained. "The era of rice MPs' rousing enthusiasm with the sole guiding principle of hiking the price of

---

[145] *Yomiuri Shinbun* (4 July 1987).
[146] The consumer price fell 0.5 percent in 1974, too little to lower retail prices.
[147] *Yomiuri Shinbun* (29 October 1987).   [148] George (1988), pp. A40–A41, A39.

rice has definitely come to an end," one newspaper declared.[149] As if in confirmation, the producer price fell an additional 4.6 percent the following year, when it was set largely in accordance with the formula used in 1987.

Although price cuts were considered a substitute for opening the market to imports, that issue now acquired a stronger international cast and a different political dynamic. When the USTR rejected the suit of the Rice Millers Association (RMA) in 1986, it had set a one-year deadline for Japan to be "forthcoming," and Japan was forthcoming – on almost every *other* agricultural dispute. The Reagan Administration won concessions elsewhere by promising Japan not to pursue the rice issue through bilateral channels. Those concessions only spurred the RMA, however. Three months after a 1988 accord that liberalized imports of beef and citrus fruits, it once again filed a formal petition, asking for a 10 percent opening of Japan's market over four years, and the USTR once again rejected its petition and expressed a preference for handling the dispute multilaterally through GATT. If the rice lobby had nothing to lose by picking a fight with Japan, export-oriented corn, wheat, and soybean growers were eager to avoid offending their best customer and feared retaliation against themselves.[150]

Faced with an upcoming election, the LDP canceled a scheduled price cut in 1989, and although the domestic–foreign price gap widened vis-à-vis the United States, Japan told America to expect no concessions on rice. Unassuaged, farmers deserted the party in droves: According to one poll, only 54 percent of farmers voted for LDP Diet candidates in the 1989 election compared with 77 percent in 1986.[151] In conjunction with an unpopular sales tax and the Recruit corruption scandal, those defections cost the party its majority in the Diet's upper house, and in the wake of that shocking defeat, continued protectionism became the key issue. A lower-house election loomed, and with parties engaged in a bidding war for the support of disaffected farmers, the LDP reaffirmed its opposition to liberalizing rice imports. George Bush had promised American voters, "Read my lips: no new taxes"; LDP candidates intoned time after time that "not a single grain" of rice would enter the country, and the party won a decisive victory in 1990 with 84 percent of the farm vote.[152]

After the government reduced the producer rice price 1.5 percent in 1990 and an additional 0.65 percent in 1991, it ignored falling costs and rising domestic–foreign price disparities to leave its purchase price unchanged for the next five years. The election of 1990 proved to be a turning point, however. As the United States and the European Community gradually bridged their differences at the Uruguay Round of GATT and rice became a symbol of all that was wrong with U.S.–Japan trade relations, international attention increasingly focused on Japa-

---

[149] *Mainichi Shinbun* (1 July 1987).
[150] Paarlberg (1990), pp. 139–40.
[151] Komari (1991), p. 13. [152] Ibid., p. 18.

nese protectionism. When Japan argued that countries should be permitted to manage trade to maintain the production of "basic foodstuffs" to ensure food security, it won little support at the Uruguay Round, and both politicians and officials began to resign themselves to some kind of market opening.

Even during the 1990 campaign, Kaifu Toshiki had been careful not to associate himself with an absolute opposition to imports, and the following prime minister, Miyazawa Kiichi, stacked his cabinet with moderate agricultural *zoku* to prepare the way for what became known as the "rice shift" (*kome shifuto*). Some LDP leaders began releasing trial balloons to test public reaction to partial liberalization.[153] If MAFF wanted to parry demands for trade liberalization and protect Food Control, both MITI and the Ministry of Foreign Affairs were willing to yield on rice for the sake of good relations with the United States and a successful conclusion of the GATT talks, and MOF strongly supported liberalization as a way to reduce subsidies.

When the LDP fell from power in 1993, Prime Minister Hosokawa presented himself as a champion of urban consumers, and at the end of the year, a poll revealed that 62 percent of Japanese favored opening the rice market, up from 41 percent in 1988. More important, export-oriented industries foresaw tangible benefits from a successful conclusion to the Uruguay Round, and agricultural protectionism was holding up a deal. On 14 December, a solemn Hosokawa announced that Japan had made a "regrettable" agreement to lift its ban on rice imports in the interest of advancing international trade negotiations. The government's concession was guarded – it agreed to import 4 percent of Japan's total rice consumption in 1995, rising to 8 percent in the year 2000, when the accord was to be renegotiated and Japan would have to make additional concessions if it continued to resist tariffication – and even that small opening was almost blocked.[154]

Whatever the sound and fury, Japan's concession was anticlimactic. Because of an unusually damp and chilly summer in 1993, the country endured its worst harvest since 1955, losing a quarter of its crop, and months before it formally lifted its ban on commercial imports of rice, the government had already opened the door to "emergency" imports. (Ironically, even in the midst of this shortage, there were places where undamaged crops were destroyed to keep within the government's rice acreage reduction guidelines.[155]) MAFF did not cede control, however. It oversaw imports, and in 1994, the ministry issued a directive that all rice be blended by a prescribed formula. Although the official rationale was to conserve dwindling supplies and ensure that all citizens share the burden of eating foreign rice, because mixing sticky, short-grained Japanese and Californian rice with other varieties led to an unappetizing result,

---

[153] Bullock (1995), p. 11.
[154] *The New York Times* (14 December 1993).
[155] *Tokyo Business* (January 1994), p. 22.

some observers wondered whether the whole scheme was not designed to sour consumers on imports. In addition, because MAFF bought foreign rice at an average price of ¥2,107 per ton and then turned around to sell it domestically for ¥20,000 to ¥28,000 per ton, it earned a tidy profit of about ¥250 billion that went to subsidizing and improving the competitiveness of Japanese rice farmers.[156]

At the Uruguay Round, "the agricultural bureaucracy yielded, yet it did so not by relaxing the Food Control System, but by *redefining* it."[157] Food Control's days were numbered nonetheless. Semicontrolled rice already comprised fully 70 percent of official rice shipments in fiscal year 1989, and to broaden its distribution channels, the government had in 1990 established exchanges where wholesalers could bid for the crops of prefectural federations of cooperatives without going through Zennō.[158] Although acclaimed at the time as a major reform, this measure was soon superseded by a much bolder shift to decontrol. A 1994 report of the Agricultural Policy Council served as the impetus for the outright replacement of the Food Control Act by an Act to Stabilize Supply and Demand and Staple Food Prices, which came into effect on 1 November 1995.

In principle, rice cultivation and distribution are finally to revolve around rice growers themselves rather than the central government and Nōkyō. The government is limited to purchasing about 1.5 million tons of domestic rice each year for stockpiles and to importing foreign rice to comply with the minimum-access agreement. Although MAFF will continue to set guidelines to prevent overproduction, producers willing to shoulder business risks and relinquish the opportunity to sell to the government can ignore their allotted acreage reduction plans. Under Food Control, semicontrolled rice flowed from farmers to agricultural cooperatives to prefectural federations of cooperatives to Zennō to wholesalers to retailers to consumers. The new law permits local cooperatives to sell directly to wholesalers and retailers, and producers themselves can trade "other than orderly marketed rice" – what was formerly black market rice – with wholesalers, retailers, and consumers, bypassing government regulation and the cooperatives altogether.

Whether the new scheme lives up to expectations remains to be seen. Combined with its Uruguay Round obligation to import rice, Japan's third bumper crop in a row in 1996 left the country with a carryover stock of more than one-third of annual consumption by the end of 1997 with no buyers in sight. And although the government cut its purchase price of rice by 1.1 percent in 1996, the first cut in six years, LDP *zoku* overruled MAFF and the Beishin's initial proposal of a 2 percent cut, and the ministry also agreed to budget ¥10 billion

---

[156] Bullock (1995), p. 14; *JPRI* [Japan Policy Research Institute] *Critique* (September 1994).
[157] Bullock (1995), p. 10.
[158] *Mainichi Shinbun* (30 April 1990).

($87 million) in subsidies to compensate farmers for the loss.[159] Ideally, however, rice is to become an ordinary commodity. Even if the government purchase price is maintained at a high level, it should not boost the price of voluntarily marketed rice, so farmers should have much less incentive to petition the government, let alone pressure the Beishin. As the *Nihon Keizai Shinbun* editorialized, "Rice in Japan can no longer be regarded as sacred."[160]

[159] *The Japan Digest* (6 November and 2 December 1996).
[160] *Nihon Keizai Shinbun* (30 October 1995).

7

Comparisons and conclusions

In 1984, the United States proposed that Japanese representatives of foreign companies be included in *shingikai*. For trade negotiator Clyde Prestowitz, the violence of the Japanese reaction "provide[d] the strongest evidence of their importance. Many in the United States viewed as hyperbole the Japanese comparison of the Industrial Structure Council to the National Security Council. In fact, it was apt."[1] Prestowitz chided Americans for presuming that *shingikai* are ineffective just because their reports are nonbinding. He exaggerated the importance of Japanese commissions – even as prominent a *shingikai* as MITI's Industrial Structure Council enjoys little real authority in itself – but he was right to get beyond legal niceties to detect influence even in the absence of authority.

Léon Dion distinguished among consultations that are "optional" (when the consulting authority is not obliged to ask for advice), "compulsory" (when the consulting authority is obliged to seek advice but is not obliged to act on it), and "executive" (when the consulting authority is obliged to seek advice and must act on it).[2] A Japanese ministry often approaches a council in order to press its own agenda, and the consultations that follow are optional or compulsory, not executive. Many councilors are clear-eyed on this point. "A *shingikai* has no right or responsibility whatsoever for how much of its report is reflected in government policy," an employer member of the Chūkishin observed.[3] That is not the whole story, however. "The Chūkishin has considerable influence within the government," another employer councilor asserted. "It may have no authority, but its influence is large."[4]

When asked to rate their *shingikai*'s influence on public policy on a five-point scale (1 = no influence at all, 5 = extremely strong influence), Chūkishin councilors put it at 3.38, members of the joint subcommittee on financial futures at 3.57, and even Beishin councilors at 3.2. Survey data echo these assessments: Participants do set store by the entrée *shingikai* provide them. Muramatsu found

[1] Prestowitz (1988), p. 130.
[2] Dion (1973), pp. 337–38.
[3] Interview with Matsuzaki Yoshinobu.
[4] Interview with Ogawa Yasuichi.

Table 7-1. *Councilor perceptions of the political process*

What do you think are the important routes for interest-group participation in the government's policymaking process? Rank the following in order of importance, from 1 to 5.

	Chūkishin (n = 17)		Kinseichō/ Gaitameshin (n = 15)		Beishin (n = 20)		All councils (n = 52)
	Generally	Here[a]	Generally	Here	Generally	Here	Generally
Ministries	2.4 (2)		1.64 (1)	1.2 (1)	1.94 (2)	2.5 (2)	2.00 (1)
Parties	2.13 (1)		2.5 (2)	3.64 (3)	1.71 (1)	1.3 (1)	2.08 (2)
Diet	2.73 (3)		3.5 (4)	4.21 (5)	3.06 (3)	3.55 (4)	3.08 (3)
Shingikai	2.93 (4)		3.0 (3)	1.87 (2)	4.06 (4)	3.3 (3)	3.39 (4)
Public opinion	4.2 (5)		4.14 (5)	4.0 (4)	4.24 (5)	4.35 (5)	4.20 (5)

[a] Not asked of Chūkishin members.

that organizations represented in councils had noticeably greater feelings of efficacy than organizations that are not represented: 53 percent of the first group reported that they enjoyed "great" or "rather large" influence compared to 32 percent of the second group, and the first group reported significantly greater success at both promoting and blocking policies.[5] (Of course, these results may also reflect the greater likelihood of more influential groups gaining representation in commissions in the first place.)

There was a consensus among members of the Chūkishin, the joint futures subcommittee, and the Beishin that ministries and parties (i.e., the LDP) are generally far more important routes for interest-group participation in government policymaking than the Diet, *shingikai*, or public opinion (see Table 7-1). In their own specific cases, though, Beishin councilors ranked their *shingikai* above the Diet, and members of the joint futures subcommittee ranked their *shingikai* above even parties. Similarly, Knoke, Pappi, Broadbent, and Tsujinaka found that in Japan's labor policy domain, *shingikai*'s reputation for influence may be lower than that of political parties and the ministries, but it is higher than that of labor unions, public-interest groups, and business associations.[6]

Given that consultative councils unquestionably do have a role to play in Japan, what does this study reveal about the different functions they perform, the representation of private interests in public policymaking, and, most broadly, the nature of the Japanese political economy?

[5] Muramatsu (1985), p. 358.   [6] Knoke et al. (1996), pp. 198, 212.

The functions of *shingikai*

In response to a questionnaire, members of the Chūkishin and several high-ranking bureaucrats of MOL's Labor Standards Bureau evaluated the degree to which the council performs various functions that are commonly attributed to *shingikai* (see Table 7-2). According to councilors themselves, the Chūkishin's primary functions are to democratize government, regulate interest conflicts, win for government the cooperation of interested parties, and provide technical knowledge. Members denied that the Chūkishin exacerbated sectionalism, acted as a final arbiter, or camouflaged government failures to any appreciable degree.

There was significant variation in the way different categories of councilors appraised Chūkishin functions. Focusing on the Chūkishin's role as a state–society nexus, employers were more likely than their colleagues to emphasize the garnering of private cooperation for public policies and the shielding of administration from interest-group conflict. Displaying the greatest cynicism, labor representatives, on the other hand, stressed the *shingikai*'s obfuscation of administrative responsibility and authorization of government decisions. Unionists were also less likely to feel that the Chūkishin makes a serious effort to improve public policymaking or that it has much influence on public policy. That is not to say that participation in *shingikai* is unimportant to labor, however.

Workers normally achieve their aims in one of three ways: through direct negotiations with management, through the Diet, or through MOL. Professor Shirai chided the labor movement for its neglect of collective bargaining. It is because Japanese unions had been lackadaisical in fighting for shorter working hours that they turned to the government to legislate reductions, he argued. What Professor Shirai's argument ignored, of course, is how the (government- and business-encouraged) prevalence of enterprise unions and the attendant strength of corporate as opposed to occupational or class consciousness have limited the scope and influence of labor agreements in Japan. It also ignored how working conditions have been adversely affected by problems that call for national solutions, like the oil crises and ongoing structural change in the economy.

On the national level, MOL and, at a later stage, the LDP coordinated the revision of labor standards. Unions and employers were active both within the councils of government, by means of the Chūkishin, and without, by means of pressure on the parties beholden to them. Less political actors with coherent aims than arenas, the Chūkishin and Diet were thus the main loci for adjusting antagonistic private interests. To the extent that council deliberations result in Diet legislation, their roles are complementary. "The basic function of the *shingikai* is to reconcile labor and management views in advance so that bills can

Table 7-2. *A comparison of* shingikai *functions*

In conjunction with the ministries, advisory councils are thought to fulfill various functions. What sort of functions did this council perform?

Did not perform at all 1 2 3 4 5 Performed to a great degree. ( ) Rank order

	Chūkishin (n = 17)	Kinseichō/ Gaitameshin (n = 16)	Beishin (n = 22)
Managing the government democratically, i.e., reflecting the popular will in legislation and administration and preventing peremptory bureaucratic decisionmaking	3.59 (1)	3.53 (4)	3.23 (3)
Mitigating and regulating conflicts of interest among interest groups or ministries	3.41 (2)	3.94 (1)	3.0 (9)
Through the explanation of policies, earning the government the understanding and cooperation of interested parties	3.35 (3)	3.25 (6)	3.05 (6)
Meeting the administration's need for technical knowledge	3.24 (4)	3.75 (2)	3.0 (8)
Heightening policies' fairness and rationality	3.21 (5)	3.44 (5)	3.1 (4)
Focusing public attention on a particular problem	3.12 (6)	2.4 (13)	3.52 (1)
Preventing confrontations among interest groups from spilling over into public decisionmaking bodies	3.06 (7)	3.63 (3)	2.25 (15)
Promoting intergroup understanding	2.94 (8)	3.07 (7)	2.73 (11)
As a kept body or supporting device of the administration, authorizing government decisions and helping the ministries to earn support	2.76 (9)	2.87 (9)	3.45 (2)
Pressuring policymakers to act favorably on council reports	2.71 (10)	2.5 (12)	2.79 (10)
As an "invisibility-working cloak," obfuscating administrative responsibility	2.59 (11)	1.87 (15)	3.1 (5)
As a window on the organizations represented, examining extragovernmental points of view and testing new ideas	2.47 (12)	2.67 (10)	2.43 (14)
By sharing responsibility for public policy with private organizations, facilitating the execution of decisions	2.12 (13)	3.0 (8)	2.72 (12)
Legitimizing compromises achieved outside of the advisory council	2.06 (14)	2.56 (11)	3.05 (7)
Camouflaging deficient or defective government operations or policies	1.88 (15)	1.47 (17)	2.45 (13)
Acting as an arbiter when political parties or conflicting interest groups are unable to arrive at agreement in the government or the Diet	1.82 (16)	2.33 (14)	2.0 (17)
Defending the plans and interests of specific ministries and agencies, thus fostering jurisdictional disputes and sectionalism	1.71 (17)	1.73 (16)	2.15 (16)

pass parliament," explained a MOL official.[7] When the Chūkishin is successful in arranging a mutually acceptable compromise, its proposals will be passed without amendment; when it is unsuccessful, the Diet stands as the final arbiter of the political conflicts of unions and employers.

The two institutions differ in the ways they adjust interests, however. The Chūkishin provides a forum in which the contending parties can confront one another directly. Once a dispute reaches the Diet, on the other hand, private interests must work through political parties, and party-political considerations extraneous to labor relations inevitably intrude. This has two important effects. First, unions have stood at a significant disadvantage when a conflict had to be resolved in parliament. Labor has not spoken with a single voice in the Diet since the DSP seceded from the JSP in 1960, and even together the two parties could not begin to match the pro-business LDP. Given its long-standing Diet majority, when the LDP resolved to pass something, it would be passed, whatever the progressive party or popular opposition (e.g., the enactment of a new consumption tax in 1988). Only LDP self-restraint and fear of being censured for exercising a "tyranny of the majority" have held this tendency in check.

Second, whereas public-interest or MOL mediation can never stray too far from antagonists' positions within the council, unions *and* employers can lose control of the situation once they entrust their interests to political parties.

> At the stage of *shingikai* deliberations, conflicting interests can be reconciled, and in that sense the *shingikai* is an immensely important forum for both labor and management. If they assert their claims sufficiently in the *shingikai*, a tolerable conclusion will result and they'll have no need to worry even if it goes to the Diet. If they leave resolution of a problem to the Diet, then workers, employers, officials – no one knows what will ensue, and they can't help but be uneasy.[8]

Some of the employer members of the Chūkishin were disgusted with the way that the *maruyū* controversy affected debate on revision of the Labor Standards Act, and one generalized that "it's better to correct government policies at the planning stage than in the Diet. Although business can use the LDP as well as *shingikai* to exert influence, we don't want to. We can use [the party] to some extent, but not completely."[9] Ōtsubo, chair of the PARC Labor Division, confirmed that "employers contact the LDP only on fundamental issues. . . . On detailed matters, they go make requests of MOL."[10]

Whether at the bargaining table or on the national political stage, organized labor is inevitably hamstrung; that leaves MOL.[11] Although MOL held both

---

[7] Interview with Nozaki Kazuaki.   [8] Ibid.
[9] Interview with Nishikiori Akira.   [10] Interview with Ōtsubo Ken'ichirō.
[11] This has only become more true over time: With the decline of the socialist parties, unions' preference for working through the ministries more than doubled between 1980 and 1994. Tsujinaka (1996), pp. 49, 52.

official and unofficial meetings with the national centers, Labor Standards Bureau Chief Hiraga himself judged that "the sending of representatives to *shingikai* is more important than direct approaches" to the ministry.[12] Participation in MOL councils offers labor a much-needed opportunity to press its demands on the government. This was especially true in the case at hand. With their problem-solving orientation, the pivotal public-interest representatives of the Chūkishin gave weight in their deliberations to technical considerations as well as to the political and organizational might of the interested parties. "We public-interest representatives didn't pay much attention to whether the employer or labor side was strong. We kept our eyes on the data."[13] Thus, as one Sōhyō representative noted simply, "the *shingikai* was the most important place for labor to have its influence felt on revision of the act."[14]

This is by no means to suggest that *shingikai* are always the most important avenue for union influence. Over time, they have come to supplement, not supplant, collective bargaining and parliamentary deliberations. "The labor movement was strong in the 1950s," reminisced one union official. "Unfortunately, the labor movement has flagged, . . . and we've had to adopt *shingikai* as another means of applying effective pressure."[15] "Because labor is a minority in the Diet, we struggle in *shingikai*," noted another official. "Unions try to participate in *shingikai* even if they have only a small effect."[16]

"Even if they have only a small effect" – that unions have no alternative to participating in *shingikai* is no assurance of the effectiveness of that participation, of course. Although labor representatives may now sit on important commissions like the Council on the Economy and the Industrial Structure Council, there are differences of opinion over the extent to which their views are reflected there, and unionists still feel excluded from many *shingikai* whose policy domains are of concern to them. Labor members in the Chūkishin were without exception dissatisfied with the status quo, regarding as insufficient their representation outside of the tripartite councils of the Ministries of Labor and Health and Welfare. "Insufficient" is not equivalent to "ineffectual," however. Japan's labor movement can make a difference in policymaking by means of advisory bodies when its basic interests are at stake.

The different categories of members of the Kinseichō and Gaitameshin's joint subcommittee agreed that its primary functions were to help mediate interest-group conflict, provide the bureaucracy with technical information, shield the government from private-sector confrontations, and promote the democratization of administration. Members were unanimous in denying that the joint

---

[12] Interview with Hiraga Toshiyuki.   [13] Interview with Wada Katsumi.
[14] Interview with Okamura Shōzō.
[15] Interview with Shimizu Eiichi.   [16] Interview with Ōtani Tatsuya.

subcommittee had camouflaged government failings, furthered bureaucratic sectionalism, or obscured officials' responsibilities. At first glance, these results might seem surprising.

Although it says as much about the way Japanese perceive America as it does about Japan, one subcommittee member observed that "unlike American society, the creation of consensus is necessary in Japan. You can't solve a confrontation between banks and security houses over futures with a decisive act by the president, as you can in America. We must move gradually, searching for the best solution. That's the role of *shingikai*."[17] And yet, as detailed in Chapter 5, *shingikai* did *not* adjust the differences between the two antagonists. Why did councilors so emphasize the regulation of conflict?

In this instance, the contribution of *shingikai* to interest adjustment was indirect but no less real. Council reports accurately reflected the contending points of view on how to organize futures markets in Japan. Beyond simply identifying alternatives, they obliged banks and brokerage houses to justify their respective arguments. "*Shingikai* clarify the demands of interest groups. . . . They function to make arguments rational."[18] Council reports thus provided MOF with the grounds on which to make a decision. The deputy director of the Securities Bureau traced MOF's final settlement to three sources: the report of the Shōtorishin, the joint report of the Kinseichō and Gaitameshin, and the fact that the TSE already handled government bond futures.[19] "It's precisely because we'd had deliberations in *shingikai* that MOF was able to adjust" the conflicting interests, according to one councilor.[20]

MOF used its commissions to designate those actors whose views it was willing to consider and to provide a framework for both the official and unofficial consultation of those views. "While deliberations at the *shingikai* itself were formal, because various discussions were being held under the table at the same time, you could say that it was a site for substantive interest adjustment, too. The formal talks and the substantive talks advanced in parallel."[21] Participation in *shingikai* and direct approaches to MOF are complementary, not mutually exclusive. The councils were suited for broad assertions of interest; direct, unofficial talks for haggling over details. "It probably wouldn't go well at the *shingikai* alone, and policymaking wouldn't have proceeded if there'd been just direct talks between the [MOF] secretariats and each industry"; "both are important – they're like two wheels of a cart."[22]

Although bankers and stockbrokers often attached as much significance to their direct approaches to MOF as to their participation in commissions, the latter has several advantages. "Even if you go to a government office and

[17] Interview with Ōyama Hiroto.   [18] Interview with Kaizuka Keimei.
[19] *Kin'yū Zaisei Jihō* (1 February 1988).   [20] Interview with Hayakawa Yoshio.
[21] Interview with Kanda Hideki.
[22] Interviews with Itatani Masanori, and Deguchi Haruaki and Kajio Akihiko.

they say something welcome, you don't know if officials will really follow through on it. Because people are responsible for what they say at *shingikai*, what's said there has the merit of being extremely clear."[23] In the same vein, as official bodies, councils document the positions that private actors have taken. "You express your opinion, put it away in a box, and it sometimes happens that that box will be of use again. Several years later, when there's a reexamination of the financial system or some other change, we can point to the minutes of [a *shingikai*'s] proceedings and say: 'At that time, we asserted this.'"[24]

All councilors, including bankers and stockbrokers, felt that positively *insulating* the bureaucracy from direct approaches by the clashing interests was one of the most important functions of the joint subcommittee. Bureaucrats concurred. Informal, private talks between interest groups and the ministries smack of backroom dealmaking, which deprives administrative decisions of legitimacy. "Having brought together the views of all such people, a report has official authority. As a result, it may not make a big difference in the end whether we listen to competing views in a *shingikai* or not, but to be able to say that we asked for views by means of that process signifies objectivity."[25] Appearances aside, direct lobbying can have undemocratic results. "When it comes to private approaches [to MOF], you end up being influenced by the loudness of each person's voice, by the strength of his standpoint; you can't strike a balance. The *shingikai* is thus necessary as an official arena. It has the role of granting a place to speak to those people who don't often come to express their views."[26]

In this case, commissions were especially useful for potential corporate buyers of futures, whose influence within MOF cannot be compared with that of banks or securities houses. Representatives of those companies considered the joint subcommittee to be far more important as an administrative window on the desires of private organizations than did the representatives of either the banking or securities industries. Conversely, MOF councils were a place for businesspeople to learn the views of bankers, stockbrokers, and financial regulators. "The *shingikai* doesn't simply pit views against one another; it's also a place where responsible authorities explain the facts on which those views are premised. Because scholars, consumers, and people from the world of industry don't regard finance as [their] business, if they don't receive an explanation, they won't be able to grasp the facts that underlie decisions."[27] As a service industry, the financial industry has a concrete stake in enhancing its clients' grasp of those facts.

> If there hadn't been *shingikai*, then trading couldn't have gone ahead so smoothly. There's a strong feeling in Japan that speculation is bad, and it

---

[23] Interview with Kaneko Tarō.   [24] Interview with Yahagi Mitsuaki.
[25] Interview with Ōyō Kyōichi.
[26] Ibid.   [27] Interview with Itatani Masanori.

was a problem that no one had ever clearly come out and said that speculative markets have a justifiable public function, too. It was important to have
this view acknowledged officially. . . .

You have to balance *shingikai* and administration skillfully. The introduction of BA [i.e., Bankers Acceptance] was a typical example of going
ahead without *shingikai*. America applied pressure through the Yen-Dollar
Committee to create a BA market and MOF complied, establishing one
without consulting a *shingikai*. The cost turned out to be high: no one was
issuing, and no investors were buying.[28]

In some ways, it is harder to explain the choices councilors did *not* make in
specifying the roles they had played. MOF *shingikai* produced two incompatible
reports, and many members attributed great influence to the joint subcommittee's secretariat. Why did they deny that the *shingikai* had furthered bureaucratic sectionalism or cloaked administrative responsibility? One group of
councilors, persons of learning and experience, did make some rather pointed
remarks along those lines. For one scholar, the Kinseichō

plays a rather formal function. The secretariat decides on the best form for
Japan's financial system, and the *shingikai* is used as a tool in order to
announce major policies officially. Whatever kind of discussion goes on
there, the actual conclusions won't change fundamentally: The Banking
Bureau's plan will be the Kinseichō's conclusion. In order to realize that
plan, the council is to search for ways of smashing opposing views.[29]

If it was scholars who felt most strongly that the joint subcommittee was
making a serious effort to improve public policymaking, scholars were also the
most pessimistic in gauging the council's actual influence. On the whole, though,
persons of learning and experience seem to have been more dissatisfied with the
part they played in the *shingikai* than they were with the *shingikai* itself. They
felt more strongly than other councilors that they were legitimizing decisions
made elsewhere. One person of learning and experience stated plainly that "we
have a role in the sense of 'authorization' [in English] vis-à-vis the public."[30]
Another described their role as one of "granting certification" (*osumitsuki
o ataeru* – literally, "bestowing a document bearing the signature of the sho-
gun").[31]

There were also cynical members among the representatives of industry, of
course. "Although there's a pretense [*tatemae*] that all major issues are decided
in the Kinseichō, almost everything follows a scenario written by MOF. Please
think of *shingikai* deliberations as essentially a ceremony," recommended one

---

[28] Interview with Rōyama Shōich
[29] Interview with Horiuchi Akiyoshi.
[30] Interview with Kanda Hideki.
[31] Interview with Ōyama Hiroto.

councilor. But even he conceded that "the ceremony is very important. Because the *shingikai* is a MOF consultative body with a legal basis, if the members voice strong[ly opposed] views in the *shingikai*, then the secretariat's plan will collapse. *Shingikai* thus can have no power at all, or immense power."[32] The difference seems to be that whereas persons of learning and experience focused on the task at hand and strove to produce an objective report as an end in itself, representatives of industry saw the joint subcommittee and its report in context, as only one stage in a multistage policymaking process.

Bankers wanted to think that the joint subcommittee had acted as a final arbiter and that it would pressure policymakers to act in accordance with its report. And yet, stockbrokers, the apparent losers, were no more negative in their evaluations of the joint subcommittee than were bankers, the apparent winners. With the Shōtorishin's favorable report in their pockets, repeated acknowledgments of their position in the joint report, and the prospect of a more balanced adjustment resulting from intraministerial negotiations, why should stockbrokers have been particularly upset with the joint subcommittee? In recent years, the need for inter-bureau coordination has mounted and, "truth be told, it might have been good for the Kinseichō, Gaitameshin, and Shōtorishin to have [all three] operated jointly."[33] Japan's "vertical administration" precluded this, however.[34] In retrospect, the progression from the Shōtorishin to the Kinseichō and Gaitameshin to MOF adjustment seems to have been inevitable and perhaps appropriate.

Why did the producer price of rice finally fall? On the one hand, the government faced crop surpluses, budget deficits, rising criticism of protectionism, and falling costs of production. On the other hand, demographic trends and reapportionment had somewhat reduced the LDP's reliance on, and responsiveness to, farmers. None of these factors was new, but as it happens, the two long-term trends intersected in 1987. Ruling-party politicians and ministry officials made the decisions; the Beishin did not play a major role. In the unsentimental but unexceptionable words of one newspaper, "When one looks at the course of government-LDP negotiations concerning the rice price decision and at the Beishin, they were repeating a farce no different from in the past."[35]

Some councilors demurred. "Although rice MPs didn't want to okay a cut, they had no choice but to respect the Beishin's opinion."[36] Others put 1987 in

---

[32] Interview with Deguchi Haruaki and Kajio Akihiko.
[33] Interview with Ōyama Hiroto.
[34] With MOF attracting criticism from around the world for its mishandling of a string of financial crises, the governing coalition in 1996 proposed to merge the Banking and Securities Bureaus and part of the International Finance Bureau, and the ministry responded with a similar offer (*The New York Times*, 26 September 1996).
[35] *Sankei Shinbun* (5 July 1987).
[36] Interview with Ara Kenjirō.

perspective. "Over the long years I've been on it, there've been times when the Beishin had power, and times when its authority vanished. It depends on each period's socioeconomic or political situation. . . . Setting the price of rice is a political issue. Because that's a fact, we can't demand an end to party intervention. It would be strange to demand such a thing."[37] Most members, however, were simply resentful. "The Beishin is futile . . . a shallow trick [*saru shibai* – literally, 'a monkey show']."[38] Chairman Nakano himself admitted to wondering sometimes whether his participation of more than a decade in the Beishin was not "meaningless,"[39] and although they relented, a number of members apparently considered quitting the *shingikai* in 1987.[40]

For the Beishin's recommendations to be changed at subsequent government-party negotiations is seen as ignoring the Beishin. For the ministries and LDP to settle on a price in advance is seen as depriving Beishin deliberations of their rationale. "Political additions are outrageous, but if the price is already decided at the start, when the government makes its inquiry, then what on earth is the purpose of spending two or three days discussing it all so seriously? It's all the same."[41] So what, if anything, *does* this council do?

When asked what functions the Beishin performs, members gave the greatest weight to how it focuses public attention, authorizes government decisions as a kept body, reflects the popular will in legislation, and heightens policies' fairness and rationality. They gave least weight to its acting as a final arbiter, fostering sectionalism, and preventing confrontations among interest groups from spilling into the government. Responses among different categories of councilors varied widely. Producer representatives were the most skeptical. They stood out in emphasizing the Beishin's cloaking of administrative responsibility and camouflaging of deficient policies, and in *deemphasizing* its reflecting the popular will, mitigating conflicts of interest, and providing technical knowledge. In contrast, retired MAFF officials were the most defensive. They tended to deny that the council acts as a kept body of the administration, cloaks administrative responsibility, legitimizes decisions reached elsewhere, or camouflages deficient policies. Consumer representatives were the most appreciative. More than other councilors, they credited the *shingikai* with earning government the cooperation of interested parties, sharing responsibility for public policy, and examining extra-governmental points of view.

The Beishin *is* a kept body that cloaks administrative responsibility. That does not prevent it from performing other, more positive functions, however. The Beishin's ability to focus public attention and reflect the popular will permits it – indirectly – to mitigate interest-group conflict and heighten policies' rationality.

[37] Interview with Ikeda Hitoshi. [38] Interview with Miyawaki Nagasada.
[39] Interview with Nakano Kazuhito.
[40] Interview with Katsube Kin'ichi. [41] Interview with Wada Masae.

In the words of one observer, "producer rice pricing has become a thoroughly institutionalized process of staged conflict involving a complex, almost ritualized, sequence of events,"[42] and the Beishin clearly performs a ritual as much as an advisory function, but rituals have their uses. Almost regardless of what happens during and after its deliberations, the very fact that these deliberations are held can help ease tensions within and among groups. As Truman noted, providing interested parties with an opportunity to be heard within the councils of government conforms to the procedural expectations of a democratic community and facilitates acceptance of the final decision among the rank and file.[43] In the case of the Beishin, "The producer view is a minority in the *shingikai*," noted a neutral councilor. "Because it's expected [nowadays] that the majority opinion will be to cut the price of rice, producers' opposition constitutes a 'gesture' [in English]. . . . It may even be that for the Beishin to decide differently from their stated position is desirable [to them individually], but they *must* display opposition in their role as producer representatives. The Beishin is thus useful to them."[44]

And despite its lack of final decisionmaking authority, the *shingikai does* influence the rice price decision. "If we didn't have a Beishin, perhaps something even more dreadful would have occurred by now," conjectured one councilor. "Hasn't the Beishin had some effect restraining the rise of the rice price? There may be limits to our influence, but it's better than nothing."[45] Every price begins as a proposal that the government must somehow justify. As political pressures gradually constricted the 9.8 percent cut to which the price formula pointed in 1987, there were opposing pressures to modify the calculation factors no more than could be plausibly explained, and when a 5.95 percent cut suddenly emerged in the wake of LDP-government negotiations, a MOF bureaucrat recalled that officials "had to think of a calculation that could be understood by the Beishin, that we could defend."[46] Even as it was negotiating this price with the LDP – precisely *because* it had to negotiate with the LDP rather than follow an objective formula – MAFF publicly professed respect for the Beishin over the party. That may seem hypocritical, but as La Rochefoucauld aphorized, hypocrisy is the homage that vice pays to virtue, and the record shows that political additions have, in fact, been more restrained when the council has approved the government's recommended price than when it has offered divided reports or no report at all.[47]

Although their answers must admittedly be taken with a grain of salt, it is interesting to note that retired MAFF officials rated the Beishin's ability to

---

[42] Donnelly (1984), p. 351; Donnelly (1977), p. 144.
[43] Truman (1971), p. 375.
[44] Interview with Mizuno Masaichi.
[45] Interview with Kishi Yasuhiko.
[46] *Sankei Shinbun* (3 July 1987).   [47] Sone et al. (1985), p. 90.

mitigate interest-group conflict and heighten policies' rationality just as highly as its ability to focus public attention and reflect the popular will.

The nature of representation in Japan

"Admitting the importance of [state] embeddedness turns arguments for insulation on their head," Evans has argued. "Connections to civil society become part of the solution rather than part of the problem."[48] Japanese have traditionally made less of a distinction between the public and private spheres than Americans have, and the growing power of private actors has only reinforced the tendency to negotiate public policies.[49] The *shingikai* system naturally reflects Japanese conceptions of interest representation.

When asked if his trade association ever lobbied the government, one official said, "No, the only lobbying Japanese trade associations do is in Washington." In other words, rather than simply petition for change from outside government, major interest groups participate directly in policymaking.[50] Few councilors saw any impropriety in including the representatives of private groups in the framing of public policies. Quite the contrary: As Professor Shirai, the chair of the Chūkishin asserted, not only is it "natural and appropriate that strongly interested groups participate in deliberative councils. What would be funny would be to exclude them."[51] One archetypal person of learning and experience, an agrobiologist on the Beishin, went so far as to observe, "*Shingikai* are a place where it's possible for interest groups to have their views reflected in the country's policies. . . . Because I'm not an interest-group representative, there's not much meaning to my participation."[52]

In defending interest-group participation in *shingikai*, councilors echoed the same sorts of justifications offered by outside observers (see Chapter 2). Clashes of interest do not rule out but positively call for the inclusion of the interested parties. Philosophically speaking, "In a democracy, it's meaningful to let interest groups contend, so it's better to include interest groups in *shingikai*, too."[53] Practically speaking, practitioners understand matters that persons of learning and experience do not, and their serving as witnesses alone would not ensure adequate consideration of their positions. Given the added presence of disinterested councilors, unjust assertions of interest are unlikely to win acceptance, and even if they do, "Things don't pass just because we say so,"[54] as one councilor noted realistically. Ease of legislation and implementation more than make up for the added complexity of policy formulation.

---

[48] Evans (1992), p. 179.   [49] Knoke et al. (1996), p. 5.
[50] Tilton (1996), pp. 26, 205.
[51] Interview with Shirai Taishirō.
[52] Interview with Yamazaki Kōu.
[53] Interview with Katō Takashi.   [54] Interview with Hondō Yoshio.

There's a view that *shingikai* should consist of neutral members without interest groups. If we were to follow that, we'd get extremely logical conclusions, but ... however splendidly logical the conclusions, when you decide policy, politicians expect that some pressure groups are going to be opposed. ... When you include them in a *shingikai* and engage in debate, [on the other hand,] representatives of interest groups come to understand views, ways of thinking, different from their own, and they understand it won't do them any good to insist solely on their own point of view. So once deliberations arrive at a conclusion, you can get by without opposition becoming too violent.[55]

One labor representative argued that the explicit recognition of self-interest was preferable to what could never be more than a pretense of disinterest:

It's appropriate because the Japanese way of thinking is different from the American and European. In any social stratum, there are few people who can make decisions objectively. Whatever the cost [to society], it's common for us to speak in favor of our own interests, so it's necessary for interest groups to represent their own opinions. It's because it's rare in Japan to consider matters fairly and objectively that [interest-group participation] is inevitable.[56]

Although this argument seems to fly in the face of reason, to say nothing of Western stereotypes of Japan, it gets at fundamental differences in attitudes about representation and the proper roles of elected and appointed officials. Americans generally accept arms-length lobbying by private actors or, conversely, the mobilization of particularistic interests by competing politicians and (to a lesser extent) bureaucrats but are suspicious of interest groups' involving themselves directly in policymaking. Japanese tend to take the opposite tack: Because they hold an ideal of policymaking as disinterested contemplation of the common good, they prefer private groups' representing their selfish interests themselves to their distracting state actors from a higher calling.

Councilors revealed some interesting attitudes when asked about the roles of interest groups, politicians, and bureaucrats (see Table 7-3). Currently, interest groups only represent interests, but they should also champion ideals, mediate among interests, and formulate public policies. They do not, and should not, execute those policies. Although politicians do represent interests, they should not, and if they now mediate among interests and perhaps formulate public policies, they should also champion ideals and execute public policies. Finally, bureaucrats do mediate among interests and formulate and execute public policies, but they ought to play a greater role in championing ideals. They do not, and emphatically definitely should not, represent interests.

---

[55] Interview with Mizuno Masaichi.
[56] Interview with Shimizu Eiichi.

Table 7-3. *Councilors' perceptions of the roles of political actors*

Do you think that interest groups, politicians, and bureaurats *actually* play the roles listed below? *Should* they?
(yes v. no)

	Chūkishin (n = 15)		Kinseichō/ Gaitameshin (n = 16)		Beishin (n = 20)		All councilors (n = 51)	
	Do	Should	Do	Should	Do	Should	Do	Should
Interest groups								
Represent interests	15 v. 0	14 v. 0	16 v. 0	16 v. 0	19 v. 0	14 v. 2	50 v. 0	44 v. 2
Champion ideals	6 v. 8	12 v. 2	5 v. 10	9 v. 6	5 v. 8	16 v. 1	16 v. 26	37 v. 9
Mediate among interests	10 v. 5	10 v. 4	6 v. 10	9 v. 7	1 v. 12	12 v. 3	17 v. 27	31 v. 14
Formulate public policies	6 v. 7	12 v. 3	7 v. 10	8 v. 7	5 v. 9	11 v. 3	18 v. 26	31 v. 13
Execute public policies	2 v. 12	3 v. 11	2 v. 13	2 v. 13	5 v. 8	9 v. 4	9 v. 33	14 v. 28
Politicians								
Represent interests	11 v. 3	3 v. 12	13 v. 1	5 v. 10	15 v. 1	3 v. 13	39 v. 5	11 v. 35
Champion ideals	5 v. 9	15 v. 0	5 v. 9	14 v. 0	5 v. 11	20 v. 0	15 v. 29	49 v. 0
Mediate among interests	9 v. 5	11 v. 3	9 v. 5	14 v. 1	8 v. 8	19 v. 0	26 v. 18	44 v. 4
Formulate public policies	5 v. 8	13 v. 0	8 v. 7	15 v. 0	6 v. 7	19 v. 0	19 v. 22	47 v. 0
Execute public policies	2 v. 12	6 v. 8	7 v. 7	8 v. 6	7 v. 6	10 v. 5	16 v. 25	24 v. 19
Bureaucrats								
Represent interests	3 v. 12	0 v. 15	3 v. 12	0 v. 16	7 v. 7	0 v. 17	13 v. 31	0 v. 48
Champion ideals	7 v. 7	14 v. 0	5 v. 9	12 v. 3	8 v. 8	13 v. 4	20 v. 24	39 v. 7
Mediate among interests	12 v. 2	13 v. 1	14 v. 1	16 v. 0	17 v. 1	15 v. 1	43 v. 4	44 v. 2
Formulate public policies	13 v. 1	13 v. 1	15 v. 0	16 v. 0	18 v. 1	15 v. 2	46 v. 2	44 v. 3
Execute public policies	12 v. 2	15 v. 0	16 v. 0	16 v. 0	18 v. 0	18 v. 0	46 v. 2	49 v. 0

To rephrase, although the representation of interests is carried out by politicians as well as by interest groups, it is rightfully the job of interest groups alone. All three political actors ought to champion ideals, but none of them actually do, except perhaps bureaucrats to some degree. Although bureaucrats and, to a lesser degree, politicians now mediate among interests, interest groups should perform that function, too. Finally, interest groups and especially politicians ought to join bureaucrats in formulating public policies, and politicians should play a larger role in assisting bureaucrats in executing those policies.

For these Japanese, model bureaucrats approach Hegel's conception of them as a universal class. Model politicians, on the other hand, would actually go beyond Aberbach et al.'s pure hybrids to share in the implementation of policies, yet they would stop representing particularistic interests – probably the function an American would consider most integral to their role. Japanese politicians thus occupy an ambiguous niche between inevitably particularistic private interests and an ideally universalistic bureaucracy.

Differences in attitudes among members of the three *shingikai* reflected differences in their respective policy domains. Private-sector labor relations are
subject to constant renegotiation from which the LDP has normally remained
aloof. Accordingly, members of the Chūkishin stood out in asserting that interest groups do mediate among interests and that politicians do not execute
policies. Despite heavy regulation, finance is still the most market-oriented of
the three sectors, the LDP has been available to appeals from banks and stockbrokers, and MOF's pursuit of financial liberalization has been utterly prag-
matic. Predictably, councilors in the joint subcommittee tended to take a more
restrictive view of the legitimate role of interest groups, and to contend that
politicians do formulate public policies and that bureaucrats do not champion
ideals. Farmers' pursuit of their self-interest has been unyielding, both the LDP
and MAFF have openly defended rural interests, and Nōkyō has long served as
an organ of agricultural administration. Thus, members of the Beishin denied
that interest groups mediate among interests and were the most likely to believe
that politicians do not mediate, bureaucrats do represent interests, and interest
groups not only do but should execute public policies. (Surprisingly, despite the
controversial role they have played in that policy domain, members of the
Beishin were also the most likely to believe that politicians should execute public
policy.)

Differences between American and Japanese conceptions of representation
and policymaking extend to the inner workings of *shingikai*. As noted earlier,
when asked to evaluate sources of interest-group power, a group of American
legislators mentioned size and electoral influence, followed by organization and
leadership, financial resources, importance of issues, skilled lobbyists, information, influence over public opinion, and prestige, in that order.[57] Japanese
councilors evaluated these factors in a very different way (see Table 7-4).
(Of course, councilors are not legislators, but the contrast is illuminating
nonetheless.)

Members of the Chūkishin and the joint futures subcommittee ranked the
factors affecting their deliberations in similar ways, stressing technical information, the ability to affect public opinion and the ministries, and the degree to
which a group would be affected by a commission report. The councilors of both
shingikai also agreed that economic resources and the number of members
boasted by a group had little influence on their deliberations. Given the greater
politicization of their policy domain, members of the Beishin, on the other hand,
followed the American legislators in emphasizing groups' electoral influence and
size.

---

[57] Kenneth Janda et al., *Legislative Politics in Indiana* (Bloomington: Indiana University Press,
1961).

Table 7-4. *Factors affecting* shingikai *deliberations*

To what extent do you think each of the following attributes of councilors' parent organizations influence advisory body deliberations?

No influence whatsoever 1 2 3 4 5 Extremely strong influence. ( ) Rank order

	Chūkishin (*n* = 17)	Kinseichō/ Gaitameshin (*n* = 16)	Beishin (*n* = 19)
Technical information presented	3.38 (1)	3.25 (4)	3.11 (8)
Ability to affect public opinion	3.35 (2)	3.44 (3)	3.21 (7)
Degree to which affected by the council's report	3.19 (3)	3.75 (1)	3.26 (5)
Ability to affect the ministries	3.0 (4)	3.67 (2)	3.37 (3)
Percent of total eligible group represented	2.94 (5)	3.0 (6)	3.31 (4)
Ability to affect the Diet	2.94 (6)	3.0 (5)	3.58 (1)
Number of members	2.82 (7)	2.5 (8)	3.58 (2)
Prestige	2.71 (8)	2.33 (9)	2.84 (9)
Lobbying skill	2.18 (9)	3.0 (7)	3.21 (6)
Economic resources	1.44 (10)	1.6 (10)	1.89 (10)
To what extent does the principle of balance influence these deliberations?	3.5	3.93	3.06

Japan's policymaking processes

At the highest level of abstraction, which models of interest-group politics best characterize the policymaking processes observed in these cases? Despite the diversity of *shingikai* and the unreasoning resistance of reality to theoretical niceties, the empirical research of this study confirms the tentative conclusion of Chapter 1.

If unions' undeniable influence over revision of the Labor Standards Act highlights the limits of a Marxist or ruling triad perspective, is a corporatist interpretation appropriate? Although the foregoing discussion treated "labor" and "management" as cohesive groups, that was a simplification: Each side did try to present a united front in its dealings with the other, but they were both characterized by internal divisions.

Business concerns varied by industry and by scale. Variable working hours were more important to service industries than to manufacturing, and a reduction in working hours was more of a problem for small- and medium-sized enterprises than for large firms. Having first worked out their demands among themselves, employers avoided the expression of separate opinions within the Chūkishin. On the issue of legal working hours, for example, if many industries were unperturbed by higher standards, their representatives were solicitous of the interests of small business nonetheless. As one councilor from the chemical industry explained, "the working hours of no chemical company exceed 40 hours a week. Even with a change in the Labor Standards Act to the shortest hours, we're all clear. I'm not thinking of the chemical industry, but of small- and medium-sized enterprises. Will they be troubled? If so, what should we consider doing?"[58] Nevertheless, a sentiment of management solidarity is not equivalent to the institutionalization of unity by means of a centralized peak organization that can aggregate various industries' interests comprehensively.

Normally fractionized and conflict-ridden, labor for once maintained its unity, even outdoing management, according to several employer councilors. Revision of the Labor Standards Act offered such opportunities and posed such threats to so many workers that the national centers successfully overcame their differences. Although the constituencies of the national centers differed some- what, their delegates met any number of times before and during *shingikai* deliberations in order to coordinate their positions, with the smaller, third-force Chūritsu Rōren federation (*chūritsu* means "neutral") helping to smooth over Sōhyō–Dōmei differences. Union representatives realized that divided counsels would carry no weight: "When the labor side is split, the employer or govern- ment position will be forced through in its entirety, so we must act in concert as much as possible. It's crucial that labor organizations work as one and not scatter."[59] That same recognition had not ensured cooperation on any number of other occasions in the past, however.

If neither side was obviously disadvantaged by its lack of a "singular, compul- sory, noncompetitive, hierarchically ordered" peak organization, does this case study bolster the arguments of pluralists? Some of the union councilors de- scribed the Japanese political system in terms that were almost Trumanesque. According to one Dōmei official:

> There are various channels open to an individual union if there is a problem in some industry. It can approach the government or Diet through a national center, or it can go to DSP or JSP Diet representatives without a national center and have the opposition parties submit a bill to the Diet. Depending on the problem, it can go directly to the LDP, or make a proposal to Keidanren or another employer organization. It's not a matter of having to strengthen the authority of the national centers indiscriminately.[60]

"Maybe approaching top organizations like Keidanren, Nikkeiren, Sōhyō, and Chūritsu Rōren isn't all that necessary," concluded a leader of Chūritsu Rōren.[61] "It's not as if there are no ways for unions outside Sōhyō, or unions

[58] Interview with Nakai Takeshi.
[59] Interview with Shimizu Eiichi.
[60] Interview with Satō Kōichi.
[61] Interview with Tamura Ken'ichi.

inside Sōhyō, to approach the ministries. There are, actually," agreed Labor Standards Bureau Chief Hiraga.[62] Not everyone found the government so accessible, however. If interest-group access has grown and labor is, in fact, acknowledged as a legitimate player in areas of immediate interest to it, the Chūkishin was not equally open to all. Still neglected by the most powerful political actors, women went unrepresented, and Communists were deliberately excluded.

How applicable is a statist perspective? When Knoke et al. collected network data from a variety of private and governmental actors on a range of labor issues in the 1980s, they found the state playing a more central, unifying role in Japan than in either the United States or Germany:

> The Japanese center thus represented a bureaucratic intermediation of communication: The peak associations mediated communications from the civil society and worked directly with the specialist government agencies to discuss labor policy, without political party interference. In turn, the Japanese government agencies located between the business and labor peaks and brokered their information flows.[63]

That revision of the Labor Standards Act revolved around MOL is indisputable. The ministry took the initiative in setting the process in motion; selected both the Rōkiken members and the public-interest members of the Chūkishin; worked with them after their appointment, conducted research for them, and was itself in direct contact with the representatives of both labor and management; and drafted the legislative bill considered by the Diet. But this case study does not support an argument for statism. MOL drafted that bill on the basis of *shingikai* recommendations that reflected the respective concerns of labor and management, and politicians freely amended that bill in the Diet.

Certain models are obviously inapplicable to this study's business case. One of the defining characteristics of Japanese finance has been its compartmentalization. Discrete banking, securities, and insurance circles are themselves subdivided, and none of these sectors directly competed with one another until quite recently. The ruling triad model ignores such divisions within big business. Although Marxism does recognize the existence of "class fractions," it is impossible to argue that capitalists, individually or as a class, imposed their will on the state. If anything, the reverse was true. Here as elsewhere, MOF was able to engage in "preemptive equilibration," first, because it has a comprehensive mandate over the financial sector and, second, because banks and security houses were uncertain both of victory should they bid competitively for LDP support and of whether the benefits of victory would outweigh the costs of bidding and possibly antagonizing the ministry.

---

[62] Interview with Hiraga Toshiyuki.
[63] Knoke et al. (1996), p. 213.

Given this context, the capacity and autonomy of MOF have been foci of controversy. Writing of the process of liberalization in general, Vogel has asserted that "only in Japan have the financial regulators been so thoroughly in charge of the 'deregulation' process. The ministry has orchestrated political bargains between industry groups, filtered its own agenda into the reform legislation, and continued to redefine the reform at the stage of implementation."[64] In this particular case, however, it was the financial community that took the initiative in introducing futures, and the ministry was, after all, mediating among private interests – and its own vertically segmented bureaus – rather than asserting statist interests of its own. "Although it didn't go the way either one of them intended, [the final settlement] was handled in such a way that the views of the banking and securities industries were included as much as possible," noted a third-party business councilor.[65]

Is this an example of pluralist decisionmaking, then, with government policy the resultant of conflicting vectors of group pressure? MOF was hardly a neutral referee: It deliberately ignored or slighted several interests (e.g., the insurance industry and the Kansai region). But if one were to make a case for corporatism, where were the centralized peak associations comprehensively aggregating and negotiating interests? Keidanren did not attempt to mediate. Although each industrial sector and subsector has its own trade association, they are primarily creatures of those sectors' larger companies, and they did not bargain among themselves. "We don't move after the Securities Dealers' Association says, 'we'll do this.' You just consider your own position, then speak," observed one stockbroker.[66]

Neither Marxist nor ruling triad models explain why Japanese business failed to contain the costs of state support for farmers, whom they regard as junior partners in the ruling coalition, if that. Schmitter has contended that agriculture "seems to have a special propensity for corporatist arrangements," and one Western analyst has noted that "in structural terms the [Japanese] cooperative system displays many institutional traits characteristic of corporatist ties."[67] Japanese agriculture *is* far more tightly organized than business, to say nothing of labor, and Nōkyō participates directly in agricultural policymaking and administration. Although relatively high, the corporatization of Japanese agriculture should not be exaggerated, however. This study has concentrated on Nōkyō, and indeed, it is unnecessary for a broad survey of Japanese agricultural policymaking to delve much further. But corporatist theory pictures monopolistic peak associations engaging in social control as well as representation, and

---

[64] S. Vogel (1994), p. 220.
[65] Interview with Imai Takashi.
[66] Interview with Satō Masayuki.
[67] Schmitter (1989), p. 68; Donnelly (1984), p. 343.

Nōkyō is neither monopolistic nor fully in control of its constituency. In addition to Nōkyō, the Beishin's producer delegation includes representatives from the National Chamber of Agriculture and the All-Japan Federation of Farmers Unions. Although they cooperate in the price-setting process, their views differ. On the one hand, the chamber is a government subsidized association that helps carry out official policies, and its leadership regards Nōkyō as selfish and myopic. "Although we submit our demand together with Nōkyō, it's Nōkyō that will pursue it to the bitter end," noted the former's executive director. "Our chamber doesn't just represent the interests of farmers: it represents the future of Japanese agriculture. Representing farmers and representing agriculture are two different things."[68] On the other hand, whereas Nōkyō faces awkward conflicts of interest as a result of its running businesses and implementing public policies as well as representing farmers, the federation can freely take a militant, unambiguously pro-farmer stance.

Nōkyō's national staff can and does make key decisions, but the ideology of the cooperative movement holds that it is local gatherings of farmers that constitute the "mother body" of the rice price struggle.[69] In the words of one headquarters official:

> The premise of Nōkyō is that each and every cooperative is an independent juridical person. Because we're a federation, even our highest decisionmaking bodies take the form of a gathering of local representatives. It's not an organization in which we can simply give orders from the top down. Until a policy's been decided, it's necessary to learn the views of localities, engage in an organizational debate, then once again send a plan out to the provinces.[70]

It sounds less exemplary when described by an official of the chamber: "Zenchū has no choice but to listen to what's said from below; it's an organization that can't persuade its own constituency. If the bottom says 'bow-wow,' it can't help but follow. It doesn't matter whether it's reasonable or not – it doesn't have the power to control."[71] Even agricultural *zoku* in the LDP have criticized Nōkyō leaders' inability to prevail on its members,[72] and at times like 1987, the executive has difficulty conveying its understanding of the national, let alone international, situation to them.

If not corporatist, is this policy domain better classified as pluralist? Given the multiplicity of economic, political, and bureaucratic organizations involved, agricultural pricing is, in the words of one of its most astute students, "a policy

[68] Interview with Ikeda Hitoshi.
[69] Donnelly (1977), p. 164.
[70] Interview with Higa Masahiro.
[71] Interview with Ikeda Hitoshi.
[72] Interview with Ōkawara Taichirō.

area as wide as economic society itself." As this observer himself noted, however, "effective power still rests with bureaucratic officials and the LDP."[73] It is this prominence of the LDP that invalidates a statist interpretation. Agriculture is highly politicized in both senses of the word – politicians routinely intervene, and policymaking is commonly conflictual – and because MAFF and MOF share responsibility for pricing yet do not share a common perspective, politicians play a more important role than they otherwise might. But then, it is almost impossible to imagine the ruling party permitting the price of rice to be settled bureaucratically. Politicians have too much at stake not to intervene: With the decision significantly and selectively benefiting a large, well-organized constituency dispersed throughout the country, setting the producer price of rice is a highly distributive policy that has a direct impact on their electoral viability.

In summary, what we see in these case studies is not Marxism or a system of power elites: Some groups are better represented than others, but representation has broadened. It is not corporatism: Interest organizations negotiate with one another and the state, but monopolistic, centralized peak associations do not control their respective sectors and enter into agreements among themselves. It is not pluralism: Many groups compete for influence, but that competition is structured and the state can play an independent role. It is not statism: Bureaucrats generally play a central role, but ministries are constrained by politicians and their own clienteles.

What we see is neopluralism: Small and fairly stable sets of well-organized, narrowly focused state and societal actors dominate relatively self-contained policy domains by privatizing conflicts and resorting to informal decisionmaking. And if the pattern naturally varies across policy domains and over time, Japanese neopluralism is most often bureaucratically led: The compartmentalization of policy domains follows the lines of ministerial jurisdiction, and agency officials are frequently able to adjust conflicts in a deliberate, self-interested way. Nevertheless, Japanese bureaucrats exercise power most frequently and effectively via, in cooperation with politicians and private actors, rather than vis-à-vis, in control of them, and when bureaucratic jurisdiction is divided or when policies are strongly distributive in nature, then politicians will play a more prominent role.

The *shingikai* system moderates as well as institutionalizes the neopluralist character of Japanese politics. By granting representation within councils, state agencies publicly acknowledge that certain interests are core actors whose involvement in policymaking is legitimate and whose preferences must be taken into account. Commissions also open doors for more peripheral interests, however. Although unions are dissatisfied with them, *shingikai* constitute a more

---

[73] Donnelly (1977), pp. 161, 144; Donnelly (1984), p. 348.

important avenue of influence for labor than for business. Rather than the bankers and stockbrokers for whom it was ostensibly assembled, it was the representatives of corporate customers on MOF's joint subcommittee that considered councils to be the most important route for interest-group participation on the issue of financial futures. And consumer representatives were the most appreciative members of the Beishin, standing out from other councilors in crediting the *shingikai* with earning government the cooperation of interested parties, sharing responsibility for public policy, and examining extragovernmental points of view. In each case, it was a concerned party that was too distant from policymakers to merit their continuous attention but too important to be ignored that derived a disproportionate benefit from participation in councils.

Another potential route for interest-group influence must be touched upon. One weakness of established models of interest-group politics is that, with the exception of some statist theories, they have tended to slight the interpenetration of foreign and domestic policymaking.[74] Precisely the opposite situation prevails in Japanese studies, however: Internationalization (*kokusai-ka*) and foreign pressure (*gaiatsu*) are among the key words (*kii waado*) of contemporary debates. Observing that its foreign economic policies are neither proactive nor rigid, Calder famously characterized Japan as a "reactive state" in which "the impetus to policy change is typically supplied by outside pressure, and that reaction prevails over strategy in the relatively narrow range of cases where the two come into conflict."[75] Other authors (and, more consequentially, many journalists and American officials) blew this observation out of proportion to assert that *gaiatsu* was necessary to break up any number of domestic political logjams in Japan.

It goes without saying that the international context cannot be ignored. As a result of Japan's growing economic impact, international attention to its policies has intensified, and more and more competitive Japanese industries have developed a strong interest in maintaining access to international markets. Thus, as both the likelihood and the potential costs of foreign retaliation have increased over time, Japanese policymakers have increasingly had to factor the reactions of other nations into their deliberations.[76] Be that as it may, in none of this study's cases did *gaiatsu* transform routine domestic policymaking.

Labor standards, financial markets, and agricultural prices all involve issues of international economic relations even if they are not the primary focus of conflict. The international context of domestic policymaking was most difficult to ignore in setting the price of rice. One MAFF official hyperbolically compared the threat of American action to the coming of Commodore Perry's "black

---

[74] The situation is beginning to change. See, e.g., Putnam (1988).
[75] Calder (1988b), p. 518.
[76] Uriu (1996), pp. 37–38.

ships" in 1853. "The Rice Millers Association's Section 301 case had an important impact; it was an extraordinarily significant trigger. . . . The suit forced us to realize that rice was no longer off-limits."[77] On the home front, coming so soon after the controversial 1986 decision to postpone a cut, the Section 301 case prodded many Japanese to question the price of rice for the first time and helped drive a wedge between Nōkyō and MAFF. Even so, as a MOF official pointed out, "We had no intention of cutting the price of rice because we were told to by a foreign country. Although we debated agricultural reform, Japan had to decide in its own way. Foreign countries haven't put in a word on the rice price decision until now."[78]

An agricultural attaché at the American embassy confirmed that this was, indeed, the case during the period described here. The U.S. government clearly preferred cuts in the domestic price of rice because that would make it easier for Japan to lower supports for other farm products. In addition, the U.S. government was approached by Japanese food processors that were unwilling to pressure their own government directly but were interested in encouraging outside pressure in order to lower the prices of their inputs and even liberalize trade in them.[79] Nevertheless, the domestic price of rice could not be the subject of official talks so long as its importation was prohibited, and the U.S. government feared a backlash: If it pushed on rice, it would hand status quo interests in Japan an emotionally charged issue with which to fan opposition to current farm imports, let alone future trade liberalization:

> The United States [government] is irked by the Japanese perception that we have an interest in the [rice price-setting] mechanism when in fact we only observe and report on it. We don't even really watch the process; we only need to know its outcome. . . . Many in MAFF have concluded for themselves that they are on a very stagnant road and need to change policies, foreign pressure or no. Although we tend to see changes as responses to foreign pressure, they're driven almost exclusively by perceived domestic needs.[80]

The threat of American intervention was important not so much in itself but in the way it was tendentiously invoked by domestic actors. Whereas advocates of reform emphasized the danger of alienating Japan's major ally and trading partner, defenders of the status quo pointed to the same threat of intervention in Japan's internal affairs as a justification for resistance to change. Although foreign pressure doubtless plays a role in facilitating some domestic

[77] Interview with Imashiro Takeharu.
[78] Interview with Matsumoto Takashi.
[79] Calder pointed to such "crosscutting communities of interest between Japanese and foreign interest groups" as a major reason for (limited) flexibility in Japan's reactive policies and he predicted that they would grow in number and political influence to make Japanese policymaking more transnational. Calder (1988b), p. 534.
[80] Interview with Geoffrey Wiggin.

policy decisions, its influence in Japan is frequently exaggerated or mis-understood.[81]

Consensus or consent?

Intended to further the integration of Japanese studies into mainstream com-parative politics in the West, this research throws new light on that old mainstay of exceptionalism, the chestnut of consensus. If consensus does get at something important in Japanese politics, it is not what most culturalists argue. Many Japanese do value harmony, but an understanding of consensus must begin with an acknowledgment of conflict. It would be unnecessary to encourage consensus if Japanese really were somehow predisposed to it. Rather, the fervor with which it is extolled suggests just the opposite: that Japanese are only too familiar with the need to curb factionalism within organizations and fierce competition among them. Take setting the price of rice: Although the cast of participants is stable and the process is repeated annually, it is marked by naked assertions of self-interest, not unanimous agreement on the need to sacrifice for the good of the group or an acute embarrassment in the face of direct confrontation. "Consen-sus, even where we find it, is the product of conflict rather than the alternative to it."[82]

When consensus emerges spontaneously, then, of course, it is likely to pro-duce the best results. But consensus does *not* emerge spontaneously in most policy conflicts in Japan, and in those cases, consensus may be "deliberately engineered," "manipulated," or "managed"; actors will often devise a "con-trived consensus" or apply a strategy of "mediation from above."[83] Because appeals to harmony can play an ideological role, buttressing the ability of indi-viduals or groups with a claim to authority to bind others to their decisions,[84] some critics go so far as to charge that outsiders mistake the results of authori-tarian control for voluntary consensus.[85] Maddeningly, the same circumstances have invited diametrically opposed conclusions: Because the formulation and implementation of public policies in Japan follow a consistent pattern of com-promise and negotiation, other observers have taken this for evidence of state actors' *inability* to achieve their goals.[86]

The key to this paradox lies in the double-edged nature of public coordination of private interests. On the one hand, the fact that the major producer and professional groups have a lively sense of their own interests and are organized to pursue them obliges the Japanese state to consider societal

---

[81] See Leonard Schoppa, *Bargaining with Japan: What American Pressure Can and Cannot Do*. New York: Columbia University Press, 1997.

[82] Samuels (1987), p, 20.

[83] Johnson (1982), p. 8; Gerald Curtis, *Frankly Speaking: The Transpacific Forum of Japan Airlines* (December 1991/January 1992, No. 77); Campbell (1984), p. 311.

[84] Okimoto (1989), p. 313.   [85] E.g., Sugimoto (1986), p. 68.

[86] E.g., Haley (1987), p. 350.

preferences. On the other hand, conflicts among interest groups permit state actors to take the initiative as an "interested mediator" and guide bargaining toward outcomes that satisfy their own distinctive preferences as well as private parties'.[87] (For that matter, even when societal interests cooperate, they may invite state actors to oversee their collaborative arrangements.[88])

In none of this study's cases did one private group win a clear-cut victory over another, and in no case did interest-group councilors arrive at a settlement unassisted. Rather, all three cases ended with the acquiescence of the concerned parties in government-sponsored settlements that recognized their respective interests (to a greater or lesser degree). Each time, "mediation from above" resulted in a "contrived consensus," with representatives approving a *shingikai* report without necessarily approving of it. This is definitely *not* to say that the private parties were coerced. The distinction is hardly unique to them, but Japanese accept that an outward pretense (*tatemae*) of consent may not reflect an inner feeling (*honne*) of agreement.[89] More to the point, once state actors devised a settlement, consultation had to involve bargaining and the mobilization of consent to succeed, and because *shingikai* deliberations constitute only one stage of the policymaking process, participating groups found it more advantageous to swallow second-best outcomes and advance the process than to stymie it.

In a history cum critique of the field, Richard Samuels argued that American scholarship on Japan has contributed little to political theory because it has been more deeply embedded in the bilateral relationship than in social science, and that even when it has joined the theoretical mainstream in the past, "the field was a concept *taker*, not a concept *maker* . . . [which] continued to respond to, rather than to create, conceptual innovations." As a result of these deficiencies, "the study of Japanese politics has evolved by accretion more than by cumulation."[90] Happily, that state of affairs has been changing.

Japan is a bureaucratized, democratic polity with a capitalist (post)industrial economy; so are the nations of the West. It clearly is instructive to look at Japan through the prism of Western political science, but to return the favor, scholars must examine Japan with an eye to generating new insights that can deepen the analysis of *other* societies. This study has attempted to "illuminate equally theory and Japan," in Samuels's words, and whether or not this author has succeeded, others surely have and will.

[87] E.g., S. Vogel (1996).   [88] E.g., Tilton (1996).
[89] Richardson and Flanagan (1984), p. 206.
[90] Samuels (1992), pp. 30, 42.

Bibliography

Publications

Abe Hitoshi. 1978. Shingikai seido no suii (Transition in the *Shingikai* System). *Chiiki kaihatsu* (160):8–14.

Aberbach, Joel D., Robert D. Putnam, and Bert A. Rockman. 1981. *Bureaucrats and Politicians in Western Democracies.* Cambridge, Mass.: Harvard University Press.

Alford, Robert R. 1975. Paradigms of Relations between State and Society. In *Stress and Contradiction in Modern Capitalism.* Edited by Leon N. Lindberg, Robert R. Alford, Colin Crouch, and Clause Offe. 145–60. Toronto: D.C. Heath.

Allinson, Gary D. 1989. Politics in Contemporary Japan: Pluralist Scholarship in the Conservative Era – A Review Article. *Journal of Asian Studies* 48(2):324–32.

Allinson, Gary D. 1993a. The Structure and Transformation of Conservative Rule. In *Postwar Japan as History.* Edited by Andrew Gordon. 123–44. Berkeley: University of California Press.

Allinson, Gary D. 1993b. Introduction: Analyzing Political Change: Topics, Findings, and Implications and Citizenship, Fragmentation, and the Negotiated Polity. In *Political Dynamics in Contemporary Japan.* Edited by Gary D. Allinson and Sone Yasunori. 1–14, 17–49. Ithaca: Cornell University Press.

Allison, Graham T. 1971. *Essence of Decision: Explaining the Cuban Missile Crisis.* Boston: Little, Brown.

Almond, Gabriel A. 1958. A Comparative Study of Interest Groups and the Political Process. *American Political Science Review* 52(1):270–82.

Almond, Gabriel A. 1960. A Functional Approach to Comparative Politics. In *The Politics of the Developing Areas.* Edited by Gabriel A. Almond and James S. Coleman. 3–64. Princeton: Princeton University Press.

Almond, Gabriel A. 1983. Corporatism, Pluralism, and Professional Memory. *World Politics* XXXV(2):245–60.

Amano Katsufumi. 1993. Seifu shingikai wa kisha no ubasuteyama ka (Are Government *Shingikai* a Dumping Ground for Reporters?). *Bungei Shunjū* 71(11):296–303.

Arikura Ryōichi. 1966. Shingikai bayari (The Popularity of *shingikai*). *Hōgaku seminā* (127):52–55.

Asahi Shinbun. 30 December 1952. Nandemo kandemo "shingikai" ("*Shingikai*" for Anything and Everything). 12.

289

Asahi Shinbun. 5–9 October 1984. Seiji shuhō: Nakasone seiken no naimen (A Political Method: Inside the Nakasone Cabinet).

Asahi Shinbun. 22 October 1984. Shiteki shimon kikan: hanazakari Kasumigaseki (Private Advisory Bodies: The Bureaucracy in Full Bloom). 9.

Atkinson, Michael M., and William D. Coleman. 1985. Corporatism and Industrial Policy. In *Organized Interests and the State: Studies in Meso-Corporatism.* Edited by Alan Cawson. 22–44. London: Sage.

Atkinson, Michael M., and William D. Coleman. 1989. Strong States and Weak States: Sectoral Policy Networks in Advanced Capitalist Economies. *British Journal of Political Science* 19:47–67.

Atkinson, Michael M., and William D. Coleman. 1992. Policy Networks, Policy Communities and the Problem of Governance. *Governance* 5(2):154–80.

Avineri, Shlomo. 1972. *Hegel's Theory of the Modern State.* Cambridge: Cambridge University Press.

Bachrach, Peter, and Morton S. Baratz. 1962. Two Faces of Power. *American Political Science Review* LVI(4):947–52.

Beer, Samuel H. 1966. The British Legislature and the Problem of Mobilizing Consent. In *Lawmakers in a Changing World.* Edited by Elke Frank. 30–49. Englewood Cliffs, N.J.: Prentice Hall.

Beer, Samuel H. 1969. *British Politics in the Collectivist Age.* 2nd ed. New York: Vintage.

Bendix, Reinhard. 1966. Social Stratification and the Political Community. In *Class, Status, and Power.* Edited by Reinhard Bendix and Seymour Martin Lipset. 73–85. New York: Free Press.

Bendix, Reinhard. 1968. Introduction. In *State and Society: A Reader in Comparative Political Sociology.* Edited by Reinhard Bendix. 1–13. Berkeley: University of California Press.

Benedict, Ruth. 1946. *The Chrysanthemum and the Sword: Patterns of Japanese Culture.* Boston: Houghton Mifflin.

Bentley, Arthur F. 1908. *The Process of Government: A Study of Social Pressures.* Chicago: University of Chicago Press.

Berger, Suzanne. 1981. Introduction. In *Organizing Interests in Western Europe: Pluralism, Corporatism, and the Transformation of Politics.* Edited by Suzanne Berger, Albert Hirschman, and Charles Maier. 1–23. Cambridge: Cambridge University Press.

Block, Fred. 1977. The Ruling Class Does Not Rule: Notes on the Marxist Theory of the State. *Socialist Revolution* (33):6–28.

Block, Fred. 1980. Beyond Relative Autonomy: State Managers as Historical Subjects. In *The Socialist Register: 1980.* Edited by Ralph Miliband and John Saville. 227–42. London: Merlin Press.

Blumenthal, Tuvia. 1985. The Practice of *Amakudari* within the Japanese Employment System. *Asian Survey* 25(3):310–21.

Boyd, Richard. 1987. Government–Industry Relations in Japan: Access, Communication, and Competitive Collaboration. In *Comparative Government–Industry Relations: Western Europe, the United States, and Japan.* Edited by Stephen Wilks and Maurice Wright. 61–90. Oxford: Clarendon Press.

Bullock, Robert. 1995. *Explaining Rice Liberalization in Japan*. Cambridge, Mass.: Program on U.S.–Japan Relations, Harvard University.

Calder, Kent E. 1988a. *Crisis and Compensation: Public Policy and Political Stability in Japan: 1949–1986*. Princeton: Princeton University Press.

Calder, Kent E. 1988b. Japanese Foreign Economic Policy Formation: Explaining the Reactive State. *World Politics* 40(4):517–41.

Calder, Kent E. 1989. Elites in an Equalizing Role: Ex-Bureaucrats as Coordinators and Intermediaries in the Japanese Government–Business Relationship. *Comparative Politics* 21(4):379–403.

Calder, Kent E. 1993. *Strategic Capitalism: Private Business and Public Purpose in Japanese Industrial Finance*. Princeton: Princeton University Press.

Campbell, John Creighton. 1975. Japanese Budget *Baransu*. In *Modern Japanese Organization and Decision-Making*. Edited by Ezra Vogel. 71–100. Berkeley: University of California Press.

Campbell, John Creighton. 1977. *Contemporary Japanese Budget Politics*. Berkeley: University of California Press.

Campbell, John Creighton. 1979. The Old People Boom and Japanese Policy Making. *Journal of Japanese Studies* 5(2):321–57.

Campbell, John Creighton. 1984. Policy Conflict and Its Resolution within the Governmental System. In *Conflict in Japan*. Edited by Ellis Krauss, Thomas Rohlen, and Patricia Steinhoff. 294–334. Honolulu: University of Hawaii Press.

Campbell, John Creighton. 1985. Governmental Responses to Budget Scarcity: Japan. *Policy Studies Journal* 13(3):506–16.

Campbell, John Creighton. 1989. Bureaucratic Primacy: Japanese Policy Communities in an American Perspective, and Afterward on Policy Communities: A Framework for Comparative Research. *Governance* 2(1):5–22, 86–94.

Campbell, John Creighton. 1992. *How Policies Change: The Japanese Government and the Aging Society*. Princeton: Princeton University Press.

Carlile, Lonny E. 1994. Party Politics and the Japanese Labor Movement. *Asian Survey* 34(7):606–20.

Cater, Douglass. 1964. *Power in Washington: A Critical Look at Today's Struggle to Govern in the Nation's Capital*. New York: Random House.

Cawson, Alan. 1985. Varieties of Corporatism: The Importance of the Meso-Level of Interest Intermediation. In *Organized Interests and the State: Studies in Meso-Corporatism*. Edited by Alan Cawson. 1–21. London: Sage.

Christensen, Raymond V. 1994a. Electoral Reform in Japan: How It Was Enacted and Changes It May Bring. *Asian Survey* XXXIV(7):589–605.

Christensen, Raymond V. 1994b (6 December). *Electoral Reform: Will It Transform Japanese Politics?* Presented to the Program on U.S.-Japan Relations at Harvard University, Cambridge, Mass.

Craig, Albert M. 1975. Functional and Dysfunctional Aspects of Government Bureaucracy. In *Modern Japanese Organization and Decision-Making*. Edited by Ezra Vogel. 3–32. Berkeley: University of California Press.

Crozier, Michel, Samuel P. Huntington, and Watanuki Jōji. 1975. *The Crisis of Democracy: Report on the Governability of Democracies to the Trilateral Commission*. New York: New York University Press.

Curtis, Gerald L. 1975. Big Business and Political Influence. In *Modern Japanese Organization and Decision-Making*. Edited by Ezra Vogel. 33–70. Berkeley: University of California Press.

Curtis, Gerald L. 1988. *The Japanese Way of Politics*. New York: Columbia University Press.

Dahl, Robert A. 1961. *Who Governs? Democracy and Power in an American City*. New Haven: Yale University Press.

Dion, Léon. 1973. The Politics of Consultation. *Government and Opposition* 8(3):332–53.

Donnelly, Michael W. 1977. Setting the Price of Rice: A Study in Political Decisionmaking. In *Policymaking in Contemporary Japan*. Edited by T. J. Pempel. 143–200. Ithaca: Cornell University Press.

Donnelly, Michael W. 1984. Conflict Over Government Authority and Markets: Japan's Rice Economy. In *Conflict in Japan*. Edited by Ellis S. Krauss et al. 335–74. Honolulu: University of Hawaii Press.

Donnelly, Michael W., et al. 1982. Shinpojiumu: Nihon ni okeru seisansha beika to seiji-teki konfurikuto (Symposium: Producer Prices and Political Conflict in Japan). *Shokuryō seisaku kenkyū* 30(2):101–31.

Dore, Ronald. 1973. *British Factory – Japanese Factory: The Origins of National Diversity in Industrial Relations*. Berkeley: University of California Press.

Durkheim, Émile. 1947 [1893]. *The Division of Labor in Society*. Translated by George Simpson. Glencoe, Ill.: Free Press.

Eads, George C., and Yamamura Kōzō. 1987. The Future of Industrial Policy. In *The Political Economy of Japan*. Edited by Yamamura Kōzō and Yasuba Yasukichi. 423–68. Stanford: Stanford University Press.

Ebashi Takashi. 1985. Shimon kikantaru shingikai ni okeru katsudō no kōkai gensoku (The Principle of Opening the Activity of *Shingikai* Consultative Bodies to the Public). *Jichi kenkyū* 61(11):3–17.

Ebata Kiyoshi. 1965. Kore ga seifu shingikai da (These Are Government *Shingikai*). *Jiyū* (7):131–41.

Eckstein, Harry. 1960. *Pressure Group Politics: The Case of the British Medical Association*. Stanford: Stanford University Press.

Eckstein, Harry. 1963. Group Theory and the Comparative Study of Pressure Groups. In *Comparative Politics: A Reader*. Edited by Harry Eckstein and David E. Apter. 389–97. Glencoe, Ill.: Free Press.

Eckstein, Harry. 1979. On the "Science" of the State. *Daedalus* 108(4):1–20.

Elliott, James. 1983. The 1981 Administrative Reform in Japan. *Asian Survey* 23(6):765–79.

Evans, Peter B. 1992. The State as Problem and Solution: Predation, Embedded Autonomy, and Structural Change. In *The Politics of Economic Adjustment: International Constraints, Distributive Conflicts, and the State*. Edited by Stephan Haggard and Robert R. Kaufman. 139–81. Princeton: Princeton University Press.

Evans, Peter B., Dietrich Rueschemeyer, and Theda Skocpol. 1985. On the Road Toward a More Adequate Understanding of the State. In *Bringing the State Back In*. Edited by Peter B. Evans, Dietrich Rueschemeyer, and Theda Skocpol. 347–66. Cambridge: Cambridge University Press.

Foote, Daniel H. 1997. Law as an Agent of Change? Governmental Efforts to Reduce Working Hours in Japan. In *Japan: Economic Success and Legal System*. Edited by Harald Baum. 251–301. Berlin: Walter de Gruyter.

Foundation for Advanced Information and Research, Japan (FAIR). 1991. *Japan's Financial Markets*. 2nd ed. Tokyo: FAIR.

Freeman, J. Leiper. 1965. *The Political Process: Executive Bureau-Legislative Committee Relations*. New York: Random House.

Fukui Haruhiro. 1970. *Party in Power: The Japanese Liberal-Democrats and Policy-Making*. Canberra: Australian National University Press.

Fukui Haruhiro. 1977. Studies in Policymaking: A Review of the Literature. In *Policymaking in Contemporary Japan*. Edited by T. J. Pempel. 22–60. Ithaca: Cornell University Press.

Fukui Haruhiro. 1984. The Liberal Democratic Party Revisited: Continuity and Change in the Party's Structure and Performance. *Journal of Japanese Studies* 10(2):385–435.

Fukunaga Hiroshi. 1995. Policy Puppet Show: How Councils of Inquiry "Debate" Key Issues. *Tokyo Business* 63(10):18–21.

Galbraith, John Kenneth. 1956. *American Capitalism: The Concept of Countervailing Power*. Revised ed. Boston: Houghton Mifflin.

Garon, Sheldon, and Mike Mochizuki. 1993. Negotiating Social Contracts. In *Postwar Japan as History*. Edited by Andrew Gordon. 145–66. Berkeley: University of California Press.

George, Aurelia. 1988. Rice Politics in Japan. *Shokuryō seisaku kenkyū* (54):166–213.

Gerschenkron, Alexander. 1962. *Economic Backwardness in Historical Perspective*. Cambridge, Mass.: Harvard University Press.

Giddens, Anthony. 1971. *Capitalism and Modern Social Theory: An Analysis of Marx, Durkheim and Max Weber*. Cambridge: Cambridge University Press.

Gold, David, Clarence Lo, and Erik Olin Wright. 1975. Recent Developments in Marxist Theories of the Capitalist State. *Monthly Review* 27(5, 6):29–43, 36–51.

Goldthorpe, John H. 1984. The End of Convergence: Corporatist and Dualist Tendencies in Modern Western Societies. In *Order and Conflict in Contemporary Capitalism*. Edited by John H. Goldthorpe. 315–43. New York: Oxford University Press.

Haley, John O. 1986. Administrative Guidance versus Formal Regulation: Resolving the Paradox of Industrial Policy. In *Law and Trade Issues of the Japanese Economy: American and Japanese Perspectives*. Edited by Gary Saxonhouse and Yamamura Kōzō. 107–28. Seattle: University of Washington Press.

Haley, John O. 1987. Governance by Negotiation: A Reappraisal of Bureaucratic Power in Japan. *Journal of Japanese Studies* 13(2):343–57.

Hall, Peter. 1983. Patterns of Economic Policy: An Organizational Approach. In *The State in Capitalist Europe: A Casebook*. Edited by Stephen Bornstein, David Held, and Joel Krieger. 21–43. London: Allen & Unwin.

Hall, Peter. 1986. *Governing the Economy: The Politics of State Intervention in Britain and France*. Cambridge: Polity Press.

Harari, Ehud. 1974. Japanese Politics of Advice in Comparative Perspective: A Framework for Analysis and a Case Study. *Public Policy* (22):536–77.

Harari, Ehud. 1982. Turnover and Autonomy in Japanese Permanent Public Advisory Bodies. *Journal of Asian and African Studies* 17(3–4):235–49.

Harari, Ehud. 1986. *Policy Concertation in Japan*. Social and Economic Research on Modern Japan Occasional Papers No. 58/59. Berlin: Verlag Ute Schiller.

Harari, Ehud. 1988. The Institutionalisation of Policy Consultation in Japan: Public Advisory Bodies. In *Japan and the World*. Edited by Gail Lee Bernstein and Fukui Haruhiro. 144–57. New York: St. Martin's Press.

Harari, Ehud. 1990. Resolving and Managing Policy Conflict: Advisory Bodies. In *Japanese Models of Conflict Resolution*. Edited by S. N. Eisenstadt and Eyal Ben-Ari. 138–61. London: Kegan Paul International.

Hayashi Shūzō. 1966. Shingikai no kōyō to sono genkai (The Utility of *Shingikai* and Their Limits). *Toki no hōrei* (586):15–17.

Hayashi Yasuyoshi. 1985. Shichōsen no shimon kikan kōseiin no sennin to shikaku (The Selection of Members of Municipal Advisory Organs and Their Qualifications). *Toshi mondai* 76(7):43–53.

Heclo, Hugh. 1974. *Modern Social Politics in Britain and Sweden: From Relief to Income Maintenance*. New Haven: Yale University Press.

Heclo, Hugh. 1978. Issue Networks and the Executive Establishment. In *The New American Political System*. Edited by Anthony King. 87–124. Washington, D.C.: American Enterprise Institute for Public Policy Research.

Heidenheimer, Arnold J., and Frank C. Langdon. 1968. *Business Associations and the Financing of Political Parties: A Comparative Study of the Evolution of Practices in Germany, Norway, and Japan*. The Hague: Martinus Nijhoff.

Heinz, John P., Edward O. Laumann, Robert L. Nelson, and Robert H. Salisbury. 1993. *The Hollow Core: Private Interests in National Policy Making*. Cambridge, Mass.: Harvard University Press.

Heisler, Martin O. 1979. Corporate Pluralism Revisited: Where Is the Theory? *Scandinavian Political Studies* 2 (new series) (3):277–97.

Hintze, Otto. 1968. The State in Historical Perspective. In *State and Society: A Reader in Comparative Political Sociology*. Edited by Reinhard Bendix. 154–69. Berkeley: University of California Press.

Hintze, Otto. 1975. *The Historical Essays of Otto Hintze*. New York: Oxford University Press.

Hiraga Toshiyuki. 1987. *Kaisei rōdō kijun hō: haikei to kaisetsu* (Revising the Labor Standards Act: Background and Commentary). Tokyo: Nihon Rōdō Kyōkai.

Hiraga Toshiyuki, Shirai Taishirō, Hanami Tadashi, and Kutani Yoshirō. 1987. Rōdō jikan hōsei o kangaeru: rōdō kijun hō no kaisei ni tsuite (Considering Working Hours Legislation: On Revision of the Labor Standards Act). *Rōdō jihō* (May 1987):4–11.

Hishinuma Seiichi. 1984. Shiteki shimon kikan o megutte (On Private Advisory Bodies). *Rippō to chōsa* (123):38–42.

Hollingsworth, J. Rogers, Philippe C. Schmitter, and Wolfgang Streeck. 1994. Capitalism, Sectors, Institutions, and Performance. In *Governing Capitalist Economies: Performance and Control of Economic Sectors*. Edited by J. Rogers Hollingsworth, Philippe C. Schmitter, and Wolfgang Streeck. 3–16. New York: Oxford University Press.

Hollingsworth, J. Rogers, and Wolfgang Streeck. 1994. Countries and Sectors: Concluding Remarks on Performance, Convergence, and Competitiveness. In *Governing Capitalist Economies: Performance and Control of Economic Sectors*. Edited by J. Rogers Hollingsworth, Philippe C. Schmitter, and Wolfgang Streeck. 270–300. New York: Oxford University Press.

Horne, James. 1985. *Japan's Financial Markets: Conflict and Consensus in Decisionmaking*. Sydney: Allen & Unwin.

Ide Yoshinori. 1969. Administrative Reform and Innovation: The Japanese Case. *International Social Science Journal* 21(1):56–67.

Imagawa Akira. 1991. Shingikaitō ni yoru kanshi (Superintendence by Means of *Shingikai*). *Toshi mondai* 82(8):53–64.

Imamura Tsunao. 1972. Shingikai to "shimin sanka" (*Shingikai* and "Citizen Participation"). *Toshi mondai* 63(11):38–52.

Imamura Tsunao. 1978. Shingikai seido no interijensu kinō (The Intelligence Function of the *Shingikai* System). *Chiiki kaihatsu* (161):38–44.

Inagawa Shōji. 1985. Sōri daijin no naikaku tōsotsu taisei: Sōmuchō no shinsetsu ni kan shite (The Prime Minister's System of Cabinet Control: On the Establishment of the Management and Coordination Agency). *Hōritsu jihō* 57(1):45–50.

Inoguchi Takashi. 1990. Conservative Resurgence Under Recession: Public Policies and Political Support in Japan. In *Uncommon Democracies: The One-Party Dominant Regimes*. Edited by T. J. Pempel. 189–225. Ithaca: Cornell University Press.

Inoguchi Takashi and Iwai Tomoaki. 1985. Jimintō rieki yūdō no seiji keizaigaku (The Political Economy of LDP Guidance of Special Interests). *Chūō kōron* (1190):128–62.

International Labor Organization. 1982. *International Labor Conventions and Recommendations, 1919–1981*. Geneva: International Labor Office.

Ishi Hiromitsu. 1994. Wagakuni ni okeru seisaku kettei mekanizumu: Shingikai hōshiki no kōzai (Our Country's Policymaking Mechanism: The Merits and Demerits of the *Shingikai* Method). *Kin'yū* (March):4–11.

Ishida Takeshi. 1968. The Development of Interest Groups and the Pattern of Political Modernization in Japan. In *Political Development in Modern Japan*. Edited by Robert E. Ward. 293–336. Princeton: Princeton University Press.

Ishida Takeshi. 1974. Interest Groups Under a Semipermanent Government Party: The Case of Japan. *Annals of the American Academy of Political and Social Science* 413:1–10.

Ishida Takeshi and Ellis S. Krauss. 1989. Democracy in Japan: Issues and Questions. In *Democracy in Japan: Political and Social Institutions*. Edited by Ishida Takeshi and Ellis S. Krauss. 3–16. Pittsburgh: University of Pittsburgh Press.

Itagaki Tetsuya. 1996. Kan Naoto Stirs the Health Ministry. *Japan Quarterly* 43(3):24–29.

Itō Daiichi. 1968. The Bureaucracy: Its Attitudes and Behavior. *The Developing Economies* 6:446–67.

Itō Takatoshi. 1992. *The Japanese Economy*. Cambridge, Mass.: MIT Press.

Japan Communist Party. 1986. *Seiji keizai sōran, 1986* (A General Survey of Politics and Economics, 1986). Tokyo: Zen'ei.

Japan Culture Institute. 1979. The Bureaucracy: Japan's Pool of Leadership. In *Politics and Economics in Contemporary Japan*. Edited by Murakami Hyōe and Johannes Hirschmeier. 79–92. Tokyo: Japan Culture Institute.

Japan Echo. 1983. Midstage in the Administrative Reform Process. 10(3):24–26.

Japan Institute of Labour. 1994. *Labour-Management Relations in Japan, 1994*. Tokyo: Japan Institute of Labour.

Japan Institute of Labour. 1996. *Japanese Working Life Profile: Labour Statistics, 1995–96*. Tokyo: Japan Institute of Labour.

Johnson, Chalmers. 1974. The Reemployment of Retired Government Bureaucrats in Japanese Big Business. *Asian Survey* XIV(2):953–65.

Johnson, Chalmers. 1975. Japan: Who Governs? An Essay on Official Bureaucracy. *Journal of Japanese Studies* 2(1):1–28.

Johnson, Chalmers. 1980. *Omote* (Explicit) and *Ura* (Implicit): Translating Japanese Political Terms. *Journal of Japanese Studies* 6(1):89–115.

Johnson, Chalmers. 1982. *MITI and the Japanese Miracle: The Growth of Industrial Policy, 1925–1975*. Stanford: Stanford University Press.

Johnson, Chalmers. 1986a. *MITI, MPT, and the Telecom Wars: How Japan Makes Policy for High Technology*. Berkeley Roundtable on the International Economy (BRIE). BRIE Working Paper #21 Berkeley: University of California.

Johnson, Chalmers. 1986b. Tanaka Kakuei, Structural Corruption, and the Advent of Machine Politics in Japan. *Journal of Japanese Studies* 12(1):1–28.

Jordan, A. Grant. 1981. Iron Triangles, Woolly Corporatism and Elastic Nets: Images of the Policy Process. *Journal of Public Policy* 1(1):95–123.

Jordan, A. Grant. 1990. Sub-Governments, Policy Communities and Networks: Refilling the Old Bottles? *Journal of Theoretical Politics* 2(3):319–38.

Kabashima Ikuo and Jeffrey Broadbent. 1986. Referent Pluralism: Mass Media and Politics in Japan. *Journal of Japanese Politics* 12(2):329–61.

Kaminaga Isao. 1986. Jichitai ni okeru shimon gyōsei no shomondai (Various Problems in Municipal Consultative Administration). *Hōritsu jihō* 58(1):60–65.

Kaneko Masashi. 1979. Shingikai, kōchōkai, iinkai to jūmin sanka (*Shingikai*, Public Hearings, Committees, and Citizen Participation). In *Jichitai mondai kōza*. Edited by Taguchi Fukuji et al. 155–72. Tokyo: Jichitai kenkyūsha.

Kaneko Masashi. 1985. Shingikai gyōseiron (The Theory of *Shingikai* Administration). In *Gendai gyōsei hōtaikei*. Edited by Ogawa Ichirō et al. 113–58. Tokyo: Yūhaikaku.

Kaplan, Eugene J. 1972. *Japan: The Government-Business Relationship*. Washington: U.S. Department of Commerce.

Katō, Junko. 1994. *The Problem of Bureaucratic Rationality: Tax Politics in Japan*. Princeton: Princeton University Press.

Katō Kazuaki. 1971. Shingikai ni tsuite (On *Shingikai*). *Toshi mondai kenkyūkai* 23(4):45–56.

Katō Kazuaki. 1978. *Shingikaitō to kōhō, kōchō* (*Shingikai* and Official Reports, Public Hearings). Tokyo: Gakuyō shobo.

Katō Yukio. 1978. Chihō no shingikai no genjō to mondaiten (The Present Condition and Problems of Local *Shingikai*). *Chiiki kaihatsu* (161):45–51.

Katzenstein, Peter J. 1978. Introduction and Conclusion. In *Between Power and Plenty: Foreign Economic Policies of Advanced Industrial States*. Edited by Peter Katzenstein. 3–22, 295–336. Madison: University of Wisconsin Press.

Katzenstein, Peter J. 1985. *Small States in World Markets: Industrial Policy in Europe.* Ithaca: Cornell University Press.

Kawaguchi Hiroshi. 1978. Shingikai seidoron no hensen (Changes in Theories of *Shingikai*). *Chiiki kaihatsu* (161):27–32.

Kawaguchi Minoru. 1987. Rōdō jikan hōseitō no seibi to kongo no kadai (Preparation of Labor Hour Legislation and Tasks for the Future). *Jurisuto* (878):4–9.

Kin'yū Seido Chōsakai and Gaikoku Kawasetō Shingikai. 1987. *Kin'yū sakimono torihiki no seibi ni tsuite* (Preparing for Financial Futures Trading). Tokyo: Ministry of Finance.

Knoke, David, Franz Urban Pappi, Jeffrey Broadbent, and Tsujinaka Yutaka. 1996. *Comparing Policy Networks: Labor Politics in the U.S., Germany, and Japan.* Cambridge: Cambridge University Press.

Komari Akihiko. 1991. *The Burden of Symbolism: Rice, Politics and Japan.* Cambridge, Mass.: Program on U.S.–Japan Relations, Harvard University.

Kōshiro Kazutoshi. 1979. Japan's Labor Union: The Meeting of White and Blue Collar. In *Politics and Economics in Contemporary Japan.* Edited by Murakami Hyōe and Johannes Hirschmeier. 143–56. Tokyo: Japan Culture Institute.

Kotaka Tsuyoshi. 1986. Gyōsei tetsuzuki kara mita shimon gyōsei (Consultative Administration in Light of Administrative Procedure). *Hōritsu jihō* 58(1):45–52.

Krasner, Stephen. 1978. *Defending the National Interest: Raw Materials Investments and U.S. Foreign Policy.* Princeton: Princeton University Press.

Krasner, Stephen. 1984. Approaches to the State: Alternative Conceptions and Historical Dynamics. *Comparative Politics* 16(2):222–46.

Krauss, Ellis S. 1989. Politics and Policymaking. In *Democracy in Japan: Political and Social Institutions.* Edited by Ishida Takeshi and Ellis S. Krauss. 39–64. Pittsburgh: University of Pittsburgh Press.

Kudo Yasushi and Kakinuma Shigeki. 1994. Bureaucrats Ready to Do Battle. *Tokyo Business* 62(4):20–23.

Kume Ikuo. 1988. Changing Relations among the Government, Labor and Business in Japan After the Oil Crisis. *International Organization* 42(4):659–87.

Kumon Shunpei. 1992. Japan as a Network Society. In *The Political Economy of Japan: Cultural and Social Dynamics.* Edited by Kumon Shunpei and Henry Rosovsky. 109–41. Stanford: Stanford University Press.

Langdon, Frank C. 1961a. Big Business Lobbying in Japan: The Case of Central Bank Reform. *American Political Science Review* 55(3):527–38.

Langdon, Frank C. 1961b. Organized Interests in Japan and Their Influence on Political Parties. *Pacific Affairs* 34(3):271–78.

LaPalombara, Joseph. 1964. *Interest Groups in Italian Politics.* Princeton: Princeton University Press.

Laumann, Edward O., and David Knoke. 1989. Policy Networks of the Organizational State: Collective Action in the National Energy and Health Domains. In *Networks of Power: Organizational Actors at the National, Corporate, and Community Levels.* Edited by Robert Perucci and Harry R. Potter. 17–55. New York: Aldine de Gruyter.

Lehmbruch, Gerhard. 1979. Liberal Corporatism and Party Government. In *Trends Toward Corporatist Intermediation*. Edited by Philippe C. Schmitter and Gerhard Lehmbruch. 147–83. Beverly Hills: Sage.

Lehmbruch, Gerhard. 1982. Neo-Corporatism in Comparative Perspective. In *Patterns of Corporatist Policy-Making*. Edited by Gerhard Lehmbruch and Philippe C. Schmitter. 1–28. Beverly Hills: Sage.

Lehmbruch, Gerhard. 1983. Interest Intermediation in Capitalist and Socialist Systems: Some Structural and Functional Perspectives in Comparative Research. *International Political Science Review* 4(2):153–72.

Lehmbruch, Gerhard. 1984. Concertation and the Structure of Corporatist Networks. In *Order and Conflict in Contemporary Capitalism*. Edited by John Goldthorpe. 60–80. Oxford: Clarendon Press.

Lockwood, William W. 1965. Japan's "New Capitalism". In *The State and Economic Enterprise in Japan: Essays in the Political Economy of Growth*. Edited by William W. Lockwood. 447–522. Princeton: Princeton University Press.

Lowi, Theodore J. 1964. American Business, Public Policy, Case Studies and Political Theory. *World Politics* 16(4):677–715.

Lowi, Theodore J. 1967. The Public Philosophy: Interest-Group Liberalism. *American Political Science Review* 61(1):5–24.

Lowi, Theodore J. 1969. *The End of Liberalism: Ideology, Policy, and the Crisis of Public Authority*. New York: W. W. Norton.

Lukes, Steven. 1974. *Power: A Radical View*. London: Macmillan.

Mabuchi Masaru. 1993. Deregulation and Legalization of Financial Policy. In *Political Dynamics in Contemporary Japan*. Edited by Gary D. Allinson and Sone Yasunori. 130–54. Ithaca: Cornell University Press.

Madison, James, Alexander Hamilton, and John Jay. 1961 [1788]. *The Federalist Papers*. New York: New American Library.

Mainichi Shinbun. 5–18 January 1985. Taitō suru burein (Rising Brains).

Maki, John M. 1947. The Role of the Bureaucracy in Japan. *Pacific Affairs* 20(4):391–406.

Marx, Karl, and Friedrich Engels. 1978. *The Marx-Engels Reader*. 2nd ed. Edited by Robert C. Tucker. New York: W. W. Norton.

Masujima Toshiyuki. 1984. Kokka gyōsei soshiki hō kaisei no igi (The Significance of the Reform of the National Administrative Organization Act). *Jichi kenkyū* 60(3):20–36.

Matsuoka Tsunenori. 1985. Shimon kikan kōseiin no sennin to shikaku (The Appointment and Qualifications of Advisory Committee Members). *Toshi mondai* 76(7):32–42.

McConnell, Grant. 1966. *Private Power and American Democracy*. New York: Alfred A. Knopf.

McKean, Margaret A. 1993. State Strength and the Public Interest. In *Political Dynamics in Contemporary Japan*. Edited by Gary D. Allinson and Sone Yasunori. 72–104. Ithaca: Cornell University Press.

Mikita Hideo. 1986. Gikaisei minshu-shugi to shimon gyōsei (Parliamentary Democracy and Consultative Administration). *Hōritsu jihō* 58(1):30–37.

Ministry of Agriculture, Forestry, and Fisheries. 1986. Agriculture in Japan. *Japan's Agricultural Review*. Vols. 13 and 14.

Ministry of Agriculture, Forestry, and Fisheries. 1987. Basic Directions of Agricultural Policy Toward the 21st Century. *Japan's Agricultural Review*. Vol. 15.

Ministry of Agriculture, Forestry, and Fisheries. March 1990. *Nōrinsui sangyō ni kan suru shuyō shihyō* (Principal Indices of the Agricultural, Forestry, and Fishery Industries). Tokyo: Ministry of Agriculture, Forestry, and Fisheries.

Misawa Shigeo. 1973. An Outline of the Policy-Making Process in Japan. In *Japanese Politics – An Inside View*. Edited by Itoh Hiroshi. 12–48. Ithaca: Cornell University Press.

Miyake Tarō. 1971. Fuken ni okeru shingikaitō no seido to sono un'eijō no mondaiten (The Prefectural *Shingikai* System and Problems in Its Management). *Toshi mondai kenkyū* 23(4):57–69.

Miyoshi Shigeo. 1971. Shingikai seido ni kan suru shomondai (Various Problems of the *Shingikai* System). *Toshi mondai kenkyū* 23(4):32–44.

Mochizuki, Mike. 1993. Public Sector Labor and the Privatization Challenge: The Railway and Telecommunications Unions. In *Political Dynamics in Contemporary Japan*. Edited by Gary D. Allinson and Sone Yasunori. 181–99. Ithaca: Cornell University Press.

Momii Tsuneki. 1987. Rōdō kijun hō kaisei hōan to rippō ronjō no ronten (The Proposal to Amend the Labor Standards Act and Points at Issue from the Standpoint of Legislative Theory). *Hōritsu jihō* 59(6):86–93.

Mori Hideki. 1987. Naikaku seiji to shingikai-shimon kikan (Cabinet Politics and *Shingikai*/Advisory Bodies). *Hōritsu jihō* 59(6):62–68.

Muramatsu Michio. 1981a. Nihon-gata puressha gurūpu no kenkyū (Research on Japanese-Style Pressure Groups). *Tōyō keizai* (2–9 May 1981):76–82.

Muramatsu Michio. 1981b. *Sengo nihon no kanryōsei* (The Bureaucratic System of Postwar Japan). Tokyo: Tōyō keizai shinpōsha.

Muramatsu Michio. 1983. Administrative Reform in a Pluralist Political System. *Japan Echo* 10(3):30–39.

Muramatsu Michio. 1985. Atsuryoku dantai no eikyōryoku: sābei deita no bunseki kara (The Influence of Pressure Groups: An Analysis on the Basis of Survey Data). *Hōgaku ronsō* 116(3):324–70.

Muramatsu Michio and Ellis S. Krauss. 1984. Bureaucrats and Politicians in Policymaking: The Case of Japan. *American Political Science Review* 78(1):126–46.

Muramatsu Michio and Ellis S. Krauss. 1987. The Conservative Party Line and the Development of Patterned Pluralism. In *The Political Economy of Japan*. Edited by Yasuba Yasukichi and Yamamura Kōzō. 516–54. Stanford: Stanford University Press.

Muroi Tsutomu. 1980. Shimon gyōsei (Consultative Administration). *Hōritsu jihō* 52(8):20–24.

Muroi Tsutomu. 1985. Shimon kikan gyōsei no arikata (The Way Consultative-Body Administration Ought to Be). In *Hōgaku seminā zōkan sōgō tokushū shiriizu*, #28. 28–35.

Naka Mamoru. 1986. Nakasone shimon gyōsei no shisō-teki haikei to yoron (Public Opinion and the Intellectual Background of Nakasone's Consultative Administration). *Hōritsu jihō* 58(1):73–83.

Nakane Chie. 1972. *Japanese Society*. Berkeley: University of California Press.

Nakanishi Tamako. 1995 (26 October). *The Under-Representation of Japanese Women in Decision-Making*. Presented to the Program on U.S.–Japan Relations at Harvard University, Cambridge, Mass.

Namikawa Shino. 1987. Rinchō gyōkaku imada narazu (What Rinchō Administrative Reform Has Yet to Achieve). *Chūō kōron* 102(14):120–30.

Namiki Nobuyoshi. 1979. "Japan, Inc.": Reality or Facade? In *Politics and Economics in Contemporary Japan*. Edited by Murakami Hyōe and Johannes Hirschmeier. 111–27. Tokyo: Japan Culture Institute.

Narita Reimei. 1967. Shingikai seido no kaizen ni tsuite (On the Improvement of the *Shingikai* System). *Jichi kenkyū* 43(1):45–56.

Nettl, J. P. 1968. The State as a Conceptual Variable. *World Politics* 20(4): 559–92.

Nihon Keizai Shinbun. 12–14 July 1995. Shingikai o tou (Inquiring into *Shingikai*).

Nihon Keizai Shinbun. 8–9 August 1996. Shingikai wa kawatta ka (Have *Shingikai* Changed?).

Noble, Gregory W. 1988. The Japanese Industrial Policy Debate. In *Pacific Dynamics: The International Politics of Industrial Change*. Edited by Stephan Haggard and Chung-in Moon. 53–95. Boulder, Co.: Westview Press.

Noguchi Yukio. 1982. The Government-Business Relationship in Japan: The Changing Role of Fiscal Resources. In *Policy and Trade Issues of the Japanese Economy: American and Japanese Perspectives*. Edited by Yamamura Kōzō. 123–42. Seattle: University of Washington Press.

Nordlinger, Eric. 1981. *On the Autonomy of the Democratic State*. Cambridge, Mass.: Harvard University Press.

Ogita Tamotsu. 1969. Shingikai no jittai (The Realities of *Shingikai*). *Nenpō gyōsei kenkyū* 7:21–71.

Ogita Tamotsu. 1972. Shingikai no jittai (The Realities of *Shingikai*). *Toshi mondai* 63(11):28–37.

Ōi Bunzō. 1965. Shingikai no kinō to rōdō kumiai (The Functions of *Shingikai* and Labor Unions). *Rōdō mondai* (87):55–60.

Okabe Shirō. 1969. Seisaku keisei ni okeru shingikai no yakuwari to sekinin (The Roles and Responsibilities of *Shingikai* in Policymaking). *Nenpō gyōsei kenkyū* 7:1–19.

Okimoto, Daniel I. 1988. Political Inclusivity: The Domestic Structure of Trade. In *The Political Economy of Japan: The Changing International Context*. Edited by Inoguchi Takashi and Daniel I. Okimoto. 305–44. Stanford: Stanford University Press.

Okimoto, Daniel I. 1989. *Between MITI and the Market: Japanese Industrial Policy for High Technology*. Stanford: Stanford University Press.

Olson, Mancur, Jr. 1965. *The Logic of Collective Action: Public Goods and the Theory of Groups*. Cambridge, Mass.: Harvard University Press.

Olson, Mancur, Jr. 1982. *The Rise and Decline of Nations: Economic Growth, Stagflation, and Social Rigidities*. New Haven: Yale University Press.

Ōmi Saburō. 1958. Shingikai no arikata: tadashii katsudō no dekiru yō na yottsu no hōsaku o teian suru (The Way *Shingikai* Ought to Be: A Proposal of Four Policies for How They Could Operate Correctly). *Toki no hōrei* (292):42–46.

Ozeki Tsuguo. 1971. Chihō kōkyō dantai ni okeru shingikai no igi to mondaiten (The Significance and Problems of Local Public Organization *Shingikai*). *Toshi mondai kenkyū* 23(4):2–14.

Paarlberg, Robert L. 1990. The Upside-Down World of U.S.–Japanese Agricultural Trade. *The Washington Quarterly* 13(4):131–42.

Panitch, Leo. 1979. The Development of Corporatism in Liberal Democracies. In *Trends Toward Corporatist Intermediation*. Edited by Philippe C. Schmitter and Gerhard Lehmbruch. 119–46. Beverly Hills: Sage.

Panitch, Leo. 1980. Recent Theorizations of Corporatism: Reflections on a Growth Industry. *British Journal of Sociology* 31(2):159–87.

Park, Yung Ho. 1972. The Governmental Advisory Commission System in Japan. *Journal of Comparative Administration* 3(4):435–67.

Passin, Herbert. 1975. Intellectuals in the Decision Making Process. In *Modern Japanese Organization and Decision-Making*. Edited by Ezra Vogel. 251–83. Berkeley: University of California Press.

Patrick, Hugh, ed. 1986. *Japan's High Technology Industries: Lessons and Limitations of Industrial Policy*. Seattle: University of Washington Press.

Pempel, T. J. 1974. The Bureaucratization of Policymaking in Postwar Japan. *American Journal of Political Science* 18(4):647–64.

Pempel, T. J. 1975. The Dilemma of Parliamentary Opposition in Japan. *Polity* 8(1):63–79.

Pempel, T. J. 1978. Japanese Foreign Economic Policy: The Domestic Base for International Behavior. In *Between Power and Plenty: Foreign Economic Policies of Advanced Industrial States*. Edited by Peter J. Katzenstein. 139–90. Madison: University of Wisconsin Press.

Pempel, T. J. 1982. *Policy and Politics in Japan: Creative Conservatism*. Philadelphia: Temple University Press.

Pempel, T. J. 1984. Organizing for Efficiency: The Higher Civil Service in Japan. In *Bureaucrats and Policy Making: A Comparative Overview*. Edited by Ezra N. Suleiman. 72–106. New York: Holmes & Meier.

Pempel, T. J. 1987. The Unbundling of "Japan, Inc.": The Changing Dynamics of Japanese Policy Formation. *Journal of Japanese Studies* 13(2):271–306.

Pempel, T. J. 1989. Prerequisites for Democracy: Political and Social Institutions. In *Democracy in Japan*. Edited by Ishida Takeshi and Ellis Krauss. 17–37. Pittsburgh: University of Pittsburgh Press.

Pempel, T. J., and Tsunekawa Keiichi. 1979. Corporatism Without Labor? The Japanese Anomaly. In *Trends Toward Corporatist Intermediation*. Edited by Philippe C. Schmitter and Gerhard Lehmbruch. 231–70. Beverly Hills: Sage.

Pharr, Susan J. 1990. *Losing Face: Status Politics in Japan*. Berkeley: University of California Press.

Poulantzas, Nicos. 1972. The Problem of the Capitalist State. In *Ideology in Social Science: Readings in Critical Social Theory*. Edited by Robin Blackburn. 238–53. London: Fontana.

Prestowitz, Clyde V., Jr. 1988. *Trading Places: How We Allowed Japan to Take the Lead*. New York: Basic Books.

Putnam, Robert D. 1988. Diplomacy and Domestic Politics: The Logic of Two-Level Games. *International Organization* 42(3):427–60.

Radin, Robert. 1997 (14 February). *Big Bangs and Whimpers: The Future of Japan's Administrative State*. Presented to the Council on Foreign Relations, New York City.

Ramseyer, J. Mark, and Frances McCall Rosenbluth. 1993. *Japan's Political Marketplace*. Cambridge, Mass.: Harvard University Press.

Reed, Steven R. 1993. *Making Common Sense of Japan*. Pittsburgh: University of Pittsburgh Press.

Richardson, Bradley, and Scott C. Flanagan. 1984. *Politics in Japan*. Boston: Little, Brown.

Richardson, Jeremy and Gunnel Gustafsson. 1980. Post-Industrial Changes in Policy Style. *Scandinavian Political Studies* 3(1):21–37.

Richardson, Jeremy, Gunnel Gustafsson, and Grant Jordan. 1982. The Concept of Policy Style. In *Policy Styles in Western Europe*. Edited by Jeremy Richardson. 1–16. London: Allen & Unwin.

Rokkan, Stein. 1966. Norway: Numerical Democracy and Corporate Pluralism. In *Political Oppositions in Western Democracies*. Edited by Robert A. Dahl. 70–115. New Haven: Yale University Press.

Rosenbluth, Frances McCall. 1989. *Financial Politics in Contemporary Japan*. Ithaca: Cornell University Press.

Rosenbluth, Frances McCall. 1993. Financial Deregulation and Interest Intermediation. In *Political Dynamics in Contemporary Japan*. Edited by Gary D. Allinson and Sone Yasunori. 107–29. Ithaca: Cornell University Press.

Rousseau, Jean Jacques. 1946. *The Social Contract and the Discourses*. Translated by G. D. H. Cole. London: J. M. Dent.

Sakuma Tsutomu, Satō Chiku, Shidano Hiroshi, and Hayashi Shūzō. 1972. Shingikai: Zadankai (*Shingikai*: A Symposium). *Jurisuto* (510):34–60.

Salisbury, Robert H. 1984. Interest Representation: The Dominance of Institutions. *American Political Science Review* 78(1):64–76.

Samuels, Richard J. 1983. *The Politics of Regional Policy in Japan: Localities Incorporated?* Princeton: Princeton University Press.

Samuels, Richard J. 1987. *The Business of the Japanese State: Energy Markets in Comparative and Historical Perspective*. Ithaca: Cornell University Press.

Samuels, Richard J. 1992. Japanese Political Studies and the Myth of the Independent Intellectual. In *The Political Culture of Foreign Area and International Studies: Essays in Honor of Lucian W. Pye*. Edited by Richard J. Samuels and Myron Weiner. 17–56. Washington, D. C.: Brassey's.

Satō Chiku. 1962. Shingikai no arikata (The Way *Shingikai* Ought to Be). *Ekonomisuto* 40(15):42–44.

Satō Chiku. 1978. Shingikai no yakuwari (The Role of *Shingikai*). *Chiiki kaihatsu* (160):2–7.

Satō Hidetake. 1978. Shingikai seido kaikaku no kokumin-teki kadai: kokka dokusen shihon-shugi to rippō, gyōsei kikan (The National Task of Reform of the *Shingikai* System: State Monopoly Capitalism, Law, and Administrative Bodies). *Keizai* (174):123–50.

Satō Isao. 1965. *Shingikai*. In *Gyōsei hō kōza* (A Course in Administrative Law). Edited by Tanaka Jirō et al. 97–117. Tokyo: Yūhikaku.

Satō Isao. 1972. Shingikai no arikata: toku ni jūmin sanka to kankei (The Way *Shingikai* Ought to Be, Particularly in Relation to Citizen Participation). *Toshi mondai* 63(11):3–16.

Satō Katsuhiro. 1986. Shimon gyōsei to jūmin sanka (Consultative Administration and Citizen Participation). *Hōritsu jihō* 58(1):66–72.

Satō Seizaburō and Matsuzawa Tetsuhisa. 1984. Jimintō chōchōki seiken no kaibō (A Dissection of the Liberal Democratic Party's Super-Long-Term Hold on Political Power). *Chūō kōron* (1185):66–100.

Schattschneider, E. E. 1960. *The Semisovereign People: A Realist's View of Democracy in America*. New York: Holt, Rinehart & Winston.

Schmitter, Philippe C. 1977. Modes of Interest Intermediation and Models of Societal Change in Western Europe. *Comparative Political Studies* 10(1):7–38.

Schmitter, Philippe C. 1979 [1974]. Still the Century of Corporatism? In *Trends Toward Corporatist Intermediation*. Edited by Philippe C. Schmitter and Gerhard Lehmbruch. 5–52. Beverly Hills: Sage.

Schmitter, Philippe C. 1981. Interest Intermediation and Regime Governability in Contemporary Western Europe and North America. In *Organizing Interests in Western Europe: Pluralism, Corporatism, and the Transformation of Politics*. Edited by Suzanne Berger. 285–327. Cambridge: Cambridge University Press.

Schmitter, Philippe C. 1982. Reflections on Where the Theory of Neo-Corporatism Has Gone and Where the Praxis of Neo-Corporatism May Be Going. In *Patterns of Corporatist Policy-Making*. Edited by Gerhard Lehmbruch and Philippe C. Schmitter. 259–79. Beverly Hills: Sage.

Schmitter, Philippe C. 1989. Corporatism Is Dead! Long Live Corporatism! *Government and Opposition* 24(1):54–73.

Sejima Ryūzō. 1983. Looking Beyond the Final Report. *Japan Echo* 10(3):27–29.

Semkow, Brian W. 1989. Emergence of Derivative Financial Products Markets in Japan. *Cornell International Law Journal* 22(1):39–58.

Shimano Fusami. 1965. *Gyōsei iinkai oyobi shingikai* (Administrative Committees and *Shingikai*). *Jichi kenkyū* (489):141–56.

Shindō Muneyuki. 1978. Shingikai tōshin no sakusei to riyō keitai (The Preparation and Use of *Shingikai* Reports). *Chiiki kaihatsu* (160):15–20.

Shindō Muneyuki. 1983. Seisaku kettei no shisutemu: shingikai, shimon kikan, shinkutanku no yakuwari (The Policymaking System: The Role of *Shingikai*, Consultative Bodies, and Think Tanks). *Jurisuto zōkan sōgō tokushū* (29):246–51.

Shingikai Kenkyūkai. 1963. Rinji Gyōsei Chōsakai (The Ad Hoc Administrative Reform Council). *Heiwa keizai* 24:54–60.

Shirai Taishirō. 1987a. Rōdō jikan hōsei kaisei o megutte (On Revision of Working Hours Legislation). *Nihon rōdō kyōkai zasshi* 29(10):2–11.

Shirai Taishirō. 1987b. Rōkihō kaisei e no Chūkishin no kengi to sono gaiyō (The Central Council on Labor Standards' Proposals to Revise the Labor Standards Act and an Outline Thereof). *Rōdō hōgaku kenkyū kaihō* (1631):1–24.

Shōji Hikaru. 1985. Chihō jichitai no shimon kikan: genjō to kadai (Local Consultative Bodies: The Status Quo and Its Problems). *Toshi mondai* 76(7):54–65.

Shōken Torihiki Shingikai. 1987. *Shōken sakimono shijō no seibi ni tsuite* (Preparing a Securities Futures Market). Tokyo: Ministry of Finance.

Shonfield, Andrew. 1965. *Modern Capitalism: The Changing Balance of Public and Private Power*. New York: Oxford University Press.

Skocpol, Theda. 1979. *States and Social Revolutions*. Cambridge: Cambridge University Press.

Skocpol, Theda. 1980. Political Response to Capitalist Crisis: Neo-Marxist Theories of the State and the Case of the New Deal. *Politics and Society* 10(2):155–201.

Skocpol, Theda. 1985. Bringing the State Back In: Strategies of Analysis in Current Research. In *Bringing the State Back In*. Edited by Peter B. Evans, Dietrich Rueschemeyer and Theda Skocpol. 3–37. Cambridge: Cambridge University Press.

Skocpol, Theda, and Kenneth Finegold. 1982. State Capacity and Economic Intervention in the Early New Deal. *Political Science Quarterly* 97(2):255–78.

Smith, Adam. 1976 [1776]. *An Inquiry Into the Nature and Causes of the Wealth of Nations*. Chicago: University of Chicago Press.

Sōhyō, Dōmei, Chūritsu Rōren, Shinsanbetsu, and Zenmin Rōkyō. 1986, 1987. *Watashitachi no rōdō kijun hō kaisei* (Our Revisions of the Labor Standards Act). Tokyo.

Sōmuchō. 1986. *Shingikai sōran* (A General Survey of *Shingikai*). Tokyo: Ministry of Finance Publishing Bureau.

Sōmuchō. 1995. *Shingikai sōran* (A General Survey of *Shingikai*). Tokyo: Ministry of Finance Publishing Bureau.

Sōmuchō. 1996. *"Shingikaitō oyobi kondankaitō gyōsei un'ei-jō no kaigō no un'eitō ni kan suru shishin" oyobi "Shingikaitō no tōmei-ka, minaoshi ni tsuite" no forō appu kekka ni tsuite* (Follow-up Results to "A Guide to the Management of *Shingikai* and *Kondankai* Meetings on Administrative Operations" and "On the Enhancement of Transparency and Reexamination of *Shingikai*").

Sone Yasunori. 1981. Tagen minshu-shugi to gendai kokka (The Theory of Pluralist Democracy and the Contemporary State). In *Seijigaku Nenpō, 1981*. 117–49. Tokyo.

Sone Yasunori. 1986a. Nihon no seisaku keiseiron no henka (Changes in the Interpretation of Japanese Policymaking). In *Nihon-gata seisaku kettei no hen'yō* (Changes in Japanese-Style Policymaking). Edited by Nakano Minoru. 301–19. Tokyo: Tōyō keizai shinpōsha.

Sone Yasunori. 1986b. Yarase no seiji "shingikai hōshiki" o kenshō suru (Inspecting the "*Shingikai* Method" of the Politics of Having Something Done). *Chūō kōron* (1201):149–55.

Sone Yasunori et al. 1985. *Shingikai no kiso kenkyū: kinō, taiyō ni tsuite no bunseki* (Basic Research on *Shingikai*: An Analysis of Their Functions and Conditions). Tokyo: Keiō University.

Sone Yasunori. 1993. Conclusion: Structuring Political Bargains: Government, *Gyōkai*, and Markets. In *Political Dynamics in Contemporary Japan*. Edited by Gary D. Allinson and Sone Yasunori. 295–306. Ithaca: Cornell University Press.

Soukup, James R. 1963. Comparative Studies in Political Finance: Japan. *Journal of Politics* 25(4):737–56.

Soukup, James R. 1965. Business Political Participation in Japan: Continuity and Change. *Studies on Asia, 1965* 6:163–78.

Stepan, Alfred. 1978. *The State and Society: Peru in Comparative Perspective*. Princeton: Princeton University Press.

Stigler, George J. 1971. The Theory of Economic Regulation. *The Bell Journal of Economics and Management Science* 2(1):3–21.

Streeck, Wolfgang, and Philippe C. Schmitter. 1985. Community, Market, State – and Associations? The Prospective Contribution of Interest Governance to Social Order. In *Private Interest Government: Beyond Market and State*. Edited by Wolfgang Streeck and Philippe C. Schmitter. 1–29. London: Sage.

Sugihara Yasuo. 1986. Burein seiji: shiteki shimon kikan (Brain Politics: Private Consultative Organs). *Hōgaku seminā* (377):78–79.

Sugimoto Yoshio. 1986. The Manipulative Bases of "Consent" in Japan. In *Democracy in Contemporary Japan*. Edited by Gavan McCormack and Sugimoto Yoshio. 65–75. New York: M. E. Sharpe.

Sugita Kenji. 1967. Shingikai o meguru shomondai (Various Problems with *Shingikai*). *Kaijō hoan daigakkō kenkyū hōkoku* 1:81–93.

Taguchi Fukuji. 1968. Pressure Groups in Japanese Politics. *The Developing Economies* 6(4):468–86.

Takenaka Heizō and Ishi Hiromitsu. 1994. Shingikai wa kakuremino ka? (Are *Shingikai* Fairy Cloaks?). *Keizai seminā* (478):38–46.

Takeuchi Yoshinobu. 1987. Rokujūninen sanbei ni kakaru seisansha beika no kettei (Deciding the Producer Price of Rice in 1987). *Fainansu* 23(5):24–33.

Tamura Kōichi. 1972. Ōsaka-shi ni okeru shingikai no shurui to mondai (The Variety and Problems of *Shingikai* in the City of Osaka). *Toshi mondai* 63(11):53–63.

Tanaka Mamoru. 1971. Chihō kōkyō dantai ni okeru shingikai seido no igi to mondai (The Problems and Significance of the Local Public Organization *Shingikai* System). *Toshi mondai kenkyū* 23(4):15–31.

Tanaka Mamoru. 1972. Seisaku keisei katei ni okeru shingikai no yakuwari (The Role of *Shingikai* in the Policymaking Process). *Toshi mondai* 63(11):17–27.

Tanaka Yōnosuke. 1979. The World of the Zaikai. In *Politics and Economics in Contemporary Japan*. Edited by Murakami Hyōe and Johannes Hirschmeier. 64–79. Tokyo: Japan Culture Institute.

Teshima Takashi. 1985. Chihō jichi to shimon kikan (Local Self-Government and Advisory Committees). *Toshi mondai* 76(7):3–20.

Teshima Takashi. 1986. Shingikai ka shin-gikai ka (*Shingikai*, Or a New Parliament?). *Hōritsu jihō* 58(1):38–44.

Thayer, Nathaniel B. 1969. *How the Conservatives Rule Japan*. Princeton: Princeton University Press.

Thelen, Kathleen, and Sven Steinmo. 1992. Historical Institutionalism in Comparative Politics. In *Structuring Politics: Historical Institutionalism in Comparative Analysis*. Edited by Sven Steinmo, Kathleen Thelen, and Frank Longstreth. 1–32. Cambridge: Cambridge University Press.

Tilly, Charles. 1975. Reflections on the History of European State-Making. In *The Formation of National States in Western Europe*. Edited by Charles Tilly. 3–83. Princeton: Princeton University Press.

Tilton, Mark. 1996. *Restrained Trade: Cartels in Japan's Basic Materials Industries*. Ithaca: Cornell University Press.

Tocqueville, Alexis de. 1945 [1835, 1840]. *Democracy in America*. Translated by Henry Reeve, Francis Bowen, and Phillips Bradley. New York: Vintage Books.

Toki no Hōrei. 1966. Shingikaitō no genjō to mondaiten (The Current State of *Shingikai* and Their Problems). (556–57):70–76.

Trezise, Philip H., and Suzuki Yukio. 1976. Politics, Government and Economic Growth in Japan. In *Asia's New Giant: How the Japanese Economy Works*. Edited by Hugh Patrick and Henry Rosovsky. 753–811. Washington, D.C.: Brookings Institution.

Trimberger, Ellen Kay. 1978. *Revolution from Above: Military Bureaucrats and Development in Japan, Turkey, Egypt and Peru*. New Brunswick, N.J.: Transaction Books.

Truman, David B. 1971. *The Governmental Process: Political Interests and Public Opinion*. 2nd ed. New York: Alfred A. Knopf.

Tsuji Kiyoaki. 1964 [1958]. The Bureaucracy Preserved and Strengthened. *Journal of Social and Political Ideas in Japan* 2(3):88–92.

Tsujinaka Yutaka. 1983. Rieki baikai kōzō no bunseki wakugumi to deita sōsu: kōporatizuma-ka to nihon no rōdō seiji no kōsatsu no tame ni (Data Source and Analytical Framework for the Structure of Interest Intermediation: An Examination of Corporatization and Japanese Labor Politics). *Kita kyūshū daigaku hōsei ronshū* 11(1):1–43.

Tsujinaka Yutaka. 1985a. Shakai henyō to seisaku katei no taiō: shiteki shimon kikan seiji no tenkai (Social Change and the Response of the Policymaking Process: Evolution in the Politics of Private Consultative Bodies). *Kita kyūshū daigaku hōsei ronshū* 13(1):1–69.

Tsujinaka Yutaka. 1985b. Shiteki shimon kikan no yakuwari to Yasukunikon (The Role of Private Consultative Bodies and the Yasukuni Roundtable). *Jurisuto* (848):67–76.

Tsujinaka Yutaka. 1989. *Rengō: A New and Last Participant in Osmotic Corporatism in Japan? Japanese Industrial Policy as a Consequence of Network Osmosis*. Airlie House, Va.: Japan Society for the Promotion of Science/Joint Committee on Japanese Studies of the Social Science Research Council and the Japan–U.S. Friendship Commission Binational Conference on Negotiating Public and Private Interests in Contemporary Japan.

Tsujinaka Yutaka. 1990. *Rengō: The Final Participant in Japan's Osmotic Corporatism: A Network Interpretation of Its Strength*. Presented at the 42nd annual meeting of the Association for Asian Studies, Chicago.

Tsujinaka Yutaka. 1993. Rengō and Its Osmotic Networks. In *Political Dynamics in Contemporary Japan*. Edited by Gary D. Allinson and Sone Yasunori. 200–13. Ithaca: Cornell University Press.

Tsujinaka Yutaka. 1996. Interest Group Structure and Regime Change in Japan. In *Maryland/Tsukuba Papers on U.S.–Japan Relations*. Edited by I. M. Destler and Satō Hideo. College Park, Md.: University of Maryland.

Upham, Frank K. 1987. *Law and Social Change in Postwar Japan*. Cambridge, Mass.: Harvard University Press.

Upham, Frank K. 1994 (unpublished). *A Tentative Model of Japanese Regulatory Style.*

Uriu, Robert. 1996. *Troubled Industries: Confronting Economic Change in Japan.* Ithaca: Cornell University Press.

Vogel, Ezra. 1978. Guided Free Enterprise in Japan. *Harvard Business Review* 56(3):161–70.

Vogel, Ezra. 1979. *Japan as Number One: Lessons for America.* New York: Harper & Row.

Vogel, Steven K. 1994. The Bureaucratic Approach to the Financial Revolution: Japan's Ministry of Finance and Financial System Reform. *Governance* 7(3):219–43.

Vogel, Steven K. 1996. *Freer Markets, More Rules: The Paradoxical Progress of Regulatory Reform in the Advanced Industrial Countries.* Ithaca: Cornell University Press.

Wada Hideo. 1986. Gikaisei minshu-shugi to shimon gyōsei (Parliamentary Democracy and Consultative Administration). *Hōritsu jihō* 58(1):30–37.

Ward, Robert E. 1965. The Commission on the Constitution and Prospects for Constitutional Change in Japan. *Journal of Asian Studies* 24(3):401–29.

Weber, Max. 1946. *From Max Weber: Essays in Sociology.* Translated by H. H. Gerth and C. Wright Mills. New York: Oxford University Press.

Weber, Max. 1947. *The Theory of Social and Economic Organization.* Translated by A. M. Henderson and Talcott Parsons. Glencoe, Ill.: Free Press.

Wilks, Stephen, and Maurice Wright. 1987. Conclusion: Comparing Government–Industry Relations: States, Sectors, and Networks. In *Comparative Government Industry Relations: Western Europe, the United States, and Japan.* Edited by Stephen Wilks and Maurice Wright. 274–313. Oxford: Oxford University Press.

Winkler, J. T. 1976. Corporatism. *Archives Européenes de Sociologie* XVII(1):100–36.

Wolferen, Karel van. 1989. *The Enigma of Japanese Power: People and Politics in a Stateless Nation.* London: Macmillan.

Woodall, Brian. 1996. *Japan Under Construction: Corruption, Politics, and Public Works.* Berkeley: University of California Press.

Yamada Hiroyuki. 1972. Shingikai seido ni tsuite (On the *Shingikai* System). *Jurisuto* (510):14–17.

Yamanouchi Kazuo. 1985. Shimon kikan no kinō to chihō jichi (The Functions of Advisory Committees and Local Government). *Toshi mondai* 76(7):21–31.

Yanaga Chitoshi. 1968. *Big Business in Japanese Politics.* New Haven: Yale University Press.

Yasuhara Shigeru. 1978. Shingikai no iin kōsei o meguru jakkan no mondai (A Few Problems in the Composition of *Shingikai*). *Chiiki kaihatsu* (161):33–37.

Zenchū. 1987. *Agricultural Cooperative Movement in Japan.*

Interviews[1]

Andō Iwao. Member of Parliament (Japan Communist Party), House of Representatives. 5 February 1988.

Ara Kenjirō. Professor, Hitotsubashi University. 18 May 1988.

[1] All interviews were conducted by the author in person in the Tokyo metropolitan area. Individuals are identified by the positions they held at the time of the interview, and where they themselves had chosen an English translation for their rank, that translation is used.

Arai Jōji. Managing Director (*jōmu riji*), Central Cooperative Bank for Agriculture and Forestry (Nōrin Chūkin). 25 November 1988.

Baba Kumao. Director (*buchō*), Management Division, Food Agency, Ministry of Agriculture, Forestry, and Fisheries. 12 July 1988.

Deguchi Haruaki. Administrative Director (*jimukyoku*), Financial and Investment Committee, Life Insurance Association of Japan. 30 November 1988.

Egashira Kenjirō. Professor of Law, Tokyo University. 16 November 1988.

Endō Yoshikazu. General Secretary (*jimu kyokuchō*), All-Japan Council of Traffic and Transport Workers Unions. 22 October 1987.

Gō Ryōtarō. President (*torishimariyaku shachō*), Nichien Chemical Engineering. 28 September 1987.

Hatakeyama Mitsuo. Political staff (*sanji*), Policy Affairs Research Bureau, Liberal Democratic Party. 22 July 1988.

Hayakawa Yoshio. General Manager (*shitsuchō*), Task Force for Financial Futures, Federation of Bankers Associations of Japan. 2 November 1988.

Higa Masahiro. Public Relations Department, The Central Union of Agricultural Cooperatives (Zenchū). 15 June 1988.

Hiraga Toshiyuki. Former Director General (*kyokuchō*), Labor Standards Bureau, Ministry of Labor. 22 February 1988.

Hondō Yoshio. Director (*kyokuchō*), Research Bureau, General Council of Trade Unions of Japan (Sōhyō). 12 October 1987.

Horiuchi Akiyoshi. Professor of Economics, Tokyo University. 16 November 1988.

Iida Tsuneo. Professor of Economics, Nagoya University. 15 November 1988.

Ikeda Hitoshi. Executive Director (*senmu riji*), National Chamber of Agriculture. 18 May 1988.

Ikehata Seiichi. Member of Parliament (Japan Socialist Party), House of Representatives. 5 February 1988.

Imai Takashi. Managing Director (*jōmu torishimariyaku*), Nippon Steel. 9 December 1988.

Imashiro Takeharu. Secretary (*jimukan*), Planning Section, Management Division, Food Agency, Ministry of Agriculture, Forestry, and Fisheries. 15 June 1988.

Inoguchi Takashi. Assistant Professor of Political Science, Tokyo University. 6 December 1988.

Ishikawa Kichiemon. Chairman (*kaichō*), Central Labor Relations Committee. 29 September 1987.

Ishikawa Toshinao. Managing Director (*jōmu riji*), Japan Economic Research Institute. 1 August 1988.

Itatani Masanori. Manager (*kachō*), Corporate Planning Department, Nomura Securities. 13 December 1988.

Iwakura Tomomitsu. Policy Affairs Research Council, Liberal Democratic Party. 13 July 1988.

Kagayama Kunio. Director (*rijichō*), Food and Agriculture Research and Development Association. 16 May 1988.

Kaizuka Keimei. Professor of Economics, Tokyo University. 25 October 1988.

Kajio Akihiko. Assistant Manager, Finance and Investment Planning Office, Nippon Life Insurance. 30 November 1988.

Kanda Hideki. Associate Professor of Law, Tokyo University. 22 November 1988.

Kaneko Tarō. President, Marusan Securities. 5 December 1988.

Kanzaki Katsurō. Professor of Law, Kōbe University. 9 November 1988.

Kataoka Hiromitsu. Dean of Student Affairs, Waseda University. 27 December 1988.

Katō Mutsuki. Member of Parliament (Liberal Democratic Party), House of Representatives. 6 September 1988.

Katō Takashi. Director General (*rijichō*), Yamaichi Research Institute of Securities and Economics. 14 July 1988.

Katsube Kin'ichi. Counselor (*san'yo*), Japanese Consumers Cooperative Union. 18 July 1988.

Kawaguchi Minoru. Professor of Law, Keiō University. 25 April 1988.

Kikuichi Mamoru. Manager (*gyōmu kachō*), International Department, Japan Securities Dealers Association. 1 November 1988.

Kikuta Yutaka. Chief Economist (*chōsa shunin*), Research Division, Banking Bureau, Ministry of Finance. 27 October 1988.

Kimura Hajime. Manager (*chōsayaku*), Planning Department, Industrial Bank of Japan. 15 November 1988.

Kishi Yasuhiko. Editorial Writer (*ronsetsu iin*), *Nihon Keizai Shinbun*. 18 May 1988.

Kitagawa Hiroyasu. Planning Chief (*kikaku kakarichō*), International Finance Bureau, Ministry of Finance. 24 October 1988.

Komatsu Tetsuo. Deputy Economic Editor (*keizaibu jichō*), *Yomiuri Shinbun*. 20 May 1988.

Konno Hisako. Attorney. 2 February 1988.

Koyama Yoshiaki. Director (*kachō*), Research Division, Banking Bureau, Ministry of Finance. 25 November 1988.

Kurasawa Motonari. Professor of Economics, Yokohama National University. 10 November 1988.

Kutani Yoshirō. Labor Relations Manager (*rōmu buchō*), *Yomiuri Shinbun*. 26 January 1988.

Masamoto Hideo. President (*kaichō*), Oita Prefectural Association of Towns and Villages. 24 June 1988.

Matsubara Haruki. Director (*kachō*), Supervision Section, Standards Bureau, Ministry of Labor. 22 September 1987, 25 January 1988.

Matsumoto Takashi. Chief Examiner (*shusa*), Agriculture, Forestry, and Fisheries Section, Budget Bureau, Ministry of Finance. 20 May 1988.

Matsuzaki Yoshinobu. Managing Director, Federation of Employers Associations (Nikkeiren). 22 September 1987.

Minaguchi Kōichi. President (*torishimariyaku shachō*), Nomura Research Institute and Computer Systems. 22 November 1988.

Miyauchi Yasuo. Executive Vice President (*torishimariyaku fukushachō*), Hitachi. 22 December 1988.

Miyawaki Nagasada. Executive Director (*senmu riji*), Japan Economic Research Institute. 1 August 1988.

Miyazaki Isamu. Chairman (*rijichō*), Daiwa Securities Research Institute. 18 August 1988.

Mizuno Masaichi. Professor Emeritus, Nagoya University. 30 June 1988.

Mochida Keizō. Professor, Wakō University. 20 July 1988.

Moriya Manabu. Chief (*kakarichō*), Securities Exchange Council Section, Securities Bureau, Ministry of Finance. 26 October, 16 November 1988.

Muramatsu Michio. Professor of Political Science, Kyoto University. 27 December 1988.

Nakai Takeshi. Director (*buchō*), Personnel and Labor Relations Department, Mitsui Tōatsu Chemicals. 23 September 1987.

Nakamura Yasuhiko. Commentator (*kaisetsu iin*), Japan Broadcasting Corporation (NHK). 27 June 1988.

Nakanishi Masao. Managing Director (*rijichō*), Safety and Hygiene Technology Testing Association. 6 October 1987.

Nakano Kazuhito. President (*kaichō*), Japan Grain Inspection Association. 20 June 1988.

Nakano Takanobu. Editorial staff, *Asahi Shinbun*. 25 January 1988.

Namiki Masayoshi. Director General (*rijichō*), Food and Agriculture Policy Research Center. 13 June 1988.

Nibuya Ryū. Senior Managing Director (*senmu torishimariyaku*), Mitsubishi Rayon. 30 September 1987.

Nishikawa Shinhachi. Professor of Public Health, Nippon College of Physical Education. 14 October 1987.

Nishikiori Akira. Managing Director (*jōmu riji*), National Federation of Small Business Associations (Chūōkai). 19 September 1987.

Nishio Masaru. Professor of Public Administration, Tokyo University. 26 December 1988.

Nozaki Kazuaki. Director General (*kyokuchō*), Human Resources Development Bureau, Ministry of Labor. 28 January 1988.

Ogawa Yasuichi. Director General (*senmu riji*), Japan Federation of Employers Associations (Nikkeiren). 29 October 1987.

Okamura Shōzō. Assistant Director (*jichō*), Center for Shorter Working Hours, General Council of Trade Unions of Japan (Sōhyō). 22 January 1988.

Ōkawa Nobuo. Director (*daihyō riji*), National Federation of Food Cooperatives. 29 June 1988.

Ōkawara Taichirō. Member of Parliament (Liberal Democratic Party), House of Councilors. 15 July 1988.

Ōmori Takehide. Director, Toda Construction. 25 September 1987.

Ōno Shōji. Director (*yakuin*), Japanese League of Livelihood Cooperative Associations. 15 June 1988.

Ōtani Tatsuya. Director (*kyokuchō*), Policy Planning Bureau, National Federation of Independent Unions (Chūritsu Rōren). 14 September 1987.

Ōtsubo Ken'ichirō. Member of Parliament (Liberal Democratic Party), House of Representatives. 2 August 1988.

Ōyama Hiroto. News commentator, Japan Broadcasting Corporation (NHK). 11 November 1988.

Ōyō Kyoichi. Planning Chief (*kikaku kakarichō*), Research Division, Banking Bureau, Ministry of Finance. 24 November 1988.

Rōyama Shōichi. Professor of Economics, Osaka University. 30 November 1988.

Saiga Shizuya. Former Director General (*kyokuchō*), Organization Bureau, Japan Confederation of Labor (Dōmei). 11 September 1987.

Satō Kōichi. Assistant Director (*jichō*), Research Bureau, Japan Confederation of Labor (Dōmei). 9 October 1987.

Satō Masayuki. General Manager (*buchō*), Investment Committee, Daiwa Securities. 5 December 1988.

Satō Mitsuo. Managing Director (*jōmu riji*), Tokyo Stock Exchange. 6 December 1988.

Satō Seizaburō. Professor of Political Science, Tokyo University. 19 December 1988.

Sawabe Mamoru. President (*rijichō*), Japanese Racing Association. 19 July 1988.

Shimada Haruo. Professor of Economics, Keiō University. 8 October 1987.

Shimizu Eiichi. Director (*kyokuchō*), Center for Shorter Working Hours, General Council of Trade Unions of Japan (Sōhyō). 26 October 1987.

Shirai Taishirō. Professor of Administration, Hōsei University. 14 October 1987.

Sone Yasunori. Professor of Political Science, Keiō University. 9 December 1988.

Sugita Ryoki. Economic News Editor (*buchō*), *Nihon Keizai Shinbun*. 4 November 1988.

Tachi Ryūichirō. Professor Emeritus, Tokyo University. 10 November 1988.

Tachikawa Masami. Executive Vice President (*torishimariyaku fukushachō*), Yasuda Trust Bank. 29 November 1988.

Takagi Tsuyoshi. Director (*kyokuchō*), Industrial Policy Bureau, Japanese Federation of Textile, Garment, Man-Made Fiber, Distributive and Allied Trades Workers Unions (Zensen). 29 September 1987.

Takei Teruyoshi. Editorial writer (*ronsetsu iin*), *Nihon Keizai Shinbun*. 4 November 1988.

Tamura Ken'ichi. Vice President, National Federation of Independent Unions (Chūritsu Rōren). 22 October 1987.

Tanimoto Takashi. General Secretary (*shokichō*), All-Japan Federation of Peasants Unions. 23 June 1988.

Tsuji Ken. Vice President (*riji*), Japan Institute of Labor. 13 November 1987.

Tsujinaka Yutaka. Associate Professor of Political Science, Tsukuba University. 10 January 1989.

Wada Katsumi. Chairman (*rijichō*), Employment Information Center. 30 September 1987.

Wada Masae. Vice President (*fuku kaichō*), Japan Housewives Association. 21 June 1988.

Watanabe Michiko. Attorney. 6 October 1987.

Wiggin, Geoffrey W. Agricultural Attaché, Embassy of the United States of America in Tokyo. 17 May 1988.

Yahagi Mitsuaki. Deputy General Manager (*jichō*), Strategic Planning Division, Mitsui Bank. 29 November 1988.

Yamazaki Kōu. Professor, Department of Agrobiology, Tokyo University. 21 June 1988.

Index